Text and Context:
Document Storage and Processing

Susan Jones

Text and Context

Document Storage and Processing

With 66 Figures

Springer-Verlag London Ltd.

Susan Jones, BA, MSc
Department of Computer Science, City University,
Northampton Square, London EC1V 0HB, UK

British Library Cataloguing in Publication Data
Jones, Susan *1942–*
Text and context: document storage processing.
1. Databases. Management
I. Title
005.74
ISBN 978-3-540-19604-4

Library of Congress Cataloging-in-Publication Data
Jones, Susan, *1942–*
Text and context: document storage and processing/Susan Jones.
    p. cm.
Includes index.
ISBN 978-3-540-19604-4   ISBN 978-1-4471-3162-5
DOI 10.1007/978-1-4471-3162-5
1. Text processing (Computer science)   2. Optical storage devices.
I. Title.
QA76.9.T48J66 1991   90–22744
005—dc20   CIP

© Springer-Verlag London 1991
Originally published by Springer-Verlag London Limited in 1991

Typeset by Saxon Printing Ltd., Saxon House, Derby
34/3830 543210 Printed on acid-free paper

Preface

This book was written to support an option course dealing with various aspects of document processing, including the technology and applications of optical storage devices. It is intended for students of computing and information technology, preferably with experience of conventional database systems, but without specialized knowledge of text analysis or information retrieval.

Its main objective is to help readers see links between topics which are still quite fragmented, but which present many interesting possibilities for future integration. The approach is pragmatic – there is (happily) no dominant formal "methodology" in this field at present and the subject is presented through descriptions of real applications and software. However the importance of ISO standards as a basis for progress is emphasised.

The coverage of many subjects is necessarily selective and sometimes superficial; those who need more detail will be referred to other sources, and suggestions for further investigations are made at the end of each chapter. Students should obviously try to make practical use of any optical storage devices, information retrieval systems, hypertext systems, and text-formatting systems which are available to them, and also take the opportunity to visit exhibitions and outside organisations where more advanced examples can be seen in action.

London, 1990   *Susan Jones*

Acknowledgements

- Figure 2.8 is taken from Collins Cobuild English Language Dictionary © 1987 William Collins & Son Ltd. with the permission of the Publisher.

- Figures 10.1, 10.2, and 10.3 are reproduced from HMSO's Technical Services Report 228 "The application of SGML to Statutory Instruments" with the permission of the Controller of HMSO.

- Figures 6.2–6.8 are reproduced by courtesy of British Airways.

- Figures 7.1–7.4 are reproduced by courtesy of Olivetti Systems.

- Figures 8.1–8.3 are reproduced by courtesy of Sony Broadcast.

Thanks are due to many people who have, directly or indirectly, contributed to this book. Firstly, to Professor John Sinclair of Birmingham University for permission to use material from the Cobuild text analysis, and to two other participants in the Collins Cobuild project – Jeremy Clear and Antoinette Renouf. Also to Inge Nicholl (Reuters), David Beaumont and John Skipsey (British Airways), Peter Butcher (City University Library), Ian Galbraith (Scanmedia), Andrew Harding and Brian Cotton (Sony Broadcast) for demonstrations, information, and illustrations. Particular thanks go to Robert Stutely of HMSO for his careful checking of the section on SGML – if any errors remain they are my own responsibility.

Some of the most valuable help came from ex-City University students Peter Tyndale (Olivetti), Quentin Cope (Xionics) and William Howard (Barts Hospital). Other past or present students who have helped widen my horizons on some topic include Anwar Fazaluddin, Ayse Goker, Kevin Bell, Colin Small, Hamendra Patel, Michael Collier, Robert Jones, Matthew Vanstone, Julie Harrison, Akbar Hossain, Rajshree Pandya, Colin Sandall and Cisillia Tay. Advice and feedback has come from City University colleagues John Snell, Jean Scott and Professor Steve Robertson, and closer to home

viii   *Acknowledgements*

John and Philip Jones have provided much practical assistance and support.

Finally, an unsolicited testimonial to my elderly but still totally reliable BBC micro which has processed thousands of words for me over the last seven years, including those in this book. I dread the day when it finally decides to cash in its chips.

Susan Jones

Contents

One
Introduction and Overview

*"Paper, you know, plays the part of a storage battery and
a conductor; it conducts not only from one man to
another, but from one time to another, carrying a highly
variable charge of authenticity or credibility."*
Paul Valéry

The primary source of information for humans is the direct evidence of the
senses – sight, hearing, smell, touch, taste. This is immediate, powerful, but
local and short-lived: it lasts only as long as the consciousness which originally
registered it.

In literate societies secondary information is also available in recorded form,
using alphabetic and other symbols. This is potentially more permanent; it
needs a recording medium (e.g. paper), and encoding and decoding processes
(writing and reading) to allow it to pass between the minds of people who may
never physically meet.

Over the last century it has become increasing common for recorded
information used for commercial and administrative purposes to be structured
into special *documents* – cheques, bills, worksheets, certificates – with a space set
aside for each piece of information. Anyone dealing with large organisations is
used to supplying and receiving information on standard forms.

As we move through the three stages described above we reduce the range of
information which may be transmitted – we can't fill in a form with a smell – but
increase our ability to exploit it to give precise control over events.

Computers have traditionally (and understandably) been most concerned
with information of the third type, enforcing even more rigid rules than the
clerical record-keeping systems on which they were based. In early data-
processing applications the idea of the "logical record" provided a useful
bridge between:

- the bundle of information previously put together on a paper form or index
  card, and
- the small amount of machine memory which was available for holding
  information to be actively processed.

Later developments in database management involved defining ever more
elaborate structures for encapsulating "meaning" in the arrangement of a few
selected, classified, and coded items of data.

Meanwhile, away from this artificial setting human beings continue to take most of their information from primary and secondary sources. And computers are increasingly required to deal with secondary information (text and pictures) in a way that is useful to the humans creating or consuming it. This book is about some of the techniques which make that possible, and applications which in one way or another go beyond the scope of conventional database management systems in the range of information which they handle. Our focus will be mainly on text, but pictorial data will also come into the discussions.

Note that we shall not be concerned with attempts to make machines "understand" textual information. This is a topic covered by the branch of artificial intelligence known as natural language processing; however in that context the material to be processed is less likely to be a sizeable chunk of raw text than an abstract linguistic structure, often with the practical objective of allowing computer systems using a restricted vocabulary and syntax to carry on apparently natural dialogue with their users.

By contrast we shall be talking mainly about texts whose structure can be fully understood only by *human* intelligence, and systems whose function is to serve that intelligence by performing large-scale but possibly quite low-level tasks. Such systems must often handle volumes of information much greater than those found in the average business database, and demand different techniques. Some real applications are presented in the following chapters to illustrate the requirements, problems and methods involved.

One important theme is the need to exploit special hardware for *data capture, storage, searching* and *presentation*. Conventional data-processing equipment was never designed for large-scale text processing, and even in academic environments users' needs have not always been well served. More recently the potential commercial importance of textual data has been recognised, and hardware has been developed which allows it to be better handled. Some basic points are introduced below, and expanded in later chapters.

Data Capture

In the past when machine-readable text was needed there has often been no alternative to re-typing it. In the late 1960s a university research project to analyse natural language required it to be laboriously punched onto paper tape (in upper case only), read into the machine reel by reel, and used without any real chance to correct typing errors. In two years it was possible to deal satisfactorily with no more than 135 000 words. Twenty years later one could walk into any secretary's office and find the same number of words on the nearest disc. As computers came to be used to originate typed and printed material, the amount of machine-readable text grew rapidly. It soon became evident that:

- Text produced for an immediate purpose (printing a newspaper, sending a letter) could be a valuable long-term resource, given appropriate techniques for storing it and finding it again when needed.
- Word-processing packages use different and arbitrary conventions to indicate how a text should appear on the printed page – these do not necessarily describe its structure in a way that is helpful for later processing.

These are points we shall return to again and again in the following chapters.

Users who wish to store or analyse printed text which is not already in machine-readable form now have the possibility of using scanning devices and optical character readers (OCRs). OCRs were first used in commercial applications such as banking, to take small amounts of data encoded in a very restricted font from a specialised document such as a cheque. Now some scanners will "read" any printed font, making it practical to generate large textual databases from any source. However, as we shall see later, it is impossible to extract the logical structure of a scanned text with 100 per cent accuracy from its physical structure, i.e. from its appearance on the page.

Storage

Having obtained the data, it is necessary to keep it somewhere, and here again we can point to a mismatch between conventional storage devices and large quantities of textual information. The magnetic disc as currently used in the computer industry is a versatile but essentially compromise medium: neither truly serial nor truly random, it contains a number of fixed-length sectors to accommodate arbitrarily partitioned blocks of information. It is easy to erase or modify the contents of one block without affecting the rest; but complex security arrangements are needed to prevent loss or corruption of the data. Except at the lowest end of the range, individual discs are expensive, and duplicating their contents is a time-consuming process.

These characteristics match fairly well the needs of the operational database for commercial or administrative use. Its overall size and shape may remain constant, but it is subject to continuous small-scale change as individual items are added, deleted and modified. It is divided into logical records of predictable size, grouping together closely related units of information, which fit neatly into the physical partitions supported by the hardware. Patterns of access to the data are often predictable, and standard techniques can be used to support them efficiently.

Consider now some of the features of a *textual* database. Basically it consists of a continuous stream of words, but these may be broken down into different grammatical, stylistic or physical units (phrases, sentences, paragraphs, chapters, lines, pages) according to the current process. It may contain internal linkages in the form of cross-references from one location to another. At the creation stage (e.g. while word-processing software is being used to draft and format it) it is subject to much low-level change, but at some point (when the article is published or the letter sent) it becomes "frozen" into its final form. Afterwards it must be available for searching.

A textual database is accumulated over time, and new data will not necessarily supersede the old (although it may be more frequently sought). So the file design must allow for increasing demands on storage space, and a diminishing probability that any particular part will be accessed. Most important, the possible ways into such a database, and the questions it has the potential to answer, are unpredictable and unlimited. The intended application, the software used to search and analyse, and the structures imposed upon the data by that software, are what make the difference.

With those ideas in mind, we can look at other storage media besides magnetic disc. Research into better technologies for holding machine-readable data in a permanent form has been, and continues to be, an important activity within the computing industry; and over the years many approaches (bubble memory, holographic memory) have looked promising but later proved to be deficient in some respect. Media which provide either higher capacity, faster access times or finer "granularity" for updating than magnetic disc may still be found uneconomic to manufacture or impractical to install.

Currently the most promising candidates are the various types of *optical disc*: video discs, CD-ROM, and "worm" discs. Optical storage was first developed for use within the entertainment industry, and the economic viability of, for example, CD-ROM for digital data storage still depends on the mass-production and widespread adoption of audio CD players. But even the most superficial survey of optical discs makes it plain that they fit many of the needs of large textual and graphical databases. Important features are their *high capacity, non-erasability, cheapness,* and ability to handle *visual data* of various kinds. These points will be explored in detail in the following chapters.

Searching

High capacity in storage devices is desirable, but it is equally important to be able to locate quickly a specific item of interest. Designers over the last thirty years have perfected a limited but powerful set of techniques for organising and searching large quantities of information on disc, and conventional database management systems depend on the use of, for example, indexing, hashing and pointer chains to support the logical data model which they present to their users. These methods were developed to minimise the notorious von Neumann bottleneck, whereby data items must be moved from disc into memory and then into one of a limited number of machine registers in order to examine their value.

The last ten years have seen the use of intelligent devices for controlling discs, able to take over some functions of the central processor, and possibly to carry out multiple searches *in parallel*. An example of such a back-end processor (described in a later chapter) is the ICL Content Addressable File Store, which is used, among other things, to improve the performance of a text retrieval package. This of course is in the context of normal magnetic storage; so far parallel searching is not an option provided for optical discs although it would obviously be an advantage to exploit their high capacity in this way.

Presentation

Once we can capture and store text on a large scale, our next consideration must be how to output it. Screen displays are enough for some purposes, and electronic mail/journal systems are designed for communications where there is no need for hard copy. However in 1990 the printed page is still the primary medium for the distribution and storage of information, and the most flexible and convenient for many people. But the production and use of printed material has a long tradition in literate societies, and its readers are used to a quality of presentation which has not always been achieved by earlier computer systems.

Until very recently the equipment most often used for output from large computers was the lineprinter – a device designed to put the largest number of characters onto paper in the shortest time, and with the least possible delay to the expensive processor driving it. Lineprinters use a limited character set (until the late 1970s it was rare to find one with lower case letters in its repertoire) and the quality of their output is more suitable for bills and program listings than continuous text. However users of information retrieval or text analysis programs have been, and sometimes still are, obliged to tolerate it.

The advent of word processing on microcomputers during the late 1970s and early 1980s resulted in the development of cheaper, slower devices for the production of letters and internal reports. The fundamental choice was between daisy-wheel and dot matrix printers, depending on the balance of requirement for "typewriter" quality on one side and speed, lower cost and flexibility on the other. The versatility of the dot matrix technology proved superior as it became possible to produce a variety of print sizes and styles in the same document.

The need for high speed, good print quality, and greater versatility is currently satisfied by various types of *laser printer*, with ink-jet printers as the poor man's alternative. Mechanically, a laser printer acts like a photocopier: the full page image is electrostatically charged onto a drum and powdered ink sticks to it; this is then transferred to paper where it is permanently fixed using heat or some other means. A much higher resolution can be achieved than with dot matrix printers, and since there are no hard-wired character shapes it is possible to use any typeface, size and orientation, and to mix graphics with text.

To make best use of these capabilities, there must be a way of conveying page image details to the printer, and the language which has been most widely adopted for this purpose is Postscript. Postscript is a full programming language which can be used to write page descriptions by calling on powerful graphics and text-handling operators. It was designed to be device-independent, and can in principle be used in connection with any printer, or indeed other display devices like screens. A look at a Postscript example will give a useful insight into the basic ideas of text "imaging".

An important result of developments in printing technology has been to narrow the gap between professionally typeset material and output from readily-available microcomputers, leading to rapid growth in the activity known as desk-top publishing. Computer users routinely produce documents with sophisticated layouts, using either wysiwyg packages or formatting programs, and we shall consider later the basic functions of software in both categories. An interesting feature of formatting programs like TeX and troff is their support for macro definition and substitution, enabling a few relatively simple instructions to generate complex formatting effects.

When creating a document, an author is concerned with two aspects:

- Its *content*, including its logical structure: how it is split into meaningful components like chapters, sections and paragraphs.
- Its *layout*: how the content is fitted into lines and onto pages.

A big advantage of computer technology is that these two issues can be separated – the author can decide what he wants to say first and worry about format later, knowing that it can be altered with very little effort. Many documents are in fact printed in several different formats, and it is becoming increasingly common to send them from place to place via electronic mail, for use in installations where the printing equipment may be quite different.

The response to these needs has been the design of yet more languages, allowing documents to be coded for transmission without losing important structural information on the way. Much of this work has gone on under the umbrella of the International Organisation for Standardisation (ISO), resulting so far in the definition of two standards (Office Document Architecture, and Standard Generalized Markup Language) which will be described and compared in Chapter 10.

This short discussion has identified three possible levels of definition for printed documents, concerned respectively with *logical structure, physical layout,* and actual *page imaging*. At each level there are now standard or widely-accepted languages for expressing the definitions. Between them they illustrate a familiar technique for handling a complex computing task – break it down into a number of discrete manageable layers and provide mappings from the high level to the low. An equally familiar problem with this approach is the overhead incurred!

Applications

The tendency in the past has been to hold machine-readable text for two main purposes: information retrieval and linguistic analysis, the prime objective in each case being to find the answers to relatively simple questions from a huge mass of data. On the one hand, a chemist may require references to papers containing particular key phrases so as to update his knowledge of the field; on the other, a lexicographer may seek instances of a certain word in order to compile an up-to-date dictionary entry for it.

These applications remain important, and are covered early on in the book, but many other interesting possibilities can now be explored. The discipline of information retrieval has broadened in scope, from being largely concerned with finding bibliographic references on the basis of a few selected keywords per document, through the provision of full-text legal or news retrieval services, to the point of dealing also with pictorial information like engineering drawings or video-frames, and so needing the appropriate devices for data capture and storage.

How should such information be presented to users in an interactive mode? The communication costs associated with remote on-line retrieval services demanded short responses, probably no more than references to printed sources which were obtained and read later. *Full-text* and *multi-media* systems should ideally allow for more leisurely browsing – economically feasible with local databases on magnetic or optical storage devices. But the potential of the medium is wasted if users can only scan through page after page of text on the screen; they would be better off with books and journals.

A more useful approach is through *hypertext* systems, supporting *non-linear* ways of moving through information based on links which the author has set up from one section to another. Hypertext systems allow readers to interact with the material in ways which would be impossible on the printed page, and open the possibility of multiple authorship and dynamically evolving texts. One obvious application of these ideas is in technical documentation and computer-based learning, where the user comes to grasp a topic by exploring it actively and individually. Such applications often need the integration of text with graphics (perhaps also sound and animation), and provide interesting examples of the use of optical storage technologies mentioned in this introduction.

To act intelligently, hypertext systems must be able to pick out and present meaningful units of text, so languages for defining logical document structure are relevant in this context as well. In fact a machine-readable document coded up with a full structural description is very versatile: it may be printed in different formats, transmitted electronically or published and sold on optical disc, converted to hypertext form or for use in an information retrieval system. If (like a Dictionary or Act of Parliament) it has a potentially long life and multiple uses, it may be an extremely valuable piece of property. In the remainder of this book we shall see how these possibilities can be exploited.

Two
Fundamentals of Text Processing

"They have been at a great feast of languages, and stolen
the scraps."
William Shakespeare

Natural Language as Data

Our first aim is to try and pin down those characteristics of natural language data which make it more tricky to deal with than data consisting only of numbers or structured records. A suitable way to begin is to survey the work of a group of users who have been using computers to process text for the last thirty years: those concerned with the study of language and literature. This chapter explains:

- Why some researchers undertake computer-based text processing.
- The basic problems faced in obtaining an accurate internal representation of a printed text.
- The kind of results required from text analysis software and the techniques for producing them.
- How certain characteristics of natural language set limits on what can be done.

Once again it should be stressed that we are not concerned with the subtleties of natural language processing as developed within the discipline of artificial intelligence. Most of the algorithms described will be very simple-minded, but the problems of producing useful and accurate results from a large body of data will give plenty of material for discussion.

From the beginning, computer technology was seen as useful for textual scholars because of its basic capabilities for sorting, searching, counting and tabulating, just as in more bread-and-butter data-processing environments. For example:

- A critic, preparing a new edition of a literary work, might find it useful to produce an alphabetical word list as a basis for a printed index.
- A researcher studying a particular author's themes and style, or comparing two or more authors or varieties of language, might wish to tabulate details of vocabulary and grammatical constructions used.

- One particular objective may be literary detection, where statistical evidence is accumulated to suggest the most likely source for a text of disputed authorship, or to question received opinion about who wrote what.

Authorship studies of the last type are usually based on easily measured factors like average word and sentence lengths, and the patterns of use for common words such as prepositions and conjunctions. These reflect choices which the author makes unconsciously, out of habit, and so are characteristic of his individual style. A famous early investigation was by Morton and Levison in the early 1960s, which concluded that certain Epistles previously attributed to St Paul were actually the work of a different writer [1].

Obviously the very tedious counting and calculation required here can be performed automatically once the material is put into machine-readable form, but that can involve considerable time and effort. Decisions about representing a text may be far from straightforward.

Why should this be so? Users of word-processing software, for example, take for granted the fact that they can enter, store and manipulate text, but their ability to do so is based on a standard simplification of a complex issue. It will be useful to go back to first principles and consider what is involved when we convert printed or written material to digital form.

Representing Text

Such material uses an alphabet – a finite (in some cases very large) set of *symbols*. Many languages use the Roman alphabet, but with national variations; other widely used scripts are Cyrillic, Greek, and Arabic. The alphabet used by a language may vary over time: Old English contains at least two letters not in Modern English. Sometimes what appears on the page is a composite symbol, e.g. a German "o" with an umlaut on top. There will often be more than one version of each symbol – the Roman alphabet has capital and small letters, and the Arabic alphabet varies the form of some letters according to their position within the word. As well as letters, text contains punctuation symbols like spaces, commas and full stops, which also carry meaning.

To represent information within computer memory, we have a limited number of fixed-length binary strings (e.g. 8-bit bytes), to which a numerical interpretation can be attached. Our only option is to establish a *mapping* between those binary numbers and our alphabet. Any computer will have at least one default mapping, but not necessarily the one we want. If the British user of English-language word-processing software sometimes finds it hard to print a proper pound sign, the researcher hoping to handle, for instance, an ancient Greek text will obviously have more preparatory work to do. One possibility is to convert or *transliterate* symbols for which no mapping is defined to existing characters. Fig. 2.1 shows a simple transliteration table, from reference [2], for the Greek alphabet.

There are now international standards, e.g. ISO 6937, described in [3], which deal with text representation and interchange in many alphabets, and life for the textual scholar is much easier than it was twenty years ago, when 6-bit characters were the norm and even the distinction between upper and lower case letters was treated as unimportant. The adoption of ASCII code and extensions to it has eliminated many problems but not all. It is, for instance, limited in size – being based on 8-bit bytes, it has a maximum capacity of 255 characters. If our alphabet contains more symbols, or we want to handle two or more alphabets simultaneously, a one-to-one mapping between symbol and code will not be possible.

α	A	ι	I	ρ	R
β	B	κ	K	σ	S
γ	G	λ	L	τ	T
δ	D	μ	M	υ	U
ε	E	ν	N	φ	F
ζ	Z	ξ	C	χ	X
η	H	ο	O	ψ	Y
θ	Q	π	P	ω	W

Fig. 2.1. Transliteration table for the Greek alphabet

The normal way around this is to use *escape* codes, i.e. codes whose function is to modify the meaning of those which follow. This principle has been employed for many years, starting with the *shift* codes which switched between upper and lower case letters in five-hole paper tape. Escape codes increase the number of possible symbols to be represented at the cost of using more space, on average, per symbol. With N codes, we can use half of them as escapes and half as actual symbols, giving a maximum alphabet size of $(N^2)/4$. Alternatively two codes can be taken to represent every symbol, giving N^2 possibilities.

Transliteration of alphabets, and the use of composite symbols, will cause extra complications when processing the data. Having entered a text using the transliteration table in Fig. 2.1, the user may wish to produce a word list in the order of the Greek alphabet, and it will be useless to sort by standard ASCII code values. General-purpose sorting software should allow the specification of a different collating-sequence for jobs of this kind.

Composite symbols are even more tricky, and may demand the use of special "own-code" routines to perform comparisons. Escape codes require that the *context*, as well as the value, of a code is considered during comparison. Even applications using very standard text representations may have to define whether the ASCII sequences for upper and lower case letters should be treated separately, or interleaved.

Tagging

So far we have considered only the question of representing raw text. The researcher may wish to count occurrences not only of individual words and phrases, but particular stylistic or grammatical features – passive verbs in the past tense, for example. The only 100 per cent reliable way of ensuring that these can be identified by software is to mark them when the data is entered. This implies the insertion of extra codes, or *tags* in the text stream, with one or more symbols reserved to identify them. For example the Greek text described in [2] contains alphabetic codes indicating such things as verb tenses and noun cases enclosed in brackets. Within tags the letters of the alphabet have a completely different significance, so the brackets in this instance also function as escape codes.

The more elaborate the tagging scheme, the more detailed an analysis is possible, but there is clearly a substantial overhead both in the original marking-up and in the design of software to recognise and act on the codes. The problems of deciding how text should be represented and tagged are familiar to anyone undertaking text processing for literary or linguistic purposes; reference [2] is one amongst hundreds that could have been selected for illustration.

Originally, the coding schemes chosen by linguistic researchers tended to be quite arbitrary, governed only by their own immediate needs and the constraints imposed by their hardware. However over the years it has been recognised that data which has been assembled so laboriously should be made available to other interested users. This implies the need for *standards* not only for character representation but also for text mark-up, and for centrally-organised sources of information about existing machine-readable text. A body which has concerned itself with these issues for many years is the Association for Literary and Linguistic Computing, which maintains an archive of potentially useful data under the control of the Oxford University Computing Service, a centre of expertise in this particular field.

As a slight digression it is worth saying that not all scholars care for the "brute-force" study of texts using statistical and computational methods. There may be a (very reasonable) feeling that time taken in wrestling with sometimes quite unaccommodating technology would be better spent on more intelligent forms of analysis. Conversely it has been suggested that the use of computers allows genuinely new and interesting questions to be asked, and could provide a scientific framework for a process which has always relied too heavily on *ad hoc* individual approaches [4]. It is not of course the computer scientist's job to argue these points, but to ensure that researchers who do want to analyse text are given the appropriate tools.

So far this chapter seems to have focused on rather specialised forms of text processing, but issues of fundamental importance have been raised. The necessity for putting extra descriptive information into texts, and the corresponding need for escape codes to identify such information, will turn up repeatedly in the following chapters. The discussion of text acquisition and analysis in the next section is set in the context of a very practical application: lexicography or dictionary-making.

Computers in Lexicography

A dictionary entry for a word in a language may define:

- Its *pronunciation* (using a phonetic alphabet).
- Its *etymology* or historical derivation.
- The *grammatical functions* it may perform in a sentence.
- One or more possible *meanings* or shades of meaning.
- *References* to *other words* with related meanings.
- The language *register* it inhabits, e.g. is it slang, colloquial, formal, archaic, obscure?

The entry may also contain quoted *examples* of the word in context, to illustrate meaning or usage. In fact this is a highly over-simplified summary, which begs the central question: what is a word? Obviously some dictionaries may present only some of the items listed here, depending on their size, scope and purpose. It is clear, however, that real text-based evidence about how words are *actually* used will be of enormous value to the lexicographer. A living language changes from day to day; the dictionary compiler is chasing a moving target, and needs all the help he can get.

The Cobuild Project

Much of the following discussion is based on a project undertaken jointly in the early 1980s by Collins the publisher and the English Language Research Centre at Birmingham University [5]. Its purpose was to produce an "Advanced Learners Dictionary", giving non-native speakers up-to-date and reliable information about the current usage of 40 000 English words. It was intended to exploit computer technology for all stages of the process, from information-gathering to the production of the final printed version (see Fig. 2.2).

As a first stage, a large corpus of contemporary English was converted into machine-readable form. It consisted of representative texts chosen from a broad range of books, journals, newspapers, etc. published around 1981. A sample of recorded and transcribed spoken conversation was also included.

Using the information gained from the corpus, dictionary compilers wrote up the details of all relevant words, using as many definitions, examples and cross-references as necessary to explain the usage of each one adequately. This information was stored in a relational database.

A compilation monitor database was also used to control information about which words had been compiled and what remained to do. As time went on, compilers were able to see details of earlier cross-references to the words they were currently considering.

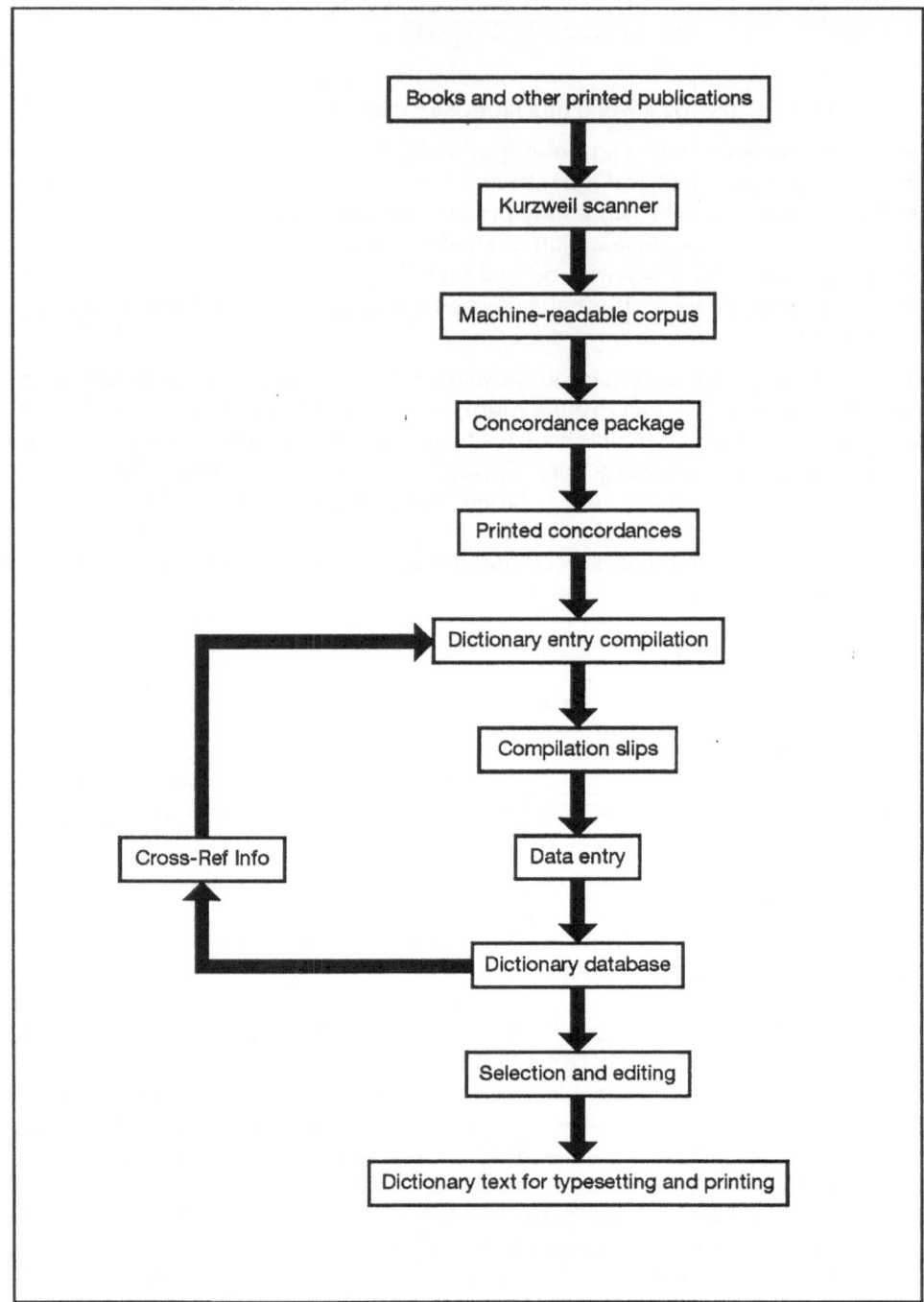

Fig. 2.2. Data flow for the Cobuild project.

At the final stage entries for the printed dictionary were selected from the dictionary database and edited to make a book of the required length. The database remained as a resource for the compilation of other dictionaries and teaching material, and for related linguistic research.

Obtaining the Corpus

A corpus (plural: corpora) is simply a body of text in machine-readable form. It can be a useful resource for the language investigator, so long as the limitations of basic text-processing techniques are well understood. An account is given in reference [6] of two earlier corpora, each of one million words, which enabled comparisons to be made between British and American varieties of English. On the face of it, a million words is a large sample of text, requiring significant computer resources to encode, store and analyse, but for reasons explained later it would not provide adequate information about the behaviour of all the words within the scope of the Cobuild dictionary. It was decided initially that 6 million words was the minimum satisfactory corpus size – this was later extended to 7.3 million, and in practice selective information from a 20 million word corpus was needed to compile some entries in the dictionary.

Entering such a large amount of data through the keyboard was not considered feasible, and because of the need to choose representative samples from different sources it was not enough simply to collect anything already available in machine-readable form. This led to a decision to use an *OCR scanner*, the Kurzweil data entry machine.

The Kurzweil was at the time the most expensive and versatile scanner available, able to scan pages of text and write them onto magnetic tape as ASCII files. It was possible to "train" it to read new print styles by going through an initial session during which its "guesses" at the identity of particular characters were either confirmed or corrected by its operator. Depending on the quality of print being scanned, its speed of text conversion was on average twice that of an expert keyboarder. It did generate systematic errors (e.g. misreading "i" for "l" and "c" for "e") but the error rate was tolerable for the way in which the data was used on the project. In 20 million words of text it was estimated that fewer than 20 000 words were wrongly spelt.

One obvious consequence of using an OCR was that the text was captured exactly as it appeared on the page. There was no chance to insert extra markers indicating either features of interest or non-English words to be ignored, as in previous corpora. Indeed some information actually on the printed page was irretrievably lost. The scanner did not, for instance, do anything special about words or phrases emphasised by italics. Another source of inaccuracy was the hyphen.

Hyphens are normally used to make up composite words, e.g. "swimming-pool", and although their usage by writers is not entirely consistent there is a reasonable level of agreement amongst printers as to when they are required.

Unfortunately hyphens are also used to break words between lines in normal right-justified text. The human reader is used to this, and will mentally rejoin the two parts of the word without worrying about it. Not so the scanner. Thus vocabulary lists produced from scanned material contain a number of spurious "words" or, even worse, real words in the wrong context which have been generated by hyphenation, as in the notorious example of "the-rapist".

In a small scanned text such errors could be corrected manually, but not in the corpus under discussion. A simple program was written to rejoin character strings split by a hyphen at the end of the line, provided that they were made up of lower case alphabetic characters rather than other symbols where the hyphen might be significant. However its use required human judgement as to when it would be useful. It was almost always worth rejoining lines in newspaper extracts, for example, where text is printed in columns and the lines are short. Elsewhere the joining process could create as many non-words as it eliminated. In fact hyphens forming composite words often do occur at the end of lines, as they are obvious break-points for either the human or software compositor.

Is there a more intelligent algorithm for removing hyphens? Routines for *inserting* them are of course used extensively in word-processing and typesetting systems, although they are never totally successful [7]. The simplest keep lists of standard English prefixes and suffixes (e.g. pre-, sub-, extra-, -ful, - tion, -ing), and split only on their boundaries. More sophisticated versions identify syllables by searching for appropriate patterns of consonants and vowels, then make a break before the start of a syllable. They refer to lists of character-pairs (such as "th") which are not normally divided, and of exceptions to the general rules (like "lighthouse").

If a text has been automatically hyphenated, a similar combination of syllable-identification and look-up should allow the process to be reversed; there will be more problems if an intelligent human compositor has done it. In fact early processing of the Birmingham corpus was carried out before the removal of end-of-line hyphens, and it was judged that the spurious words generated by hyphenation should form an insignificant proportion of the whole. Effectively they were "noise" which could be ignored in such a large volume of data. But as a general issue, hyphenation is a good example of the problems raised when automatically converting printed material into machine-readable form.

Basic Text Analysis

Let us now consider what information can be automatically produced from a corpus, and how it helps the lexicographer.

Word Frequency Distributions

The first and most obvious output is a list of all the words which occur there, with their frequencies. (See the example in Fig. 2.3.) This will suggest which words are common enough to deserve inclusion in a selective dictionary. In addition, frequency lists from different source texts can be compared to show how some words predominate in particular varieties of English (e.g. British

authority	1673	attempt	1774	slightly	1886
appear	1674	interesting	1775	david	1889
hell	1681	difference	1777	kitchen	1891
killed	1682	chief	1778	forces	1900
grow	1683	military	1778	army	1903
brown	1684	considered	1781	leaving	1904
forms	1687	daughter	1782	neither	1905
smile	1688	growing	1782	television	1907
somewhere	1691	let's	1782	instance	1909
direct	1692	provided	1785	arm	1911
nobody	1692	produce	1788	chair	1912
relationship	1692	liked	1790	basic	1916
silence	1693	aware	1794	river	1921
direction	1694	corner	1794	fall	1923
minister	1694	bill	1796	huge	1923
france	1702	choice	1796	closed	1928
obvious	1702	sign	1797	attack	1930
ordinary	1702	reasons	1801	theory	1933
talked	1702	impossible	1802	added	1941
type	1702	fast	1809	returned	1946
average	1706	older	1812	wants	1947
council	1706	hospital	1813	flat	1948
plan	1707	required	1813	cases	1957
agreed	1708	foreign	1814	arrived	1965
surface	1708	showed	1814	security	1968
ment	1709	eight	1816	committee	1973
touch	1712	strange	1816	apart	1974
despite	1713	according	1824	played	1975
visit	1716	entirely	1827	garden	1976
programme	1717	rose	1831	watch	1976
member	1719	pressure	1842	caught	1985
remained	1720	becomes	1847	couple	1990
sight	1720	student	1849	physical	1990
holding	1721	department	1851	completely	1992
complete	1724	training	1852	increase	1992
carefully	1730	income	1855	wind	1992
ahead	1742	interested	1857	legs	1994
based	1742	playing	1857	german	1996
recent	1743	developed	1858	lady	1999
freedom	1745	quality	1859	ran	2000
carry	1747	cover	1860	news	2001
range	1749	conditions	1861	mass	2008
telephone	1749	parts	1861	staff	2008
wide	1752	population	1865	expect	2009
gets	1753	break	1867	size	2009
thank	1754	usual	1867	writing	2011
throughout	1755	ought	1868	afraid	2012
lower	1757	worth	1870	international	2013
offer	1757	degree	1874	changes	2015
capital	1761	milk	1876	looks	2021
pass	1761	final	1877	growth	2023
success	1762	prepared	1882	value	2023
practice	1765	picture	1884	pretty	2024
we'll	1770	tax	1885	material	2026

Fig. 2.3. Extract from a word frequency list.

rather than American, spoken rather than written, technical rather than literary). These are helpful points to make in a dictionary for a language learner, who will not have a natural instinct for them.

This is a suitable point to introduce a distinction between two possible meanings of the word "word". If we say that a text contains 500 words, what do we mean? The statement is ambiguous unless we know whether we are talking about tokens or types.

- *Tokens* are the "running words" of a text, as given by the familiar word-count facility in a word-processing package. No account is taken of the fact that some sequences of characters occur more than once.
- *Types* are the individually recurring words in the language, the ones identified in the example frequency list. The word "the", for instance, is one type, but represented by many identical tokens in any normal piece of English.

To give another concrete example, the first verse of the British National Anthem contains 29 tokens but only 19 types, because of its repetitive nature. Obviously the longer the text, the more repetition of types will occur.

A statistic which is sometimes of interest when studying a text is its *type–token ratio*, i.e. number of types over number of tokens. A small ratio implies that the author has a restricted vocabulary, and re-uses the same words often, as in a school reading-book. A large ratio implies a wider vocabulary and avoidance of repetition. The ratio will vary according to the sort of language being used, but comparisons are valid only where the texts are about the same length.

From a data processing point of view, the production of word counts, frequency lists and type–token statistics from a text is conceptually simple. It requires:

- A *linear scan* through the text to identify tokens. A token here is simply a string of (alphabetic) characters between spaces or other punctuation symbols. Although not entirely satisfactory, this definition is still the only feasible one for efficient large-scale analysis of arbitrary texts.
- A *sorting process* to bring all tokens for the same type together for counting and listing in alphabetical order. The precise algorithm will depend upon the amount of data and the memory available – with small texts a comparison tree may be built up during the scanning process, while with larger texts it will be necessary to write tokens to a file and sort as a separate operation.

Before considering the other useful forms of text analysis, it is necessary to say something about word frequency distributions in natural language.

If for any text we plot a graph of type frequency against the number of types occurring at that frequency, we shall find them inversely related, as in Fig. 2.4. This is based on data from 18 million words of the Birmingham corpus; only words with frequency 4–180 are included to display the most characteristic part of the curve clearly. There is a clear increase in population from the top to the bottom of the frequency range, giving an approximation to a rectangular hyperbola. This is the *Zipfian* distribution [8]. An alternative presentation (Fig. 2.5) shows for each word in the text: log(frequency) against log(rank), where the rank of a word is its position in a list ordered by descending frequency. This should approximate to a straight line.

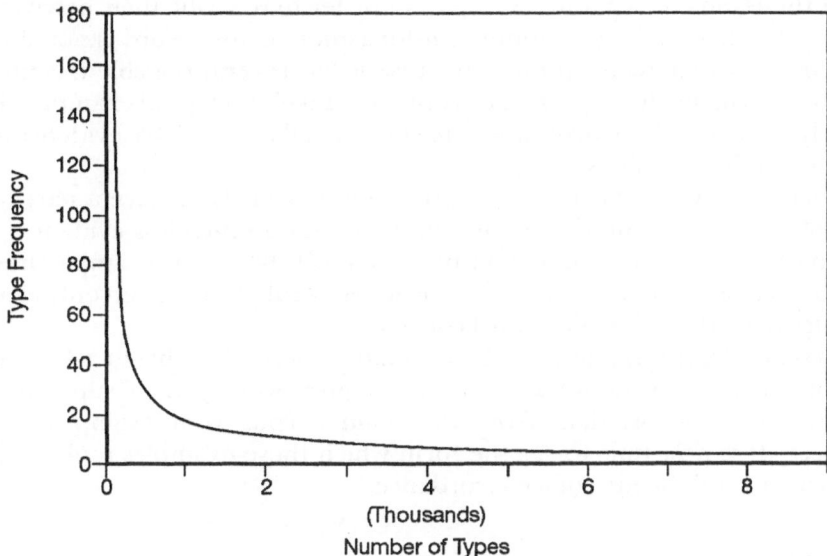

Fig. 2.4. Word frequency distribution. Type frequency against number of types.

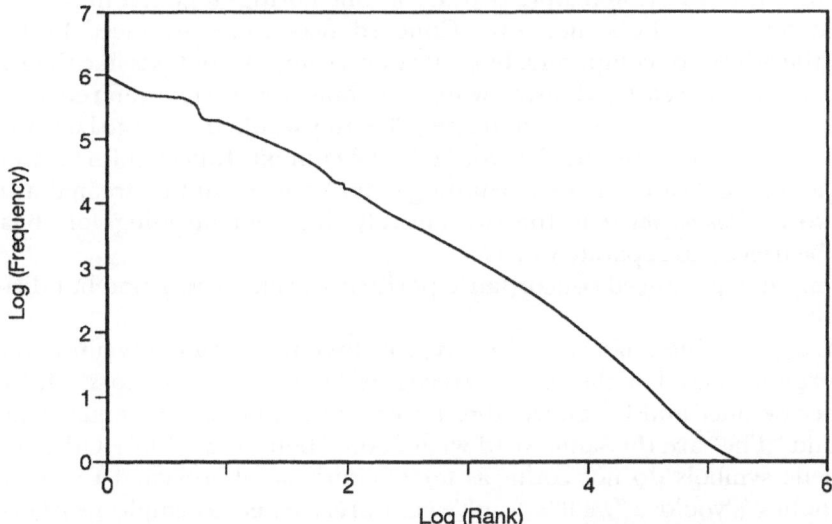

Fig. 2.5. Word frequency distribution. Log (frequency) against log (rank).

In practice it does not matter much whether frequency distributions in a natural language text can be predicted mathematically, so long as we understand how much information it is reasonable to expect from it. A basic fact of life for the language investigator is that whatever the size of text there will be too little data about some words, and far too much about others.

Some words are frequent because of their grammatical function – it is hard to write a sentence without "the", "of", and "and". And it is clearly unnecessary to look at thousands of separate examples in order to describe their behaviour. On the other hand a large amount of information about a word is not always unwelcome. It may turn up often because it has several possible meanings, which are normally distinguished by context. ("Like" is a typical example.) It is precisely the job of the lexicographer to consider all the available evidence and separate out the meanings.

Conversely a word which occurs infrequently is likely to have a narrower range of possible meanings, so one can define it on much less evidence. An account of the Cobuild compilation process in [5] shows, for example, how a quite satisfactory dictionary entry for "veritable" could be based on only eleven examples from the 7.3 million word corpus.

In practice, lexicographers on the Cobuild project were able to ask for less than complete context samples about very frequent words, and to supplement, for infrequent words, data from the main corpus with examples from elsewhere. It is now time to see the form which these examples took, and to discuss in general the idea of a concordance.

Concordancing

A concordance is a printed alphabetical list which brings together in some way all occurrences of the same word. Concordances were produced by hand before the advent of computers, but only to very important texts like the Bible and Shakespeare. With each listed word were one or more text references, e.g. chapter and verse, or act, scene and line. The user would have to go back to the original in order to examine the word's actual context. Inflected forms would be *conflated*, e.g. "run", "runs", "running" and "ran" would be treated as the same word. *Homonyms* (e.g. the two entirely different meanings of "bear") would be treated as separate words.

A computer-produced concordance performs a similar function but differs in detail.

First, the definition of a "word" (or type or token), is, as already hinted, very much cruder – based on the ability to recognise spaces as terminators. The user must decide once and for all whether lower and upper case are equivalent: if "the" and "The" are the same word what about "bob" and "Bob"? Other non-alphabetic symbols do not count as terminators, so abbreviated forms with apostrophes ("you'd", "we'll", "can't" etc.) are treated as single words – in practice quite useful for analysis. Conflation of inflected forms is not usually performed by concordancing software; although theoretically feasible, it is error-prone and time-consuming – a point to be taken up again later. Automatic separation of homonyms is an even less realistic possibility, since it requires far too much genuine natural language understanding.

```
be any. It's like the boy learning to ride a bicycle who sees a rock in the
ree times, admitted that he could not ride a bicycle, or at any rate if he
rcome their fears and learn to swim or ride a bike or walk home in the dark.
ed Epping Forest. There William could ride about dressed in a tiny suit of
McCurry's deep voice made the question ride across the room like a wave, coll
damaged bike which he may, or may not, ride again. The Public Safety Democrat
ame clattering out with his friends to ride against the City, up Ludgate Hill
 grateful for what little there is. We ride again and what comes to me now is
adeleine in her cloak and with my dawn ride a grim rehearsal for the present
nce. And she still had a sixteen-mile ride ahead of her. She said, "I must
contact with other people. You say you ride a horse--good exercise, but what
have ever seen tense people trying to ride a horse for the first time. They
e's at least old enough in meanness to ride a horse race, and wropped up enou
." "Much obliged," Otis said. "Can you ride a horse?" Ned said. "I been livin
um- ber of years," Otis said. "Can you ride a horse?" Ned said. "Nemmine wher
six in the evening and had managed to ride all the way from Ipswich station
hardly own this even to myself, and I ride alone over these beautiful hills
fifteen minutes they would, they must, ride along side by side, and speak, ju
of quip- sters. "Anyone who's going to ride and do things like steeplechasing
or Fell pony, will do. They are fun to ride and drive, and make a pet of too.
ill teach you bad ways.' "Is it bad to ride and shoot and fly a hawk, mother
belonged to them so far as they could ride and sing out "Tally-ho!" It was
settled into its own kind of feel and ride and sound, completely different
e us our presents and let's have a cab ride and tell us about the time you we
long, the way an older child wants to ride a new bicycle. If you pick up the
under the automatic fine rule. If you ride another's bike without permission
n as it became apparent that he could ride anything on four legs, Mohammed
ungs in the middle of a roller coaster ride are having a Child-Child transact
ficiently in league with the police to ride around in police cars. In one pla
or broken line squalls you can try to ride around them, but this one isn't.
ho didn't mean a fart in hell to me to ride around in and the spring came and
joint account. He then continued his ride as far as Shepherds Bush Green.
what it was, nor did anybody else ever ride as its jockey, even after Ned beg
a right to be. Hilary permitted her to ride astride, and for two happy years
de by side. I dread horses and cannot ride at all, and since I had to have
dified by character. It doesn't pay to ride a theory too hard, you lose sight
e whatever. By the late afternoon, you ride at last into the lower gorge wher
st in time to see a swarthylooking man ride away down the street on Daisy. No
led, take the lump out of the idle and ride back to the hotel. Sylvia and Joh
ight when the company started the bus ride back to. the Astoria. The buses,
ir war leader, they told Bull Bear to ride beside him to make sure that in
d. They play football and hockey, they ride bicycles and tumble about on skat
those sets of rollers on which people ride bicycles indoors. By lunch-time
g, wear western clothes, carry radios, ride bikes and speak French to confoun
glass, and little elegant ship-models ride buoyantly in mid-air, for the chu
stand at this window and see the Blues ride by, the sun shine and the tourist
lder, where kids wave to you when you ride by, where people look from their
smile. They were accompanied on their ride by Cal who, having completed the
ed. An investor who goes along for the ride can make a good deal of money. Bu
my pillow on Bub's saddle so I could ride comfortably, and slung my rifle
them for yourself, and even missing a ride didn't matter compared with takin
visiting friends. First I took a taxi ride direct from the docks to the main
said, to cover up for Willie. "I got a ride down," Rudolph said. Plainly, he
all rolled into one - a roller coaster ride down an avalanche of white water.
```

Fig. 2.6. An example KWIC concordance extract for "ride".

The second difference is in the form of the output from a computer concordance. For lexicographers and other language investigators, a KWIC (Keyword in Context) index is likely to be preferred to a list of references, so that there is no need to keep going back to the original. An example section of a KWIC index is given in Fig. 2.6. The keyword is centred in each line, with as much context as will fit before and after it; there may also be a location reference to the text in which it appears. Extra information about the word's frequency overall, and its representation in separate texts making up the corpus, may also be shown.

Concordances of this kind are conceptually simple to make, involving once again a linear scan through the text to identify each token and its desired context, followed by sorting and printing. The main practical problem arises from the enormous expansion of material involved, with a whole line of characters being generated, potentially, for every single token. Twenty years ago the output of KWIC indexes was a major activity for those involved in text processing of any kind, but in many areas (e.g. library and information retrieval applications) they have been largely superseded by on-line keyword searching facilities.

For the Cobuild project, the decision to use printed concordances was based on practical necessity and convenience. The computing facilities available at the time would not have allowed simultaneous on-line browsing through a massive corpus by up to twenty users; and lexicographers needed the material in a portable form, where they could scan rapidly through hundreds of lines without being confined by terminal screen capacity, and, perhaps most important, where they could annotate the material while working on it.

Standard concordancing packages were stretched to their limits by the Cobuild corpus, and it is worth discussing in a little more detail the techniques involved in dealing with such a large mass of material. Traditionally the three stages in concordancing involve:

- Scanning the text, identifying tokens, and for each token a stretch of text corresponding to the desired line-length for the final printed concordance. Part-words at the start and end of lines may be blanked out, but all lines must be of fixed length, with the word of interest starting always at the same character position. Each line is written to an external file.
- Sorting the concordance lines, using a standard external sort algorithm such as selection replacement.
- Scanning the sorted file, identifying "breaks" where the keyword changes, and printing out concordance lines with appropriate spacing and headings.

One difficulty about the above process is that it is hard to partition. If the computer system is not physically capable of concordancing a complete corpus at one time, for example, there are two possibilities:

- Partition by text. Produce concordances for separate texts, then merge all the concordance lines together.
- Partition by keywords. Go through the same large corpus repeatedly, producing concordances for words beginning with each letter of the alphabet separately.

Neither solution is satisfactory because both demand more processing in total than for a one-off task. Either the same corpus is repeatedly scanned, or concordance lines are repeatedly read and written during the merging process.

At the same time it is impossible to envisage a system with the capacity to concordance any text, however huge. Since corpus acquisition is naturally something which happens over a period of time, an incremental approach is clearly desirable. The solution eventually adopted on the Cobuild project was to split the work in a different way. The process (as described by Clear in [5]) involved:

- Creation of an index to the location of every token in the text.
- Complete alphabetical sorting of the index file.
- Generation of concordance lines for each token in the text.

Not only does this solution avoid the large-scale sorting of corpus lines altogether, it is potentially more flexible. When new material is added to the corpus, it is possible to create an index to it and merge with the existing index. Moreover there can be more choice about what concordance lines to print, and in what order and format. Below are some options which concordance software can provide, and an indication of their relevance within the Cobuild project.

Length of Concordance Line.   Normally, line-length is set to fit the available printer width, e.g. up to 130 characters on a standard line printer. This allows the keyword and its immediate neighbours to be picked out easily, but it is sometimes useful to provide more context. Users on the Cobuild project found that words whose function typically involved linking one sentence with another needed to be seen within two lines instead of one.

Stop-Words.   It is not always appropriate to print a concordance entry for every character string in the corpus. The user may wish to ignore numerals or other non-alphabetic strings, or very high-frequency words, and will therefore declare them as "stop-words". Alternatively he may wish to make a positive selection of "pass-words" for which information is wanted.

Sampling.   An alternative to suppressing information about frequent words altogether is to reduce the sample size, e.g. to print every tenth concordance line. This option was used by the Cobuild team in some cases. It is obviously rather crude, however, as interesting examples of rare usages could go unnoticed.

Sort Order: Keyword.   A normal sort routine uses the letters of the keyword in left-to-right order. Researchers studying a highly inflected language are sometimes interested in grouping words by their grammatical endings, and thus require a so-called "a tergo" concordance, based on right-to-left order. This option was not required by or provided for the Cobuild team.

Sort Order: Context   After selecting on the keyword itself, concordance lines can be sorted either by the left half-line (in right to left order) or the right half-line. This allows certain word sequences to be identified easily. For example an important feature of English is the use of "phrasal verbs" like "ring up", "set off", "carry on", where the meaning of the whole phrase cannot be deduced from its separate parts, and which need to be carefully explained to a learner. Sorting on right context conveniently brought most instances of the same phrasal verb together for examination. Conversely other language patterns (e.g. phrases ending with the word "time") were more easily identified with a concordance sorted on left context.

We now return to a question raised earlier in the discussion of concordancing, about the difficulty of applying automatic procedures for the conflation of inflected forms.

Conflation

Modern English is not a highly inflected language but it does use a fairly regular set of rules for processes like making nouns plural, or changing the tense of verbs. As an example, let us consider some rules for plurals:

- The default action is to add "s" as a suffix to the noun.
- If the noun already ends with "s" (or letters like "x", "sh", "ch"), the suffix becomes "es", giving plurals such as "boxes" and "churches".
- Nouns like "lady" or "spy" change their final "y" to "ies", but only if the "y" is immediately preceded by a consonant, so "boy" has a simple "s" suffix.
- Some nouns ending in "lf" or vowel and "f" ("wolf", "leaf") get "ves" as suffix, but not all of them ("thieves" but not "chieves").
- A number of common nouns have irregular plurals (like "mice" and "men") which extend to some of their compounds – we have "dormice" and "snowmen" but not "humen".
- There are also nouns which retain a sufficiently foreign flavour to demand the application of quite different inflections, e.g. one "alumnus" but many "alumni".

The situation, then, is that there are basic rules with exceptions, and exceptions to the exceptions, down to several levels. Similar principles apply when putting -ing or -ed onto the end of verbs, forming comparatives and superlatives of adjectives with -er and -est, and making adverbs from adjectives with -ly.

Since words varying only in their suffixes are closely related (and will appear as part of the same headword entry in a normal dictionary) it might seem a useful step to conflate them by performing a *suffix-stripping* or *stemming* algorithm. Such algorithms do exist; their purpose being to take away common suffixes in a consistent manner so that all related forms are reduced to a basic stem, which may or may not be a word in its own right. In the case of noun plurals, this could involve removing "s" or "es" in suitable contexts. On its own this would leave forms like "hous", "ladi", or "leav", so there should be a further option to change the stem ending as well. More unusual forms of the plural can be dealt with in look-up tables.

A general point about stemming algorithms is that they are subject to a law of diminishing returns – perhaps 70 per cent of cases can be handled easily with a very few rules, another 20 per cent with rather more, and the last 10 per cent require very great effort to get right. Even more serious, any process which works correctly for some words will actually generate errors for others – think about the problem of "cruisers" versus "trousers", or "cruises" versus "crises". Moreover even where correctly done in a grammatical sense, conflation can lose important semantic distinctions. It will be more confusing than useful, for instance, to mix the most commonly used sense of "glasses" (or "spectacles" for that matter) with all the other meanings carried by the singular form of the word.

In deciding whether to attempt conflation in a text processing application, then, the following general points must be considered:

- What algorithms are theoretically possible. We have already noted that rules can be specified which will deal with large numbers of cases, but as each new exception is handled, the rules becomes more complex and may generate errors elsewhere.
- What it is feasible to perform on a given volume of data. A suitable point to carry out stemming procedures is after individual tokens have been extracted from the text, but before they are sorted. This allows related index entries to be merged automatically, without destroying the text itself. It is an extra stage requiring substantial resources, but not beyond the scope of any system capable of carrying out the rest of the concordancing task.
- The needs of the application. Conflation involves deliberately throwing away some information so as to achieve conciseness of description. In information retrieval applications, as we shall see in the next chapter, stemming may be used, along with other look-up procedures, to increase the power of a search term in a query. By contrast a lexicographer needs to look at language examples in a more concrete way, and conflation (even if it could be performed with 100 per cent accuracy) will blur the picture slightly.

The Cobuild project did not make extensive use of automatic conflation, and it was the task of the lexicographer about to compile a dictionary entry to collect together the relevant concordance lines for all related forms. It turned out that these provided valuable insights about grammatical variants, which could feed into the compilation process.

Comparisons of relative frequencies showed that often one grammatical form was more prominent than the others and thus the most likely to be met by the language learners, so it was appropriate that definitions and examples in the dictionary should concentrate upon it. For example "tadpoles" occurred much more frequently than "tadpole", and there was a strong preference for certain forms of verbs – "backslid*ing*", "encrust*ed*", tak*en* aback" – over their relatives. Some usages were more closely linked with particular grammatical forms than others: although the adjective "lame" was equally freely used in the context of legs or excuses, the adverb "lamely" was invariably found in the more metaphorical sense.

So the lexicographers were better off without automatic conflation, although in other text-processing applications, concerned with more abstract recognition of meaning and structure, it may have a greater value. Interestingly, a later stage of the Cobuild project made use of the opposite process: a routine to generate grammatical variants automatically. When the draft dictionary text was extracted from the database, a skeleton entry was produced for each headword, containing all regular inflexions for its word-class. This created many erroneous forms, but the effort of editing these out was considered to be less than that of entering all the regular forms manually.

Collocation

Some of the most important evidence from large texts is about *co-occurrences* or collocations between words, i.e. what words have a habit of appearing close together? We have already seen that sorting on right or left context can reveal some typical patterns but it is possible to do more: to list, for any given word, what other words occur in its vicinity and how often, perhaps selecting only those where the number of co-occurrences goes over a certain threshold. Note that this is another case of discarding information in order to obtain a more selective view of general trends. The actual context is lost; we are left with the information, for example, that "bicycle" occurred 13 times near to "ride".

The importance of this fact depends upon the size of the text, and how often the two words occur in it anyway. Given these figures it is possible to calculate the number of times they could be expected to come together if the words were in random order, and then test whether they actually co-occur *significantly* more often. Fig. 2.7 shows collocates which occurred more often than expected with "ride" within a span of four words, and an associated measure of significance.

In fact the list has been shortened by the removal of proper names and very frequent words – those with more than 10 000 occurrences in the text from which the data was taken. At that level the information provided was mainly grammatical, showing for instance the prominence of common prepositions and some personal pronouns. Collocation with lower frequency words, as shown in Fig. 2.7, provides evidence of the *lexical* functions of "ride", which were of primary interest to the compiler of a dictionary entry.

Interactive and Dynamic use of a Corpus

Reference [5] repeatedly emphasises the value of textual evidence for the Cobuild lexicographers – the examples appearing in dictionary entries were all derived either directly or indirectly from the concordances rather than artificially created. Building the corpus involved considerable effort at the start of the project but it remains as a valuable long-term resource for research and the production of later dictionaries and teaching material.

The discussion so far has focused on rather static forms of analysis – the production of complete KWIC indexes or other tabulations on paper or microfiche, as a massive one-off effort from a fixed-size corpus. Practical necessity dictated that kind of use originally, but over the time span covered by the Cobuild project more emphasis was placed on selective investigations of the corpus, and the available hardware became better able to support interactive use.

| Collocate | Frequency | Co-Occurrences | | Significance |
		Expected	Actual	Level
again	7556	2.170	7	0.00695
ain't	321	0.092	4	0.00001
airport	482	0.138	2	0.00874
along	3004	0.863	5	0.00196
bet	321	0.092	2	0.00400
bicycle	190	0.055	8	0.00001
bicycles	50	0.014	2	0.00010
bike	98	0.028	2	0.00039
automobile	163	0.047	2	0.00106
bus	656	0.188	9	0.00001
cab	87	0.025	4	0.00001
car	2659	0.764	9	0.00001
coaster	5	0.001	3	0.00001
distant	413	0.119	2	0.00650
dogs	421	0.121	2	0.00675
else	2549	0.732	5	0.00096
english	1553	0.446	3	0.01062
faster	335	0.096	2	0.00434
fly	422	0.121	3	0.00027
give	4396	1.263	5	0.00949
going	6974	2.003	9	0.00024
gonter	48	0.014	3	0.00001
got	7201	2.068	8	0.00135
hard	2643	0.759	4	0.00760
hitch	28	0.008	2	0.00003
horse	719	0.206	13	0.00001
horses	398	0.114	4	0.00001
hours'	48	0.014	2	0.00009
joy	366	0.105	2	0.00515
long	7760	2.229	7	0.00797
motorcars	5	0.001	2	0.00001
mount	312	0.090	2	0.00378
mule	61	0.018	2	0.00015
north	1595	0.458	4	0.00128
permitted	228	0.065	2	0.00205
ponies	61	0.018	2	0.00015
preferred	305	0.088	2	0.00362
reckon	81	0.023	2	0.00027
returning	317	0.091	2	0.00390
roller	30	0.009	3	0.00001
school	3305	0.949	5	0.00294
shake	257	0.074	2	0.00259
shall	2176	0.625	7	0.00001
shoot	277	0.080	3	0.00008
sleigh	8	0.002	2	0.00001
storm	287	0.082	2	0.00322
swim	212	0.061	2	0.00178
taxi	311	0.089	2	0.00376
through	9226	2.650	8	0.00595
walk	1261	0.362	3	0.00605
want	5800	1.666	6	0.00728
who's	304	0.087	2	0.00360
wouldn't	1804	0.518	4	0.00199

Fig. 2.7. An example collocate list: collocates for "ride".

Now when examining the corpus interactively, the user selects a word or pair of words for which concordance information is required, then scrolls backwards and forwards through a KWIC display on the screen, expanding the context if he wishes for any concordance line. He can use typical pattern-matching facilities (based on regular expressions) to select concordance lines, so as to pick out all instances of a particular phrase. Alternatively concordance output may be written to a file, and scanned to produce the collocational information described above. This is a great advance on the rather inflexible once-and-for-all concordancing methods used originally.

A more recent development is the decision to set up a *dynamic* corpus at Birmingham University. As we have already seen, word frequency distributions in natural language text are such that one must analyse large texts in order to find out enough about some words, but can be swamped by the amount of information on others. Creating larger and larger static corpora is thus subject to the law of diminishing returns.

The dynamic corpus consists of existing electronic texts (e.g. from national newspapers), which are not stored permanently but processed by software "filters" to extract data on less frequent words and identify changing features in the language. Unfortunately this interesting new approach cannot be explored further here, but it can be seen as an extension to the basic idea of exploiting computer power to study large-scale linguistic patterns. Note that it was not a feasible proposition until machine-readable text became so readily available that it was possible to throw away most of the information while pursuing items of interest.

Following our discussion on concordancing and text analysis, the later stages of the original Cobuild project will be described more briefly. Our account will make connections with ideas current in conventional database management, and introduce some ideas about relationships between words, and structural representations of complex texts, which will recur in later chapters.

Building the Dictionary Database

The basic unit in a dictionary is the *entry*, the identifying attribute or key to which is the *headword*. Entries are of varying lengths, depending upon the number of senses of the word, and the number of examples to be recorded. When building the Cobuild dictionary database, however, it was found necessary to split the information about each headword into smaller fixed-size units.

Dictionary compilers recorded information about a word by completing a number of separate paper slips. These were of two types: *main* and *subsidiary*. The first type held basic information about one sense of a headword, including its definition, its grammatical form, and cross-references to other words. Following this might be any number of subsidiary slips holding real text examples of the word in use, with related explanatory material. These slips formed input records for a relational database.

As any standard textbook on the subject will explain, relational database design requires *normalisation*: dividing information into a set of flat files or tables containing records of the same size and shape. Links between related records in different files are represented by matching "key" values. In any application, normalisation has a tendency to fragment a database, separating items which at some stage must be joined together again. Its advantage is that it creates simple structures on which powerful general-purpose operators can be defined.

Following this principle, the Cobuild dictionary database was built out of three main tables:

- Categories. Key fields were the headword, and a category number labelling one sense of the headword. Dependent fields included the definition, and syntactic and semantic information. A system-derived sequence number was attached to each record, to be used for recording cross-references.
- Examples. Key fields were the headword, category number, and example number. Dependent fields were the example string itself, plus syntactic and semantic information specific to that example. There would normally be a one-to-many relationship between a category record and its example records.
- Cross-references. This table held details of many-to-many relationships between words. Identifier fields were the sequence number of the category record *from* which the cross-reference was made, and the actual headword *to* which it was made. The dependent field was a code indicating the type of cross-reference.

Cross-references

Cross-reference between items is an important feature of any dictionary; to be successful the language learner must build up a picture of the many syntactic and semantic relationships which exist between words. One useful consequence of using a database was that lexicographers about to compile an entry for a set of words could be given information about all the references made to them so far. And when the dictionary text was finally extracted from the database, cross-references could be followed up automatically to check that they all had a valid "target", and that there were no loose ends.

Cross-reference was used to handle issues like variant spellings, derived forms (e.g. "national"/"nationalise"), and irregular inflections (e.g. "go"/"went"). It also set up *semantic links* from one word to another, of which the most important were:

- Synonym: a word with (broadly) the same meanings, e.g. "vermin":"pests". There are of course very few pairs of words which can be substituted for one another in all circumstances.
- Antonym: a word of opposite meaning, e.g. "long":"short".
- Superordinate: a word with a broader range of meaning, one higher up in a semantic hierarchy, e.g. "robin":"bird".
- Collocate: a word which frequently occurs in the same context, e.g. "heal":"sick". We have already seen that information about collocation was directly obtainable from the corpus database.

These relationships are obviously important to language understanding; and in the final version of the dictionary they were shown in an extra column next to the definition and example text for each headword, along with the grammatical notes. They thus formed part of a more abstract linguistic framework, which learners could explore after gaining some understanding of the meaning and usage of individual words.

Some of the above ideas will be encountered again in the discussion of information retrieval systems, where a common technique is to use a thesaurus recording information about synonyms and broader and narrower terms in a query language, so as to increase their potential for extracting relevant material.

Generating a Dictionary Text

The story so far is that lexicographers examined information from a corpus or text database, then constructed a relational database containing records for headwords/senses, examples, and cross-references. The final stage was the extraction and arrangement of material to make a book of the desired length. Software was used to generate draft dictionary entries, and editing and formatting programs were available to help in the very labour-intensive task of selecting and rewording the final text.

In order to generate dictionary entries, data in separate records, fragmented by relational normalisation, had to be joined together again. The various record fields were then re-ordered; some to form part of the main definition and example text, some to go into the extra column alongside. As already described, regular grammatical variants were generated automatically by the addition of suffixes to the headword. Individual fields and entries had to be strung together to form a continuous text, with delimiters which would eventually carry typographical meaning – headword and derived forms going into bold type, examples into italics, grammatical notes into capitals.

This process was carried out successfully, and the *Cobuild Advanced Learners Dictionary* was finally printed and published in 1987. An example page from the dictionary is shown in Fig. 2.8. In concluding the account of the project it may be useful to stand back from this achievement and consider in a more abstract way the underlying problem of representing dictionaries and similar reference books. We have seen that the data went through various transformations in its evolution towards a final form, mainly because of the constraints and limitations of the available software.

To a printer, a dictionary is a book like any other, a long sequence of printable characters embedded with typographical directives. The editing and formatting programs used in the final stage of the Cobuild project were based on that idea. To the user, on the other hand, there are thousands of ways into and paths through a dictionary; the normal alphabetical sequence is merely an aid to finding what he wants and there is only a chance relationship between adjacent entries on a page. This situation is much better modelled by a database in which entries are directly accessible by headword. However the demands of specifically relational database software made it necessary to fragment the data to attain structural regularity. Even the lexicographers assembling the original dictionary information were required to break it into units which were manageable by data entry and storage routines.

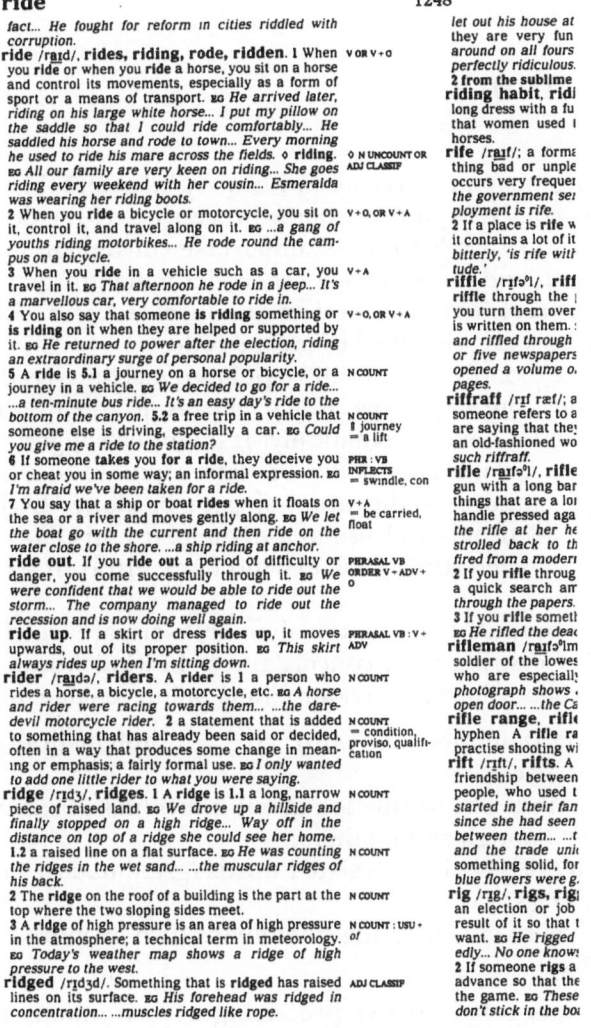

Fig. 2.8. An extract from the Collins Cobuild Dictionary.

The question is whether it is possible to design a single representation for text with a complex structure, which is equally suitable for all purposes. For example, one which allows it to be treated as a linear sequence when necessary but also supports the possibility of multiple entry points and internal relationships. This requirement goes well beyond the field of lexicography, it probably applies to the bulk of text being deliberately put into machine-readable form today. Some obvious developments to consider are hypertext systems and the use of generic mark-up languages, which are discussed fully in later chapters, and the making of dictionaries will also provide relevant examples there.

Chapter Summary

Natural language text is represented with an *alphabet*, and this must be mapped onto a set of *internal codes* for computer processing. If the default mapping is not suitable for our needs we must undertake conversion (*transliteration*) for input and output, and possibly use *escape* codes to handle extended alphabets. If we wish to represent grammatical or structural features of a text we may do so by *embedded tags*, also signalled by escape codes.

Apart from keyboarding, text can be put into machine-readable form using an OCR scanner, but some inaccuracy will result and the insertion of tags obviously cannot be done automatically. It might be suggested that there is a *trade-off* between *volume* and *quality* of data captured – what is acceptable depends on the nature of the processing to be done. Large-scale surveys looking for broad trends will use automatic text entry and tolerate errors; small-scale but detailed studies will expend more effort in accurate transcription and tagging.

Some typical outputs from text analysis software are word frequency lists, word frequency distributions, concordances showing words in context, and summaries of collocational behaviour. Some points to come to terms with are:

- A very crude definition of "word", e.g. an alphabetical character-string delimited by spaces.
- Unequal amounts of information about individual words: too much about some and not enough about others.
- The difficulty of associating related words (grammatical variants) with 100 per cent accuracy.
- The impossibility of separating homonyms (two or more "words" with the same spelling).

The above points relate to the processing of continuous text, which was intended to be read through sequentially. Many texts to be created and processed, like a dictionary, have a more complex structure and their component parts are commonly accessed in random sequence. Conventional database software forces a rather artificial fragmentation on the data, and a more flexible format is desirable.

Investigations

Examine any facilities for large-scale text-processing at your educational institution:

- Is there an OCR scanner? How does it work? Does it have a fixed repertoire of fonts or will it "learn"? How many pages can it read in an hour? What is the error rate?

- What equipment is there for dealing with texts in a non-standard alphabet? How is the alphabet mapped onto your machine's internal code? What part is played by escape codes?

- Is there any text analysis software, e.g. the Oxford Concordancing Package? What options does it provide? Does it deal with non-standard alphabets? What are the practical limits on the size of text it will handle? How easy is it to partition a large concordancing task?

Compare the type–token ratios and plots of word frequency distributions for several different texts. Do you find any substantial differences if you look at:

- Texts from tabloid/quality newspapers?
- Technical/general texts?
- Texts in different languages?

Write and test algorithms for:

- Hyphenation.
- De-hyphenation.

References

1 Morton AQ (1978) Literary detection. Scribner, New York
2 Davidson M (1983) Computer analysis of verb forms in the Greek New Testament. ALLC Bulletin 11(3):68–72
3 Smith J (1983) Transmitting text: A standard way of communicating characters. ALLC Bulletin 11(2):31–38
4 Crawford TD (1981) Towards a science of literary theory. ALLC Bulletin 9(3):6–8
5 Sinclair JM (ed) (1987) Looking-up – an account of the Cobuild project in lexical computing. Collins ELT
6 Johansson S (1980) The LOB corpus of British English Texts: Presentation and comments. ALLC Journal 1(1):25–36
7 Pringle AM (1981) Justification with fewer hyphens. Computer Journal 24(4):320–323
8 Zipf G (1949) Human behaviour and the principle of least effort. Harvard University Press, Cambridge, Mass

Three
Information Retrieval I

"Life is rather like a tin of sardines – we're all of us
looking for the key."
Alan Bennett

Definitions

"Information retrieval" is a very loose term, so we must start by setting some limits to our subject. We are not concerned, for instance, with systems which respond to requests for specific facts, e.g. "What time is the next train to London?" Enquiry systems like that undeniably supply useful information, but they do not necessarily store and manipulate it as *text*, so they are outside the scope of our discussion. It is more accurate to say this chapter is about text retrieval systems: those where a short text (perhaps only a single word or phrase) is used as a way in to a much longer one, which may contain the information that the user is seeking. Even more narrowly, it begins with an account of document retrieval systems, whose function is to hold only enough data to point the user in the direction of texts kept elsewhere in printed form.

Having said that, we shall continue to use the phrase "information retrieval" (IR), since it is the one preferred by information scientists concerned with this activity. It will not be possible to cover all aspects of the current discipline, which has undergone many developments over the last twenty years. For more exhaustive treatments, covering, for instance, research into automatic document classification, please refer to a standard textbook (e.g. [1]).

All readers will be familiar with library catalogues; many will have used an on-line searching system to identify a book or article of interest, so informally the ideas of IR should be well understood. Some basic principles, which predate the computer by hundreds of years, are:

- It is a universal practice to attach to any document at least one piece of "indicative text": its *title*. In more formal publications (like scientific journals), articles will be assigned extra keyword descriptors.
- Any large collection of documents will have an associated *catalogue* or *index*, allowing potential readers to scan through quickly to see what is available.

- Librarians and information scientist have long been in the habit of *classifying* books and other documents by *subject*, so that they may be more easily found.

All these ideas carry over into computer-based IR systems.

Information Retrieval Services

Students are perhaps most likely to have used a big on-line IR system from a college library to a remote database, via a dial-up service such as DIALOG or DATASTAR. Bibliographic databases are available for all scientific disciplines, many dating back to the 1960s when computers were first used for printing indexes and abstracts of scientific journals, and it was realised that automatic searching would also be possible. More recently, services have been extended to include business and financial information. Such databases are very large, typically accumulating a million new items a year, with each item being 2000 or more characters long. They need special hardware and software configurations, since their pattern of use is unlike that of a large administrative database.

They are stored on a number of host machines throughout the world, run by specialist bureaux, and accessed by users via an X25 packet switching network. Packet switching has made the cost of on-line retrieval for customers less expensive than when IR services first came into being, but the design of these systems is still based on the principle that the user needs to minimise communication costs while obtaining the maximum useful information. The dialogue, and the general style of interaction, is remarkably terse in comparison with that of more recently developed software.

A bibliographic database holds discrete records of variable length, each containing full identifying data for a particular document. Typical data fields are:

- Article number: a unique record key within the system.
- Author and author's affiliation.
- Source, i.e. journal or conference proceedings, volume number, pages, etc.
- Year of publication, language.
- Title.
- Abstract.
- Subject index terms.

Of these only the title and abstract could be described as continuous text; the remaining fields contain numbers, codes or short character strings such as might be found in any conventional database record. Subject index terms are assigned by a professional indexer, using a special indexing language devised for the discipline covered by the database. This language consists of lists of terms and rules for their use, and may have quite a complex structure in its own right.

Query Languages

Normal use of an on-line system is through a query language. A *query* consists of a combination of *search terms* identifying documents of interest. It can be built up interactively, with the system reporting at each stage how many documents in the database will satisfy it. To aid this process, each step in the query is given a sequence number, and previous part-queries may be combined using *Boolean operators* to create more complex expressions.

The following fragment of dialogue shows a simple search on words occurring in any field. Subject index terms would be identified more specifically.

```
? factor              : user enters first keyword at the prompt
1 2753                : system reports number of occurrences
? analysis            : user enters second keyword
2 3972                : system reports number of occurrences
? combine 1 and 2     : Boolean "and" of queries 1 and 2
3 253                 : number of co-occurrences of both terms
```

The user can continue to refine the query by entering more search terms, perhaps setting extra constraints based on a particular field's contents. For example only papers with a publication date later than 1988 may need to be considered, or those by an author whose work is already known may be eliminated. The objective is to end up with a manageable number of potentially useful references.

The next stage is to scan through the list of retrieved papers, perhaps with a selective display showing only authors and titles. If they appear relevant, full details may be noted or printed out so that the actual documents can be found later. An initial literature search will aim to be fairly inclusive, but users of the service may return to it periodically to check references or look for new material. Some systems offer a "current awareness" service, whereby the same query is automatically presented to the database from time to time to keep researchers abreast of new developments.

Although their surface syntax may differ, Boolean query languages are all very similar in their basic principles, involving the combination of search terms like keywords with the operators "and", "or" and "not". Queries can be directed to particular fields such as publication date or author, and include numeric comparisons if appropriate. It is generally possible to truncate keywords in order to pick up all grammatical variants, so "pollut" matches "pollute", "pollution", "polluting", etc.

These ideas are now commonplace in general-purpose database applications, but they originally appeared in the context of on-line information retrieval. When these systems were first introduced it was thought necessary for casual enquirers to be assisted in their use of a Boolean query language by a trained intermediary, but the spread of database packages on small machines has made some of the basic ideas much more familiar to the public. However an intermediary may still be very useful when deciding which of the many available databases to search, or learning the structure of a complex indexing language.

One difference between a bibliographic database and, say, a typical relational database is in the number of secondary keys or *descriptors* for each record. This will depend, for instance, on how many keywords and index terms have been assigned, and on the length of the abstract. Any combination of descriptors can be used for searching, hence the phrase "co-ordinate indexing" which is sometimes used in connection with IR systems. This marks a contrast with earlier methods of cataloguing and indexing, where documents were assigned to a fixed position within an existing structure, for example the hierarchical arrangement of the traditional Dewey-Decimal scheme.

Co-ordinate indexing clearly provides greater flexibility, but it also has more potential for inaccuracy, particularly where searches are based on keywords occurring in continuous text rather than specially assigned index terms. The question of how to assess and improve the relevance of references obtained from an IR system will be discussed shortly, after a brief account of implementation techniques.

Database Design for a Co-ordinate Indexing System

The basic problem to be solved is that the database contains many-to-many relationships: one document is defined by multiple keywords and one keyword applies to many documents. Neither is it possible to put any upper bound on the number of such relationships. Some keywords (e.g. "human" in a medical database, "distribution" in a statistical database), will occur very frequently indeed, and although they are unlikely to be used for retrieval on their own they will undoubtedly form part of longer search expressions. The classic method for handling this problem is the *inverted list* organisation, which involves at least three levels of reference from keyword to document (see Fig. 3.1):

- At the top level is a sorted "dictionary" of keywords. With each keyword is stored its frequency in the database, and a pointer to the first appropriate entry in the inverted list at the next level down. Keywords include subject index terms, descriptors, words occurring in titles, abstracts, etc. Contents of other fields such as author and publication date may be indexed separately if a different search procedure is supplied.
- The inverted list file contains at minimum a sequence of relevant article numbers for each keyword. Many IR systems code a more complete

reference, indicating the field in which the keyword appears and its exact position within a continuous text field. This allows the possibility of "proximity searching", an option described later.

- At the lowest level come the articles themselves. They are uniquely identified by article number so a conventional indexed sequential or hashed file organisation is possible, provided it can handle variable-length records.

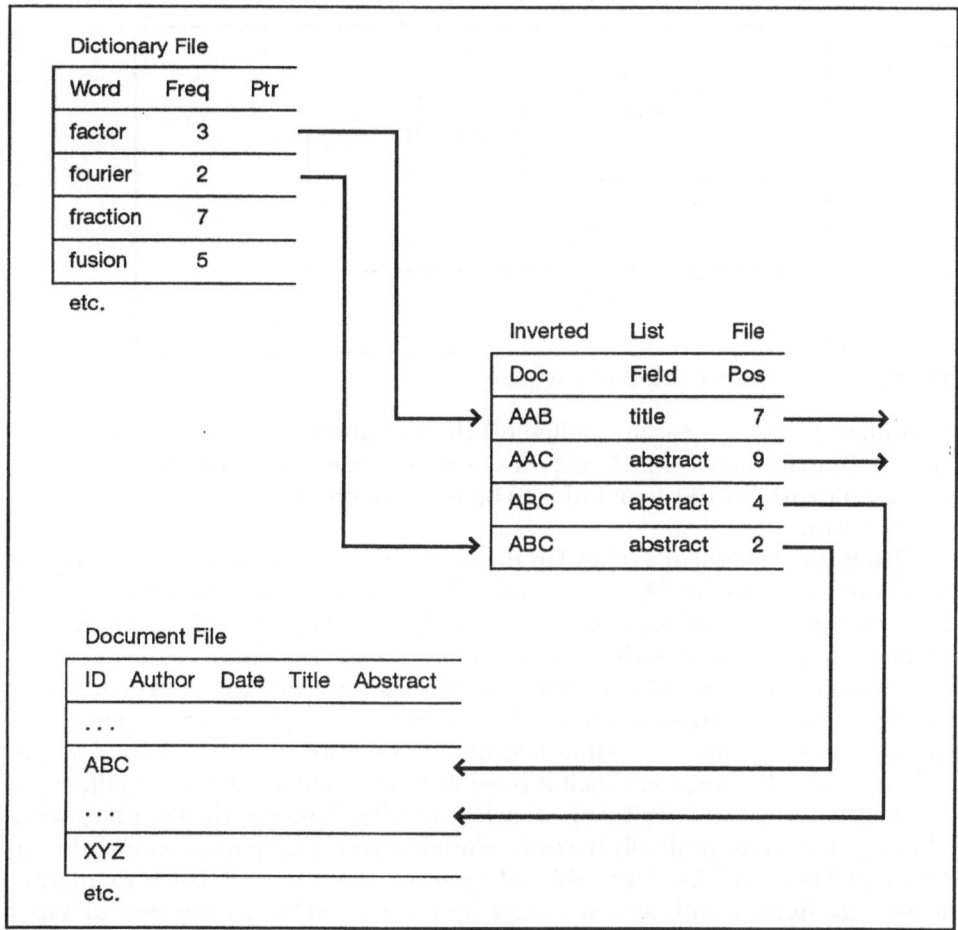

Fig. 3.1. Inverted list file organisation. (Three-level path from keyword to document.)

The search process involves moving through these three levels. When a user enters a query term, it is identified in the dictionary, and immediate feedback can be given about its frequency. If a truncated term is used, all the entries which match it will be adjacent in the dictionary so they can be identified easily. Wild-card matching whereby characters in the middle of the string can be ignored will obviously require more dictionary scanning, a possible reason why this facility is not always provided on remote IR services.

Dictionary entries point to a list of associated article numbers. An important feature of the inverted list organisation is that documents satisfying queries containing Boolean expressions can be identified easily. "And", "or", and "not" can be mapped directly onto the operations of *intersection, union* and *difference*, which are applied to the sets of article numbers for each query term. So the set of matching references for the current query can be built up incrementally, and at each stage the system can report how many members it contains (see Fig. 3.2).

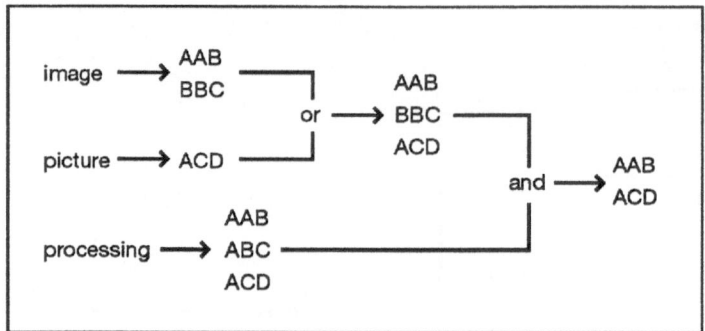

Fig. 3.2. Interpretation of a Boolean query.

Complete article records are pulled off the lowest-level file when the user asks for details to be displayed. He may choose to look only at the first few in the list, and then to ask for the remainder to be printed and mailed, so as to minimise connect time.

That is the skeleton of a typical implementation, but it is customary to impose additional structure on the files at each level, in order to speed up searching. For example a b-tree may be used to index the keyword file, allowing the dictionary to grow in a uniform way as new entries are added.

Any decisions about physical file design must take into account the fact that an IR database is always growing. The normal assumption in an operational database for business or administration is that insertions will be roughly balanced by deletions, and that it is possible to set some upper limit on file sizes. By contrast it is not customary to delete entries from an IR database, since although they may gradually become of less interest to enquirers they could still be needed occasionally. A possible solution is to allow those records to migrate to storage devices with slower access times, e.g. exchangeable disc or tape, rather than be held continuously on-line. Hardware configurations for IR systems tend to allow for a higher than usual proportion of storage devices to processing units, simply because the "hit rate" on some files is so very low.

Another general point to make about IR database organisation is that retrieval efficiency is optimised at the expense of updating efficiency. On-line retrieval must be fast, as users are paying connection costs, but it is not necessary to do on-line updating. Instead batches of updates (new records) can be applied periodically, and the dictionary and inverted list files re-organised accordingly. Decisions about updating frequency are essentially economic –

long intervals between updates are efficient in machine terms but customers will not continue to pay for access to systems which are seriously out of date. The shelf-life of the information is also relevant – typically a news database is updated daily, while intervals of a week or even a month are tolerable for a database of research literature.

Word Occurrence Vectors and Document Signatures

There are alternative ways of representing occurrences of index terms in documents, which can be explained by beginning with a simple hypothetical example. We create, for every document, a binary string where each bit position stands for a possible term. Bits are set to 1 if the corresponding term occurs in the document, otherwise zero. Assume our dictionary contains keywords as in Fig. 3.3.

Keyword	Bit Set
data	000001
disc	000010
file	000100
information	001000
storage	010000
tape	100000

Fig. 3.3. Keyword coding by bit position.

The occurrence of keywords "data file storage" in a document is now coded as [010101]. Query matching can be performed by assembling a similar binary string for the query terms, then scanning through word occurrence vectors applying appropriate bit-wise logical operations. In this example, a query asking for both "tape" and "disc" would match B and D. For speed of searching, vectors may be held on a separate file in sorted order, together with pointers to the relevant document (see Fig. 3.4).

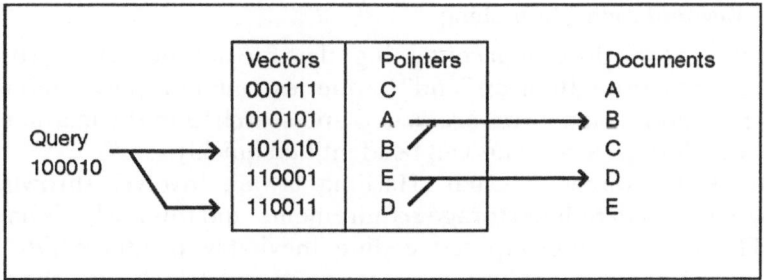

Fig. 3.4. Matching document signatures.

This looks like an interesting approach, but there are obvious practical problems. Firstly, it depends on having a fixed set of index terms which are known before the database is set up; if more are added later all the existing vectors must be recreated. There are systems which satisfy this requirement but they use hundreds of keyword terms rather than half a dozen, so the vectors in practice will grow very long. Moreover a binary vector cannot hold additional information about the field or position in the document where the word occurred, or even its frequency of occurrence.

Experimental systems based on occurrence vectors have developed in different directions. A system described in [1] uses vectors recording not only what words occurred in what documents, but numeric weights which reflect their importance as indexing terms. (One possible weighting could be based on word frequency.) These are long vectors, but because they are also sparse (i.e. have few positive entries) standard techniques can be applied to store them economically. Queries can be coded in the same way, and calculations performed to indicate which documents match them best.

Further investigations in this area take in techniques of automatic document classification, based on the theory that documents with similar occurrence vectors will be relevant to the same set of queries and may be profitably grouped together within the database. Reference [1] has a full discussion of these topics.

A different development of the occurrence vector idea involves creating document "signatures" by superimposed coding. The object here is to hold binary occurrence vectors which do not need one bit position for every possible keyword. Instead, each keyword is mapped to a fixed length bitstring by a hashing algorithm, then all relevant keyword bitstrings are superimposed using Boolean "or", giving a signature or summary string for the whole document. Fig. 3.5 shows a coding for the keywords in the original example.

Keyword	Hash Code
data	0001
disc	0101
file	1001
information	0110
storage	0011
tape	1010

Fig. 3.5. Keyword coding by hashing

The signature for a document containing "data file storage" is now [1011]. This can be matched, using Boolean "and" by queries containing any combination of those terms, and if signatures are stored and searched in the manner already described, relevant documents can be identified quickly.

There is, of course, a catch. Hashing always involves throwing away information so as to reduce storage requirements, and this is what is happening here. The use of superimposed coding inevitably produces *false drops* – instances where document and query terms do not match even though their signatures do. In the above example the bitstring for "data file storage" also matches "tape", for instance.

Performance can be improved by creating separate signatures for sections or fields of long documents, and of course by increasing the size of bitstrings and experimenting to find the optimum hashing algorithm for a particular set of terms. But any system based on signatures must check for false drops before documents are presented to the user.

There has been a recent revival of interest in signature search methods because they can be applied very efficiently on parallel processing hardware. In general, however, mainstream developments in IR over the last twenty years have been based on inverted list indexing, and most of the following points about assessing and improving the usefulness of retrieval systems are made in that context.

Assessment of IR Systems

At the time when IR systems first began to be developed, the other main uses of large mainframes were for heavy number crunching or data processing, and strong justifications were needed for putting resources into an application which was less obviously essential or cost-effective. The performance of IR systems in comparison with human information-finders – the relevance of the document references they produced – was regarded as a matter to be investigated very rigorously. More recently the economic value of computer systems which exist merely to supply information has been better recognised, but measurement and assessment of IR systems is still seen as significant, and the issue is always discussed in textbooks on this topic. Hence the following brief survey.

Two measures of particular interest are:

1. Recall ratio:
$$\frac{\text{relevant items retrieved}}{\text{all relevant items}}$$

2. Precision ratio:
$$\frac{\text{relevant items retrieved}}{\text{all items retrieved}}$$

Intuitively these indicate how far the query has:

1. successfully found most of the relevant references,
2. avoided picking up too many irrelevant ones on the way.

In practice there is generally some trade-off between the two objectives. The measures are calculated for an individual query, but values for a set of queries can be averaged to say something about the overall performance of a system, or to compare the usefulness of different databases or indexing methods.

On the face of it there are two difficulties:

- How to identify relevant items not retrieved without scanning the whole database? This is possible only as part of a specific investigation; it is not a statistic which can be routinely collected as the system is used, or there would be little point in using automatic searching.
- How to define relevance? This can be determined only by the user, perhaps at the end of the retrieval session, although a later reading of the complete documents may cause a change of opinion. The decision about whether to follow up a reference depends partly on personal factors, e.g. whether it comes from a source which the enquirer rates highly.

Strictly speaking these are questions for the information scientist, although the computer scientist implementing an IR system may be asked to set up mechanisms to enable relevance measures to be calculated. There are no technical problems about this so long as he has a clear specification about the statistics to be collected and reported.

It may be enlightening to pursue the issue of relevance a little further by comparing the process of retrieval from a bibliographic IR system and a conventional structured database. In the design of a personnel system, for example, prior analysis will be applied to decide what queries need to be answered, and accordingly what record fields to define and how to code data values. Assuming that data is coded and entered correctly, using Boolean expressions to identify employees with more than five years service who speak French and have a computing degree presents no theoretical problems since the system simply looks for a combination of string or numeric values in certain well-defined positions. The user's expectations about relevance are based entirely on these assumptions.

In bibliographic retrieval, there is a much less direct link between the information content of a document and any descriptors which can be applied to it, especially if these are keywords derived from continuous text. The difficulties of treating natural language words as data items were discussed in the previous chapter; we can sum up the problem within the IR context by saying that there is no one-to-one correspondence between a "word" and a "concept". In detail:

- Words in continuous text vary greatly in *frequency*. Some are very common because they have a grammatical rather than semantic function; in general these will not be of much use in the retrieval process.
- Some words have *variant spellings*. More seriously, most words are part of a "family", the members of which vary only in their grammatical endings, e.g. "factor", "factors", "factored", "factorise", "factorisation". For retrieval purposes all members of this family may be equivalent. Simple truncation to a root form will not always have the desired effect however; users would not normally wish to combine "factory" with the above list, even though etymologically it is a distant relative.
- Most words are *ambiguous* to some degree, in that their precise meaning can be determined only from their context. And the context for understanding

may be very broad: words like "analysis" or "solution" denote very different processes in, say, chemistry and mathematics.
- Conversely, there are many *synonyms* for the same idea, or at least words which can sometimes be substituted for each other. "Information" and "data" are possible alternatives, although "information" is a more inclusive term than "data".

IR systems work best within bodies of literature, e.g. scientific or legal texts, where writers make a conscious effort to avoid word-sense ambiguity. Even so it is hardly surprising that queries based on combinations of de-contextualised keywords fail to find all relevant documents, and do bring in some which are irrelevant.

Improving Search Performance

We now suggest some extensions to the basic techniques of co-ordinate indexing and retrieval, developed to try and overcome some of the problems just discussed. In general they involve applying more human intelligence to the task of indexing the database, and/or improving the algorithms for automatic keyword generation and searching. The first approach exploits more of the semantic properties of natural language data and fits in with the tradition of librarians and information scientists who have long experience in devising knowledge structures and classifying documents. The second approach involves cruder techniques, which are cheaper to implement. They are used in traditional document retrieval, but are even more essential in the context of full-text retrieval, especially where there are no trained indexers or search intermediaries to service the system.

In practice all the extensions described below require some combination of human intellectual effort and software support, but there is a difference of emphasis. For example the design and use of a thesaurus, or of a "faceted" indexing language, relies very much on natural language understanding by human experts.

Thesauri

A thesaurus for a document retrieval system is a file which records relationships between words – hierarchical, associative, or equivalence. In the discussion of dictionary cross-referencing in Chapter 2 we saw that words might be related as superordinates, common collocates, or synonyms; here we have exactly the same ideas. Some large IR databases in medicine and chemistry use a controlled indexing language in which there is a *preferred term* for every set of synonyms;

the indexer must select the preferred term, even if the author has used a different one. He may also assign, if appropriate, broader, narrower or related terms from the thesaurus hierarchy. For example, in the field of computer science, "programming language" is a broader term than "Cobol" but a narrower term than "application development tool". For the best results, the searcher also needs to know the thesaurus structure, which is why intermediaries are often employed to help casual users with databases of this kind.

However, a thesaurus can be used within any text retrieval system, not just one with a controlled index language. Its function then is to extend the scope of query terms entered by the user. When a query is entered, its keyword terms are looked up in the thesaurus, and – either automatically or as a user option – the system will also find documents containing synonyms, or broader, narrower and related terms. This is likely to improve the recall ratio of a query, but perhaps at the expense of its precision! There are no major technical difficulties in consulting a thesaurus while processing a query; the main system overhead is in the expertise needed to devise and maintain a coherent thesaurus structure within the field covered by the database. If intellectual effort is lacking here the thesaurus may degrade rather than improve retrieval performance.

Faceting

A more complex structure is exhibited by a "faceted" index language, where the indexer not only assigns terms, but their "roles" in a document description. The one described here is *Precis* (Preserved Context Indexing System, see [2]); in practice most often used to catalogue books in a specialist library but in principle suitable for any set of documents

A Precis index entry may contain up to four *core terms*, with the roles of "action", "object", "agent" and "location". So the phrase: "solution of murders by detectives on railways" would be coded as:

action: solution
object: murders
agent: detectives
location: railways

A core term may have subsidiaries with the role of "part", "member" or "assembly": in the above example *Orient Express* should be coded as a "part" subsidiary to "railways". The system is open-ended, with new terms being added by indexers as required, but they should be linked into an existing thesaurus structure, e.g. "crimes" specified as a broader term than "murders". A "type" code may also be assigned to terms, for instance to indicate whether they are proper names or geographical locations.

The Precis index entry attempts to summarise the content of a document more accurately than a collection of separate keywords; and fortunately it is not then necessary for the searcher to reproduce the indexer's train of thought in order to find it. The complete entry is automatically permuted in various ways so that in turn each core term becomes the lead, and all the others its qualifiers. Each variation so formed is inserted in the index, providing a number of ways to find a document while maintaining the structural relationships between its index terms.

Clearly neither indexing nor look-up can be completely automated with this system, although software aids have been produced to assist in both processes, and there is scope for application of artificial intelligence techniques. Retrieval performance tends to be better than with a simple keyword method but there is a high price to pay in terms of human time and expertise.

Where it is not possible or economic to devote such resources, IR systems must make the best of words extracted automatically from the text. But the keyword list may be processed in various ways, with the aim of counteracting the extremes of frequency found in natural language words, and concocting a set of terms, each of which covers a reasonable range of documents. This means eliminating some words altogether, and grouping others together.

Stop-lists

Stop-words are those which occur in continuous text but are not expected to be search terms, and so do not figure in the inverted list index. When processing new text the system must compare each word it meets with the stop-list, and ignore any which appear there. Alternatively, systems with a controlled indexing language may have a pass-list, and ignore everything else. Stop-words entered as part of a query are also ignored, with an informative message to the user.

Virtually all text retrieval systems use a stop-list. It consists of a few hundred common words whose elimination will make automatic indexing and searching more efficient without much affecting retrieval quality. Obvious candidates are members of "closed" word classes like conjunctions, pronouns, and prepositions – whose function in the sentence is mainly grammatical.

An extremely crude method of getting rid of grammatical words is to throw away those with fewer than four letters. This requires no human effort whatsoever, and will rarely have any adverse effect on retrieval, but it still leaves a number of obvious candidates behind. Neither is it possible to identify stop-words on the basis of high frequency alone. We have already noted that some very common words are used for retrieval as part of a combination. In fact a hard and fast distinction is difficult to make. The kind of words which turn up in titles and abstracts often carry useful meanings in some contexts while elsewhere they are just part of the verbal machinery: compare "A new method for factor analysis" with "An analysis of some new factors identified in..."

There is little alternative, then, to having the stop-list devised by an expert in the subject discipline, perhaps guided by example word frequency lists. In that respect it is not very different from the thesaurus; however it is worth noting that stop-lists are necessary evils, rather than positive aids to retrieval. Elimination of grammatical words constitutes a loss of information, since the user cannot ask about phrases which contain them. This is a relatively small price to pay for a substantial gain in efficiency, but given sufficient machine resources to index every text word there would be no advantage in a stop-list.

Dealing with Variant Spellings

From the system developer's point of view, the simplest way to deal with variant spellings is to throw responsibility back to the user – allow him to look at the dictionary and identify them for himself. Alternatively they can be recorded in the thesaurus, if there is one. For systematic variations exhibited by a large number of words, the system can arrange to normalise (or normalize!) them before placing them in the dictionary.

A special form of normalisation is sometimes applied to proper names, for instance those of document authors. A difficulty here is that the enquirer may be unsure of the precise spelling, is it "Phillips" or "Philips", "Davis" or "Davies"? It may be tedious to enter Boolean expressions covering each possibility. The "Soundex" system allows variations of this kind to be reduced to a common phonetic form by applying a few simple rules, e.g. ignoring vowels, reducing double letters to single letters, putting groups of consonants into equivalence classes. This is helpful for names but too drastic for ordinary words.

Conflation, Suffix-stripping, Stemming, Lemmatisation

The above are all synonyms for the same process: removing grammatical endings from words so as to produce a root form which will act as a more powerful search term. The impossibility of doing this with total accuracy was discussed in the previous chapter, where it was suggested that although automatic conflation was too crude a process to be helpful to lexicographers, it might have more of a place in IR. Let us consider in a little more detail what is involved.

As well as direct grammatical inflexions (-s, -ed, -ing, etc.) many words take common suffixes to produce derived forms. For example:

- Suffixes to form verbs: -ate, -ify, -ise, as in activate, codify, normalise.
- Suffixes to form nouns: -hood, -ism, -ist, -ity, -ment, -ness, -ship, -tion.
- Suffixes to make adjectives: -able, -al, -ant, -ary, -ful, -ic, -ish, -ive, -ious.

The above list is in no sense complete; because of its historical development English is very rich in formative endings, with the result that a substantial tree may be grown from a root form, as in the example in Fig. 3.6. It will be seen that the suffixing process is recursive, in that one ending can be added to another, perhaps with some mutation like the loss of a final "e". Moreover any new verb or noun so formed can take the normal grammatical inflexions for its class so the number of possible variations is rather greater than Fig. 3.6 suggests.

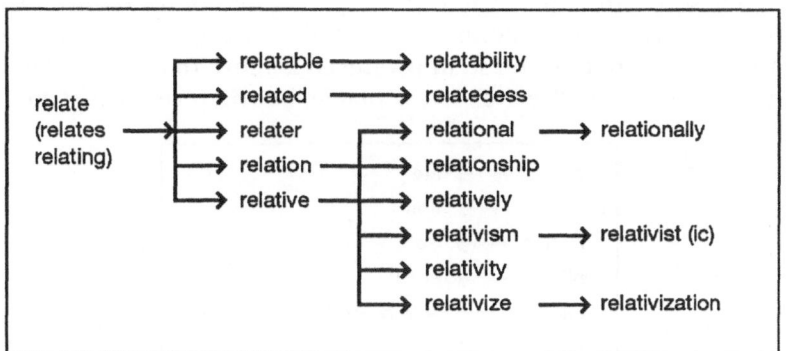

Fig. 3.6. Derivation tree from root form "relate".

The use of formative suffixes allows ideas to be expressed concisely, and they are especially evident in prose which deals with abstractions, using a vocabulary largely derived from Latin. This type of language is very characteristic of scientific papers, so the application of suffix-stripping here is likely to make a substantial reduction in the number of index terms to be handled. Some of the first major IR databases were in the field of chemistry, a discipline which has its own precise rules of term derivation with special endings such as -ine, -ol, -ium, -ide, etc. Perhaps the early adoption of suffix-stripping in this context paved the way for its acceptance elsewhere – at any rate it is a technique which is widely available on large systems. In theory similar principles could apply to formative prefixes like over-, un-, re-, etc. but in practice there appears to be less enthusiasm for this within the IR community.

One simple-minded way of ignoring suffixes has already been mentioned: allowing the user to enter a truncated form as a query term. Alternatively, related forms can be grouped together as synonyms in a thesaurus. But it is quite common to do the suffix-stripping once and for all when keywords are added to the system dictionary. This can be managed by using a large look-up table containing both basic suffixes and all possible combinations of them, e.g. "icalization". Alternatively rules for suffix detection and removal can be applied repeatedly, reducing words to a root form in a series of steps. Porter [3] describes an algorithm which takes this approach.

Rules take the form of substitutions to be applied on the basis of certain conditions, e.g. what is the stem ending? Consider for example the -ing suffix. When this is added to a verb, a final "e" preceded by a consonant is removed, while a final "t" preceded by a single vowel is doubled. Thus we have "sit" → "sitting" but "site" → "siting". Conversely the rule to strip off the suffix must replace the "e" and eliminate the double "t".

Derived forms are simpler to handle than grammatical inflexions, but complications arise where a word contains a composite suffix. Individual rules must be ordered to give the optimum results, with a general rule that the longest possible substitution is applied. A typical selection of rules is given in Fig. 3.7. These ensure that, for example, "organisation" reduces through "organise" to "organ", "exhibition" to "exhibit". Once again the substitution is subject to a condition, that the stem produced is more than one syllable long. Reducing "relational" to "relate" is acceptable, but then removing the "ate" is not!

```
ational   ⟶   ate

tional    ⟶   tion

ization   ⟶   ize

ation     ⟶   ate

ion       ⟶   –  if preceded by "s" or "t"

ize       ⟶   –

ate       ⟶   –
```

Fig. 3.7. Example of suffix-stripping rules.

In retrieval from scientific text, suffix-stripping rules can reduce the number of terms to be indexed by about a third [3], even when certain more difficult transformations (e.g. "reception" → "receive") are not attempted. However it is important to realise that some information is being lost on the way. Consider again the derivation tree for "relate". Granted that all the words there are members of the same family, their reduction to a single root will almost certainly impair retrieval precision. It is pointed out in [3] that a theoretical physicist would prefer not to mix "relativity" with other forms, and the same could be said of the computer scientist with "relational" or the philosopher with "relativist". In fact it is arguable that words towards the bottom of the tree are the only ones with a narrow enough meaning to be valuable as search terms. The other point to be made is that suffixes provide useful information about word-class, so should certainly not be eliminated by systems which attempt a more intelligent syntactic analysis of a text to be searched.

So much for operations on the keyword list. We now consider some practical extensions to the querying and searching procedure itself.

Proximity Searching

In the discussion of co-ordinate indexing techniques, the assumption was made that matching a document to a query was a simple matter of checking whether or not the search term(s) occurred anywhere in the document. This may be unrealistic when the amount of continuous text held in document records exceeds a short paragraph. Often it is not enough to know that two words turn up somewhere; the user is also concerned with their order, and how close they are to each other. Suffix-stripping and elimination of stop-words may have made it impossible to check for complete phrases like "analysis of variance" through the index, but provided information has been kept about the positions of words in the original text, it is possible to specify proximity searches. Some possible options are that words should be:

- In the exact order given, e.g. "value added tax".
- Adjacent, e.g. "added value" or "value added".
- In the same sentence, paragraph, or other text unit.
- Within a specified distance, e.g. "value(3:3)added" will match a phrase containing the two words in either order with up to three words between.

What is possible depends on what information is held in the inverted list index; systems may store a simple word offset from the start of the text or hold more detail about sentence and paragraph boundaries. Additional pattern-matching functions can be applied once potentially relevant records have been read from the database, but searching in that way will be somewhat less efficient.

Ranking Retrieved Documents in Order of Relevance

In a long document, one or two occurrences of a query term or phrase may not be particularly significant; the user may be more interested in those where it turns up repeatedly. However it is probably not sensible to ask him to set a threshold value beforehand. Instead the list of retrieved documents can be presented in the order of some *score* arrived at by counting how often his search terms appeared. A system which maintains details of keyword occurrences in full will obviously be able to do this.

This is one method for ranking retrieved documents according to their likely relevance. Another one involves allowing a looser query specification, which does not demand an exact match. The user might have six independent search terms and not necessarily expect to find them all together, but be interested in documents containing any combination of three or more. It is possible, though cumbersome, to express this with a Boolean query, but easier to use a language which supports the option directly. The retrieved documents can again be presented in order of likely relevance, with those having five of the original search terms being ranked higher than those with four or three.

A further extension to this idea is to assign *weights* to query terms in order of their perceived importance, and to use them in calculating the rank of retrieved documents. Some systems allow users to set the weights, others calculate them automatically. A simple but effective method is to use some inverse of overall frequency, since frequently occurring terms are likely to be less discriminating selectors.

Term weighting may be used in conjunction with another technique described as *relevance feedback*, whereby the user's judgement on the relevance of one set of retrieved documents is used to modify the query formulation before searching again. The general principle is to find new documents which are in some way "like" those originally deemed relevant, and "unlike" the others. This may be done by using all descriptors of relevant documents as new query terms, or by re-assigning the weights so as to favour terms which retrieved relevant queries and downgrade the others.

Methods involving weighting are somewhat experimental by comparison with those described in previous sections. They are often associated with the use of word occurrence vectors for keyword searching rather than the more common inverted list file organisation. Only a very brief outline has been given here and the reader is referred to [1] for details of experiments to test their effectiveness.

Exploiting Connections Within the Database

The final technique to be described for improving search performance is not based on keyword retrieval, but on the use of other database information to extend the range of a query. We know that once a relevant document has been found, it is always possible to find others which are related to it in some way by following up its references. Similarly it is possible to consult a *citation index* to see later articles which referred to it. A computer-based retrieval system has the potential for following up such links automatically – at least within the same database – but the publicly available on-line services do not exploit this possibility as they might. One early and otherwise quite limited system which did so to good effect is described in [4].

The database consisted of articles from 17 statistical journals. Each article entered was assigned a unique key indicating the journal, year, volume, and starting page number. All references to other articles within the same set of journals were coded in the same way, making it easy to incorporate citation details into any article referred to. The cross-references could be followed up when a query was made, so that users retrieving articles by keyword or author had the option of seeing also full details of citing and cited articles. In principle the process could continue indefinitely, identifying other references to the references, other citations from the citations, and so on.

The option to obtain details of references and citations was popular with users of the system, and extended the scope of queries in a useful way. Its effectiveness depended on the initial identification of a self-contained set of journals with a comprehensive coverage of the subject; as references outside these journals were ignored it would not be possible to change such decisions later without producing some inconsistency in the database.

The main overhead came at the updating stage: whenever a new batch of records was added to the database it would entail the updating not only of author and keyword indexes but of citation details in existing document records. In a massive on-line system this might be unacceptable, but separate files of cross-reference information could be held instead.

That concludes the general survey of basic IR techniques, and some of the extensions which have been tried to improve the effectiveness of retrieval. It is perhaps fair to say that they are all very pragmatic; there is no way of proving their correctness in a mathematical sense. All that can be done is to implement them and investigate their value to a sufficiently large group of users. Those which show good results will eventually be incorporated into working systems; the others – whatever their theoretical justification – will remain as footnotes in the research literature.

Chapter Summary

Text retrieval systems enable users to find documents of interest by entering *queries* consisting of *keyword terms* linked by *Boolean operators*. Such systems are commonly implemented using an *inverted list* file organisation, which allows documents indexed by any combination of keywords to be identified without scanning the document file. This organisation is designed for fast, frequent retrieval but slow, periodic updating, reflecting the expected usage of an IR database.

Keywords extracted from natural-language text do not always represent the subject matter of a document precisely, so queries will sometimes fail to find all relevant documents, or find ones which are irrelevant. *Recall* and *precision* ratios are sometimes used to measure the effectiveness of a query, and aggregated to indicate the overall performance of a system.

The retrieval power of keyword search terms can be improved by: the use of a *thesaurus*, *suffix-stripping* to identify root forms, *spelling standardisation*, and *proximity searching* to set specific conditions about co-occurrences between keywords in text. It is possible to find other relevant documents by exploiting *cross-references* within the database.

More experimental IR systems use *word occurrence vectors* or *document signatures* rather than inverted list files to record the occurrence of keywords within documents. They may implement a system of scoring rather than exact matching, with documents presented to users in order of their likely relevance to the query.

This chapter has concentrated on document retrieval systems where abstracts rather than full texts are held, but the principles described here are equally applicable to full-text systems, which are introduced in the following chapter.

Investigations

What famous literary quotation is 90 per cent stop-words?

Try out an on-line information retrieval service through your college library. Choose a database relevant to your subject of study. Find out how many references it contains and how far back they go. Get to know its query language and note which of the options described in this chapter are offered. Do a literature search on a topic of interest and see how many references you obtain. Were they all relevant, and if not, why not?

Implement a suffix-stripping algorithm, based on the method described in this chapter. Try to avoid "brute-force" matching of every suffix combination by applying several rules in order, setting them out as a state-symbol table. Do you end up with real words or truncated roots? If you are fluent in a language other than English investigate whether similar principles can be applied there. Alternatively, consider the effectiveness of a prefix-stripping algorithm.

References

1 Salton G, McGill M (1984) Introduction to modern information retrieval. McGraw-Hill, Maidenhead
2 Austin D (1984) PRECIS: A manual of concept analysis and subject indexing. British Library, London
3 Porter MF (1980) An algorithm for suffix stripping. Program 14(3):130–137
4 Jones S (1974) The London School of Economics computer-based bibliography of statistical literature. Journal of the Royal Statistical Society Series A 137(2):219–226

Four
Information Retrieval II

"To your text, Mr. Dean! to your text!"
Queen Elizabeth I

This chapter extends the basic ideas of information retrieval in several directions. The emphasis moves away from remote services and bibliographic databases, towards full-text retrieval application, set up by large organisations for their own purposes. A short case study will describe how one company acquired, selected and indexed data for its own internal requirements. General-purpose commercial software is normally used to implement such systems, and an account will be given of two different packages and the facilities they provide for setting up and querying databases; these will be linked, respectively, to the use of parallel processing hardware, and integration with conventional relational database technology. The final topic to be discussed is text compression: as longer texts are stored it may become very desirable to reduce the database size as much as possible, and so this is an appropriate point to give an overview of the relevant techniques.

The Move Towards Full-text Systems

The original retrieval systems held information about huge numbers of documents, but stored a very small proportion of the text in each case. Any other method was impractical because of the expense of putting full texts into machine-readable form, and limits on available disc storage. At least one reason for the emphasis given to retrieval relevance in this context is that after making a query the user must still obtain the documents he has been told about, at the cost of his time and possibly his money. Systems where whole texts can be examined on-line are not only more convenient but make the issue of precision rather less urgent, since non-relevant documents can be eliminated from consideration more quickly.

The first public on-line full-text systems were set up in the mid-1970s to serve the legal profession. First in the field was *Lexis* in the USA; a comparable service for British and European law was *Eurolex*, which came into operation in 1980. Here the advantages of IR were obvious, since lawyers are intensive users of specialised printed sources such as statutes, case law reports and legal commentaries. As a group they were influential, able to pay an economic price for information services, and for the convenience of consulting them from their own offices. So full-text systems were financially and technically feasible, but the employment of special intermediaries between the subscriber and the database was not.

It turned out that legal documents fitted well into the pattern already set for bibliographic databases. They displayed a standard structure familiar to lawyers: statutes being divided into sections and subsections, each with a well-defined scope; case reports into units containing, for example, headnotes, citation, opinions, judgment, along with other fields denoting title, date, counsel, and so on. Legal vocabulary is intended to be unambiguous (or at least to take on only one meaning at a time!), and it was possible to search on keywords extracted from the text, without the need for prior indexing, but exploiting the use of a thesaurus, and of preliminary suffix-stripping. A standard Boolean query language was used; obviously with long texts the options for proximity searching would be very important. (Legal texts are also characterised by an extensive network of internal and external cross-references; the potential use of citation information in retrieval was suggested quite early on [1], but the following of cross-references is still not an option in the legal IR systems generally available.)

During the 1980s, the balance of interest shifted decisively towards full-text systems, which were no longer seen as a novelty, nor, in comparison with other computer applications, particularly extravagant in their use of resources. Large quantities of machine-readable text became available as a by-product of printing and electronic mail, and this applied not only to professionally published material but also to reports and correspondence circulated within and between commercial and industrial organisations.

The result was the development of a number of large-scale general-purpose IR packages, designed for organisations to run their own internal text retrieval services. Some typical examples are Status, Basis, and BRS Search. These packages provide the kind of retrieval functions already described; like other general-purpose database software they also include housekeeping facilities to enable systems to be set up, updated, re-organised, and tailored to users' needs.

Such packages are still intended to run on reasonably large machines, since the kind of systems they support are not worth running unless they cover several thousand documents. There are simpler approaches for smaller databases which do not demand the establishment of elaborate inverted list file structures. Unlike other database (and text processing) applications which can be satisfactorily scaled down for small machines, IR systems are out of place on PCs unless in connection with optical storage devices – a topic which will be introduced in the next chapter.

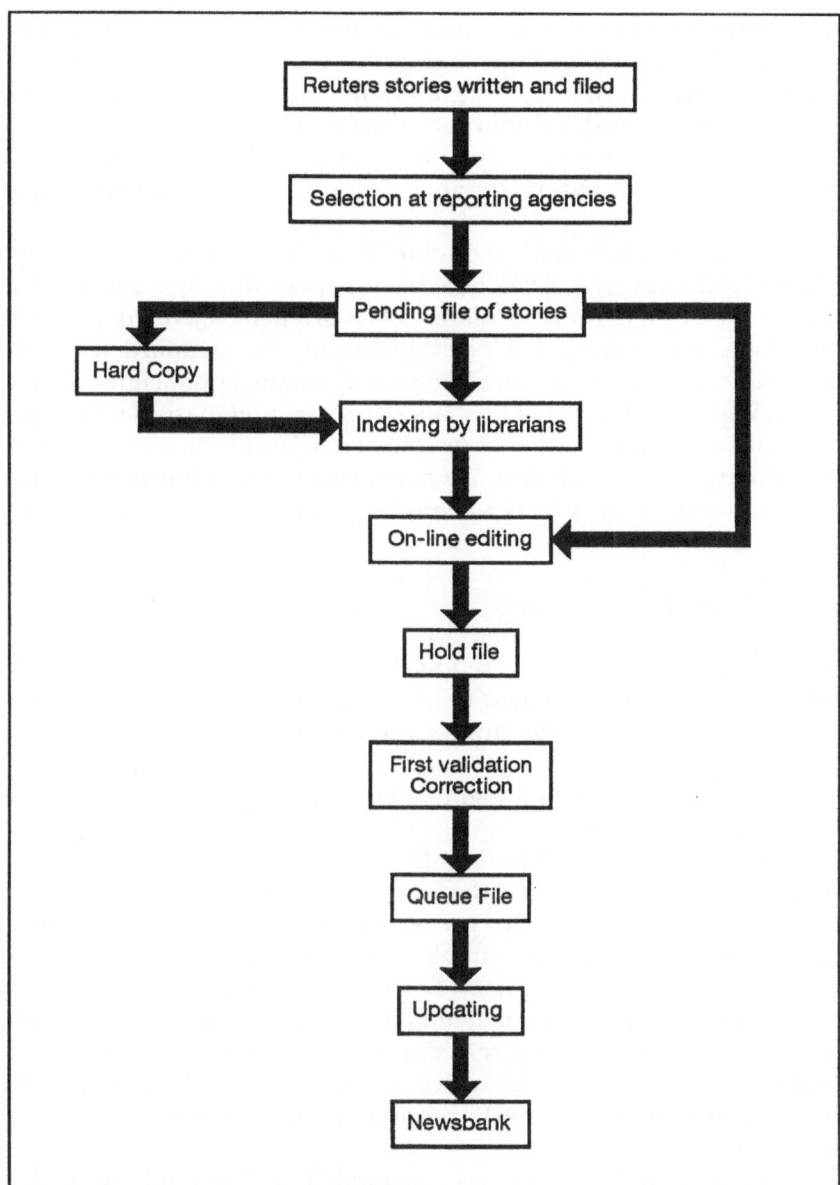

Fig. 4.1. Data flow for Reuters Newsbank.

Reuters Newsbank

We now consider an interesting example of full-text retrieval in action, and in particular the processes whereby current material must be selected and indexed before being placed in a database. Reuters is a large and well-known news agency, having reporting bureaux throughout the world. It runs an international network for transmitting news and other information, mainly financial and commercial. All journalists need to obtain background material on events which they have to cover, and for Reuters staff its own archives form an important source of that material. This is clearly a suitable application for full-text searching.

The account given here is of an on-line service which ran between July 1984 and April 1990, and which has now been superseded by a more advanced system operated by a Reuters subsidiary. The original Newsbank was set up on Vax machines using Basis – a package having the standard text retrieval functions described in the previous chapter. A summary data flow diagram for the system is given in Fig. 4.1. The main structural unit in the database was the "story": a news report from one or two short paragraphs to several pages long, filed by Reuters journalists from anywhere in the world. Some human decision-making was needed before stories could be placed in the Newsbank.

Selection and Indexing

The first level of selection occurred at the reporting bureaux. About 30 per cent of stories filed were deemed to be of global or long-term interest; these were marked as potential candidates for the Newsbank and sent over the network to a "pending" file on the machines which serviced the system. They arrived throughout the day and night, but the cut-off point from one day to the next was set at 2 a.m. GMT.

Stories carried some descriptor information along with their main text, including a *headline, date, dateline* (the location from which the report was filed), *by-line* (the journalist's name), plus provisional *topic* and *country codes*. They were assigned an internal sequence number as a unique identifier while going through the initial processing phase. Each night the stories on the pending file were printed out, sorted and collated before being examined next day by the librarians. Here some further selection might take place, mainly to avoid duplication. If several stories on an active news topic had been filed within 24 hours, the most up-to-date and comprehensive was selected, with minor rewriting being done if necessary.

The main task at this stage was to modify and extend the descriptor information. All stories were indexed by at least one "topic" code indicating a broad subject category of the type "DIP/MIL" for "Diplomatic/military", and one country code. Extra countries might be added, for instance if the report covered some international agreement or dispute. Although it was always possible to identify references to other countries by a full text search, it might pick up too many irrelevant documents, as in the case of an air-crash involving victims of many nationalities. So the use of specific country descriptors improved search precision.

Other possible descriptor fields were "company" and "sport", optional depending on the nature of the story. A company name field was used if appropriate to distinguish stories "about" a specific company from those making casual references to it; the same applied to stories about a particular sport. Four thesauri were defined within the system to support indexing, validation and retrieval on the descriptor fields.

One further special descriptor – the "name" field – was sometimes used to overcome a common difficulty in IR systems: that certain character strings are stop-words in some contexts and useful keywords in others. In a chemical database for instance it is impossible to look for "vitamin a" in a keyword search because "a" is also the indefinite article. The Reuters stop-list contains the word "Reuter" itself, since it occurs in the introductory phrase for every story. Common prepositions, pronouns, etc. were also eliminated from the keyword list, as were character strings containing nothing but numeric digits, since these were very frequent but rarely significant for searching.

Under normal circumstances, then, it would be impossible to look for news items about a Reuters journalist being expelled from a country, a concert by the rock group "The Who", or developments following "Resolution 242". The name field was designed as a catch-all for words and phrases like these, to be assigned by the librarians when the normal rules about stop-words were not applicable.

Librarians made decisions about selection and indexing by reading paper copies, then called up the stories by sequence number and edited them on-line. The maximum document size on Basis was 16k characters; longer stories were accommodated by linking successive records together. Stories came from two sources: the "media" file, which carried general news reports, and the "commercial" file, containing company information supplied as part of Reuters financial services. The latter were split into screen-sized units of text, which had to be joined together again to make complete documents for the Newsbank.

Validation and Updating

Selected and indexed documents were moved to a "hold" file and a printed copy was produced for reference. The records then went through a first validation procedure to check for structural correctness, i.e. fields being complete and in the right order. Any errors at that stage were reported and corrected. Valid records went onto a "queue" file to await the next stage of validation and updating.

Updating took place overnight. As usual with an IR system this involved not only adding new records to the database but extracting keywords and updating dictionary and index files. Values in topic, country, company and sport descriptor fields were validated against the relevant thesaurus. A report was produced about possible errors here but the records concerned were not held back since they might still be retrieved in other ways.

The general problem with IR database management – that during updating the system is not available for retrieval – was overcome by so-called "volume shadowing". Copies of the database were held on several machines; during the night updating was performed on one while the others continued to service search requests, then the updated version was copied back to the other machines. This sort of duplication was of course essential for a service accessed by journalists from many different time-zones.

In fact two databases were held: a short-term one covering the most recent six months and a long-term one holding all previous data. Operating the system involved periodically moving records from one to the other, when some data compression also took place. The purpose of holding two databases was to ensure fast retrieval of more recent material. The user was required to choose which database to see when logging on to the system, but the search facilities offered were the same. To give an idea of overall size, in August 1989 there were over 130 000 stories in the short-term database, and about a million stories in total.

Searching

Journalists using the system logged in over dial-up lines. They were presented with a choice between a standard Boolean query language supplied by Basis and a menu-based interface. In the first case, the dialogue was very similar to those already described in the previous chapter. Users could *look* at the list of words occurring in any field, using typical wild-card matching; so the command: *look name* = * produced a list of all the specially indexed phrases like "Resolution 242" described above.

Keyword searching could address the whole document or one field, e.g. *find 'opec'* or *find headline* = *'opec'*. The system responded by giving the total number of relevant references, and the query could be refined by further Boolean expressions, e.g. *find 1 and dateline* = *'geneva'* combined the first query entered with the new condition. Proximity searching and word truncation were also supported.

Where a field to be searched had an associated thesaurus, the system reminded the user of the preferred term or standard name. Thus the query *find co* = *'ici'* produced the response *USE co* = *'Imperial Chemical Industries'*. Any thesaurus could be consulted by entering the *browse* command, and selecting the relevant thesaurus name. Search terms were not automatically expanded; decisions to use synonyms or related terms were taken by the user when refining a query.

Retrieved documents were presented in date order, the most recent first. Fields could be displayed selectively, and any search terms in the text were highlighted. The story field was treated as a whole – individual paragraphs were not separately identified – but it was possible to display any section of it by referring to line numbers.

The alternative menu-based system simply presented a set of choices based on field, i.e. headline, story, dateline, country, company, sport, topic, by-line, or date. Selection of one of these took the user down to the thesaurus or list of terms recorded in that field, when a further choice could be made. Although useful when becoming familiar with the system, menu-based searching proved somewhat slower and experienced users tended to prefer the query language.

The above is a user's-eye view of a typical on-line full-text retrieval system of the 1980s. A point that emerges very clearly is that the process of scanning and indexing stories to improve subsequent retrieval performance was quite labour-intensive, requiring the skills of a traditional librarian or information scientist. Documents generated for one purpose (the fast transmission of news stories for publication) were later used for the secondary purpose of on-line retrieval. Not surprisingly, there was some mismatch, making it necessary to carry out reformatting and validation. The capture of the bulk text, and basic keyword matching, could be achieved automatically and economically, but intellectual effort was needed to allow meaningful searches of the material.

Reuters has now expanded its activities in the provision of on-line news retrieval very considerably, offering three commercial public services: *Textline* (general news), *Country Reports*, and *Company Newsyear*. These sources are potentially as important to Reuters clients as those for purely financial information, providing a context within which to evaluate market trends and make appropriate decisions. And the growing perception of the commercial value of text retrieval services has justified a corresponding investment in hardware and software to improve their timeliness and ease of use.

Standard IR techniques have been extended by the use of AI software which allows the automatic selection and classification of incoming stories. (Taking a simple example, rules were specified to identify company names which were the main subjects of a story, rather than casual references. The names can then be looked up in the company name thesaurus and if necessary standardised for insertion in an index field.) Nonetheless, human editing and indexing is still an important feature of the extended systems.

Having looked at an example application, we now consider in more detail the characteristics of two contrasting packages. One is a conventional text retrieval system which has been in use for over ten years (although undergoing progressive development); the other is a more recent product in which text retrieval functions have been added to a standard relational database system.

The Status Text Retrieval System

Status was first developed at the Atomic Energy Research Establishment at Harwell. Because of its origins it was suited to handling legal documentation, and was used to set up the *Eurolex* system, mentioned earlier. The software has been implemented on a number of mainframes, and the first part of the following account is quite generally applicable. (For further implementation details, see also [2].) However one particular version (for ICL VME) has an interesting enhancement involving the exploitation of parallel searching hardware and a brief description will be given of the principles involved there.

Status provides facilities for system set-up, allowing the database manager to define:

- Physical parameters, e.g. disc space allocation, maximum record and field sizes.
- Logical database structure (see explanation below).
- System users and their access rights.
- "Concordable" characters: taken into account when creating indexes. Numeric strings may be ignored, for instance, and upper and lower case letters treated as equivalent.
- Common word lists (stop-lists) or fixed vocabulary lists (pass-lists).
- The thesaurus, if one is used. Status does not assume a system of preferred terms, but allows the setting up of "synonym rings" in which each member is equivalent.

Status supports a standard hierarchy of: database, chapter, article, named section, paragraph, and word. Articles are analogous to records in conventional databases, but may be grouped into chapters to allow selective searching within broad topics. The database manager can control the order in which articles are stored, putting related ones together to provide a convenient "browsing chain" for users. This might be arranged, for instance, to make the recent material most easily accessible.

Articles are divided into separate named sections to reflect the structure of the stored documents. User access controls, common word lists, indexing and searching can all be separately defined for each named section. A text section is normally divided into paragraphs and words but articles may also have *keyed fields* of type integer, real, date, etc. which allow searches with numeric comparison operators, and can act as sort keys if necessary. *Positional keyed fields* are declared when it is desired to hold a list or table of values to be searched.

A "concordance" in Status terminology is an inverted list file rather than a KWIC concordance. For each indexed word a four-level reference is held: to the chapter, article, paragraph and word number. As usual there is a top-level dictionary recording the frequency of every word in the database and this may be consulted by the user.

Searching takes place through a typical Boolean query language, which covers proximity searching and reference to named sections and key fields. Typical queries are:

Q *Copper Sulphate?*
A   complete phrase to be matched.

Q *Sulphate + (Iron , Copper) − Zinc?*
A Boolean expression: + = "and" , = "or" − = "not".

Q (Earnings/1,5/Supplement) @ ABSTRACT?
/n1,n2/ denotes a proximity search within a paragraph, @ is a named section selector.

Q Pubdate > 23/5/88?
Numeric comparison on a keyed field of type date.

The output from a query can be directed to the terminal or to a printer, and the user can select which fields are to be shown. On the screen, query terms are highlighted in any displayed text. On the printer, report generator facilities can be used to specify detailed layout.

As usual, complex queries can be built up in stages, saved and re-used. In addition, *query macros* with parameters can be specified, allowing lengthy command sequences to be repeated easily, perhaps with minor variation in search terms. Macros may either be publicly available, or private to single users.

For making queries, then, the user has similar facilities to those on a remote IR service. The important difference with an in-house system is that he could also be modifying and adding to the database on-line. Documents or articles may be composed over a period of time, and in general are likely to be much more variable in size than records in a relational database, for instance. So a fairly dynamic storage structure is required, and an organised approach to updating.

In fact, for security reasons the database itself is not updated immediately when a user changes or extends an article. Modifications are placed on an *intermediate file* and made permanent later by the database manager using a batch update facility. Text on the intermediate file is accessible once the article to which it belongs has been located, but until it has been indexed and the concordance file re-organised, it cannot be found directly by querying.

In the earlier discussion on IR database design, it was noted that there is a conflict between the efficiency of updating and of querying, and that the inverted list organisation favours the latter process. The expected pattern is that many users access the database simultaneously with queries and require a rapid response, but that new material is added less frequently and involves the lengthy process of keyword extraction, possibly suffix-stripping, and updating of both index and text files. During this time the database is not available for queries. This contrasts with other on-line applications like airline reservations, where both updates and queries must be handled in real time.

The Status method of intermediate files represents a compromise, which gives users the convenience of interactive updating but allows the database manager to decide when and how often it is worth taking the system out of commission for the addition of new material. The ICL Content Addressable File Store (CAFS) extension was designed to improve the situation further by making text on the intermediate files immediately available for searching.

The ICL CAFS Extension

The Content Addressable File Store is an example of a back-end processor, a piece of hardware designed to sit between a disc datastore and a mainframe computer, and improve the performance of database functions by applying local intelligence. A general account of such devices is given in [3]. CAFS is in fact a *hardware filter*, capable of making multiple key comparisons in parallel. Its value for IR applications is that comparisons can be set up to implement standard Boolean queries directly, and only records which satisfy all the comparisons are passed to the mainframe. The filtering process takes place at speeds approaching that of straight disc transfers, without tying up the central processor. So a set of relevant records can be retrieved rapidly without the overhead of keyword indexes. The components of CAFS are:

- An array of registers, each holding a key value, and with a corresponding low-level processor able to compare the key with an incoming bitstring. Mask-bits can be specified to enable part-matching of variable-length strings.
- A search evaluation unit, which receives a one-bit result from each comparison, and applies logical operations to determine whether the keys match the query. The unit in fact holds a small microprogram generated in the mainframe for each query and sent to CAFS.
- A retrieval unit which, on the basis of the search evaluation, either does or does not send the current record through to the mainframe. This unit is able to select a subset of record fields for transmission.

When a CAFS query is initiated, the comparison registers are loaded with the key values to be matched, and the comparison operators ($=,<,>$) to be used in each case. At the same time the search evaluation unit is loaded with the microprogram to perform the appropriate logical tests. The file to be searched is then scanned sequentially. For each record, the fields required for retrieval are sent to a buffer in the retrieval unit, and the key values are picked out and sent to the comparison registers, using as many as are needed for the query. Up to 14 key comparisons may proceed in parallel; when their results are evaluated a signal is sent to the retrieval unit to indicate whether or not to release the current record. For a diagrammatic representation of the system see Fig. 4.2.

CAFS files must be held in a standard format so that the retrieval unit can pick out individual data items. Records may be of variable length, and consist of one or more "self-identifying" fields, each preceded by an identifier code and a length, and holding a set of fixed-length items followed possibly by a variable-length item. Status records are of course very variable in format; at least some fields will contain continuous text and individual keywords must be identified within those fields, so this flexibility is certainly needed. The system provides a special utility to convert files into the CAFS format.

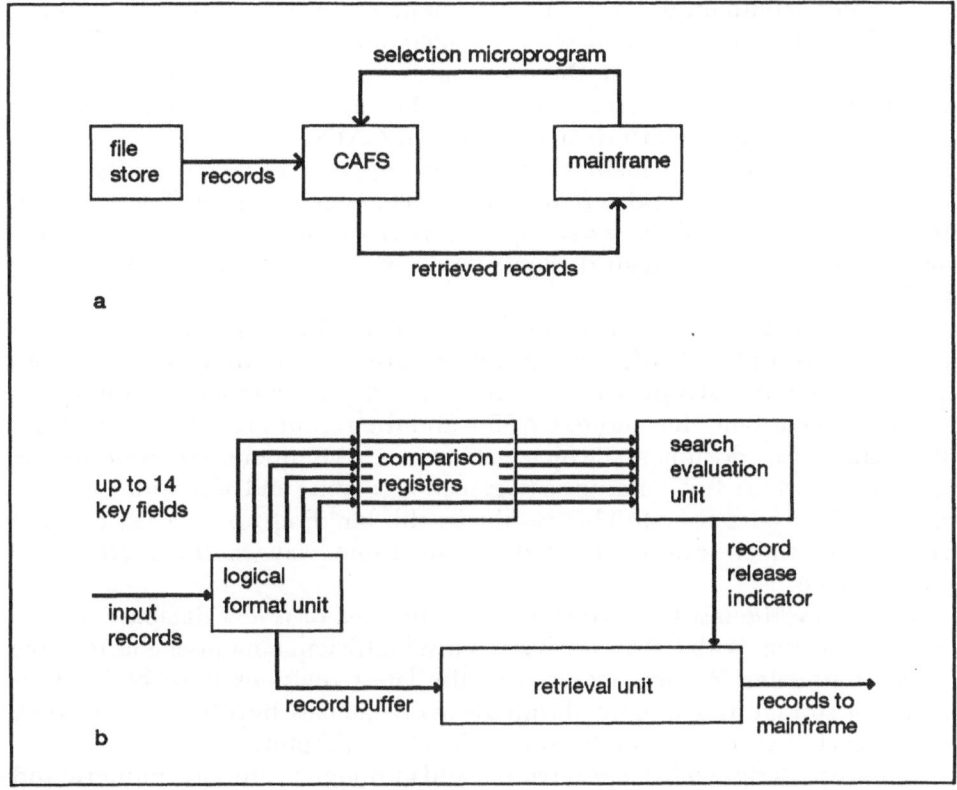

Fig. 4.2. a CAFS overview. **b** Data flow for CAFS selection.

CAFS can be interfaced with any database search software; it also includes a "file correlation" unit to support fast relational joins between two files, and will perform counting and aggregation functions on records as they are read. Searches may be specified through the ICL operating system control language, or, more flexibly, by routines called from user programs. (In the Status implementation, the language used is Fortran.) The basic routines supplied allow the programmer to: open and close a CAFS file, define a file buffer and a record layout, prepare a search by defining a Boolean query, and repeatedly read the file, with the effect that each read will return one record satisfying the query.

The Status database manager with access to CAFS may choose to use it in one of two ways [4]. Small databases may be held entirely on a CAFS file, with the advantage that there is no need to hold extra index information, or go through the time-consuming process of keyword extraction and index updating. However functions associated with the concordance (e.g. interrogation to find word frequencies) and with a thesaurus are not available. Moreover although CAFS searches quickly, a sequential scan through a whole file is implied, so performance degrades as the database increases in size.

The more common use of CAFS is to allow keyword searching of material recently added to the database, for which no concordance has yet been produced. Under this system the user makes his changes, which go onto the intermediate file as usual. After validation, the database manager issues an *online update* command and the text goes onto the CAFS file, which the system will search along with the main database during any retrieval session. The concordance file is not updated, however, so changes are not reflected in word frequency lists. Periodically a *batch update* is performed, when the amendments are transferred to the main database, the concordance is updated, and the CAFS file cleared.

The user making a query need not know whether his output comes from the main database or CAFS; often it will be a mixture of both. After translation into a convenient internal representation, the entered query is sent in two directions – to the concordance file and to CAFS – and the results are collated together. References for documents which satisfy a CAFS query are sent to the mainframe, where further criteria (e.g. section scoping and user authorisation) may need to be satisfied. This results in the building up of a list of valid references, which can be treated in the same way as those from the concordance.

This is not the last time we shall meet the idea of a text database on two different media. With CD-ROM, it is not just inefficient but impossible to make periodic updates for new material so the latest revisions must be held on magnetic storage and integrated with the main database by software at the time of retrieval. A specific example appears in a later chapter.

Status was designed for text retrieval, and although it supports numeric and coded data fields, and could be used to run operational or administrative databases, it would not be particularly efficient or convenient. The other package to be considered in this chapter had a different starting point. In Oracle, text retrieval has been grafted onto a conventional relational database system, normally used for straightforward business applications.

Oracle SQL*Textretrieval

The relational data model is described in many standard textbooks, and will be summarised extremely briefly here. All information in a relational database is represented by flat files or tables of data; every entry in a table has the same regular structure. Powerful relational operations can be defined to act upon and produce tables, and these allow answers to queries to be extracted from the database. A number of query languages have been defined based upon these operations, of which the best known is SQL, developed by IBM. Suppliers of current relational systems find it essential to support SQL as one possible interface, and the language is subject to ANSI/ISO standardisation [5].

At first sight the relational philosophy is incompatible with that of text retrieval, where variability of size and structure is much more in evidence. The original relational model stressed that values held in tables were "atomic". So if a six-digit code number had an internal structure such that some queries need refer only to its first two digits, the sub-field should, strictly speaking, be defined separately. For practical reasons real relational systems do not impose this constraint, and SQL supports features like substring and wild-card matching to look at characters within fields. But while this is useful for identifying short strings such as names and product descriptions, it is not enough to handle the sort of IR application we have discussed so far.

In business environments where relational systems are most used, a need has been identified to store and search longer text fields, along with numeric and coded data. The personnel example so often used to illustrate database concepts can be extended to include the need for a free-text résumé of employees' job experience. A construction company might wish to hold in its database lengthy descriptions of work to be done and materials to be used, for selection and merging with the results of calculations to produce tenders for jobs and bills of materials. And there are the obvious text-handling business functions already noted, i.e storage and circulation of reports, correspondence and legal documents. Many companies elect to standardise on database software to minimise overheads in support and training, and are likely to prefer a product which can satisfy a wide range of needs. So the addition of text retrieval facilities to a relational system might be expected to give it a commercial advantage over its competitors.

Extensions to the Relational Model

In Oracle [6], the standard relational model has been extended in three main ways, by providing:

- Definitions of new text datatypes.
- Utilities for text loading and indexing.
- Extensions to SQL to support keyword retrieval, and to the user command language to support the creation and use of keyword queries.

Datatypes relevant to text retrieval are:

- Character: the standard type, for strings < 256 bytes.
- Keyword: for fields containing a variable-length list of separately delimited keyword strings.
- Long text: for blocks of continuous text up to 64k bytes.

Only one long text field may be defined for any table. Data in these fields is stored on a separate disc location, linked to its home record by a pointer field. Long text must be divided into "rows" or lines delimited by a special character like linefeed, so that the semblance of a tabular structure is maintained. The normal expectation is that text will be generated outside Oracle (by word processor or e-mail); then incorporated in the database and indexed using a utility program running in batch mode.

As far as indexing and searching is concerned, Oracle has imported the traditional text retrieval functions wholesale. All text words may be indexed, with either a stop-list or pass-list option. The result of indexing is the creation or updating of two underlying database tables: the "word-list" and the "locations-list". These are like the files referred to in other contexts as the dictionary and the inverted list (or concordance), implementing the traditional three-level access method. Locations-list entries hold: *word, record or document number, field-name* and *word-number*. A thesaurus may be used to represent relationships between words as synonyms, preferred terms, broader, narrower or related terms. This information is held in the "word-link" table.

Extensions to SQL

The database can be queried by: straight keyword searching, proximity searching, Boolean expression, left or right truncation and wild-card matching, soundex matching, and expansion of query terms through the thesaurus. Queries can be built up in steps, saved, re-used, and deleted from the database.

These ideas are already familiar; the question is how they can be presented in a relational context. Often the database will consist of a mixture of text and non-textual data, and the full range of relational queries must be supplied along with those specific to text-searching. Oracle integrates the two by defining extensions to SQL, notably the extra keyword "contains". The following example query from a personnel database is taken from the Oracle documentation:

select name, job, salary from emp-table
where résumé contains ("speak" OR "spoken") AND
("cantonese" OR ("mandarin" AND NOT "orange"))

Proximity searching is specified by a pair of numbers in brackets indicating permissible distances between words in either direction:

select title from document
where abstract contains ("coffee"(5,5)"consumption")

Expressions with "contains" are translated into standard SQL denoting relational operations on the underlying tables. In practice one such simple query could generate many lines of lower-level SQL. To find documents containing a single word requires that relevant entries in the locations-list are selected and then joined with the document file over document number. Testing whether two words co-occur demands that the locations-list is joined with itself. So ignoring all the housekeeping, security checks and optimisation which must also go on behind the scenes, the lower-level version might look something like this (using a temporary renaming function to allow a self-join on the locations-list):

select title
from document, location-list, location-list temp
where location-list.word = "coffee"
and temp.word = "consumption"
and location-list.doc-number = temp.doc-number
and temp.doc-number = document.doc-number

Proximity searching would require further selects based on the word-numbers of matching entries, to ensure that they were sufficiently close in value. Looking at this laborious specification of a simple query it is clear that considerable effort is required to implement keyword searching in a relational context. However it is not necessary for the user to know about the underlying operations, and the advantage of translating into SQL is that from then on the standard compilation and searching routines can be used, and queries can freely mix references to text and non-text fields.

Other forms of string searching are denoted by functions. For instance:

select title from document
where soundex(author) = soundex("Coles")

will find all documents by authors Coles, Cooles, Colls, Collis, etc. Tests on numeric and date fields, and the use of wild-card matching, are of course already part of normal SQL.

To use thesaurus information in matching, a special suffix must be added to keywords named in the contains clause. Thus:

"coffee"&   asks for coffee plus synonyms.
"coffee"<   asks for coffee plus broader terms.
"coffee">   asks for coffee plus narrower terms.

Further dialogue may be used to refine such queries, e.g. if the keyword is part of several synonym rings the system will ask which one to use. Likewise there may be a choice as to how many levels up or down to go in the hierarchy of broader/narrower terms. Note that hierarchical relationships, of the sort that appear in a thesaurus, can be stored and searched using relational operations. Oracle SQL already has the necessary functions, but once again it is not necessary for users of SQL*Textretrieval to refer to them explicitly.

Handling Queries

Extending and translating SQL are only part of the story. Once a query based on keyword searching has been executed, it may be inappropriate to simply display the fields named in the select clause, especially if they contain long text. Instead the user must be allowed to scan through and check their relevance.

Suppose the following query has been run:

select story from document
where story contains ("big" AND "bad" AND "wolf")

What is returned is a hitlist of references satisfying the query. The user may now issue the command "Display Hitlist" to see the first line of each relevant story retrieved. Any one of these can be selected by cursor. The command "Display Text" causes a screenful of the relevant text to be displayed, with query terms highlighted. These facilities are obviously very like those provided in earlier IR systems.

Even in its simplified form, it is unlikely that users will be able to enter syntactically and semantically correct SQL every time, so Oracle provides a set of commands to help in composing and running queries. The most important are:

- Create Query: in the buffer, using a screen editor.
- Edit Query: in the buffer, using a screen editor.
- Run Query: produce the hitlist for the current query.
- Refine Query: add extra clauses to the current query.

There is an option to run a query and report how many documents satisfy it, without forming a hitlist. In addition there are commands to *save* and *drop* queries, *list* and *rename* stored queries, *get* a query and make it *current*. Several queries may be "active" simultaneously, in the sense that their hitlist is still in existence; these can be listed and restored along with their hitlists. Two or more existing queries can be combined to form a new one, and it is possible to display the text of a query along with a *history* showing how it was built up.

During an interactive session the user may also examine thesaurus and word frequency information with "Browse Wordlist", and alter a piece of text on screen after a retrieval. Like Status, Oracle does not perform a complete update of underlying word-lists after an interactive edit; this must wait for a batch program to be executed later. Addition of new text causes extra entries to be added to the word-list and location-list, but references to deleted text are not removed until the whole document file is re-indexed.

We therefore see most of the functions provided by a standard text retrieval system, with the advantage that they can be combined with those more common to relational systems. In practice however the query/command language interface described above is not expected to be suitable for many potential users. Oracle presents SQL*Textretrieval, and the library of routines support- ing it, as a development tool for creating simpler interactive applications, tailored to a particular organisation's requirements. The normal interface would be "Query by Forms" – a general facility whereby the entry of data onto a particular screen form "triggers" the execution of predefined SQL code to answer the query. This gives the same effect as the macro facility mentioned in connection with Status; with the SQL code referring to variables or formal parameters whose actual values are supplied by the user at execution time.

This follows a general trend within the database community. SQL began as a simple language to make the relational operations available to naive users, but it has over the years acquired much of the power and complexity of a full programming language. The first ANSI standard (very much a subset of that available in commercial systems like Oracle) contains nearly 100 keywords, many of them for use in situations where SQL statements are "embedded" in procedural third-or fourth-generation language programs. Under these circumstances SQL provides a standard set of facilities to update and query the database, but the end-user will never see it. The same is likely to be true of the Oracle text retrieval extensions.

Text Compression Techniques

Text compression is often employed by general purpose IR systems, so can appropriately be discussed at this point, but the techniques are applicable wherever a large amount of text must be accommodated with limited storage capacity. They were found necessary, for example, by the writers of adventure games on 8-bit micros with 64k of RAM at their disposal. They are often also available as an operating system facility, applied automatically to users' files which have not been accessed within a certain period of time.

The basic compression techniques involve either substituting short strings for longer ones or exploiting repetitions in the data. Methods of the first type are mainly applicable to continuous text; the others have a wider area of application. Both produce typical space–time trade-offs; conversion algorithms are used when data is read and written, and a balance must be struck between the need to save storage space and the processing overheads incurred. In an IR application it is useful if decompression (which will occur many times) can be faster than compression (which only needs doing once).

It is possible to compress text without losing information for two reasons. Firstly, the standard data representation method used in most machines is fairly extravagant. Recall the discussion in Chapter 2 about alphabet codings. English text needs codes for 26 letters (52 if upper and lower case are held separately), plus 10 for numeric digits and another 12 for necessary punctuation symbols. But each character is normally held in an 8-bit byte with 255 possible values.

The second reason is that any language, whether natural or artificial (e.g. a programming language), is in a statistical sense highly *redundant*. In terms of standard information theory [7], the most efficient code is one where at any point in the message there is an equal probability that any one of the available characters from the alphabet could follow – this is clearly not true of English text. After a "q", for instance, the next letter is a virtual certainty; in other cases there may be a choice only between the vowels or a selection of the consonants.

Even within the constraints of what is pronounceable many perfectly plausible character strings simply do not occur. And there are wide variations in frequency for both words and letters, the pattern for which will vary from one language to another.

Redundancy in languages is a useful property in that it enables codes to be cracked and messages to be reconstructed even when garbled by misprints. And it is notable that extra redundancy in the form of parity bits and block headers is commonly used when storing and transmitting digital data, in order to test for and possibly correct errors. Conversely we can reduce redundancy in stored text by applying one or more compression techniques. Only general principles are discussed here, but enough to provide a basis for detailed algorithms.

Compression by Substitution

One general principle is to use a look-up table in order to substitute short character strings for longer ones. Consider first the problem at word level. Some words are very frequent in natural language text, and one form of data compression we have already seen involves eliminating common words from the keyword index. It would be too drastic to remove them from the text itself, but they may be held more economically. They are generally short words anyway (Zipf's "principle of least effort"), but if they can be made to occupy only one or two bytes each there will still be a substantial saving. This is an idea analogous to "tokenisation" in the compilation or interpretation of programming languages.

If we have, say, 150 spare character codes, they can be used to represent the 150 most common words. A further 250 words can be coded into 2 bytes using an escape code as prefix. A useful property of word encoding is that it is unnecessary to store space characters before or after encoded words, as they can be inserted automatically by the decoding routine. This form of compression obviously fits well into the IR context: stop-words must be identified by look-up anyway in order to construct the keyword index, and code substitution can be done at the same time. When the text is decompressed, each code is used as a table index to pick up the corresponding word, so there is no searching to slow down response time.

Huffman Coding

At the other end of the scale are compressions based on the frequency of individual characters. The principle here is to devise a substitution such that the more frequently a letter occurs, the shorter its code. A well-known standard method for doing this is Huffman coding, which works at bit level. To begin with we require "weights": percentage frequencies for all the characters to be coded. Fig. 4.3 shows some estimates for the 26 letters of the alphabet – these are taken (slightly modified) from the distribution of letter tiles in the game of Scrabble and are chosen not for their accuracy but because they provide easy numbers to work with.

A	8	E	12	M	3	Q	1	U	4	Y	2
B	2	F	2	N	6	R	6	V	2	Z	1
C	2	G	3	O	8	S	4	W	2		
D	4	H	2	P	3	T	6	X	1		

Fig. 4.3. Estimated weights for letter A–Z.

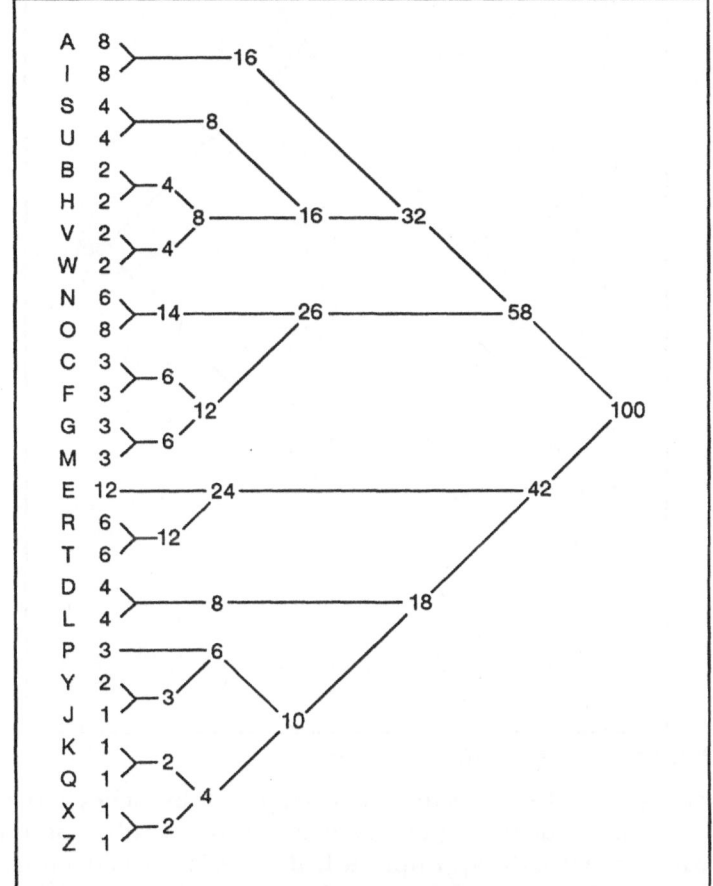

Fig. 4.4. Huffman coding – tree of combined weights.

The next step is to build a binary tree by repeatedly linking together pairs of nodes, starting with the lowest weights and working upwards. Nodes at the leaves of the tree are single letters, those higher up represent combinations. Combination nodes take on the sum of the weights of their constituent parts; the combined weight of the whole tree must be 100. Obviously a program can be written to produce such a tree; the results will differ slightly depending upon the order in which the data is scanned to find matching nodes to combine. The general outcome is that the higher the weight, the shorter the path required to reach it. Fig. 4.4 shows one possible arrangement of the data, displayed in such a way that the lines do not cross.

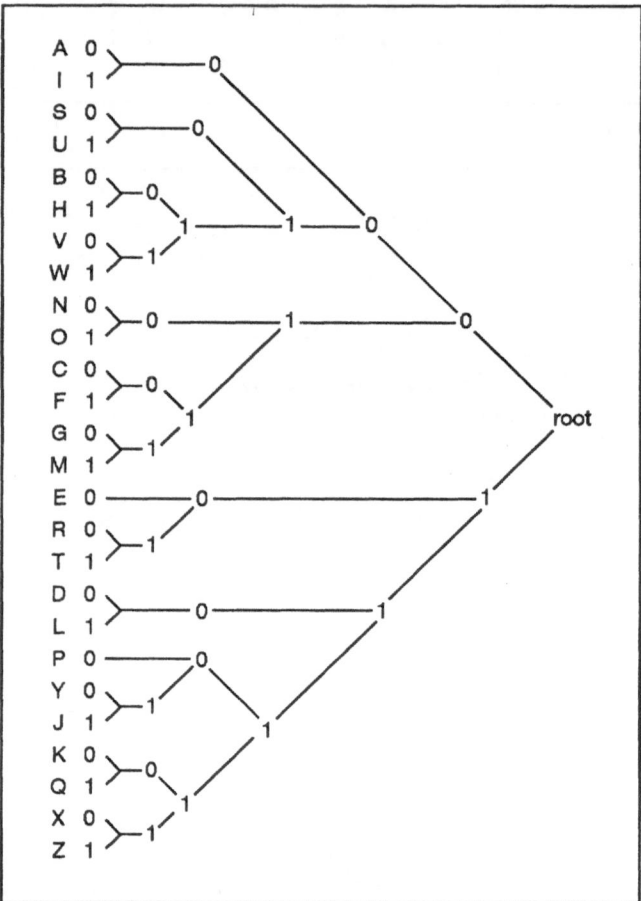

Fig. 4.5. Huffman coding – equivalent binary tree.

We now assign 0 and 1 respectively to each pair of branches in the tree, as in Fig. 4.5. The binary code for any character is found by reading off the digits on the path from the root to the appropriate leaf node. When laid out as in Fig. 4.6, it will be seen that the length of the codes bears a good relationship to the letter frequency, with E coded into three bits and Q, X etc. into 6. The greater the frequency range, the greater the difference between the longest and shortest codes produced by this system.

Huffman coding is economical, but the fact that it uses character codes of different sizes implies that a text can be decoded only by starting at the beginning and working through to the end. This may be no disadvantage when, for instance, transmitting messages through a network, but it will cause more difficulty where it is required to decode and display from an arbitrary starting point. Here it may be better to base the coding on fixed length units. Working only on individual characters (and remembering that there are more than just letters of the alphabet to deal with), we can store the most common in 4 bits and less common ones in 8 or even 16 bits. We thus end up with a "flattened" form of the standard Huffman coding tree.

Letter	Weight	Code	Letter	Weight	Code
E	12	100	B	2	001100
A	8	0000	H	2	001101
I	8	0001	V	2	001110
O	8	0101	W	2	001111
N	6	0100	Y	2	111010
R	6	1010	J	1	111011
T	6	1011	K	1	111000
D	4	1100	Q	1	111001
L	4	1101	X	1	111110
S	4	00100	Z	1	111111
U	4	00101			
C	3	01100			
F	3	01101			
G	3	01110			
M	3	01111			
P	3	11100			

Fig. 4.6. Huffman codes, with lengths relative to weights.

Whatever variant of Huffman coding is used, it is important to see that assignment of a short code to a character precludes the use of that same bit-pattern as the start of a longer code. In the example above, for instance, there can be no 4-, 5-, or 6-bit codes beginning with "100". Likewise if we use, say, 12 4-bit codes for the 12 most frequent letters, we shall have only 64 8-bit codes at our disposal. As always in computing, you don't get anything for nothing!

Modified Huffman Coding

In between word coding and character coding come methods for coding letter sequences, some of which like "th" and "ing" actually occur much more often than single letters such as "q" and "x". It is obviously possible to analyse a sample stretch of text to obtain statistics on "digraphs" (letter pairs) and perhaps also "trigraphs" (three-letter strings). Bear in mind that the frequencies of individual letters must then be adjusted as the sequences in which they occur are extracted and treated as characters in their own right. Knowing the frequency distribution of common sequences, it is once again possible to assign shorter codes.

Such a method is used to implement the "compress" function available on many versions of Unix and based on reference [8]. The algorithm identifies the most common substrings (based on the first section of the file), and puts them in frequency order. It then builds a replacement dictionary, using all 9-bit codes, then 10-bit codes, and so on up to a limit which is between 12 and 16 depending upon the machine's address space. As the text is compressed, the performance of the replacement dictionary is checked periodically; if the compression ratio deteriorates, the old dictionary is thrown away and a new one built on the basis of the current block of text. For English text the algorithm appears to give a 40%–60% compression ratio; however it is another method which demands linear scanning of the whole file, and so could be unsuitable where it is required to move straight to an arbitrary position in a long text.

A general question which arises in text compression is what to do about upper and lower case. Whether representing words, sequences, or individual characters, it is probably more efficient to ignore case differences when assigning letter codes, and use one or two shift codes instead.

Run-length Encoding

We now consider more briefly other compression methods which are not specific to text. One which is applicable to any linear sequence of data is run-length encoding. If several successive elements have the same value we can store instead one copy of that value and an associated count field. So "aaaaaaaacccccccdddddddddd" is represented more compactly by "a/8/c/6/d/9/" (where / is an escape code delimiting count fields). Such repetition is rather unlikely in natural language text, so the technique is useful there mainly to compress strings of blanks. It may however have a place in other IR data files – recall the need for storing sparse word occurrence vectors or document signatures efficiently. We shall also see in a later chapter that it provides an effective way of compressing binary coded graphics images, where the likelihood of repeated sequences is very high. An advantage of run-length encoding is that compression and expansion is performed with reference to the data sequence only; no looking-up is required.

Two-dimensional Encoding

Another general method is to treat the data as a set of blocks, and for each block to hold information only about its differences from the previous block. Once again this is a useful technique for raster graphics encoding, where blocks may consist of successive lines of pixels in a bit-map, or even successive screens in an animation sequence. In either case many points will stay the same from one block to the next. This is of course less likely with successive lines of continuous text, even if treated at the bit level, but it is extremely likely in an alphabetical list making up a keyword index. Here it is necessary to record only where each word starts to diverge from the one before, and the actual letters which are different. Fig. 4.7 shows an example.

Full Word	Compressed Form
discipline	??????
disclose	5, lose
disclosure	8, ure
discolour	5, olour
discomfort	6, mfort
disconcert	6, ncert
disconnect	7, nect
discontent	7, tent
discontinue	8, inue
discord	6, rd
discordant	8, ant

Fig. 4.7. Two-dimensional compression for an alphabetical word-list.

The use of text compression can compensate to a large extent for the space overheads incurred by the inverted list organisation. As a rule of thumb, given a text data file of size M bytes, auxiliary information will increase the total database to about 2.4 × M. This assumes that the inverted list will need another M bytes, the dictionary (in b-tree format) 0.3 × M bytes, and the document index 0.1 × M bytes. But character compression on the original text and on the inverted list could reduce them each to around 0.5 × M bytes. Thus the total packing could give a 1.4 × M sized database.

Chapter Summary

This chapter has considered some of the issues which arise when organisations undertake to set up and manage their own full-text retrieval systems. As the Reuters case study showed, textual information originated for another purpose can be captured and stored for later retrieval, but in order to exploit it fully some human intelligence is required to identify its most important facets.

As the requirement for full-text databases grew, commercial packages became available to handle the tasks of data definition, creation, updating and retrieval. They covered broadly the same scope as DBMSs for structured data, but dealt with records which were potentially much more variable in length and format, and which required pre-processing and indexing before they were readily accessible. Traditionally, software to handle structured databases and text databases has developed along separate lines, but the Text*Retrieval facilities introduced into the Oracle Relational DBMS allow the two sorts of data to be combined, presenting a unified query facility via extensions to SQL.

Full updating of an IR database cannot normally be combined with on-line retrieval, so efficient strategies for making recent material available are required. For the Reuters application, volume shadowing (hardware duplication) was the solution. The Status package holds un-indexed intermediate files whose contents are accessible only through links from other documents; the ICL CAFS implementation goes further in allowing keyword searches on intermediate files by exploiting parallel processing hardware.

Textual databases need to be fairly large if they are to provide a useful resource, and the associated indexes occupy at least as much space as the original text. Space is saved by the application of text compression techniques, based on the principle of reducing redundancy. Frequently occurring words or characters are translated into shorter bitstrings; and repetitive sequences are re-coded more concisely.

Investigations

Find out whether any PC-based package available to you has facilities for storing and accessing textual data. Check what are its limitations on field, record or file sizes, and if possible its average speeds for updating and retrieval.

If there is a text compression utility on your operating system, try it out with different types of data file and note the best and worst compression factors obtained. If you have time on your hands, write and test your own text compression program using code substitution or run-length encoding, and compare its performance against the system utility.

Find out about other attempts to exploit hardware parallelism for improving IR search performance. (Start with a literature search on a suitable database!)

Consider the problem of translating typical queries based on keyword searches into basic relational operations. Suppose we have a database containing the following tables:

- Word-list (word, frequency).
- Locations-list (word, document-key, field-name, word-pos).
- Thesaurus (word1, word2, association-type)
  (where association type may be "synonym", "broader", or "narrower").

Write standard SQL statements to:

- Count how many documents contain both "red" and "green" anywhere in the text.
- List keys of documents containing both "red" and "green" up to five words apart in the abstract field.
- List keys of documents containing the word "red" or any broader term, e.g. "colour", or narrower term, e.g. "scarlet", "crimson", etc.

References

1 Tapper C (1980) Citations as a tool for searching law by computer. In: Niblett B (ed) Computer science and law. Cambridge University Press, Cambridge

2 Teskey FN (1982) Principles of text processing. Ellis Horwood, New York
3 Su SYW (1988) Database computers. McGraw-Hill, Maidenhead
4 ICL Status Reference Manual, ICL
5 Yannakoudakis EJ, Cheng CP (1988) Standard relational and network database languages. Springer-Verlag, London
6 Chellone P, Edwards J. Introduction to SQL*Textretrieval (Version 1.0). Oracle Corporation
7 Shannon C, Weaver W (1949) The mathematical theory of communication. University of Illinois Press, IL
8 Welch T (1984) A technique for high performance data compression. IEEE Computer 17(6):8–19

Five
Introduction to Optical Storage

"The Moving Finger writes; and, having writ,
Moves on: nor all thy Piety nor Wit
Shall lure it back to cancel half a Line,
Nor all thy Tears wash out a Word of it."
Edward Fitzgerald

In comparison with magnetic discs, the most significant points about current optical storage media are that:

- They have a high capacity.
- They hold non-erasable information.
- They are robust and durable.
- They have a relatively slow response time when read.

This chapter provides a brief overview of optical storage principles and introduces three widely used types of optical disc. The following three chapters look at each one in more detail, in each case considering how logical data structures may be designed to exploit its physical characteristics effectively. Some typical applications areas are described, generally focusing on the use of databases with a high textual content.

The three main forms of optical storage in current use are video disc, CD-ROM, and "worm" disc. *Video disc* was the first to be developed, originally intended as an alternative to video-tape for the delivery of home entertainment. This is an analogue medium, storing the signals to generate a series of frames for display in TV format. It is also possible to hold digital data interspersed with each frame – a capability exploited by, for example, the Acorn/BBC "Domesday Disc" which allows a mixture of video stills and computer generated graphics and text to be displayed.

In the event video disc did not challenge tape for use in the home, mainly because as a read-only medium it does not permit users to record their own television programmes, but it did prove to have a useful application in computer-based training where it is required to display frames in random order. For this purpose it is arranged that one video frame coincides with one revolution of the disc, allowing for a much higher quality of still image than can be achieved on videotape. A 12-inch video disc, for instance, carries 36 minutes of video when played consecutively. It contains around 55 000 tracks per side, each track corresponding to a single frame, any one of which may be accessed individually.

CD-ROM is currently the best documented and the most widely used optical storage medium, and the one for which the establishment of industry standards has gone furthest. Once again the basic device was designed for home entertainment: audio compact disc, which has enjoyed considerable commercial success and for which playing equipment is now comparatively cheap. As a digital medium compact disc had obvious potential for computer data storage, although its adoption required the imposition of extra layers of software to handle formatting and error-checking.

As its name implies, this is another read-only medium as far as the user is concerned; data is recorded on it once in a mass-production operation and it is then distributed and sold in much the same way as a book or audio CD. So it is very suitable for textual databases which are not subject to continual modification, and is sometimes a cost-effective alternative to the use of on-line retrieval services.

A standard compact disc is 4.72 inches in diameter, and information is recorded on one side only. It contains about 20,000 physical data tracks, but these may be grouped into up to 90 "logical" tracks, which are separately addressed and indexed on a "run-in" section at the start of the disc. As an audio medium, CD provides 60 minutes of playback time; when used for computer data storage, it has a capacity of 550 megabytes for user data. We shall see later that its method of data representation requires substantial redundancy in order to ensure accuracy of playback.

Worm discs are used only for computer data storage and have no connection with the entertainment industry. The acronym "worm" stands for "write once, read many times". This is a digital medium which allows information to be recorded piecemeal by the user as if on a magnetic disc, but once written it cannot be erased. So worm discs are principally used for *archiving* large quantities of data which will never need changing.

Such data may come from conventional databases. It may be primarily textual; often it will consist of scanned document images which must be held over a period of time for legal or financial reasons, and which would occupy too much space in paper form. Until recently these images would have been held on microfilm or microfiche, but optical disc provides a more compact form of storage, with the added capability for computer-based searching and display. Standards are much less well-established than for CD-ROM, and several large system suppliers are in conflict for a major share of the market.

Worm discs come in several sizes, the most common being the earlier 12-inch and the more recent 5.25-inch. Because they are written individually rather than mass-produced, the equipment needed to use them is considerably more complex and expensive than for CD, since it must selectively address and record on a particular sector using a high-power laser. Both sides of the disc are used; current 12-inch discs can hold up to 4 gigabytes of data, 5.25-inch discs 600 megabytes.

The obvious next step is the *erasable* optical disc, on which information may be repeatedly overwritten and changed. The necessary technology exists to do this, although at the time of writing there are few examples in everyday use. For many purposes, e.g. in CAD/CAM applications, it will clearly be useful to have a robust high-capacity updatable medium, even if access rates remain comparatively slow. However the techniques for handling files and databases are likely to be similar to those for magnetic disc.

By contrast the non-erasable media to be discussed now are suitable for different purposes; for instance CD-ROM is a publishing medium like a book or record; worm disc is an archiving medium which satisfies a lawyer's or auditor's requirement that it should be impossible to falsify records. They all present opportunities for handling information in new ways, and interesting technical problems about how best to exploit their capabilities.

The Physical Level

Data is recorded on optical disc in the form of small marks or "pits" burnt or otherwise scored onto a reflective metal coating. This surface is covered by a transparent protective layer so that it cannot be damaged, but the pits may be detected through it by a laser beam. As the beam is focused on a part of the disc, light is either reflected back directly from the unmarked surface (a "land"), or, if there is a pit, scattered widely in several directions. The difference in reflected light level from pits and lands is the basis of the reading mechanism. Dust and other marks on the outer surface of the disc should not affect the readings in any way.

Designers of disc technology have a basic choice to make between two recording modes: *constant linear velocity* (CLV) or *constant angular velocity* (CAV). The difference between them is shown diagrammatically in Figs. 5.1 and 5.2.

Magnetic discs always use CAV, involving the familiar arrangement of a series of independent concentric tracks. Although tracks on the outside of the disc are longer than those in the middle, the same amount of data is recorded on each, the bits being more tightly packed as the write head moves to the centre. This allows the disc to rotate at constant speed and provides a fast random access mechanism. Worm discs, which as we have seen are designed only for computer data storage, are also normally recorded in this way; likewise interactive video discs, which require the advantage of random access and one-to-one correspondence between tracks and frames.

By contrast, CLV uses a continuous *spiral* track with the same density throughout, and so makes maximum use of the available recording area. It is the best method to choose where the data is to be accessed sequentially, as in commercial recordings on media such as LP records, video discs designed only

Track 1, Sector 0 ——————

Track 0, Sector 0 ——————

Track 0, Sector 1 ——————

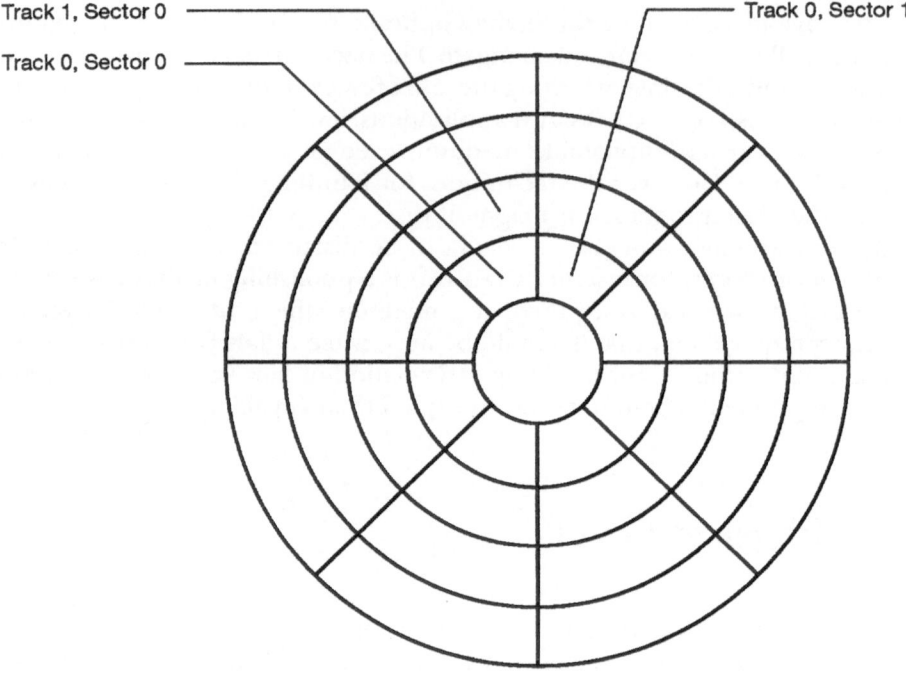

Fig. 5.1. Sector organisation on a CAV disc.

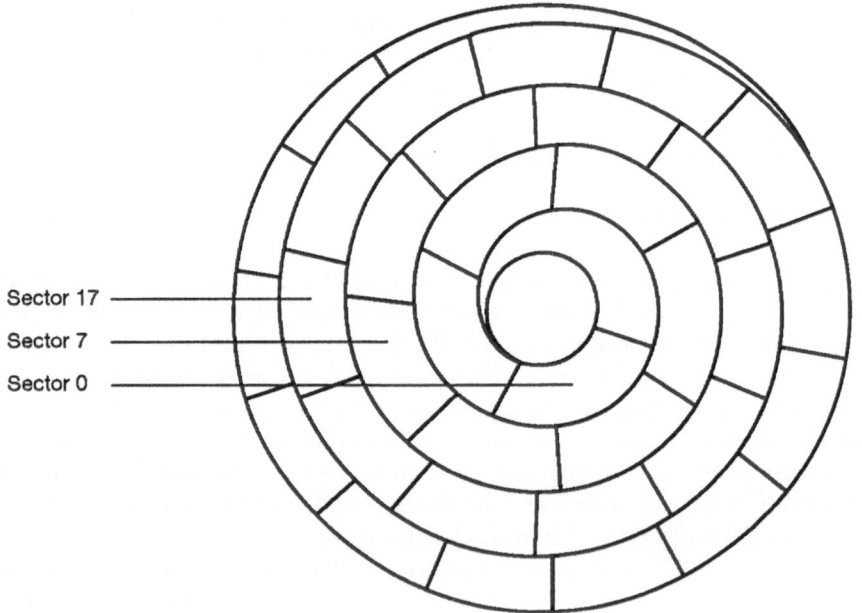

Sector 17 ——————

Sector 7 ——————

Sector 0 ——————

Fig. 5.2. Sector organisation on a CLV disc.

to show films, and audio compact discs. CD-ROM, being based on identical technology, also records at CLV but here the increased storage capacity is achieved at the cost of access speed – a typical example of the space–time trade-off often encountered in computer-based information processing.

For more detailed treatment of optical storage technology at the hardware level the reader is referred to [1] and [2]. The following three chapters consider data representation and applications in more detail, but treating each type of disc separately. We begin with CD-ROM, probably the most widely used of the three media, and certainly the one where efforts at industry standardisation have been most effective.

Investigations

Optical storage technology is developing very rapidly and some information given in this chapter, and the next three chapters, about speeds, capacities and current applications will change drastically within one or two years. Although some basic principles should remain in force, it will be necessary to seek more up-to-date information in the popular press and academic journals, and suppliers' literature.

For example, look at the current situation on erasable optical discs. Are they commercially available, and if so at what price and with what machines? Has their performance improved sufficiently for them to supersede magnetic discs? For what applications are they considered most useful?

Further suggestions for updating investigations are given in the following three chapters.

References

1 Hendley AM (1988) An introduction to the range of optical storage media. In: Oppenheimer C (ed) CD-ROM – Technology to applications. Butterworths, London
2 Laub L (1986) What is CD-ROM? In: Lambert (ed) CD- ROM: The new papyrus. Microsoft Press, Ropiequet

Six

CD-ROM

"... the dream of capturing the universe of the intellect in
concentric systems ..."
Hermann Hesse

CD-ROM is the cheapest and most widely used form of optical storage, based as we have seen on the commercially successful audio compact disc. This chapter explores its development at several levels. It considers briefly how digital data is physically stored on compact disc, and how conventions for data representation were extended to allow random access on an essentially serial medium. At the logical level, there is a more detailed section on the standards established to allow CD-ROM data to be seen by a computer operating system in terms of files, directories and volumes. Finally two CD-ROM text retrieval applications are described, indicating the problems and advantages of this method of supplying information.

Physical Data Representation Methods

The previous chapter described briefly how data was recorded onto optical disc tracks in the form of pits and lands. Compact disc is a digital medium so its contents must be interpretable as binary data, a series of ones and zeros. As the read head moves around the track, it is possible to detect at each clock interval whether a pit or land has been detected. A transition from pit to land or vice versa represents a one, no transition represents a zero.

The timing is such that it is impossible to read two ones in succession, indeed there must always be at least two zeroes between any pair of ones. So when data is recorded each 8-bit byte is expanded to a corresponding 14-bit code with the desired property, and these are then separated by a further 3 *merge* bits. A group of 24 such codes makes a *frame*, preceded by synchronisation bits and followed by error correction bits. A frame in fact represents 24 bytes of raw data by 588 bits at the physical level. Higher level data groupings are based on these frames.

When CD is used for audio playback, the data read from the disc is treated as a series of values to go through a digital to analogue converter and create an audio signal. Digital recording gives very accurate reproduction for this purpose and errors not found by the basic detection/correction mechanism at frame level are not audible to the human ear. When the same medium is used for computer data storage it is necessary to incorporate more powerful error checking, and to address individual units of data with complete accuracy.

CD-ROM data frames are therefore grouped into physical 98-frame *sectors*, corresponding to one seventy-fifth of a second of *playing time*. Each sector has a unique 4-byte identifier indicating its distance, in terms of actual playing time, from the start of the disc. Apart from identification and synchronisation bytes, a sector holds 2048 bytes of real user data and 288 bytes for error detection and correction. The CD-ROM driver reads and transmits these sectors to the operating system, handling errors *en route*. See [1] for a description of the algorithms used – a sophisticated form of cyclic redundancy check.

CD-ROM data is recorded at *constant linear velocity* – which is the main reason for its relatively slow access rates. We have seen that data sectors are identified not by an absolute address but relatively, on the basis of their distance from the beginning of the disc. When seeking a block in a random location, the read head must move across the disc in order to locate the right physical track, but the correct rotational speed for reading that track will vary according to its distance from the centre, so there will be some delay each time it is adjusted. Such delays are unimportant for audio CD, but significant for a computer peripheral.

Standards for CD-ROM Logical Structure

As already noted, the development of audio CD has been marked by a strong emphasis on industry standards. Initially these were set out in the Philips/Sony *Red Book*, which defined the necessary capabilities for both recording and reproduction equipment. The compatibility of different discs and players within the market was the basis for the early commercial success of CD. When it was adopted for data recording, an extension to the standard was specified (the *Yellow Book*), which dealt in particular with the additional error checking required at sector level. The next important standard concerns the laying out of bits and bytes as records and files.

Here again it is worth stressing the difference between optical and magnetic media. A magnetic disc, whether hard or floppy, will start life by being formatted by the operating system for which it is intended, and will normally continue to be read and written by the same, or a similar, system throughout its lifetime. In use, a part of the disc is set aside for housekeeping data about the files it holds, and this will be dynamically updated as they are created, modified and destroyed. The files themselves may also be periodically re-organised in order to maintain performance.

By contrast, a CD-ROM will generally be created on one machine for use on a number of others. The data is recorded using special *origination software*, the basic function of which is to write physical sectors onto a *master* disc to be used for mass-production. All decisions about organisation and content are implemented, irrevocably, at this stage. Many thousands of identical copies may then be made, and the product will sell better if it is usable with a wide variety of players and operating systems. Moreover the recorded information may well be a bibliographic database or document archive which remains useful over a long period of time, so that the lifetime of the disc itself is potentially longer than that of the equipment for which it was originally purchased.

A useful standard for the logical organisation of CD-ROMs must therefore take into account three main factors:

- Interchangeability between current systems.
- Forward compatibility as the technology, and the standard itself, develops in future.
- Efficient data access on a medium which has comparatively poor random-access performance and no capability for dynamic re-organisation.

The standard currently adopted within the industry had its origins in 1986 with the publication of a report [2] by the High Sierra Group of interested equipment manufacturers and software companies within the US. Their proposals were clarified and endorsed by the European Computer Manufacturers Association, and finally formed the basis of ISO Standard 9660, published in 1988. The account given here is intended to suggest how the specification satisfies the objectives listed above, along with some others to be mentioned later. In order to write relevant software a much more detailed study of the original documents would of course be needed.

A standards specification is rather like a program without the supporting design documentation: it does what it does but the reasons behind it, the requirements, constraints, arguments and strategic decisions which influenced its production, must be deduced from the final result. It is often necessary to read between the lines to understand why some things are there. One point immediately evident to the reader is the number of special terms used to refer to different subdivisions of the recorded information. The standard begins by defining, for instance:

- A *logical sector*: the user data field from one or more consecutive physical sectors, normally 2k bytes long.
- A *logical block*: a group of 256, 512, 1024 or 2048 bytes, treated as a logical unit for input–output, and uniquely addressable by a logical block number.
- An *extent*: a set of contiguous logical blocks.

On these are based further divisions such as *units*, *sections*, *partitions*, the significance of which will be explained shortly. Clearly some complex information structures are expected here, with a large number of possible variations. We can contrast this with an earlier widely used standard medium for information interchange – magnetic tape. In that case some basic physical parameters had to be set: number of tracks, parity, density, block size, character code, etc. but all further interpretation was left to the applications program reading the data. Now many more rules are laid down about data formats and structures.

Volumes

The standard does not assume a one-to-one relationship between a disc and a database. CD-ROM is a high-capacity medium, but many bibliographic databases are a whole order of magnitude larger, so could stretch over several physical discs. Conversely it is quite feasible to store two or more databases of modest size on the same disc. In the standard, a single CD-ROM is referred to as a *volume*, and there is provision for putting several together in a *volume set*, or for defining two or more *partitions* of the same volume.

Members of a volume set are assigned a sequence number, and each one must hold details about the structure of all volumes with sequence numbers less than or equal to its own. This allows periodic additional discs to be issued (e.g. for a typical growing bibliographic database), with the latest volume always having complete up-to-date information about the whole set. A *volume group* is defined as a series of volumes created all at the same time, and with consistent structural descriptions.

Two or more volume *partitions* may share the same disc or set of discs. Each partition consists of discrete set of files used together for some application, and while one such partition is in use all the others are "invisible".

The standard defines the layout of one or more *volume descriptor records* which must be recorded in the first available data space on the disc (from sector 16 onward, after any operating system specific information). These may be either boot records (allowing system start-up from CD-ROM), volume descriptors, or partition descriptors. For each volume the information to be recorded includes:

- Identifying information – for the standard itself, the operating system, volume, set, publisher, application, and data preparer; also names of files holding related information such as copyright notices, abstracts, and details of standard bibliographic record formats.
- Dates and times of volume creation and modification, and delimiting the period during which the information is to be considered current.
- Locations of a root directory and path table defining a full directory structure; also parameters such as volume space, set size, block size (standard throughout the volume), and path table size.

The volume descriptors, then, label disc contents in a way analogous to that of other published works, while providing the first level of access for any system using the data. Space is also set aside for application-specific information whose format is not defined by the standard.

Directories and Path Tables

The standard supports the idea of a hierarchical directory structure, as used in operating systems such as DOS and Unix. There is a root directory for each volume or partition, and a *root directory record*, as we have seen, in each volume descriptor record. But though CD-ROM is apparently organised in the same way as magnetic disc, the implementation is quite different. To understand why, we need once again to remind ourselves of the characteristics of CD-ROM: high capacity, non-erasability, and relatively poor performance at random access, particularly on "long seeks" where rotational speed must be adjusted. It was evident to CD-ROM developers before the standard emerged that these characteristics must be taken into account when designing file and directory structures [3].

On a magnetic disc, files and directories are created and destroyed dynamically, so considerable flexibility is needed. A newly-created entry may be placed wherever there is room, and a move through several levels of the directory structure could involve several seeks across the disc to locate the appropriate sequence of directory records.

That strategy is unlikely to prove satisfactory on CD-ROM, where random seeks can take up to a second to perform. Nor is it necessary, since at the time when the disc is first produced the set of directories and files it will hold is already predetermined. There is then every incentive to make the optimal arrangement beforehand even at the cost of using extra space. This is the function of the *path table*.

The path table holds details of all directories in a volume in such a way that logically moving through the hierarchy is actually accomplished by a sequential scan of a table. The relevant fields in a path table entry are:

- Length of directory name.
- Address of the relevant directory record.
- Parent directory number.
- Directory name.

The important field to consider here is the parent directory number. Entries in the table have an implicit sequence number and this is used when flattening-out the tree-structure into a linear order. Consider the example in Fig. 6.1.

To search for a file with pathname *A/Q/Z/f*, the system would:

- Find directory A in the path table and note its sequence number (0).
- Search for the next entry where that number occurs in the "parent directory" column.
- Search sequentially forward for directory name Q, and note its sequence number (2).
- Search for the first entry where that number occurs in the "parent directory" column.

- Search sequentially forward for directory name Z. Pick up the relevant "directory record" location. The directory record points to a file containing file records, which in turn point to file locations.

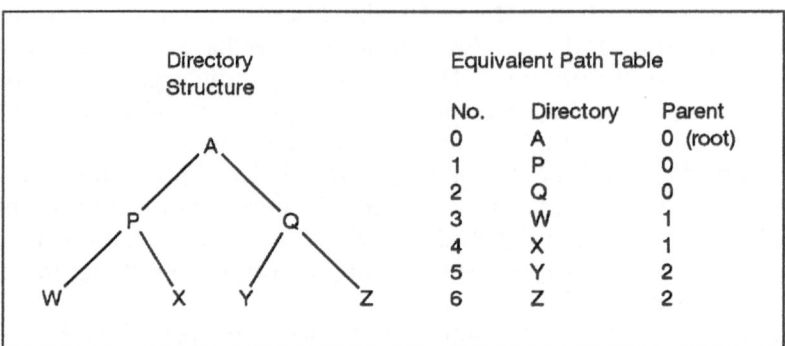

Fig. 6.1. Directory structure and equivalent path table.

It is therefore possible to locate any file in the same number of moves through path table and directory record. In principle the path table could hold a hierarchy of any depth, but the standard imposes a maximum number of 8 levels, and a maximum length of 255 bytes for any full pathname. Two bytes are set aside for the parent directory number, allowing for more than 32 000 directory names. Obviously this arrangement involves some duplication of information – each directory still holds descriptors for all its subdirectories so the hierarchy is represented both explicitly and implicitly – but time is more important than space in this context. Note also that it will give an improvement in speed only if users and applications refer to full pathnames; there is no advantage if they carry out searches in a step by step manner.

This method of handling directories illustrates an interesting point about computer-based information processing – that it is always possible to separate *logical design* from *physical implementation*. For the CD-ROM standard it was obviously useful to mimic currently used data formats; there is for example provision for file read/write/execute permission bits and creation/modification dates which on the face of it are not applicable to discs which cannot be altered. Perhaps they are there in anticipation of the development of erasable optical storage, but more likely to provide maximum compatibility with magnetic media as used on Unix or, even more important, DOS.

At the same time it was necessary to take into account the fact that optical disc could accommodate perhaps thousands of files but would use them very inefficiently if magnetic disc based methods were adopted uncritically. So the path table presented a useful way of avoiding random seeks. Similar efficiency considerations apply when selecting individual file organisations for CD-ROM applications, where decisions about trade-off will normally be resolved in the direction of using space to save time. A few suggestions on that issue are given later, after consideration of basic file formats.

Files

The standard allows the setting of general file parameters, indicating, for instance, levels of protection and whether the existence of the file is to be made known to the user or kept secret. Files may be preceded by an *extended attribute record* containing fields to say whether records are of fixed or variable length, their maximum size, and how they are delimited. For a document file, conventions for separating lines and indicating vertical spacing may be selected; there is room also for describing how extended alphabets are to be represented with escape sequences. For numeric codes, the standard allows either "most significant byte first" or "least significant byte first", to cater for different machine architectures.

Two pieces of terminology associated with files have yet to be explained. The first is the file *section*, which is a part of a file occupying an *extent* or series of contiguous blocks. It is possible to have a file of more than one section, and it will be necessary to do so if the file happens to stretch across two or more physical discs. Every section has an entry in its parent directory. An interesting option is that the same section may be logically part of more than one file, i.e. two different names, perhaps in two different directories, may lead to the same data. A possible reason for this is to avoid duplicating information where one file is a minor variation on another but the two have substantial data in common.

The other division of a file is a *unit*, which is used if *interleaving* is adopted for a particular application to improve sequential processing speed. This involves spacing out data records so that when processing the file each one is read at the optimum time, with no rotational delay. The technique is similar to the "spiral" file organisation used on magnetic disc for many years. The standard allows the definition of interleaved files with a fixed unit size and *interleave gap* size; moreover the gaps between units may be used to store units from an entirely different file, which must also of necessity be interleaved. Whether such an arrangement will improve performance depends of course on very careful timing calculations by the file designer.

Within the limits described, the normal record access mechanisms like indexing, hashing and chaining may be implemented. The standard has nothing to say about this beyond setting aside fields within the extended attribute record for system and application use, where information about file organisations could be recorded.

In practice the designer of a single file must decide how to map the information onto disc, considering all the points already made in connection with directory structures. Because the information will not change, it is worth trying to predict likely patterns of access so as to ensure that the most frequently needed records are most favourably placed. Likewise an analysis should be made of key distributions to arrive at the best choices for blocking factors or hashing algorithms. In general it is wise to be quite generous with space in order to save time. Some interesting strategies are suggested in [3].

The Standard in Practice

Like other standards in the computing industry, the one proposed by the High Sierra Group and ratified as ISO 9660 was very much a compendium of existing practice, defined by representatives of companies that already had extensive technical and marketing experience in this field. It in fact specifies three *interchange levels* for originating and receiving software: level 3 has no restrictions, at level 2 files may consist only of a single section, and there is a further restriction at level 1 on lengths of directory and file names.

Most of all the standard reflects the fact that the great majority of CD-ROM products at the time when it was written were intended for use with DOS systems – a state of affairs which its publication had the effect of consolidating. Microsoft produced an extension to MS-DOS version 3 based on the standard, and this now enables the operating system to treat a CD-ROM reader as if it were just another disc drive.

The MSCDEX software consists of two parts: a device driver specific to a particular manufacturer's CD-ROM reader, and a set of interrupt-driven input routines, called whenever the operating system needs to access the device. It is normally purchased along with the CD-ROM hardware; once installed it allows the user to examine and move through directory structures, and read (but not write) files using normal DOS commands.

For some purposes this is all that is needed. The standard defines CD-ROM as an *interchange medium*: it is there to transfer large data files from one machine to another. This is indeed one possible use – publishers sell discs containing public domain and sample software or collections of clip-art and scanned images, for example, which are copied onto a hard disc and then accessed in the normal way. Likewise files of financial information are sold for use with certain modelling packages or spreadsheets. The distribution method is cheap; the cost of the physical disc is very low, and the price charged reflects the value and timeliness of the information for the buyer.

The issue becomes more difficult when the CD-ROM contains textual databases which are too large for a hard disc, and which are intended to be read *in situ*. It must now be considered as a package containing both information and essential software. A number of examples can be given:

- Providers of the remote chemical, medical or legal retrieval systems described in earlier chapters now also sell CD-ROM databases plus retrieval software, with the advantage that users can search locally for past material, and incur communications costs only when they return to the on-line service for the most recent references.
- Similar techniques are now applied to less academic publications, such as the popular computing magazines indexed by the Ziff-Davis publishing company.

- A CD-ROM may be distributed as a supplement to or substitute for complete printed or microfilm-based catalogues, so for instance libraries and bookshops can regularly receive details of currently available British and US books in this form.
- Reference books can be packaged in the same way. The Microsoft Bookshelf, for example, holds ten works of reference, including a dictionary, *Roget's Thesaurus* and a book of quotations. The first edition of the *Oxford English Dictionary* is available on CD-ROM, and the second edition will become so within two years.

All these texts are usable only with the software sold with them, and for the more traditional databases a mainframe retrieval package is often adapted for the new environment. Alternatively a new interface may be designed which better exploits the possibilities of the PC, for example the Bluefish package used to access the Ziff-Davis library. In any case, the programs are sent to the buyer either on the CD-ROM itself or on accompanying floppy discs, and must be installed on the hard disc before use.

In theory there are now three layers of software between the user and the CD-ROM: the device driver, the MSCDEX routines, and the applications software. All is well so long as the writers of that software actually use the input routines, but there are instances where they go below the operating system and address the device directly. It can then happen that the files on a disc are quite visible through the DOS interface, but the retrieval program supplied with it will not work on some manufacturer's equipment.

Failure to keep to standards is of course common in the computing industry, and the motive for suppliers of CD-ROM products is much the same as elsewhere. Either the programmer is trying to get a better performance from the device by low-level control, or using tricks to implement protection against illegal copying.

To safeguard themselves against such problems, organisations needing a particular CD-ROM product will often be advised to purchase the whole system – hardware, software and CD-ROM – from the same supplier, who must guarantee that it will all work together. It is an interesting reflection on the value of information as a resource that purchasers may be willing to pay three or four times the cost of the disc itself for the hardware which will enable them to use it satisfactorily. In fact an industry survey taken in 1989 revealed that 70 per cent of CD-ROM users owned only one disc – they had bought their equipment for the sake of a single database application.

So the ISO 9660 standard provides a platform for interchangeability, but a text or database on CD-ROM is not as portable as recorded music on audio CD, and even less so than a physical book or microfilm. Even where standard calls are made to operating system routines, the retrieval software expects a particular arrangement of data and it is certainly not open to a user to buy a database which interests him and then independently select the interface which he prefers.

A frequently-quoted statistic is that a single CD-ROM holds the equivalent of 250 000 pages of A4 text, but it must be remembered that the larger the text, the more attention must be paid to its structure if it is to be a valuable resource. However to represent structure the data supplier has only a few basic techniques at his disposal: embedded codes within the text itself, or the familiar mechanisms of record layout and file organisation: directories, indexing, chaining, and so on. At present, with few exceptions, the conventions used are quite arbitrary, and the particular techniques adopted are known only to the designers of the database and accompanying software.

The best current example of a more universal standard is the MARC interchange format used by libraries. This was devised during the 1960s, originally for data on magnetic tape. It defines fields to include everything which libraries need to record about a book e.g. ISBN, author's name (personal or corporate), title, publisher, edition, date of publication (actual or projected), original/translation language, and physical descriptors such as size, number of pages, illustrations and binding.

The use of this standard has proved advantageous to the library community over the years in enabling data to be shared easily. In Britain details of all newly-published books are recorded in MARC format by the British Library. Other libraries, e.g. those in universities, can obtain the data to add to their own computer-based files and avoid the cost of re-keying. The standard also provides for local variations according to the needs of individual institutions.

The ISO 9660 standard caters for the interchange of MARC records on CD-ROM by including a special field in its volume descriptor record which may be used to hold the name of a file containing bibliographic record definitions. This is obviously useful within the library community, and CD-ROM has been adopted as one means of distributing the British Library data. It will enable libraries who do not wish to invest in communications links for on-line access to obtain the information more cheaply, although with an inevitable time-lag.

However this is only one amongst a large number of possible applications, and one where the data itself is not highly structured beyond the level of individual records and fields. There is no equivalent common format for retrieval databases. For continuous text there are ISO standards for character representation covering different national alphabets (e.g. ISO 8859 Latin1), and the Standard Generalized Markup Language (ISO 8879) potentially enables texts to be recorded with some indication of their higher level structure. But at present most CD-ROM databases are seriously accessible only with the software they are sold with, and that software may turn out to be usable only with a subset of the available hardware.

Before leaving the question of CD-ROM standards, it is worth mentioning briefly some further developments in the area of multi-media systems. The principle of the self-contained turnkey system has been adopted for an extension of the Red and Yellow book standards, for compact discs holding integrated text, sound, and image data for the entertainment or education market. The CD-I standard, as defined in the Philips/Sony *Green Book*, lays down formats for these different kinds of data, and protocols for programs to control the interaction. It gives a complete specification of the CD-I player: a microcomputer system with its own memory and processor, and ports for peripheral equipment such as screen, mouse and joystick, as well as the drive itself.

The CD-I standard is based upon the original principle that any compact disc should be playable on any equipment, but it clearly cuts out the possibility of using the data except as dictated by the creators of the entertainment or education package. There are now several rival products in this area, where the main technical challenge is how to deliver video sequences of a satisfactory quality. Examples of their everyday use are not available at the time of writing, so they will not be discussed here, but a useful survey of this rapidly developing technology appears in [4].

Example Applications

We now return to the main theme of the book and consider examples of the use of CD-ROM for text storage and retrieval. Two products are described, a catalogue and a manual, both previously supplied only in microfilm or print. In both cases using the CD-ROM is not an isolated task, but has links, actual and potential, with other operational activities. The first example is of a bibliographic database, commercially available to subscribers, and consisting of short records accessed through conventional retrieval software. Following a brief account of the product and its use within a particular academic library, some more general points will be made about the likely impact of CD-ROMs on library services.

Whitaker's Bookbank

Bookbank is a CD-ROM version of the *British Books in Print* catalogue, consulted in libraries and bookshops. It holds details of books currently available in Britain, along with forthcoming titles notified by publishers. There are over 550 000 records, occupying about 50 megabytes of a single disc, representing books published over, roughly, the last three years. Around 5000 new titles are added each month. A similar product, Bowker's *Books in Print*, is also available for books published in the US. The following account reflects the experience of a typical academic library, which uses both databases.

Subscribers pay about £900 per year for the service, and a new disc is received every month. (The suppliers of CD-ROMs on subscription may, but do not necessarily, require the old disc to be returned each time.) There are no intermediate updates. The identical information can also be received on microfilm, and in practice libraries will often prefer to have it in both forms. The main advantage of the CD-ROM version is that records can be downloaded from it to another database in MARC format. They are also used for automatically generating purchase orders, so very little data entry by library staff is required. However details of forthcoming books may not always be complete and accurate, so the final version of any book record stored in the library database will be the one received from the British Library.

A typical sequence of events might be:

- The library receives a reader request for a new book. A full reference will consist of ISBN, author, title, edition, publisher, and date of publication, but not all readers will have completed the request in full.
- The Bookbank is consulted on-line. If the book cannot be found the corresponding US database (Bowker's) is searched.
- When the book is found, a purchase order is generated. A copy of the record, in MARC format, is downloaded onto the PC hard disc.
- At the end of a session, downloaded hard disc records are modified to fit the local system and sent off to the main library database, where they are held pending the arrival of the book itself and the "official" MARC record from the British Library. The ISBN is used as the unique record identifier throughout the process.

For searching, Bookbank uses BRS software, adapted from a mainframe-based retrieval package. This provides three modes of use: novice, intermediate (both menu-driven) and expert (command driven). The command language is somewhat inflexible in not allowing the user to display a book record on the screen and then download it, so intermediate mode is preferred.

The search options allow retrieval by ISBN, author, title keyword, publisher, date, and subject index. (The subject index consists of a small number of very broad categories, e.g. Law, Humour, History, which are no doubt more useful to a general bookshop than an academic library.) One index is used for all fields so it is unnecessary to specify fields in the query. In practice where the ISBN is not known the option most often used is to enter the first four letters of the author's name followed by the first four letters of the title. This returns results very quickly – for more complex queries there is a noticeable drop in retrieval speed.

The book record as used here is of course much shorter and simpler than those discussed in earlier chapters – there are no keyword or abstract fields, and the only scope for keyword search is within the title. The retrieval process is correspondingly less problematic – the searcher is normally looking for a single book which is known to exist rather than a set of documents of possible relevance. Because the application uses a standard retrieval package, a full query language is provided with Boolean operators and various options on adjacency between keywords, but in practice it is seldom necessary to qualify searches in this way. It is also notable that the stop-word list is barely a dozen words long.

The system provides several ways of displaying sets of output records (including a sort option), but once again this is a reflection of the general-purpose nature of the software rather than the needs of the application. Normally the one or two records retrieved by each query will fit comfortably on the screen, and after briefly ascertaining which one matches the reader request, the user will immediately ask for the "download" option. At this point the name of a DOS file must be given, and a choice made as to whether to overwrite or append to any existing file of that name.

Bowker's *Books in Print* presents very similar facilities, although with another retrieval package and a different user interface. Here it is generally necessary to specify the fields to be searched in a query; several separate indexes are held and these can be browsed by the user. Complex queries may be built up in stages, with the system reporting on the number of hits each time. Following retrieval there are options to display, print, or download the relevant records.

Between them the two products are certainly useful to the librarians, but not yet ideal for the context in which they are used. Specifically, two very similar databases come with two different retrieval packages which supply essentially the same set of options through different interfaces. The user must carry out two different installation procedures each time a new disc is received, and moving from one database to another means switching to a different set of commands.

Here is a concrete example of the current lack of CD-ROM applications software portability, and because the two products are being used side by side on identical PCs the incompatibility is more obvious than it would be in other circumstances. As a step towards integration, the Bookbank software includes a utility to "switch" to *Books in Print*, essentially by resetting default pathnames for data files and software. So a user wishing to run both systems on the same PC could install them both on the hard disc. However when changing from one database to another he would still need to: exit to DOS, run the switch utility, put a different disc in the CD-ROM drive, and then execute the required system.

General-purpose retrieval software is supplied for a task which could be more precisely defined and streamlined. The most frequent choices cannot be set as the default, and extra keystrokes are needed to back up from menus and reselect the same options each time. The requirement to continually re-enter a file name for downloaded records is particularly inconvenient.

The library handles on average 50 new readers' requests every working day, and goes through a similar search/download sequence for each. Many of the Bookbank software options are in fact never used. By contrast a traditional IR package might serve 50 different researchers in a day, each following an individual search pattern, and in this situation a wide range of options is desirable. The dilemma of general-purpose versus specially-tailored software is not new of course, but the fact that CD-ROM is a mass-produced read-only medium means that there is no scope for distributing different versions. A positive advantage of sending out a complete new database disc every month is that it gives the suppliers the opportunity to upgrade and improve the software frequently, but it will always be identical for everyone.

The obvious next step for an academic library is to allow readers to search the Bookbank and perhaps generate some form of request automatically. For this a streamlined interface, preferably common to the two databases, would be desirable. Other practical requirements are a server machine capable of handling several CD-ROM readers daisy-chained together, and networking versions of the retrieval software.

The Possible Impact of CD-ROM on Libraries

We have seen that CD-ROM databases may substitute for on-line retrieval systems and for specialised catalogues which in their printed or microfilm form are unlikely to be seen outside large libraries or bookshops. CD-ROM is also a suitable medium for distributing reference books such as dictionaries and encyclopedias. Once the database is assembled multiple copies can be reproduced and sold cheaply and – given reasonable standardisation of the interface between databases and retrieval software – individuals and small organisations should be able to accumulate fairly large electronic libraries, giving them some independence from the institutional sources of information on which they previously relied.

These trends have been investigated over the last few years by Project Quartet [5], a collaborative research project financed by the British Library to consider the application of information technology within its area of concern. In relation to CD-ROM, the group identified two significant points: the build-up of private libraries as described above, and a corresponding change in the services demanded of academic libraries. The expectation is that they will become providers of expensive specialist resources rather than general bibliographies or works of reference, and that at least some of their more specialised material will not be printed in the conventional way but electronically published and stored on optical disc with one-off printed copies being produced on demand.

Reference [5] describes a database used for experiments with a prototype document delivery system based on these ideas: two years' output from 220 biomedical journals held on 80 CD-ROMs. The journals (which included half-tone images) were electronically recorded in full by scanning each page in fax format, but then professionally indexed for normal keyword search. The Project Quartet investigations focused on the technological developments required to automate all the tasks involved in searching for, ordering and delivering scientific documents electronically. Three phases were identified:

- References to relevant papers are found, using either an on-line retrieval system (via a packet-switched network) or a local bibliographic database on CD-ROM. The principles here are already familiar.

- Copies of the required documents are ordered from an academic library. The process is analogous to Electronic Data Interchange between commercial organisations, in that the receiving system must check that it can supply the "goods" and handle billing and payment. An X400 e-mail network is likely to be an appropriate communications channel for this part of the task.
- Finally the document image is retrieved from the library's CD-ROM database and sent to the user's local workstation, where a copy is output onto laser printer. Broadband public ISDN fax networks are considered necessary for this to be technically and economically feasible in future.

With particular reference to CD-ROM developments, the Quartet Project has identified the need for jukeboxes and automatic handling devices for multiple CD-ROMs, supported by efficient retrieval and caching software to overcome the inherent problems of slow access times. Library administrators will face the problems of physical management – cataloguing, labelling, circulation control, security – for objects with different characteristics from those of books and journals. And there are the more intangible problems raised by using a different circulation mechanism, like establishing copyright and ensuring fair revenues to publishers and authors.

Some of the technical issues touched on here – document image scanning, jukeboxes, caching, networking – are discussed in more detail in the following chapter on worm disc technology. Meanwhile, this account of CD-ROM is concluded with a second case-study. We describe an application where a CD-ROM database containing both textual and diagrammatic information was created for internal use within an organisation, and can now be presented through a sophisticated user interface.

British Airways Technical Publications

Background

Airlines have a statutory duty to maintain and repair their aircraft, and to do so correctly their staff require technical manuals. These contain both text and engineering drawings, and provide detailed instructions on the procedures to be followed for any engineering operation.

The manuals are supplied by the aircraft manufacturer. They are laid out in accordance with ATA (Air Transport Association of America) Specification 100, so that the same class of information (e.g. installation of firefighting equipment) always appears in the same position, under the same reference number, for every aircraft type. There are minor variations in manual content for each individual aircraft, since no two are precisely the same. Moreover some airlines have local modifications in their manuals where they have installed their own special equipment for any purpose.

Airlines carry out a continual programme of modification to aircraft fleets, to incorporate improvements in technology and satisfy changes to operational requirements, and also as a result of monitoring the condition of aircraft during maintenance work. As a result the manuals are subject to continual change. There is a legal obligation to use the most up-to-date version, and to retain copies of each revision, to allow retrospective investigation as to whether past maintenance procedures were carried out properly.

Over the last 20 years it has been customary for manuals to be supplied on microfilm reels rather than paper. Pages of the manual on microfilm are only accessible sequentially, and paper copies can be produced from them if necessary. Temporary small-scale revisions are supplied in the form of paper supplements, which must always be consulted by the engineer starting a maintenance task. Typically, there is a cycle of between 90 and 120 days between the issue of one complete microfilm revision and the next.

Clearly the above represents a complex text processing application where a high standard of accuracy and control is required for a large volume of data. The following is an account of a pilot study, undertaken at the instigation of British Airways, to consider CD-ROM as a medium for storing and using engineering manuals in an operational environment.

The Feasibility Study

The study focused on the Boeing 757 and two of its manuals. These were:

- The Maintenance Manual, containing 11 000 pages, including 5000 pages of diagrams.
- The Illustrated Parts Catalogue, containing 23 000 pages, including 5400 pages of diagrams.

About 170 copies of these manuals are required throughout the organisation, but the pilot study was concerned only with supplying seven copies, to maintenance engineers and the Technical Publications department at Heathrow Airport.

To be considered satisfactory, the CD-ROM version would have to be usable by engineers while carrying out maintenance procedures, and to allow the handling of both temporary and complete revisions, and archiving. The content and structure of the information should be identical to that of the paper/microfilm version, fast access to both text and diagrams should be achievable, and hard copy should be obtainable when needed. It was also hoped that the CD-ROM would provide substantial advantages over existing methods:

- In speed and convenience of access.

- In quality and legibility of displayed and printed information.
- In reduction of space occupied by manuals in current use, and in the archives.

The participants in the investigation were British Airways as users, Boeing, the aircraft manufacturers, who agreed to provide manual information in a form which would be usable for CD-ROM, and Maxwell Data Management, who took on the role of systems integrators.

The systems integrator plays an important part in the production of a CD-ROM, having responsibilities ranging, perhaps, from supply of hardware to market research and publicity. A very informative account of this role is given in [6]. In the case currently under discussion the work undertaken by MDM included:

- Selection and supply of equipment and system software, including the basic "search engine" package to retrieve data from the CD-ROM. This was KRS from Knowledgeset.
- Design and implementation of the particular application, including the user interface.
- Conversion of the data into a suitable format. The text was already in machine-readable form for output onto microfilm, but the information had to be prepared so that it was convenient to consult in the new way. Diagrams had also to be included.
- Management of CD-ROM mastering and reproduction. This involved an important issue of legal responsibility. Boeing as manufacturer is required to supply manuals and guarantee their accuracy – it had to be satisfied that a third party would convert and transmit the data correctly. Throughout the trial period the manuals continued to be supplied on microfilm, but where the CD-ROM was the primary reference source all the normal statutory safeguards had to be applied.
- Liaison with other airlines as part of a long-term marketing strategy. Unlike commercially published CD-ROMs, aircraft manuals have a limited potential market. A shift to the new technology is economic in the long term only if the majority of airlines adopt it.

It is clear that the investigation involved many different issues: technical, legal and commercial. We now consider the developed application in a little more detail.

Structure of the Manuals

As already stated, two manuals were used: the Maintenance Manual and the Illustrated Parts Catalogue for the Boeing 757. The data, which in all occupied 34 000 pages (30 hard-copy volumes or eight microfilm reels), fitted onto about 60 per cent of the 550-megabyte disc. As one would expect with CD-ROM storage, a high proportion of the space was used for indexes, pointers etc. to give fast and flexible access to the data.

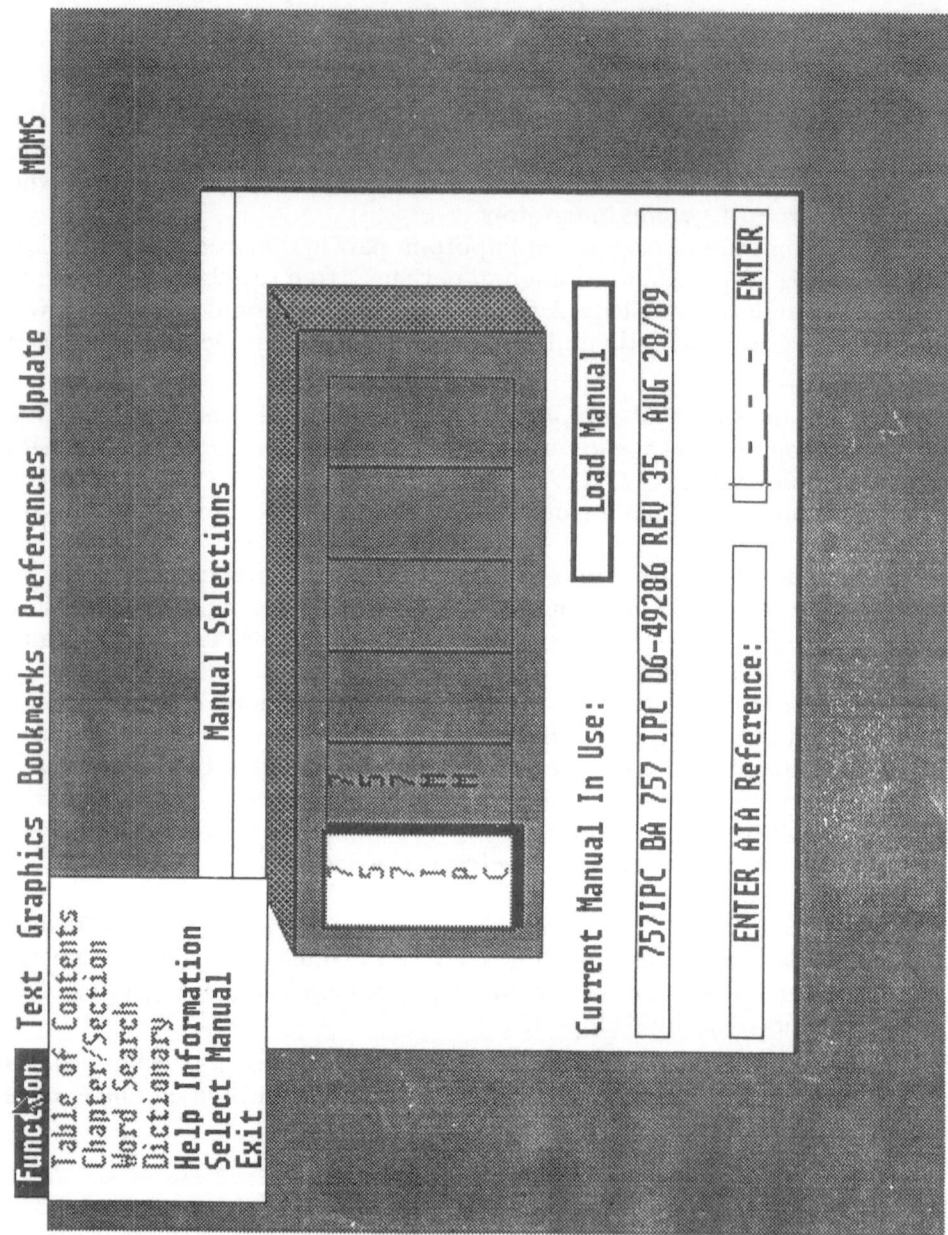

Fig. 6.2. BA maintenance manual – opening screen.

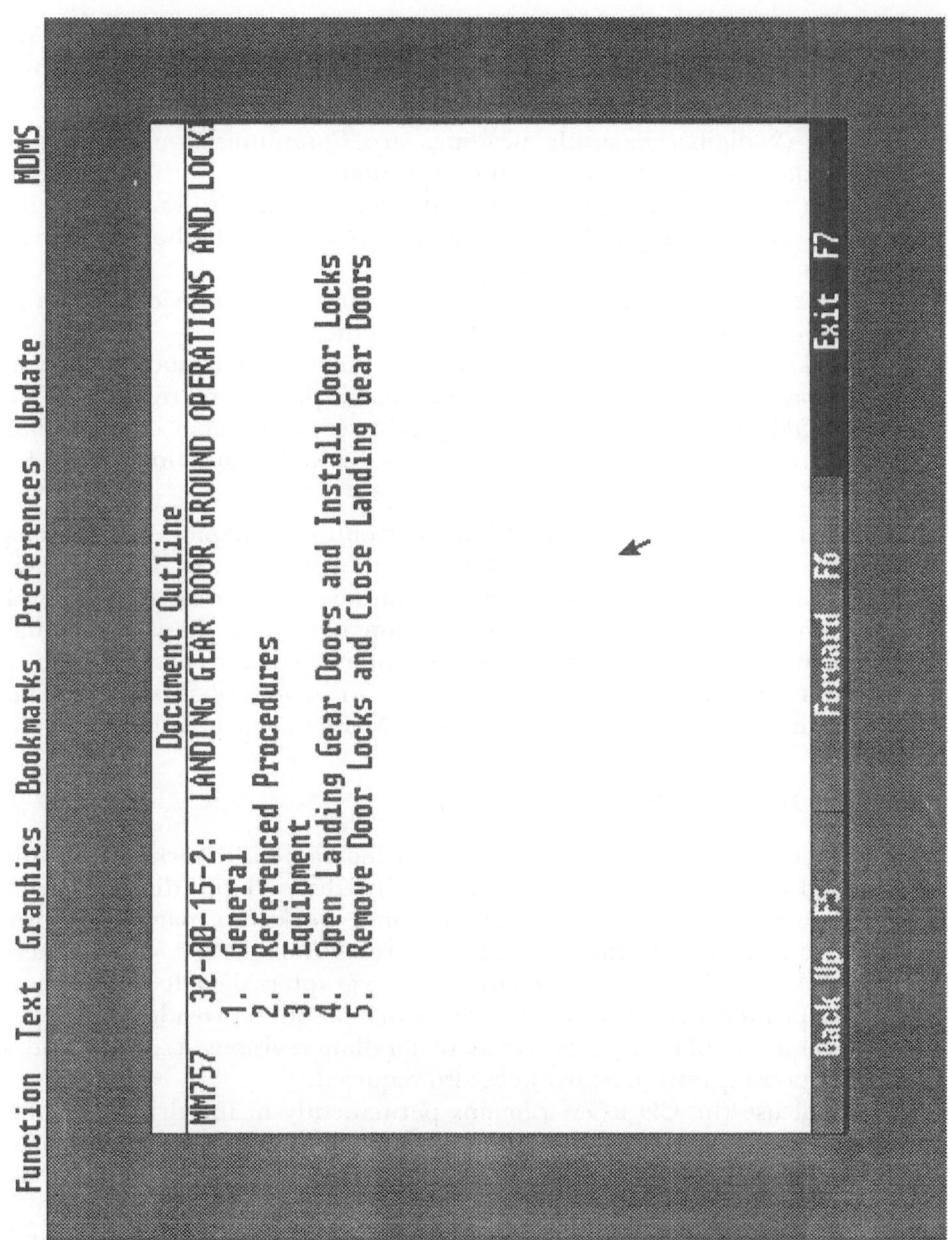

Fig. 6.3. A document outline.

The manuals have a fixed hierarchical structure, as laid down by the Air Transport Association. The maintenance manual is split into divisions identified by reference number, i.e.

- Chapters (2 digits). Example headings are Communications, Electrical Power, Equipment/Furnishings, Fire Protection.
- Sections (2 digits). Example headings (under Communications) are Data Transmission, Passenger Address and Entertainment, Radio and Video Monitoring, Speech Communications.
- Subjects (2 digits). These headings go down to the level of individual items of equipment and conditions which may arise in them.
- Pageblocks (1 digit). A pageblock is the basic unit of text, containing one or more paragraphs about a particular maintenance procedure. In the transfer to CD-ROM, the notion of a physical page as seen on paper or microfilm disappeared, since the amount of text to be viewed at any time would be variable.

The Illustrated Parts Catalogue has a similar layout, with chapters and sections as in the Maintenance Manual. The third and fourth levels are "Unit", which takes the reader down to individual part numbers and descriptions, and "Figure", which presents one or more illustrations of the unit. Thus the manual structures provide a mechanism for fast interactive searches through a hierarchy, as well as other methods of access to be described shortly. The account of the system will focus mainly on the Maintenance Manual.

System Operation

The equipment used for the pilot system was a 286-based AT workstation, with a mouse and wimp interface, a 110 megabyte hard disc, a floppy disc drive, and CD-ROM drive. Good visibility is essential in a workshop, particularly for diagrams, so 16-inch or 19-inch screens with a resolution of 1280×1024 pixels were used. A special board was used to speed up graphics data decompression and a laser printer was supplied with each workstation to provide hard copy. For the Technical Publications department handling revisions, a scanner and a graphics data compression board were also required.

In normal use the CD-ROM remains permanently in the drive, and the application runs continuously. There should be no need for users like maintenance engineers to interact with the underlying operating system. Operationally the most important point is that the latest revision of the manual shall be used; to this end the revision date is printed on the ROM disc itself, and is also displayed on the screen when the application starts up. There are several ways to get at a piece of information: by going down the chapter/section hierarchy, by using word search facilities, or by following cross-references.

Hierarchical Search

The opening screen shows a bookcase (see Fig. 6.2), where a manual can be chosen by clicking with the mouse. This leads to a table of contents, from which the user can move through the hierarchy of chapter, section, etc. in the way naturally implied by the manual structure. Alternatively a 6 or 7 digit ATA reference number can be typed to move directly to the relevant subject or pageblock. So the manual can be quickly searched in traditional ways, using the mouse and function keys to move up and down through the table of contents. At the lowest level "document outlines" can be displayed, showing the paragraph headings within a chosen pageblock (see Fig. 6.3).

Word Search

The word search facility is based on standard ideas for full-text information retrieval, but with a very wide range of options once the query has been matched.

All the words in the manual (except for stop-words) are indexed, and a word-frequency list can be examined (see Fig. 6.4). This will show up variant spellings and misspellings, which the user may need to take into account. There is no thesaurus, but words can be right-truncated to search for several related grammatical forms. Boolean expression occupying up to five lines may be used, and there are options to look for words co-occurring in the same paragraph, up to *n* words apart, or in the exact order given. They can be looked for in the whole document or part of it, e.g. only in title lines or in tables (see Fig. 6.5).

As a query is entered, the system shows how many pieces of text satisfy it, and additional query terms may be typed in to pinpoint the required one more accurately. Up to 1000 pointers into the text can be generated by a query. A list is displayed showing all the relevant pageblock reference numbers and titles (see Fig. 6.6), and the document outline option is used to give an overview of any selected pageblock. Finally the full text of a referenced pageblock can be displayed, with the actual search terms highlighted on the screen. The user can move from one to another by pressing the "next match" key. Keyword queries developed in this way can be filed and re-used on another occasion, although in practice this is not encouraged.

Cross-references or "Hot Links"

The manuals contain many cross-references, since it often happens that one task consists of several subsidiary tasks which are perhaps described elsewhere. Thus under pageblock MM757 79–11–03–4 (Oil Tank Gravity Filter Installation) we find the instruction to "Align ... filler cap housing ... then secure with three bolts". There follows a reference to MM757 70–51–00, a section which somewhere contains details about how to secure bolts. The link is followed up by clicking with the mouse on the highlighted reference. Example screens showing highlighted hot links are shown in Figs. 6.7 and 6.8.

Note that the reference is only to a section (as in the above example) or at best a pageblock, and the user must continue his search through a document

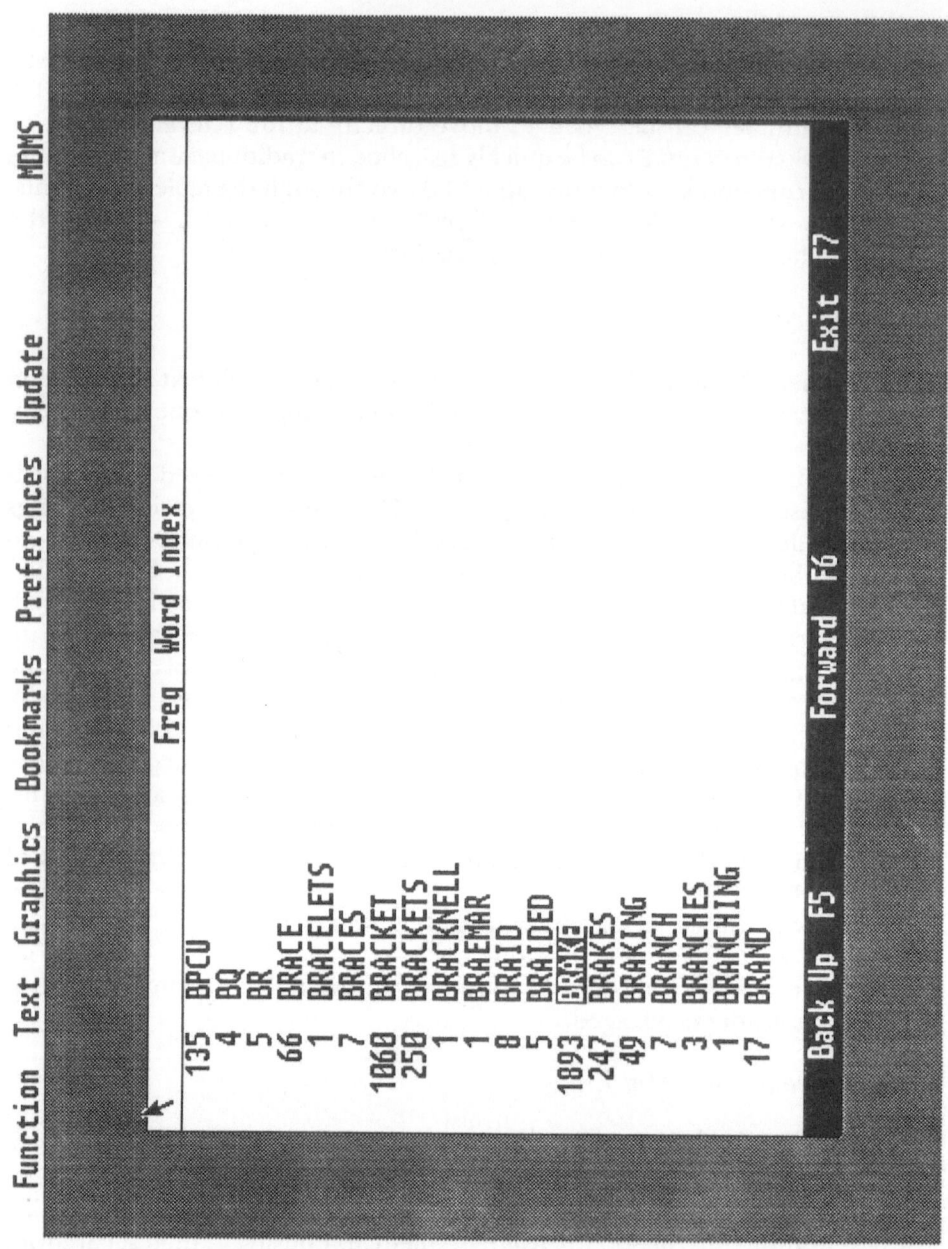

Fig. 6.4. Part of a word-frequency list.

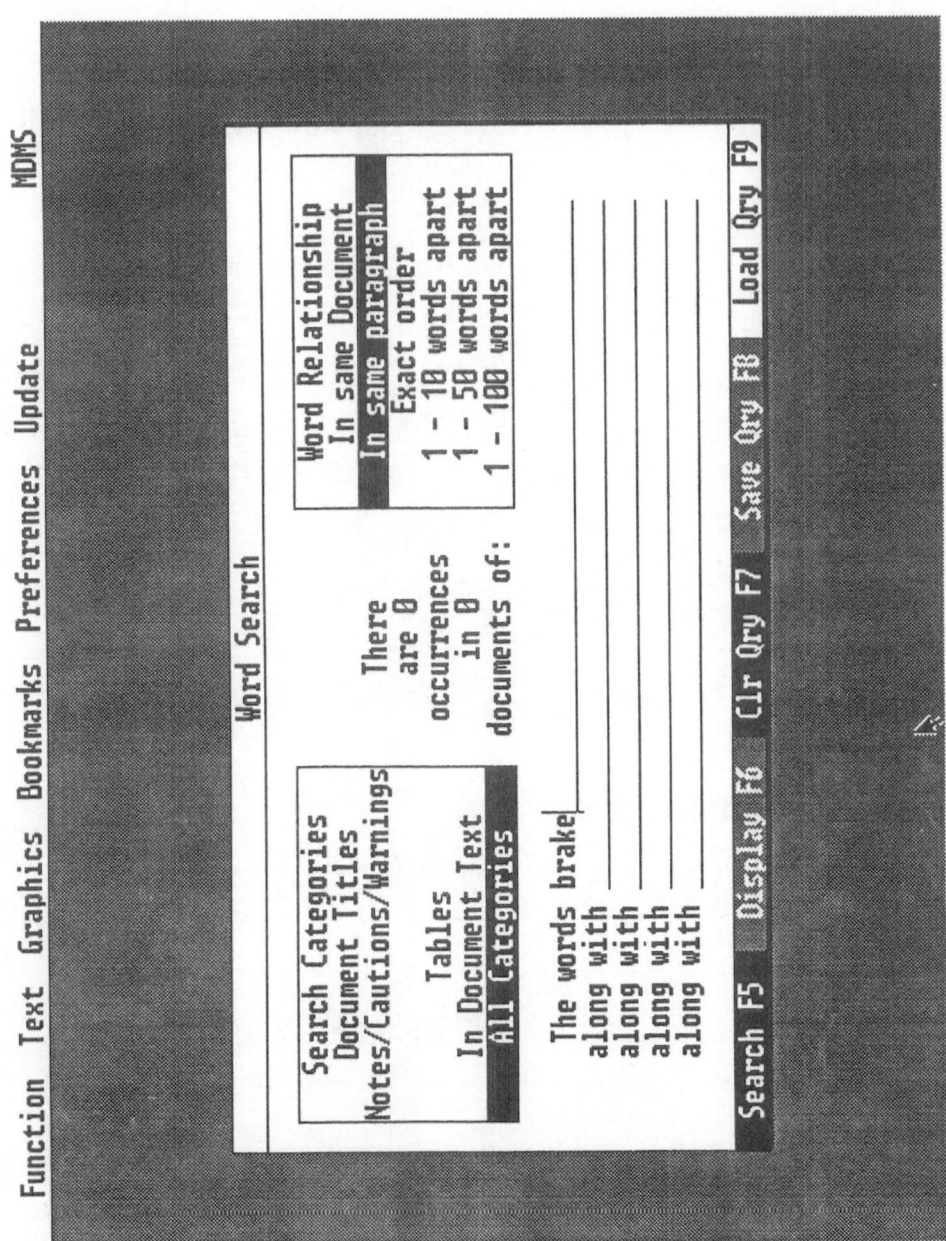

Fig. 6.5. The word-search screen.

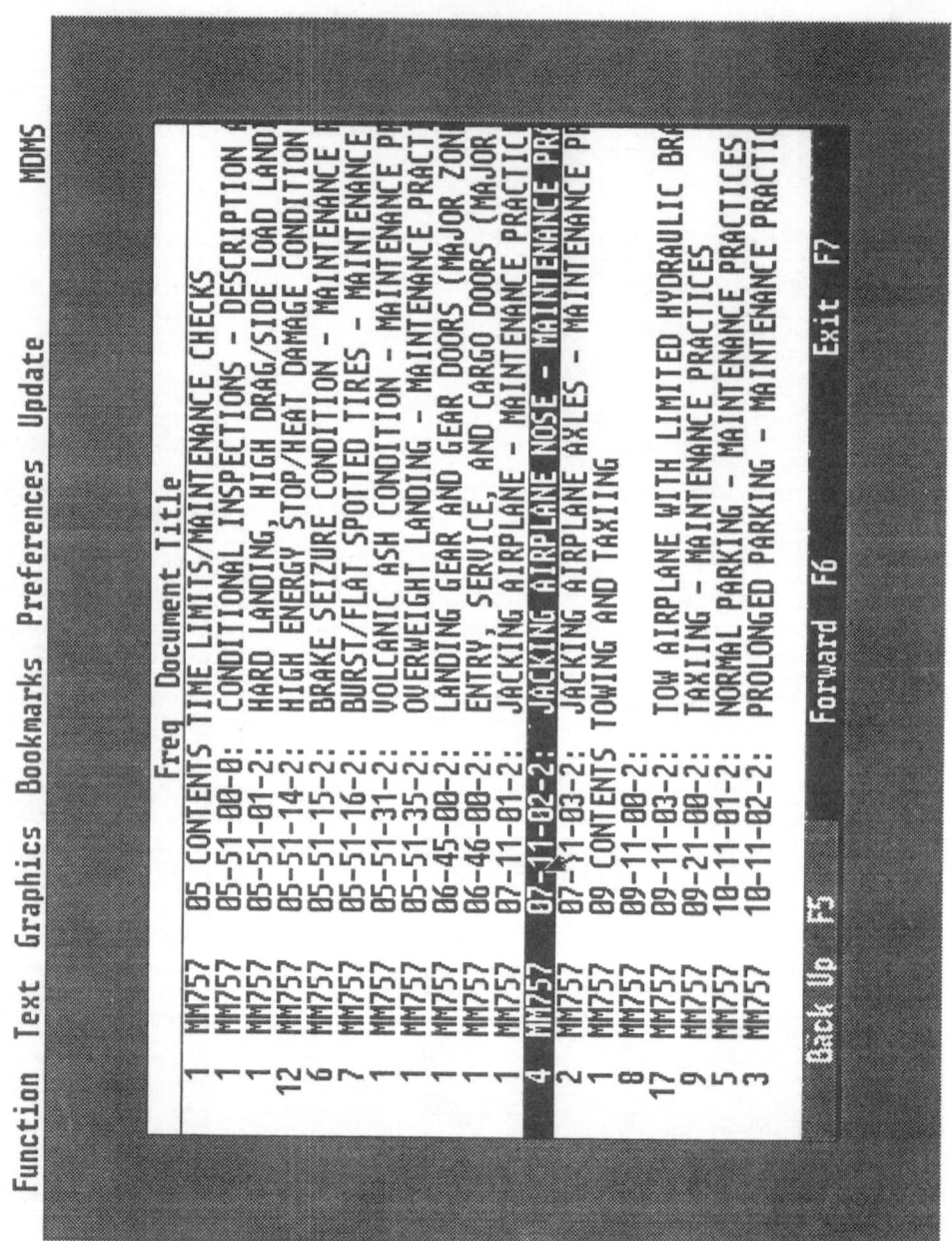

Fig. 6.6. Hits from a word-search.

outline. Pageblocks themselves are quite lengthy pieces of text which are further subdivided into numbered and labelled paragraphs relating to particular tasks, so finding the exact target of a hot link may take time. A likely future development is that manuals will be structured using AMTOS (Aircraft Maintenance Task Oriented System); this will extend the current standard subdivisions down to the individual task, allowing a lower level of reference and giving greater precision.

The CD-ROM used for the pilot study is taken directly from the current manual, which was obviously not originally designed for this interactive use. Links were generated automatically from explicit textual references, and no others were added. However one beneficial result of conversion to CD-ROM was the identification and correction of spurious cross-references.

Following a chain of cross-references through a text may cause the user to lose his bearings and forget his original objective. To avoid this problem the system provides a "Path to Document" option, which shows a list of pageblocks read so far. Clicking on an item in the list causes a return to that point, and the deletion of the last part of the path. A related option allows a display of all references *from* the current pageblock and all references *to* it (i.e. citations). This is of particular value when producing revisions to the manual, a process which will be discussed a little later.

Viewing Graphics

The other important use of the hot link is to view figures or illustrations. On the CD-ROM, graphics are not seen when simply scrolling through the text. They are held on separate files, and require a different set of routines to access them, decompress the data, and display them on the screen. This is probably the most demanding software function in terms of processing power.

There are two ways to encode diagrams in digital form: *vector* and *raster*. Both are used in the manuals under discussion, vector graphics for the Maintenance Manual, raster graphics for the Parts Catalogue.

With *vector* graphics the only data to be stored is the set of X,Y co-ordinates for the start and end points of the lines in the drawing. This is economical in processing time and storage space (one figure occupies about 7k bytes on the disc), and produces a clear image on the screen. Standard transformations can be applied to the data to scale, shift, or rotate a drawing. Illustrations originated using CAD or drawing packages are in vector form, and this data should be directly transferable for use in a retrieval system.

Raster graphics are used where it is impossible (e.g. with a photograph) or uneconomic to capture an image in terms of lines. Instead it is scanned and stored as a matrix of dots. At a typical rate of 300 dots per inch this obviously demands more storage space, and provides less flexibility for subsequent data manipulation. Compression algorithms can be used to reduce storage requirements, and this was done for the Parts Catalogue Illustrations. For the trial application, hardware decompression was used to enable a picture to be displayed within five to six seconds.

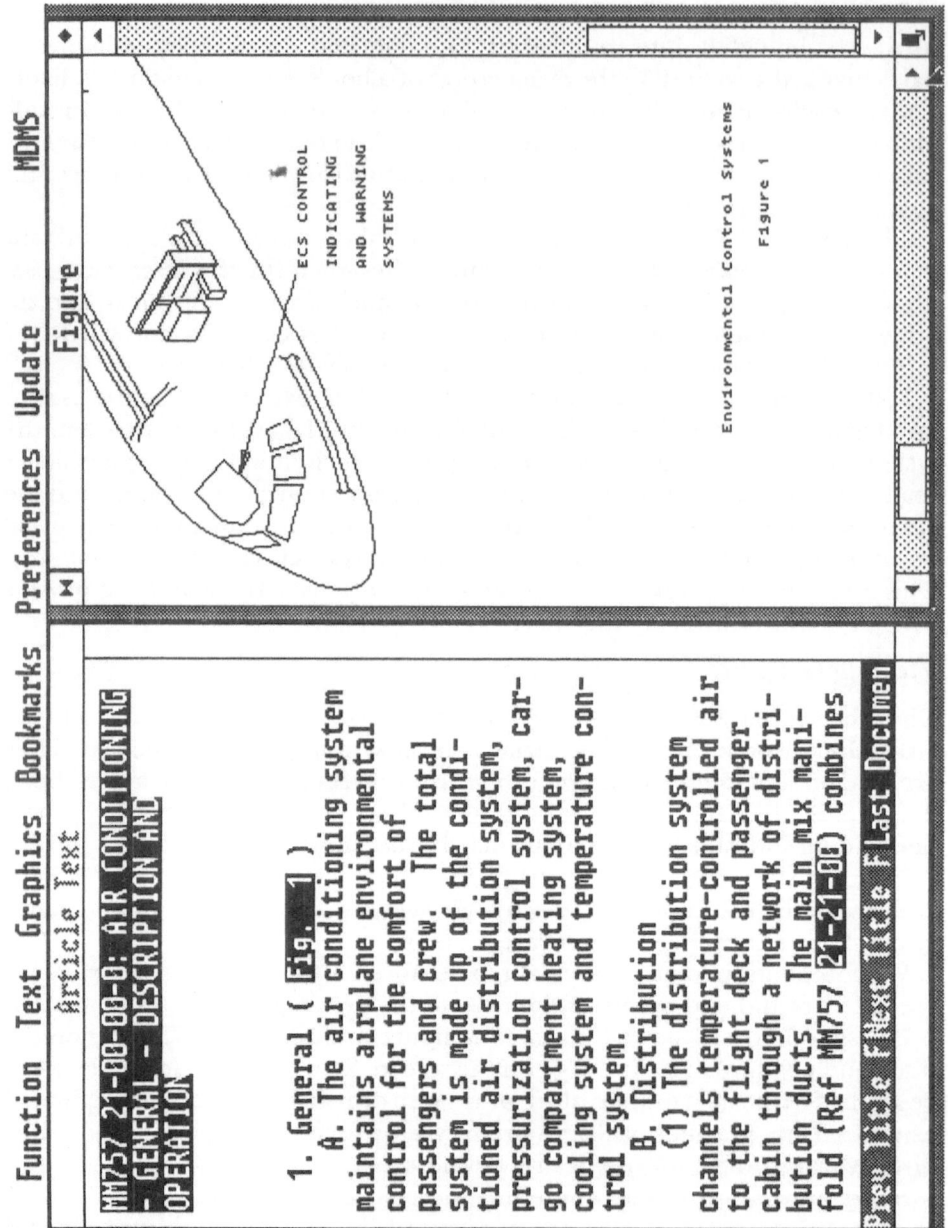

Fig. 6.7. Multi-window screen showing hot-links for references to text and graphics.

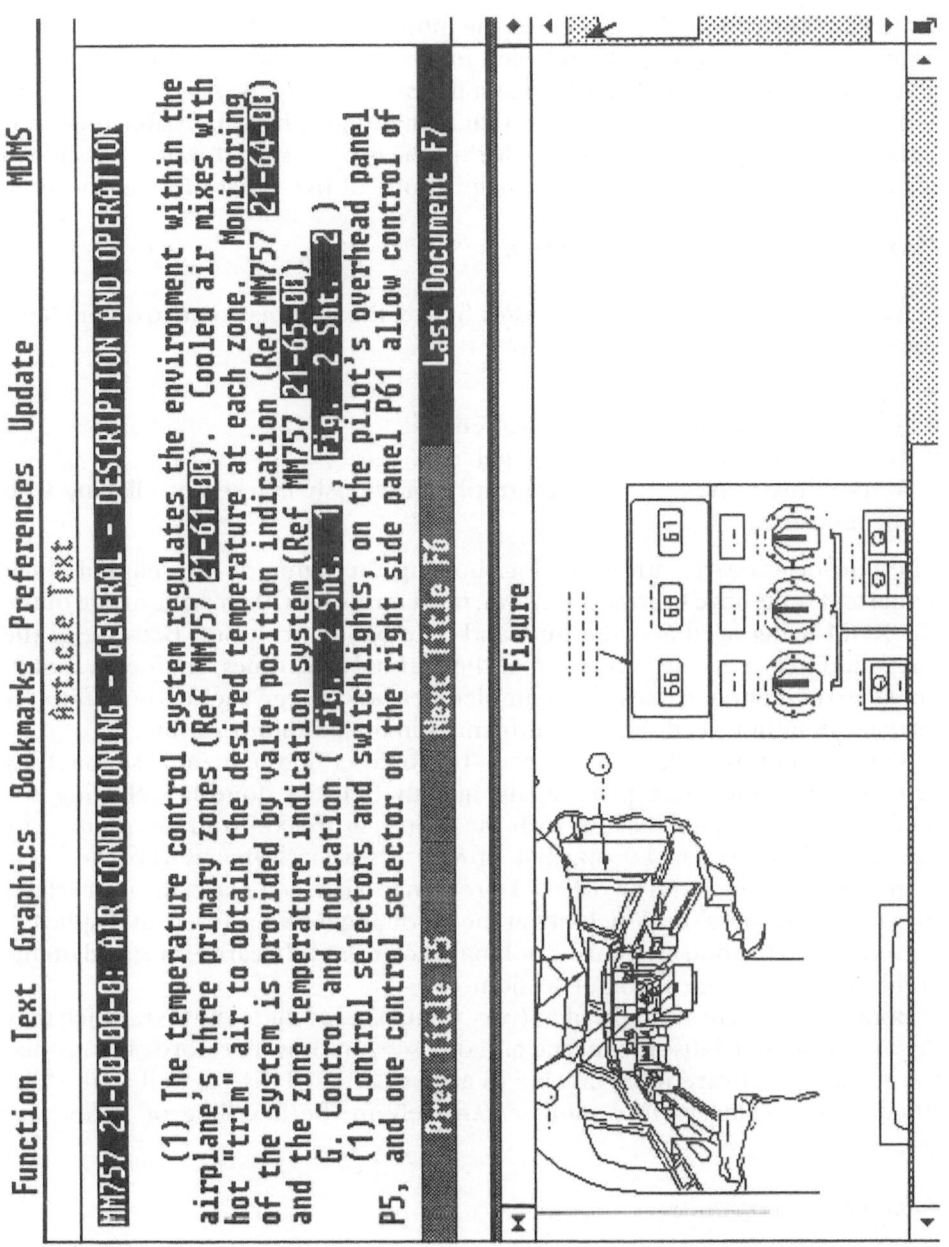

Fig. 6.8. Multi-window screen showing hot-links for references to text and graphics.

To see an illustration, the user clicks the mouse on a highlighted reference to a figure, and this brings up the relevant image, in a new window overlaying the text. The screen may be split horizontally or vertically into two independent windows (as in Figs 6.7 and 6.8), so that text and graphics are visible together. Either window can be scrolled, and within the graphics window it is possible to "zoom" in or out, so as to see the image at one of five levels of magnification.

Printing and Saving Information

Having found the required text and/or figure, the user may wish to obtain hard copy. The available options are to print:

- Graphics: the current figure.
- Screen: the text on the current screen.
- Whole document: the current pageblock.
- Marked text: one or more paragraphs previously marked by clicking with the mouse.

The output appears with a header showing the name of the manual, what actual text units have been printed and, most important, the revision date of the CD-ROM being used and the time and date of the print-out. Because of the obligation to use the latest revision of the manual at all times, engineers should not keep their paper copies after completing a task, but go back to the computer system when they need the same information on another occasion.

They are however allowed to insert "bookmarks" in the manual so that they can return to the same place again quickly. This is done by selecting the bookmark option and clicking with the mouse at the appropriate point. Any number of places can be marked during a session; what is recorded is a pageblock reference and an offset. To return to a marked place, the user selects the "use bookmarks" option, looks at the list of pageblock references displayed, then clicks on the one he wants. Bookmarks can also be cleared, or saved on file and loaded for re-use at a later session.

Bookmarks can be thought of as (very minor) revisions to the text, which may be saved onto hard disc files at the end of a session. It is therefore obvious that the retrieval software must be able to access the hard disc as well as the CD-ROM. This facility is used more extensively in the handling of temporary revisions.

Temporary Revisions

These were a vital issue for the investigation of CD-ROM feasibility. Under the microfilm-based system, they are produced on paper and those which take the form of a "safety alert" must be distributed within 24 hours. The disadvantage is that maintenance engineers have two places to look for information – a reel of microfilm and a large binder full of revision pages – so it is possible for something important to be missed. By contrast the CD-ROM system shows temporary revisions already incorporated in the main text. They are displayed in a different colour to emphasise the fact that they are recent changes, but they do not require the engineer to look elsewhere.

This is a great improvement for the user, but it cannot, obviously, be achieved by directly "updating" a read-only optical disc. Instead the software provides a special set of functions for the data administrator in the Technical Publications department. His procedure is to mark the stretch of text where a revision is needed, and select from a special "update" menu. This causes a file containing the marked text to be written to a "revisions" directory on hard disc, where it can be edited with a standard word processing package. On any subsequent use of the database the new revision will appear. Throughout a session, the software is continually checking the revision directory while taking data from the CD-ROM, and, if necessary, modifying the text as it is shown. Temporary revisions remain in force until a complete new revision is received on another optical disc.

There is also a facility to add new diagrams, at least in raster form. The image to be inserted in the manual is scanned, and the file written to the hard disc, again in a special directory and with a unique sequence number. The data administrator must make an explicit connection between this number and a figure reference within the text. Future versions of the software will allow all revisions (text and graphics) to be set up under control of the application, without the need to interact with the operating system file directories.

The investigation clearly established the technical feasibility of handling temporary revisions with CD-ROM, but some operational problems remain, for instance how to achieve rapid distribution of the update files to all users. Within one site this can be done by installing them from a floppy disc, but full networking may be required when the system is in use at linestations throughout the world.

Extensions

To complete this account of British Airways Technical Publications, we will briefly mention some extensions to the system set up for the trial period, suggesting a few of their long-term organisational implications.

Each aircraft has three (smaller) manuals associated with it: the Fault Isolation Manual, the Wiring Diagram Manual and the Structural Repair Manual. It is obviously desirable to include them, and there is space to hold the data on the same disc as the other two manuals. However this involves a change of policy on revision schedules – where the production of microfilms was *staggered* in order to spread the workload of the staff producing them, all new versions coming out on the same CD-ROM must be *synchronised*.

The system will be progressively extended to handle Engine Overhaul manuals from Rolls-Royce, manuals for other Boeing aircraft, and from other aircraft manufacturers. Selection of the correct disc before carrying out maintenance will involve either a manual operation (as with the microfilm reels) or, more likely, the installation of several CD-ROM drives daisy-chained together on each machine.

The production system will use 386-based workstations with 20-inch screens; the special decompression board for raster images will no longer be required, as acceptable performance can be achieved with software on the faster processors. The equipment will be needed at up to 300 sites, about 150 of which are overseas. The problems of distributing the data have already been mentioned. Temporary revisions can be sent via networks or on floppy disc but CD-ROMs must be physically delivered, and an airline obviously has the resources to do this internally. There are some overseas locations where it is difficult to site computer equipment; one solution may be to install it in the aircraft itself so that it is always available where needed.

The arrival of a complete revision should trigger off a series of housekeeping activities on each machine in use. All temporary revisions, bookmarks, etc. become obsolete and must be deleted. In the Technical Publications department, the old CD-ROM must be archived, along with all associated temporary revisions. Since the retrieval software is also held on the CD-ROM, it is of necessity archived with it. To comply with legal requirements it may in future be necessary to archive operating system software, and even, eventually, hardware!

Although the workstations will be used mainly in a stand-alone mode, there are plans to link them to a large mainframe database controlling engineering applications. One possible application concerns the handling of faults detected while an aircraft is in flight. Using ACARS (Aircraft Communication Addressing and Reporting System), Fault Report codes can be sent directly to the mainframe, where they are interpreted to indicate the repairs likely to be needed. This information can be transmitted to the relevant workstation where, using the CD-ROM manuals, parts requisitions and other details can be printed so that the maintenance engineers are already prepared to deal with the aircraft when it arrives.

For the user organisation, then, the investigation showed that to adopt CD-ROM instead of older media for large-scale technical publications was not only feasible but presented many advantages, enabling information to be accessed more conveniently and archived more economically. It was possible to handle both text and graphics, and to deal with the important issue of temporary revisions. This application illustrates some of the text retrieval techniques described earlier, as well as other more sophisticated features which will be discussed again in a later chapter on hypertext. However the details of legal and organisational constraints, and the possible long-term consequences of adopting the new technology, may be considered no less important.

Chapter Summary

CD-ROM was developed using an existing standardised digital recording technology. The mass-market for audio compact disc ensured low manufacturing costs for playing equipment, leading to its rapid and widespread adoption as a computer peripheral. The corresponding disadvantage was that random access data structures had to be mapped onto a sequential medium, where tracks were recorded at constant linear velocity and the block-addressing mechanism was based upon actual playing time.

Efforts at industry standardisation for higher levels of data representation resulted in the High Sierra Group proposals adopted as ISO Standard 9660. These defined how logical structures (such as volumes, directories and files) should be physically encoded, so that applications software could access data through standard operating system routines rather than player-dependent functions.

CD-ROM is a read-only medium, and hence used to distribute fairly static databases, including textual and bibliographic material. The equipment is commonly attached to stand-alone PCs and workstations; larger scale databases with multiple users will require the adoption of automatic handling devices and the establishment of broadband networks for document delivery.

Two example applications were described, in which CD-ROM was a substitute for microfilm/printed versions of a book catalogue and an aircraft maintenance manual. The second case involved a full-text database incorporating engineering diagrams, accessible by chapter and section, by keyword search, and the following of cross-references. The system also managed auxiliary material held on magnetic disc. The kind of features illustrated here will be discussed again in a later chapter on hypertext systems.

Investigations

Make a survey of published textual or bibliographic databases currently available on CD-ROM, and note the price-range both for the discs themselves and the playing equipment. Are individual discs usable on a range of PCs and workstations, or specific to a particular system?

Look at facilities available for users to create their own CD-ROMs, or to have them produced in small quantities for internal use rather than published for sale. What sort of costs are involved?

Find out about recent developments in the use of CD-ROM in turnkey systems for the entertainment and education market. Look particularly at capabilities for interactive video. Can you sort out the rival claims of, for example, CD-I, CD-V, DVI and CDTV?

References

1 Hardwick A (1986) Error correction codes: key to perfect data. In: Lambert S (ed) CD-ROM: The new papyrus. Microsoft Press, Ropiequet, pp 73–83
2 High Sierra Group Report, May 1986, reprinted in Holz F (ed) CD-ROM: Breakthrough in information storage. Tab Books, pp 145–200
3 Zoellick B (1986) CD-ROM software development. Byte, May:177–200
4 Frenkel K (1989) The next generation of interactive technologies. CACM 32(7):872–881
5 Tuck WR (9189) New directions for document delivery: Quartet's experiments with Adonis. Interlending and Document Supply 17(3):94–100
6 Gibbins P (1988) The role of the systems integrator. In: Oppenheimer C (ed) CD-ROM – Technology to applications. Butterworths, London, pp 49–79

Seven
Worm Disc and Document Image Processing

" ... lambs could not forgive ... nor worms forget!"
Charles Dickens

Overview of Worm Disc Characteristics

Like CD-ROM, worm disc is a digital non-erasable medium, but there are significant differences in its characteristics and use:

- The technology has no other purpose but to hold computer generated data, and the recording conventions are designed for doing so as efficiently as possible.
- Worm disc is an archiving and storage medium rather than a publishing medium; there is no mastering/mass-production process, and the contents are not usually for public sale.
- The same equipment is used to read and write the data, and discs are normally filled up over a period of time rather than written all at once.
- Both the storage and retrieval process may be integrated with other information processing tasks within the user organisation.
- Industry standardisation is not yet a powerful force. The most commonly used disc sizes are 12-inch and 5.25-inch, but even basic physical parameters such as cartridge thickness vary from one manufacturer to another, and so, at the system level, do parameters such as recording density and data formats. Worm discs are not intended for interchange of data between machines of different type; they are normally formatted, written, and afterwards read on the same system.
- Worm discs currently represent the highest capacity mass storage system available within the data processing world. A typical 12-inch disc holds 2–5 gigabytes of data; and up to 280 discs may be installed in large "jukebox" devices, with a worst-case access time of 25 seconds. 5.25-inch discs have a capacity of from 600mb to one gigabyte; jukebox storage is more compact and typical access times are 7–10 seconds.

Because of the lack of standardisation, we shall spend much less time on physical formats and logical organisations than in the case of CD-ROM. At the physical level, the basic method of interpreting pits and lands in terms of bits is the same, but the data is recorded at CAV rather than CLV, i.e. rotation speed remains constant, and division into separate sectors is similar to the arrangements on magnetic disc.

Nevertheless access times are an order of magnitude slower than those of a standard hard disc, i.e. 150–250 milliseconds for a random seek and 200–500 kbytes per second data transfer rate. This speed difference is due to a number of factors, for instance that the read/write head is heavier than on a magnetic disc, and the rotation rate slower. In turn these characteristics result from the work that must be done when data is written or read. Writing in particular needs a high-power laser, and since data is recorded by heating up the disc surface, the rotational speed must give time for this to take effect. Because the track density is higher than on a magnetic disc, it also takes longer to manoeuvre the bulky read/write head into the correct position.

Logical Data Organisation – Requirements and Strategies

Given the performance characteristics described above, the simplest way to treat the disc is as a *sequential* medium like magnetic tape, an appropriate option for users who are mainly interested in a compact off-line storage medium. Suppliers of optical disc drives and controller boards will also provide *emulation* software enabling a computer operating system to address the disc drive as if it were a tape drive. A typical application might then involve straightforward copying from an existing tape archive so as to reduce the need for storage space. A single 1-gigabyte surface holds the equivalent of 30 full tapes written at 1600 bpi, for example, so the saving will be substantial, and data transfer can be carried out as a background job on a mini or mainframe, with little operator intervention.

Even in that context it is desirable to impose some structure on the disc, for instance to enable the contents of related tapes to be conveniently grouped together. So the emulator software allows the creation of *logical reels* on the disc, defined by a start and end block number. Before using the disc, the operating system is instructed to "mount" a particular logical reel as though it were a tape. Reels may be of any convenient size, and it is possible to keep more than one reel "open" on the disc while it is being filled so that new files can be appended at the most appropriate place. (Obviously care must be taken not to run off the end of one reel and onto the next, making data on both reels unusable.) When the space allocated to a reel is exhausted, or there is no more data to be added, it may be permanently closed and write protected.

Within a logical reel, the operating system may carry out typical tape operations, e.g.

- Rewind to start of reel.
- Backspace one file/logical record.
- Skip forward one file/logical record.
- Read/write a record.
- Write a "tape mark" to indicate end-of-file.

It may also emulate overwriting one file with another, the effect being to make the original file inaccessible and write the new one further along the reel. Note that rewinding and skipping forwards and backwards between files can be carried out more rapidly than on tape. The tape-mark separating one file from the next is a record holding backward and forward pointers (to the start of the previous and following files), as well as information about the length and status of the current file. Any file can be quickly located by a series of random seeks, although records within a file are sequentially organised.

An application using the sort of facilities just described will not, obviously, expect to provide fast on-line data retrieval. Typically the optical discs themselves will be held off-line, although there will probably be an index on magnetic disc holding details of the location of each file in terms of surface, logical reel and file number. When a particular file is needed, the appropriate cartridge will be found, the logical reel mounted, and the data read back onto magnetic tape or disc for processing. That is quite satisfactory for some purposes; we will now go on to consider what are the requirements for more interactive uses.

Even when an optical disc is used as a random-access device, it is unlikely to hold a miscellany of directories and files like an active DOS or Unix magnetic disc. It is more likely to hold many thousands of records of the same or similar type. Often these records will be documents – ASCII text or images or a mixture of both. The normal record size will be large by conventional database standards, for example 50k bytes for a single A4 scanned page image in compressed form. Obviously some kind of housekeeping information must be kept to locate these records, but this will vary according to the pattern of use.

If it so happens that all the data to go on one optical disc can be assembled beforehand, the file design task is similar to that for CD-ROM. Using the Small Computer Systems Interface (SCSI) data bus, an optical disc can be randomly accessed as if it were a magnetic disc. So file organisations can be worked out to exploit the capabilities of the medium, knowing that there is no need to consider later insertions, deletions or updates. Simulations, e.g. [1], can show how to optimise performance by selecting indexing structures, hashing functions and packing densities for efficient search, while maintaining a reasonable usage of the available space.

In practice however, in the archiving applications for which optical storage is most often used, the process of data capture is integrated with other organisational tasks, and filling a particular disc can take place over a period of days or weeks. In that case housekeeping information must be amended as new batches of records are added, and this cannot be done by overwriting. Information must be held somewhere, for example, about the locations of records currently on the disc, and the next available free space for writing.

A simple and common approach is to write new data records sequentially, starting on the outermost track of the disc and moving inward, while the housekeeping information begins at the innermost track and moves outwards. The next available write position is known as the "high water mark", and this is re-recorded every time new data is added. Data records and housekeeping information "grow" towards one another, and when they meet the disc is known to be full. This system is very economical of space, with records being grouped together purely on the basis of the time when they were written.

Some applications may require data recorded at different times (e.g. correspondence received from a certain customer) to be brought together for one enquiry, and performance will be better if it has all been placed together. By predicting beforehand how documents will be distributed, the designer can pre-partition the disc so that separate areas are allocated for related sets of records – a technique known as *clustering*. If the predictions are correct it will improve access performance; if not it may result in an unacceptable waste of space. The only way to re-organise a database is to read it all off one disc and write it to another, but given the volumes of data involved and the actual cost of the discs themselves (about £400 for a 12-inch cartridge), this is a time consuming and expensive option.

We have considered the possibility that an optical disc may be filled up all at one time, or in stages. Many archiving applications involve both processes – the first during *backfile conversion* from some other medium such as paper, microfilm or magnetic tape, the second when data is captured at the time of its arrival within the organisation. The two methods must obviously produce compatible results for later retrieval, and for the optical discs themselves a fairly simple data organisation will normally be preferred, with higher-level indexing structures based on auxiliary magnetic discs which can be efficiently searched, updated, and re-organised. Any copies of the index on the optical disc are there only as a back-up. However there are systems (more frequently those based on PCs and 5.25-inch discs) where working indexes are kept on the worm disc itself, providing immediate protection against magnetic disc corruption, and the ability to export individual discs more easily from one installation to another.

Worm Disc Applications

What sort of data goes onto worm disc? As already suggested, scanned document images form the majority of records on many systems. And with good reason – this is the only medium with sufficient capacity to hold the bulk of data likely to be generated if a decision is taken to move from paper-handling to complete on-line working. A good overview of the long-term potential of document image processing appears in [2].

- Any organisation dealing extensively with the public – hospital, local authority or government department, bank, building society or insurance company – will still receive a high proportion of its input on short (often handwritten) documents, and there is no realistic way to convert these into machine-readable form except by image scanning.
- Some of the documents received: application forms, hire purchase/mortgage agreements, have a legal status which requires their retention for a number of years in case of dispute. A printout of a scanned document, held on a non-erasable medium, may be found acceptable in court as the "best available image" if the original document has been destroyed.
- In many cases the text to be stored includes photographs (e.g. in a newspaper cuttings library [3]), X-rays, charts (medical records [4]), engineering drawings or other diagrams (patent documents [5]). One insurance company holds an indexed cuttings library of all advertisements from and news items about rival organisations, to support its market research activities.

One obvious reason to hold scanned images on optical disc is to save paper storage – if office space in a capital city is costed by the square foot there is every incentive to get rid of filing cabinets! Even where at least one original must be retained (as in the case of patent documents), other copies can be more economically stored and distributed on disc.

The other advantage for many organisations is that with properly networked retrieval several people can access the same image simultaneously, so avoiding the delays which occur when a paper file is out of the office or even lost. In practice paper files are usually looked at to enable staff to make decisions. If the retrieval system lets its users record their decisions centrally, or pass paperwork automatically to another member of the team, it should improve communications within the organisation and avoid the familiar problem that the left hand doesn't know what the right hand is doing.

As well as scanned paper documents, an optical disc archive may include data from other sources, namely:

- Microfilm records. Large backfiles on microfilm can be scanned with special equipment and entered in the system like paper images.
- Fax images received within the organisation, which are already in a suitable format for storage.
- COLD. This acronym stands for *Computer Output on Laser Disc*, and was coined by analogy with the earlier COM (*Computer Output on Microfilm*). Many messages to customers are computer generated – for example a bank or building society sends regular statements as well as word processed letters – and a COLD facility allows this information to be extracted automatically from active account and correspondence files and written to optical disc. It is

saved in ASCII form, and so is economical in storage – several hundred such records are batched together to form an optical disc block of appropriate size. Note also that when COLD records are retrieved the system must simulate the original document on the screen. For the user, the display should be the same whether it comes from an old paper image or a COLD record.

- An alternative to COLD is that *ASCII* files, e.g. from a word processor, may be automatically converted to *raster form*. They are more compatible with other image data, but obviously occupy more space.

A typical retrieval system for a bank or building society, then, could hold the following record types:

- Signed customer applications/agreement forms, legally retainable for a period of fifteen years, acquired by scanning backfiles, perhaps on microfilm, or by data capture at the time when the agreement was processed.
- Correspondence *from* the customer, in the form of scanned handwritten or typed letters, or fax images.
- Correspondence *to* the customer, saved directly from word processing files in raster or COLD form.
- Customer statements, again either converted from paper or microfilm files, more recently captured using COLD.

The volume of data to be stored is extremely large – a building society, for instance, may handle 50 000 new mortgage applications per year, and need to hold application forms, survey reports, agreements and miscellaneous correspondence. A national clearing bank may generate a million customer statements in a three-month cycle, quite apart from other inputs to the system. So the application designer must consider how to distribute the information in the optimum way, bearing in mind that not all inputs have a predictable time pattern, and that the retention periods for different document types will vary.

A simple arrangement involves keeping different document types on separate discs, but using a jukebox with multiple drives to get an acceptable response time when data is assembled from different sources. Alternative methods already mentioned involve pre-partitioning and clustering related records on the same disc. In fact if the required set of documents can be identified in advance, the application software may pre-select them overnight and *cache* them on magnetic disc to allow fast retrieval during the next working day. A retrieval system managing an optical disc mass-storage system must look for data in four places in descending order of priority: the magnetic disc cache, the cartridges already in the drive(s), other cartridges in the jukebox racks, and, as a last resort, cartridges held off-line which must be mounted by the operator. A well designed application will ensure that the last situation doesn't arise too often.

An Optical Storage Archiving and Retrieval System

It should be obvious by now that setting up an interactive document handling application on optical storage involves more than simply attaching a worm disc drive to an existing computer installation. The various activities involved – scanning and other types of data entry, indexing, storage, retrieval and printing – need to be supported by a network linking peripheral equipment, servers and user workstations, with specially designed software to direct the flow of information between them.

One example of such a system is *Olivetti Filenet*, an account of which will provide a framework for discussing the relevant ideas. A diagrammatic overview of the Filenet system is shown in Fig. 7.1. For a large-scale document handling application, the following components are required:

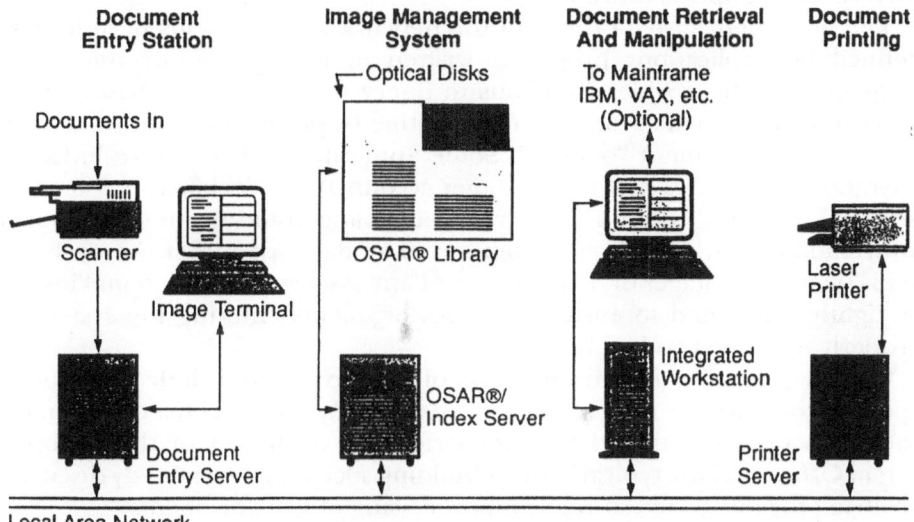

Fig. 7.1. Overview of the Filenet document image processing system.

- A document entry station, with scanner, server, and operator terminal.
- An OSAR jukebox, capable of holding between 64 and 280 cartridges, with from one to four separate drives.
- A laser printer for outputting document images, once again with an associated server.
- A number of workstations for checking and indexing documents as they are entered, and for image retrieval. These would be served by the following databases on magnetic disc:

(i)   A database of logical indexes, enabling interactive retrieval of unique document identifiers.

(ii)   A database of physical indexes, mapping each document identifier to an optical disc cartridge, surface, and sector.

(iii)   A database of cached document records, either recently read or written, or "pre-fetched" for a particular day's work. Access to cached records is fast, and applications will be designed to exploit the cache files as much as possible.

The separation between the two magnetic disc indexes allows some flexibility: the logical database software can be chosen to fit the application and in particular the nature of the indexing used. A bank or building society archive where access is geared to customer account numbers or similar keys can be handled by a standard relational database system, whereas a newspaper cuttings library where multiple keywords have been assigned as document descriptors may require a full inverted list index. In either case, once a unique document identifier has been found, the physical index can be used to find the corresponding optical disc address.

The movement of data through the network to the various peripherals is defined by applications programs written in the special-purpose *Workflo* language, which provides functions to query the various databases, and to move records from one workstation to another by putting them into and taking them out of document "queues". Some applications also require links with operational databases (e.g. for customer accounts), so Workflo can also open a terminal "window" onto a mainframe, enabling some document indexing information to be copied over from a remote database rather than rekeyed. Thus the various stages of data entry, and any associated decision making, can be tightly integrated to ensure that all documents entering the system are properly processed and archived.

We now consider the various parts of the process in a little more detail. Specific examples are mostly taken from two areas: the backfile conversion of patent documents currently being carried out on behalf of the European Patent Office, and the typical bank or building society system already discussed, involving the integrated storage and processing of live documents.

Document Preparation

When converting backfiles, the sequence of documents must be complete and in order. They will be put into batches of a suitable size (e.g. 50 pages), and normal clerical controls will be applied. Documents must be checked for legibility and physical condition, i.e. that they are not too crumpled to go through a sheet feeder. If they are bound or stapled the pages must be separated. There are in fact three sorts of scanner: *sheet-feeders, flat-bed scanners* and *camera-based scanners*. Those of the first type will normally be preferred since they require less operator attention, but where documents cannot be unbound or are in fragile condition one of the other two methods must be used. (A particular advantage in converting fragile documents to machine-readable form is that the paper only needs to be physically handled once; thereafter all reference can be to the stored image.)

Scanning

Scanning involves turning a document image into a bit-map where ones and zeroes stand for black and white points on the page. Fig. 7.2 shows a screen-dump taken while a scanning operation was taking place. In practice scanned images often do not consist purely of black and white dots, but of continuous lines in various shades of grey. The scanning process therefore involves various options including the following:

Thresholding

The operator must select a particular shade of grey as the threshold; everything below this level is treated as white, everything above it is treated as black. The choice of threshold depends on the faintness of the document, just as it does in the analogous process of photocopying. Where straight black and white images do not provide enough subtlety (e.g. in scanned photographs), each point must be represented by an 8-bit byte holding a *grey scale* level. This provides the opportunity for much more sophisticated image processing, but the storage space and processing time required is not justified for the kind of document storage being discussed here.

Density

Typical scanning densities are 200, 300, and 400 dots per inch. There is an obvious trade-off between the quality of the image and the storage space needed to hold it. Once again the choice depends on the nature of the document – size of print, scale of diagrams, etc. For comparison, a high resolution screen on a workstation or PC displays at about 80 dots or pixels per inch, standard fax images are scanned at 200 dpi, standard laser printers print at 300 dpi. On the face of it there is little point in storing at a higher density than can be displayed or printed afterwards; however for images with a long life expectancy it may be worth saving a better quality image in anticipation of future developments.

Compression

A page of A4 text scanned at 200 dpi takes half a megabyte of storage – impractical even for the largest optical disc capacity. Data compression

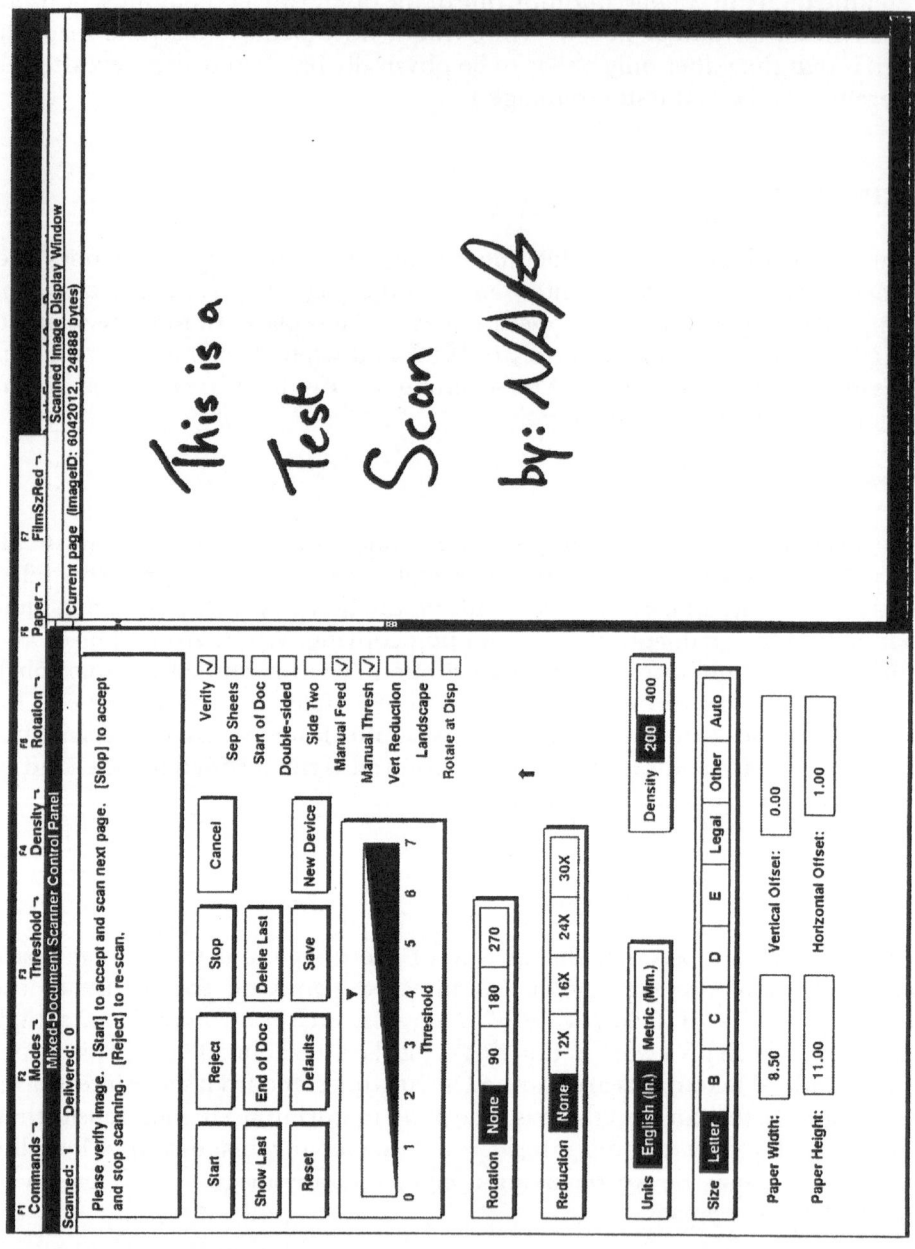

Fig. 7.2. Scanning a document.

techniques are used to reduce the number of bits to about 10 per cent of the original requirement – hence the often-quoted figure of 50k bytes for a stored document image. The methods most often used are based on the CCITT Group4 facsimile standards [6], defined to allow efficient fax transmission over data communications networks but equally applicable for this purpose. They combine two techniques which were mentioned earlier in connection with text-compression but are actually more significant in this context: run-length encoding and two-dimensional encoding.

Run-length Encoding

This obviously has excellent potential for image compression, particularly where there is a high proportion of white space. For each line of data it is necessary to hold only a short binary "code word" for each run of black and white dots, and since black dots are likely to be clustered rather than scattered randomly across the page the method will produce a substantial reduction. For example, white run-lengths from 29 to 63 bits long are all represented by 8-bit code words, and black run-lengths in the same range by 12-bit code words.

Two-dimensional Encoding

The algorithm here is rather more complex. In principle two-dimensional encoding involves holding, for each line of the image, only the *differences* between itself and the previous line. However because the method is always used in conjunction with run-length encoding for individual lines, these differences cannot be represented on a bit-by-bit basis. Instead the algorithm identifies the position of each *changing element* (the point where black switches to white or vice versa) and codes it with respect to the position of a corresponding *reference element*, i.e. the nearest changing element on the preceding line. The code word used will vary according to the relative positions of the two elements, and how many pixels apart they are.

This method depends on absolute accuracy when data is stored or transmit-ted; if bits are lost it is not just a single line but the whole image which is corrupted. Compression and decompression can be performed either by software or hardware, using a special-purpose card. The fact that images can be accurately reduced in this way has great practical significance, since the kind of systems now being discussed would not be feasible without compression. The portability of fax images into and out of a document storage system may also be important in some cases.

Verification/Processing

Document images must be checked for legibility to ensure that they will be usable again when they are needed, and for this there is no alternative to human judgement. It is particularly important if, as is the intention in many applications, the original document is to be destroyed once its image is stored. Verification can be performed at the time of scanning, but it is normally a more economical use of equipment and manpower to do it later as a separate stage. We can usefully distinguish two possibilities here: one where the scanning takes place during backfile conversion and there is no immediate need to use the image, the other where a live document has been received and needs some work done on it.

In the first case it will be arranged that documents are entered in large ordered batches, with as little manual intervention as possible. For example when converting patent documents into machine-readable form indexing is performed beforehand, using cheap equipment without a high-resolution display. Quality control is then a separate operation, with a 5 per cent or 10 per cent sample of images being visually checked after transfer to magnetic tape; if any document is unsatisfactory a complete batch must be rescanned.

In the second case verification must be integrated with other processing. In the typical bank or building society application, batches of correspondence are received daily and entered into the system via the scanner workstation. The images are held on temporary disc storage, identified only by a batch/sequence number, and not yet written to a permanent database. They are later examined by a responsible member of staff. Possible actions at this stage are:

- Check the visual quality of the image. Issue instructions for re-scanning if it is unsatisfactory.
- Give the document a permanent index number.
- Look at what the document actually says, and trigger off any necessary actions to process it. This may involve passing it to a supervisor or another member of staff.
- "Commit" the document image for permanent storage.

A system supporting such actions must allow users the same freedom of action as they would have with paper documents – the "desktop" metaphor is here perhaps less artificial than in other areas of computing. Users must be able to accept a queue of documents into the equivalent of an "in-tray", call up a "background file" of existing documents, "annotate" a document image, and look at existing annotations. They therefore need a large multi-window screen with zooming and scrolling so that documents can be examined in detail. To reply to correspondence, they must be able to call up and complete standard letters, or write one-off letters, and records of these letters must also be automatically stored. For example, Figs. 7.3 and 7.4 show multi-window screens for a medical application, containing scanned documents, menus for various processing and re-routing options, and a window onto a mainframe patient database.

Indexing

This involves assigning a unique key to each document, but perhaps also ensuring that there is a usable path to that key, starting with identifiers which the user will know at the time of retrieval. As usual that path is application-dependent. For example:

- Patent documents are indexed by a unique *patent number* and type. In addition each *page* of each document is indexed according to whether it contains a bibliography, abstract, description, diagram, claim, exception definition or blank space. Held quite separately are keyword databases which allow retrieval of references to patents in particular subject areas, but this level of indexing does not occur when the patent document is scanned for storage.
- Paperwork associated with a particular bank or building society client must be indexed first on that client's *account number* (which may require a prior look-up on name and address). It is further identified by the date and time of its arrival (including the original data entry station and batch number), and on document class, i.e. agreement, claim, letter; these indexes lead to the physical locators like disc family, surface and sector.

The important question is how identifying information is entered into the system and how much it is possible to automate. In the case of the patent office backfiles for example, bar-coded sheets are filed into the sequence of documents before scanning takes place. Alternatively, pre-printed forms may have identifiers bar-coded on them, or be designed so that OCR can be applied to a small area of the scanned document. For instance an insurance company, on receiving a claim by letter, will generate a laser-printed form with reference numbers in OCR format for the customer to complete. When the form is returned it is scanned and indexed automatically – only then is the claim processed.

For miscellaneous correspondence, however, or where indexing is integrated with other tasks, some data entry procedure will be carried out by a workstation operator. As already suggested, this may involve accessing a mainframe database to check and transfer customer details like name, address and account code, and perhaps consulting background files of previous customer information so as to maintain continuity of reference numbering for papers on the same topic. Entry dates and batch codes may also be used to make up a set of document identifiers which lead to a unique key, and in turn to a physical disc location.

For some purposes, e.g. the handling of newspaper cuttings, *keyword* descriptors must also be assigned for each new document. Where only a document image is stored, full-text keyword indexing is obviously not feasible – that requires optical character recognition on the scanned documents. When selecting equipment for a document image retrieval system, it may be important to ascertain what are the facilities for optical character recognition (i)

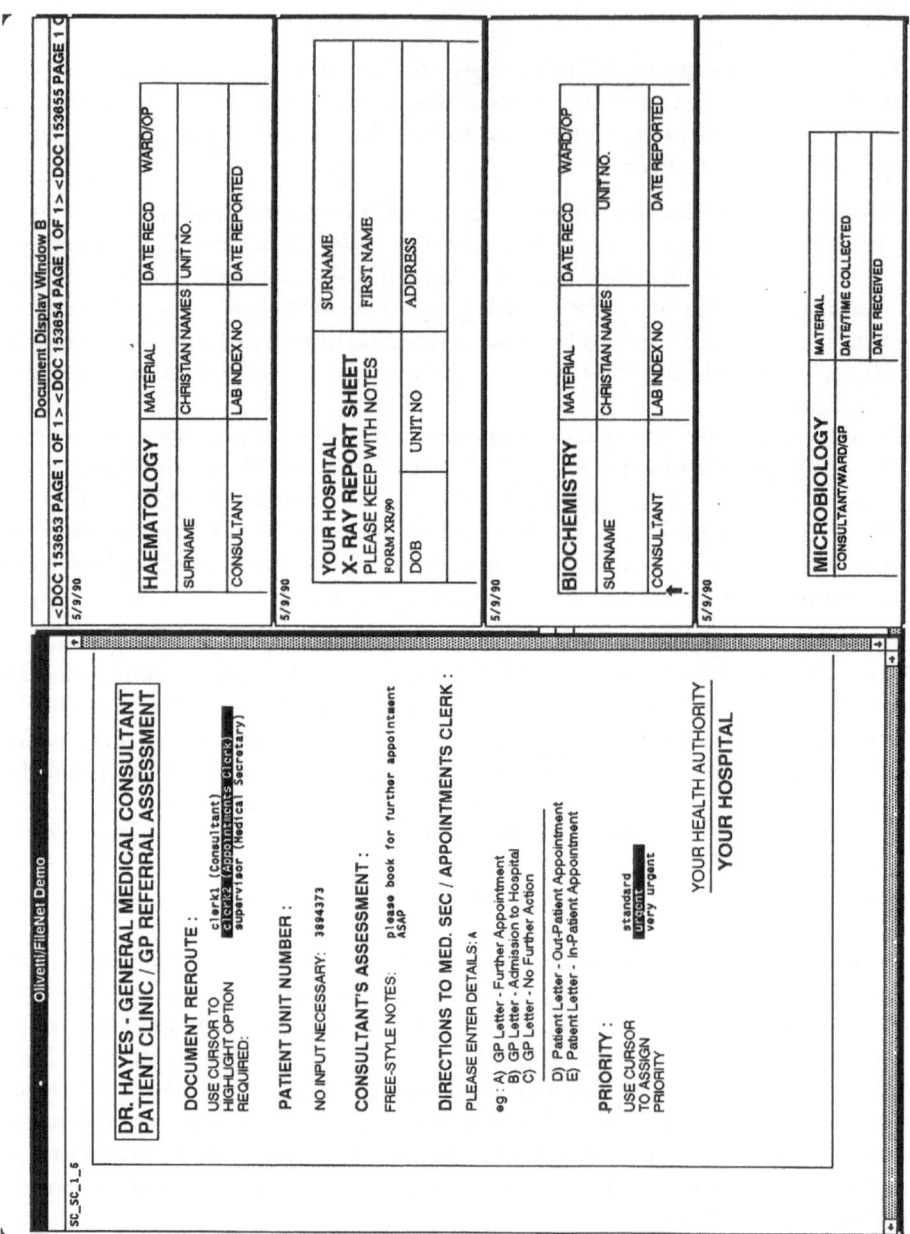

Fig. 7.3. Multi-window document processing – rerouting.

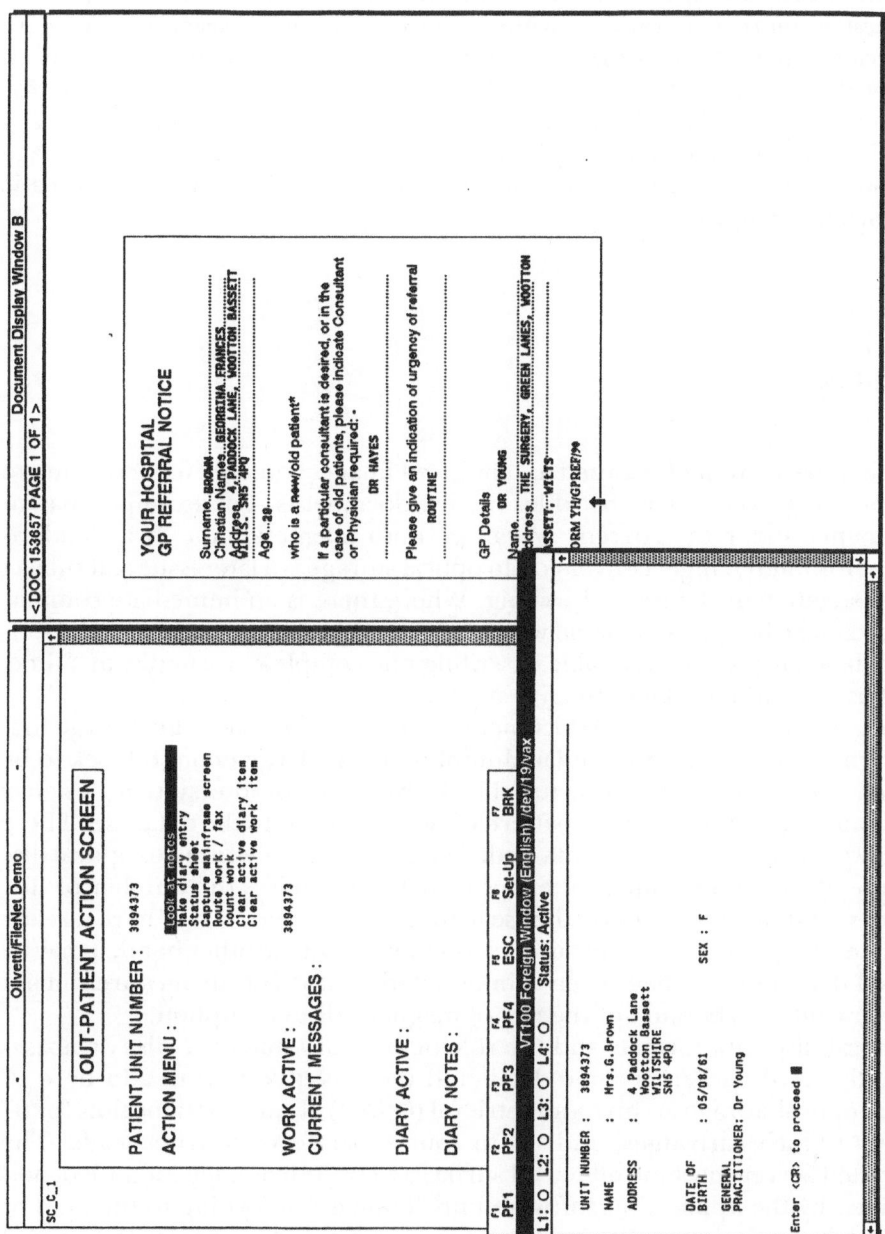

Fig. 7.4. Multi-window document processing – action menu, scanned referral notice, window to mainframe database.

at the time of scanning and (ii) after the event, on the scanned image. At present the first is more generally provided – technically it is easier to recognise characters when all the information is still present than when some has been removed by the sampling process. There is however a potential demand for systems which handle both straight document images and subsequent (perhaps selective) optical character recognition on those images, giving the advantage of more easily manipulated ASCII versions of documents, including automatic keyword indexing.

Storage

The first destination of scanned and indexed images could differ according to whether they come from backfiles or live documents. For example, patent documents under the current system go onto magnetic tape in a standard format for interchange; conversion to optical storage is a later issue still subject to investigation at the time of writing. Where there is an immediate commitment to make backfiles available within a live system, it is possible to use stand-alone data entry stations capable of writing one complete worm disc at a time, which is later imported into the live system.

Images from newly arrived documents, by contrast, are more likely to go first to magnetic disc, to be accumulated until there is a large enough block to be written to optical disc. The actual block size is set by the system designer depending upon the expected pattern of new additions to the database. There is as always a balance to be maintained. The advantage of writing to optical disc in large blocks at infrequent intervals is that it minimises the number of disc accesses, and of updates to the housekeeping area, where (as we have already noted) each update irrevocably uses up disc space. On the other hand, it may be argued that until they have been committed to optical disc, images are still not 100 per cent safe, because of the risk of magnetic disc corruption.

Optical disc data formats and the role of auxiliary magnetic disc databases were discussed earlier in some detail and there is little new to add here. A typical optical storage archive and retrieval (OSAR) library contains slots for 64 to 280 12-inch cartridges, and up to four separate read/write heads. The associated server machine allows all surfaces to be individually identified, and classified by the application software into "families" according to the kind of information stored upon them. For security, particularly of data with financial and legal implications, it is normal to hold a separate "transaction" disc as a permanent running record of documents written to all the other discs. This will provide an *audit trail* when necessary. In some cases also a special disc of "linkage" data may be held, to associate related records scattered over several different surfaces.

Retrieval

Retrieval from optical disc, as we have seen, involves going through one or more magnetic disc databases to find the physical location of the required documents. Linkage records may be consulted if documents from several optical discs must be assembled, to simulate the effect of consulting a large historical paper file on a customer.

In a live system both storage to and retrieval from optical disc will occur simultaneously. With four read heads for 200 cartridges, and a typical access time of 20 seconds to select a cartridge and get a record from it, it is obvious that the response time for a multi-user on-line retrieval system would not be adequate using optical disc alone. So magnetic disc *cache* files, as mentioned earlier, are used to minimise delays.

Cache files are essentially *queues* of records which will be required for later retrieval, and which have been selected in advance by the applications software. This often happens overnight for use the following day – thus the cached image is initially "locked" for something like fifteen hours. Thereafter the basic principle is the same as that for paged memory systems: when new records are read into the cache they overwrite those which were least recently used. Every time an image is again referred to or "touched" by the software its currency is updated.

Printing

With adequate retrieval and processing facilities many conventional office tasks should be feasible using documents in their electronic form, but paper versions are sometimes needed, especially for sending outside the organisation. An image handling system must include one or more laser printers on the network, with associated servers, to generate hard copy. Printed output will be spooled, with options to set priorities and specify paper size, scaling factors, and other formatting parameters. It is then an organisational problem to prevent paper copies building up in departmental filing cabinets, thus negating the original aims of the system!

It is important to ensure before adopting an image handling system that any printed output will be adequate for its purpose. The quality of a scanned image can never be as good as the original, because some information has been thrown away. In terms of resolution it also compares badly with microfilm, although laser printer output is often superior to photographic paper. Notions of adequacy will obviously differ according to the expected usage, e.g. whether the image is of a letter to be read and answered, or an intricate diagram which must be used to repair a machine.

Another relevant criterion is whether there is an intention to destroy the original document or whether it remains to be consulted as a last resort. In the Patent Office application, for example, scanning is performed to allow easy interchange of information from one country to another, and eventual distribution and sale via optical disc. The objective is to avoid the very expensive process of publication in printed form, but one paper copy of each patent document will always be retained. On the other hand banks, building societies and insurance companies use document imaging precisely to avoid the expense of storing the original.

The difficulty arises if it becomes necessary to produce a legally binding document as evidence in a court case, and it now exists only in electronic form. A similar issue arose many years ago in respect of microfilm, and there is a British Standard (BS 6498/6398) on the admissibility of microfilm evidence. At the time of writing a similar standard is in preparation for scanned documents, but at present in Britain at least, there is no guarantee that an electronic image will carry equal weight with an original.

From a technical point of view it is clear that a scanned document is potentially more vulnerable to interference than a microfilm. We have seen that scanned images tend to be put on magnetic media *en route* to or from optical disc, and we know that pixel-editing software exists which would enable subtle alterations to be made on them. Although data cannot be altered on optical disc itself, it is theoretically possible to update an entire disc by making a copy which incorporates changes, insertions and deletions.

This is not to say that large-scale fraud does or is likely to occur when commercial document imaging is adopted; but the safeguards against it must as usual be based on good system control, the separation of functions between different departments and persons, and the maintenance of audit trails for the detection of irregularities. Organisations wishing to present evidence based on a scanned image must be able to show in principle that there was no scope for tampering in the system from which it was obtained. They will also need to weigh any potential losses because of the unavailability of original documents against the savings to be made in the costs of paper storage. Risk assessment of this kind is a necessary aspect of any feasibility study whenever a new computer-based application is envisaged.

Conclusions

As the above discussion has shown, an integrated document image handling system has many of the characteristics of a conventional data processing system: efficiency of operation and security of data are no less important. It follows that some capability is needed for generating control information: statistical and summary reports, exception reports and so on, to monitor the performance of the system and indicate how it should be developed and enhanced. The principles are similar to those of any other management information system, and will not be elaborated here.

That concludes the discussion of worm disc technology and applications. The focus has been mainly on document imaging, where the characteristics of the medium are seen to best advantage. There is enormous potential demand for a cheap, compact, secure form of storage for machine readable documents,[1] and the next few years should see systems of the kind described in this chapter more widely adopted. However it is important that further progress be made in:

- Techniques for automatic indexing via optical character recognition, perhaps even on handwritten documents.
- Clarification of the legal validity of scanned document images.
- Standardisation of physical and logical data formats like that achieved for CD-ROM. At the physical level, standardisation is most likely to occur in the context of the newer 5.25-inch discs. Important standards for document formats are ODA and SGML [7] – these will be discussed in a later chapter.

Another open question is that of the "shelf-life" of worm discs. Ten years is a figure sometimes quoted, more recently Philips have guaranteed their discs for 30 years, but as yet obviously these claims are impossible to verify. As with other archiving media, it will be necessary to make periodic checks to ensure that data is still readable, and re-write onto new discs if there is any sign of deterioration.

Chapter Summary

Worm disc is a "write once, read many times" medium, used for archiving digital data. There are at present no widely-accepted standards for data formatting, but tracks are normally recorded at constant angular velocity. The discs are often kept in jukeboxes on-line to a computer, providing high capacity storage with rather unfavourable access times. They may be used simply as less bulky substitutes for magnetic tape; if they are treated as semi random access devices it is often necessary to maintain auxiliary indexing information on magnetic disc, and to employ caching techniques to improve performance.

Worm disc databases are most often used for document image storage. Organisations which handle large quantities of paper in the form of correspondence, reports etc. can save space by scanning them and archiving the images.

---

[1] To get an idea of the volumes of data which such systems may have to handle, consider the European Patent Office application, which has been mentioned at various points in this chapter. In 1990 the database consisted of 65 million pages of scanned documents comprising patents from five European countries published since 1920. With the addition of patents for other European countries, and including everything up to the year 1993, it is expected to grow to 135 million pages, which will require 15 000 gigabytes of storage, equivalent to 80 000 magnetic tapes. Some of the most recent patents are now commercially available on CD-ROM but for a complete mass-storage archive very high-density worm disc is the most likely option and some large-scale feasibility studies are currently in progress [5].

When the database is linked to a number of workstations on a network, any document can be used without being taken out of circulation, and a flow of work can be organised which carries out the functions of a clerical paper-handling system more efficiently. The database can also include scanned microfilm records, fax images, and COLD documents.

Document image databases are created by scanning backfiles of paper or as part of day-to-day operational procedures which include image capture. Important stages in the process are: document preparation (to ensure that scanning will result in a legible image), scanning, data compression, verification, indexing, storage, retrieval and printing. There is a range of possible scanning densities, with a trade-off between quality of the stored image and space occupancy. Data compression methods used are those for Group4 fax encoding, incorporating run-length and two-dimensional encoding.

Optical character recognition may be used to perform automatic document indexing, but manual indexing will often be required, particular if any kind of keyword retrieval is needed. Storage of document images on worm disc implies also the updating of associated magnetic disc databases which are used for subsequent retrieval, with images being placed in intermediate cache files for faster access. Images can be printed on laser printer; at the time of writing the legal issues about admitting scanned documents as evidence are unresolved.

Investigations

Identify possible requirements for document image processing in any company or organisation with which you are familiar. Produce a cost-benefit analysis based on the storage space to be saved and productivity gained versus the cost of equipment and backfile conversion.

Look at the details of the CCITT Group4 fax image encoding, and try to write an efficient program to do compression and decompression.

In the time since this book was written, what progress has been made towards standards for worm disc physical/logical data formats, or the admissibility as evidence of scanned documents?

References

1 Hanson O, Fu Z (1988) Determining optimum file structures for optical disc storage. In: Trapp R (ed) Cybernetics and systems 88. Kluwer Academic Publishers, Dordrecht, pp 1191–1198
2 Hendley AM (1987) Document image processing systems. Cimtech, Hatfield Polytechnic

3 Beard K (1989) Managing press cuttings with the Harland Simon Opal system. Proceedings, OIS International, Meckler, pp 178–183

4 Pratt M (1989) Automating the control and distribution of hospital records. Proceedings, OIS International, Meckler, pp 192–201

5 Dintzner JP (1990) Some experiences of planning and installing DIP for very large, geographically dispersed applications. Proceedings, DIP 1990, Blenheim Online Publications, pp 83–88

6 CCITT (1984) Recommendation T.6, Facsimile coding schemes and coding control functions for Group4 facsimile apparatus. Fascicle VII.3, Malaga-Torremolinos

7 White M (1990) Standards – the key to DIP progress. Proceedings, DIP 1990, Blenheim Online Publications, pp 137– 143

Eight

Video Disc and Computer-Based Training

"What is the use of a book", thought Alice, "without
pictures or conversation?"
Lewis Carroll

Physical Characteristics

Video discs represent the earliest use of optical storage technology. In contrast to CD-ROM and worm disc their primary purpose is to hold *analogue* rather than digital data, i.e. the signals to generate a PAL 625-line television display. Data is recorded in the form of pits and lands, the length of the pit indicating the voltage of the signal. It is thus feasible to hold 36 minutes of video on a 12-inch disc – one second of colour video in analogue form requires one megabyte of storage, whereas the same information in digital form would require 30 megabytes. Obviously this also affects the speed of reading and display. Compact discs are expected to be the eventual successors of video disc for multi-media systems, but at the time of writing their data transfer rate is too slow for showing good quality video sequences.

Video discs may be recorded at constant linear or angular velocity, and many players are capable of handling either mode. The ones of interest to us here – those used in interactive computer-controlled systems – use CAV, to allow easy random access to individual frames. For this purpose a disc holds 55 500 tracks per side, each corresponding to one numbered frame. It rotates at 1500 rpm, to display at the required rate of 25 frames per second. Speed of access is very player-dependent, but to address a frame out of sequence may take about one second in the worst case.

Video players are commonly classified according to the level of service they provide. Level 1 players can be used with a hand-held controller which allows functions such as freeze, fast-forward, backward etc. Level 2 players have a built-in processor which runs general purpose software, recorded on the sound track of the disc in digital form. Level 3 players can be controlled from an external processor, connected through a standard RS232 interface. This obviously provides for more flexible and powerful software systems, and it is these which will be discussed from now on. Early video disc applications in Britain were often based on the BBC Micro, which was strongly represented in the education market. More recent developments have been concentrated on IBM PCs and clones.

An important requirement in interactive systems is that text and graphics generated from a computer can be *overlaid* on the video picture. This requires a "genlock" IVA (*interactive video adaptor*) card, which combines the two signals correctly onto a single screen. The basic principle here is that one or more of the colours on the logical palette from the PC is deemed to be "transparent", so that wherever it is used the underlying video picture shows through. A recent advance on the IVA is the DVA (*digital video adaptor*) which reads the video image from disc and converts it to digital form in memory before displaying it. This allows more precise synchronisation of the two signals, and useful manipulations – zooming, enlarging, shrinking, four-way splits – of the video image.

Video Disc Control Functions

A video disc can be controlled from a PC by sending signals through the RS232 serial interface. These take the form of bytes which, for instance, stop and start the machine, move to a particular frame number and begin playing. The genlock card itself must also be controlled. As with other peripherals, a *device driver* is used to handle these tasks in a standard way, providing a set of routines callable from operating system or user program. One example is the VideoLogic command library for DOS machines known as MIC (*Multi-Media Interactive Control System*). This is installed on a PC hard disc along with device configuration files, and gives a programmer-level interface to the video player and associated genlock software.

A survey of the MIC commands indicates what basic facilities are needed to handle an interactive video disc application. They include system initialisation and equipment control (e.g. Video On/Off), and parameter settings to control the genlock card, specifying the type of screen output from the PC, the vertical displacement of the video signal in relation to the PC-generated output, and which colours on the PC palette are to be treated as transparent. Access to the contents of the video disc is handled by commands such as *Play*, *Still*, *Fade* and *Step*, quoting frame-numbers, output levels, and timings.

Since video frames are addressed by an absolute number, the system must provide a way to identify each one individually, so that the start of each distinct video sequence can be directly accessed. They can be calculated from the time codes on the original tape used to master the disc; alternatively indexing information may be obtained while the disc is playing. In MIC, for instance, there is an *Index On/Off* command which switches on or off a display of the current frame-number. Speed of playing can be adjusted to allow this to be seen and noted. There is also a *Report* command, which returns the current frame-number to a calling program. When designing an application, the relationship between a particular video sequence and a pair of frame numbers can be determined, in a rather labour-intensive manner, using these mechanisms. Any higher level logical indexes must be built up from there.

There are also MIC functions for colour settings, simple user interaction, and error handling. An error will occur, for example, if the software tries to address a frame number which does not exist on the currently mounted disc. A disc in totally analogue format has no identifying information that software can check, so it is difficult to safeguard against such errors.

It is within the scope of video disc technology to hold digital data alongside the TV images, and thus to store disc identifiers and higher level indexes to logical groupings of frames. Some self-contained products are designed in that way, for instance the BBC *Domesday* disc which runs on a Laservision player specially adapted by Philips electronics. However there are no widely-adopted standards in this area, and it is usually simpler and more flexible, as with other forms of optical storage, to maintain indexing information on magnetic disc where it may be corrected and refined easily. The two systems described later in this section use that method.

Video Disc Applications

Development of computer-controlled video discs is concentrated in a few rather specialised areas, namely:

- *Computer-based training.* Video-disc may be useful, for example, where the trainee must become familiar with the appearance and function of a piece of equipment, and the manual procedures for operating and maintaining it. These can be shown directly on film rather than through stylised computer-generated diagrams. In a quite different area, medical students learning anatomy can see detailed views of the human body in action. The video images (and associated soundtrack) are incorporated into a learning package where the display sequence is varied according to user response.
- *Interactive manuals.* This application is really a variation on computer-based training. Video sequences on, for example, equipment and operational procedures are held and indexed, as before, but users are free to move about in any sequence, rather than being forced to enter the "correct" response before going on.
- *Interactive catalogues.* This is a form of information retrieval where what is sought is not a document but an image or video sequence, as a route towards a physical object or even a person. A museum, for example, may hold a database of its artefacts, including video images classified by keywords or

other descriptors. In a different area, an electronic "casting directory" contains details of television actors' and actresses' skills and experience, along with samples of their work.

- *Point-of-sales/point-of-information terminals.* These can also be thought of as electronic catalogues for the retail trade – particularly useful in large discount stores where it is impossible to put all the goods in stock on display. Customers can look at video sequences as a more realistic alternative to photographs in printed catalogues, then select and order goods automatically through the same terminal.
- *Entertainment.* Some arcade games have been based on video images rather than computer-generated graphics. There is enormous potential scope for the use of interactive video in entertainment, and in more open-ended education or information products such as the "City Disc" produced by the BBC Interactive Television Unit.

The remainder of this chapter focuses on computer-based training (CBT) and interactive manuals, making relevant links and comparisons with the more text-oriented systems described in other parts of this book.

Educational Software Overview

Educational software and CBT packages are sometimes referred to as "courseware", and as we shall see the specification of a training session or computer controlled "lesson" has something in common with programming. (The phrase "programmed learning", once used in connection with this activity, now has unfavourable connotations which are best avoided.)

The use of computers for education has quite a long history, and as with other applications its nature has changed over the years. Early systems were of course mainframe-based; one of the best known being CDC's *PLATO*, which ran in the early 1970s. PLATO was a general-purpose system, which allowed lessons on any topic to be constructed and presented using interactive terminals. It used large amounts of memory and disc space, and was essentially concerned with delivering screens of text, testing and acting upon user responses, and maintaining records of learners' progress. Because of its size and expense it was available only in some large higher education institutions in the US.

The development of smaller and cheaper machines, and in particular the 8-bit micro, made it feasible to provide computers at all levels within the formal educational system. The main advantages of the microcomputer were its immediacy of response for both programmer and user, and its ability to display graphics, often in colour. On the other hand it was limited in terms of memory and disc space, and so unsuitable for presenting hard information in the form of large amounts of text. The most successful packages were those – like educational simulations for the primary school age group – designed to develop general problem-solving skills or stimulate discussion and investigation. Programs were often written in an idiosyncratic way so as to exploit special machine characteristics, and many of the techniques involved were not portable or easily generalised.

CBT has more specific aims: to put over a body of information or to inculcate a set of well-defined skills. It needs large data files containing text, diagrams, and sometimes, as already suggested, video sequences and soundtrack as well. Its function is to present information in a structured way, accept and evaluate user responses, adjust the progress of the training session accordingly, and keep records of individuals' work. It tends to be aimed at older students or adult trainees, not only because of content and presentation but because it requires at least a PC-level machine with a hard disc for each learner.

CBT: Authoring Systems

An effective piece of courseware is expensive to develop, and requires two sorts of skill. The subject expert and/or educator must determine what information is to be taught, its structure and order of presentation, what questions are to be asked, the range of likely answers and how they should be treated. The notion of "flow of control" is relevant in the sense that different paths may be followed, or sequences repeated, on the basis of user responses. Meanwhile at the systems level the conventional skills of the programmer and database designer are needed to ensure efficient and accurate data access, fast display, and prompt and "idiot-proof" handling of user input. It goes without saying that one person is unlikely to have equal expertise in both fields.

As in other areas of computing, the solution has been to split the task and handle the aspect of machine control with general-purpose software. We thus find a number of *authoring languages* or *authoring systems* enabling domain experts to construct courseware without a detailed knowledge of normal programming. The best analogy is with *fourth generation languages* as used in business information systems, where the application logic is specified as far as possible in a non-procedural and machine-independent way.

Over the years, general-purpose authoring systems have developed from languages barely more high-level or structured than Dartmouth Basic to wimp-based packages where much of the design is specified through screen diagrams. A brief account will be given of two systems: both PC-based and incorporating video disc control facilities, but otherwise presenting many contrasts in respect of their applications areas and their user interface.

One thing that they – and all other CBT software – have in common is that their basic unit of information is a "frame". This is not a frame in the sense of a single video picture, but a structure for presentation which may include any or all of: text, graphics, video/audio sequence, and instructions for user interaction and moving to the next frame. Three main software functions are required, to: accept from the author a set of frame specifications, validate and translate them into files of interpretable data, and deliver a training session based on these files to an actual learner.

Example System 1: MacAid

MacAid is an authoring language developed over several years as a joint venture between McMaster University in Hamilton, near Toronto, and the Medical School of St Bartholomew's Hospital, London [1]. It forms part of a set of programs to support medical student education, but it is general-purpose and can be used to create any CBT application.

A MacAid *script* consists of a series of *numbered frame definitions*. These must be entered and modified using a text editor; however the authoring system can be instructed to display a frame at any time while a specification is being created. The method of defining an exercise is at quite a low level, and on the face of it is a labour-intensive task. With experience, however, it is possible to generate large numbers of similar exercises by copying scripts and making global edits, whereas in a menu-driven authoring system the same series of interactions must be used repeatedly to generate similar structures.

Frames

The authoring system recognises a number of *frame types*, and a number of *parameter settings* which affect a frame's appearance and behaviour. For instance the author can specify the screen columns and rows it is to occupy, its colour scheme and border style, the length of time for which it is to be displayed, and what is logically the "next" frame to follow it. Some basic frame types are:

*G *Global*: for specifying global event handling, and declaring and initialising variables. For example:

*G 'Revision',600 'End',700
DEF question,answer,score=0

This maps the first two function keys to keywords, and specifies the destination frames associated with each. It also sets up three variables and initialises them to zero. There is only one global frame per exercise.

*T *Text*: for displaying text at a fixed position within the frame. For example:

*T 100 R=10,15 C=20,60 B=2 P=2 N=110

~CEnter a number in the range 1 to 5

This creates a window in rows 10 to 15, columns 20 to 60 with background colour 2. It pauses 2 seconds before going on to the "next" frame, which is 110. The output text will be centred – embedded escape codes like ~C are used to indicate style and formatting: newline, centre, underline and reverse video.

*Q Question: for accepting user input and matching against possible responses. Answers may be numeric or string values, sets or ranges of values may be grouped for similar treatment, and default actions may be set for all answers not handled specifically. Matching an answer causes transfer of control to a related frame. For example:

*Q 110 (1:3),120 'Y',130 'N',140 (),150

Input in the range 1 to 3 brings up frame 120, "Y" or "N" bring up 130 or 140, and anything else brings up 150.

*R Return: analogous to a subroutine in that it performs a task, then returns control to the question frame from which it was "called". Each wrong answer to a question might be handled by a return frame, commenting in such a way as to guide the learner towards the correct answer,for example:

*R 150 R=20,25 C=20,60 B=1 P=5
That number is too small. Try again.

These frame types provide the basis for a simple lesson but more complex facilities are sometimes needed. There is, for example, a **A (Answer)* frame, which writes a user's answer to a log file for later analysis by a teacher, and a **U (Utility)* frame which performs calculations and directs flow of control.

Programming Commands

In fact, using the full set of MacAid's functions is like conventional programming, in that there are both system-and author-defined variables, given values either by accepting user input or by calculation and assignment (possibly within the scope of a simple "if ... then" statement). A typical use for these facilities might be to keep scores of right and wrong answers, or to save a series of user responses so that the logic of moving from one frame to another is based on more than the most recent answer. The next frame to be shown can be selected according to a variable value, which in turn was derived from previous conditionals and assignments.

As well as simple variables, the author may define *tables* to hold series of values for calculation and display, and *dictionaries* for looking up and translating user inputs. A dictionary here is like a thesaurus in an IR system, in that it allows variant spellings or synonyms to be converted to a preferred term before an answer is tested. In practice predicting all possible responses and dealing with each one appropriately is one of the most difficult aspects of courseware design. Multiple-choice questions are easy to handle; but when words, phrases, etc. may be entered it is hard to distinguish between genuinely wrong answers and correct answers wrongly spelt. For total flexibility, of course, an intelligent language parser or recogniser would be required, but this is rather outside the scope of current authoring systems.

Finally, there are extra facilities to handle the user interface. These include commands to activate the mouse driver, hide or show the mouse cursor, and map mouse buttons onto input values; likewise to define *screen buttons* in terms of position, style, colour, legend, and the number and string value to be returned when each is selected. To produce other graphic displays the author defines *shapes* – in terms of lines delimited by X,Y co-ordinates – which can be placed anywhere on the screen and manipulated in various ways. There are also commands to plot graphs based on input or calculated values.

So MacAid provides a high degree of control over visual effects and application logic – the price paid being the relatively low-level specification language, which demands a programming approach from its user. Like any other useful piece of general-purpose software MacAid has gained many extra features over the years, with a consequent increase in complexity, so that the complete manual is now a massive document. Software design often demands a trade-off between power and simplicity – something we shall see again later when we consider desk-top publishing packages. The courseware production system to be discussed later in this chapter presents an interesting contrast in that respect.

Use of Video Disc in MacAid

Facilities for video disc control were added to the MacAid language in 1988 and are now used to generate commercially available courseware in the medical field. One product is a set of advanced anatomy tutorials, aimed at students of various disciplines. Each group (e.g. doctors, dentists, physiotherapists, nurses) sees a different subset of the material. Their progress through it is directed by a set of multiple-choice questions, which give immediate feedback on right and wrong responses, and allow revision frames to be viewed on demand.

A second product is less typical of CBT courseware, since it is designed not for individual learning but for group discussions and training sessions. The disc contains a series of interviews with cancer patients and their families, recounting their symptoms, and is intended to familiarise medical staff with the problems of caring for such patients and their relatives. However from the technical point of view the principles are fairly standard. The video disc holds only the filmed interviews; software and frame specifications are stored on magnetic disc. The group's progress through the material depends on the answers given to questions posed at various points during the training session.

We now consider how the task of video disc control fits into the language and system described above. The MacAid designers needed to ensure that their products would run on all the players and adaptor cards currently available with MS-DOS – they therefore wrote a library of routines to interface with both the VideoLogic and the alternative Visage V:EXEC command set, using only low-level functions which were likely to be universally supported in future. Commands in the authoring language itself are mapped onto these routines, providing a somewhat higher level of control and interaction.

At the basic MIC command level, for example, the instruction to play a series of frames is *asynchronous*: control returns to the PC program as soon as it has been initiated. However it is likely that a courseware designer will want to wait for the end of the sequence before the next interaction, or maybe allow it to be interrupted part way through. So MacAid gives options to synchronise on a particular frame number, and to recognise a keyboard entry as a signal to escape from the sequence. The underlying routine to support this goes into a loop which continuously monitors the current frame number and the keyboard, returning control to the MacAid script at the appropriate time.

The video driver routines are activated from MacAid in a *V frame, followed by one or more specific instructions with relevant parameters and option settings. Like the underlying MIC or V:EXEC routines they perform initialisation, colour settings and so on, but their main function is to specify which video frames to display, and how to present them. The range of possibilities here is best illustrated by discussing the principal commands in order of complexity.

At the simplest level, the PLAY command sets the player in motion, beginning with the current frame. It takes parameters indicating whether the rate should be *slow*, *normal* or *fast*, and the direction *forward* or *reverse*. Playing will normally continue until another motion command is issued. The STILL command stops the motion of the player at the current frame. The SHOW command takes an absolute frame number as parameter and displays the corresponding frame.

The SEQUENCE command takes a pair of absolute frame numbers as parameters and plays the sequence of frames between them. As already noted, this is basically an asynchronous action; in order to wait until the sequence is completed before doing anything else one must associate it with a SYNC command. This specifies the frame number to synchronise on, and indicates, via the option list, whether the user may ESCAPE from the sequence prematurely and, if so, whether the sequence is to stop on the current frame or COMPLETE by moving to the last frame in the sequence.

More complex sequences and interactions are described with the commands STEP, DISPLAY, and GALLERY. STEP is a relative move, e.g. STEP 100 plays the next 100 frames and then stops. However this action is also modified through the option list, e.g. indicating whether the user is allowed to escape part way through, and whether or not to complete the sequence by moving to the last frame. In addition the PICTURE option says whether or not the picture is to be turned off at the end of the sequence, and the DELAY option sets the delay time (in tenths of a second) between frames. If DELAY is set to zero, movement from one frame to the next is controlled by the user pressing the *Enter* key. And the

INTERACT option gives a further possibility – that the user can move freely forwards and backwards through the sequence with the left and right cursor keys.

The DISPLAY command is used to present a sequence of non-contiguous still frames; e.g. "DISPLAY 10 25 120 70 45" will show those frames in that order. Within this sequence the same options apply as in the case of the STEP command – for setting delay times, allowing user interaction and escaping, stopping immediately or completing, turning off the picture at the end or not. Finally the GALLERY command presents a whole series of non-contiguous stills and sequences (referred to as *scenes*), subject to the same option settings. Along with each scene it is possible to specify text messages to be displayed, and the position of those messages on the screen.

Effects commands are available to control fading and mixing of audio, video, and PC-generated graphics. The three basic commands AUDIO ON/OFF, VIDEO ON/OFF, and GRAPHICS ON/OFF are extended to allow specification of either absolute or relative intensity levels. For example, "GRAPHICS 50" sets the intensity level to 50 points, within a scale going from 0 (off) to 255 (full on). Alternatively "GRAPHICS +50" sets it up by 50 points from the current level. One can also ask for a FADE between the current and target levels, together with a DURATION over which that fade is to be performed. Consider the following series of commands:

- VIDEO ON
- SEQUENCE 1000 1250
- SYNC 1200
- VIDEO FADE OFF DURATION = 20

This switches the video on, searches for frame 1000, and starts playing to frame 1250. The SYNC command forces the driver routines to wait until frame 1200 before doing anything else. Then the video picture is faded off over 2 seconds (50 frames at 25 frames per second). More complex fading and mixing of video and graphics can be specified with the CROSSFADE and MIX commands.

The above commands give precise control over playing and user interaction, together with more error protection than is provided by the underlying routines. Moreover the command interpreter optimises communication with the video player. At 2400 baud through the RS232 interface this is relatively slow, so any unnecessary operations are best avoided. The software maintains a set of internal flags saving the state of the player – current frame number, current audio, video and graphic intensity levels, whether indexing is currently on or off, etc. These flags are always checked when a video command is issued, and the corresponding driver routine is called only if a state really needs to be changed.

Use of MacAid for Video Databases

The software originally written to handle video instructions within MacAid proved to have more general applications. It is used, for example, to support a command line interpreter allowing direct control of a video disc from the keyboard or through batch files. An interface to the underlying routines has also been grafted onto a PC-based IR package (IdeaList), enabling video sequences to be indexed by keyword, searched for using a Boolean query language, and then immediately displayed.

The principle behind this is simple. An IdeaList database is held on magnetic disc and contains free-format records with text fields. Details about each video sequence are held in these records; in particular one field holds a description of its contents and another the actual MacAid instruction, e.g. "SEQUENCE 100 200", to play it. The user interacts with the IR package in the normal way but, having retrieved a record satisfying a query, has an extra option to see the relevant frames. The IR software extracts the MacAid command from the record and sends it to the video control routines which put it into execution. This is obviously a valuable aid for courseware designers looking for sequences with certain characteristics. It requires a prior indexing effort to record frame descriptions, but the text can be derived from original specifications written when the disc was designed and before the video material was shot.

A more ambitious long-term project involves the setting up of a database to hold the entire contents of the Wellcome Museum of Medical Science. This will include, for example, about 22 000 transparencies and 1000 display panels providing teaching material on the subject of tropical medicine, which will be put onto video disc. Associated text will go onto hard disc and CD-ROM. The material will be accessible via keyword searching and weighted retrieval techniques, but there will be associated CBT modules for directed learning. The intention is to make the museum's contents more readily available to medical schools, both in the UK and abroad.

MacAid represent one possible approach to the problems of courseware production using material on video disc – there are of course others. Fundamentally, CBT applications need the ability to select and present frame-sequences under user or program control, while at the higher level of design those sequences must be identified and structured in a meaningful way. The following account of the Sony IKS system focuses mainly on that aspect of the problem.

Example System 2: Interactive Knowledge System

Interactive Knowledge System (IKS) was developed within Sony Broadcast to create training material about Sony equipment – cameras, recorders, mixers and so on – used in the broadcasting industry. The final products are *interactive manuals* which are usable in an open-ended way both for initial training and for later consultation, giving the user some choice about the order in which information is presented. The fact that there is no need to detect "right" and "wrong" answers, or specify very complex flow of control, has implications for the design of the authoring tools.

The objectives and operation of the system are described in reference [2]. The kind of equipment supplied by Sony to broadcasting organizations is expensive and complex, and requires long professional experience to exploit all its capabilities. It is generally reliable in operation, but on those occasions when repairs and maintenance are necessary they must be carried out quickly. The technology is changing rapidly so engineers and technicians need frequent retraining in the details of new equipment; at the same time knowledge about earlier products still in use must be preserved somewhere.

These objectives have traditionally been satisfied by a combination of practical training sessions and printed manuals – interactive video can supplement the first and act as a more satisfactory substitute for the second. Video sequences have an obvious advantage over text or diagrams in being able to show the actual equipment in operation, from any angle, at any range, and with an accompanying spoken commentary. An additional advantage for this application is that the screen can display sample waveforms, showing what electronic signals ought to be output by various parts of the equipment. So a maintenance engineer can be guided through his task in a step-by-step manner, comparing ideal waveforms with those actually output onto an oscilloscope, and making any necessary adjustments to bring them into line.

Training discs are run on a Sony player controlled by an IBM PC, and the IKS system follows the principle described earlier that all digital material (files and programs) is held on magnetic disc. There is an authoring system (IAS) which allows domain experts to design and produce courseware, and a delivery system which presents the finished product to the user. All interaction with the delivery system is carried out through a *touch-screen* – there is no text input at that stage, so the engineers are not required to use the keyboard.

IAS: Page Structure Definition

Once again there is a basic unit of information like a frame – here it is actually called a "page" but the principle is the same. Initially a page is specified with some or all of the following information:

- A unique number indicating its position in the information hierarchy.
- Page type.
- Title.
- Description of a video sequence.
- Description of overlaid graphics and text.
- Text of the spoken commentary.

- Duration.
- Additional help text, if appropriate.

Pages are built into a hierarchical structure which will eventually allow the user to navigate up, down, and sideways through the information. The system provides a graphic interface for defining the structure, so that the outline logic of a set of instructions can be seen and altered dynamically. An example screen can be seen in Fig. 8.1. Each page has a title and a type, indicating the function which it performs. The most common types are:

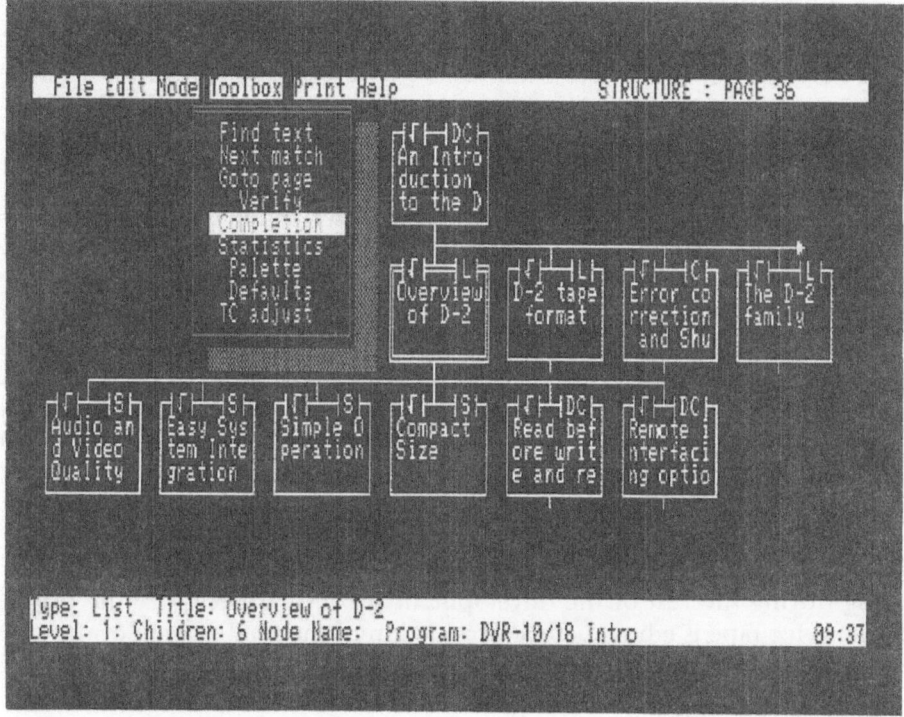

Fig. 8.1. A hierarchical page structure.

- *Choice*: a menu page presenting a set of possibilities for further expansion. For example, the user may choose which component of the equipment to look at next.
- *List*: also presents possibilities for further expansion but this time with the implication that they should be seen in a certain order. A series of tasks to remove, check, adjust and replace a particular component might be defined here – the list could be used as a quick reminder about the whole procedure or to give access to more detailed instructions about each stage.
- *Sequence*: a page at the bottom of the hierarchy, a sequence of video frames presenting detailed information, and not expanded further.

Additional page types allow a departure from flow of control based on a strict hierarchy. A *repeated list* page cycles through a list indefinitely – probably to guide the user through a repeated series of adjustments to the equipment until a correct outcome is achieved. A *terminate sequence* page then lets him escape from such a loop by entering a response in a dialogue box. A *jump node* page specifies a direct jump to another page, identified by its number. Finally, a group of pages can be named as a *macro*, and called from elsewhere in the hierarchy.

Page specifications are entered into a *storyboard*, and saved on a database which is used to control the rest of the production process. As tasks relating to each page are completed they are signed off, so that it is always possible to see what remains to do.

Video/Audio Production

The next stage is to create video sequences as described in the storyboard. The Sony Broadcast training department has all the equipment needed to record this material, so the process can be closely integrated with the rest of the courseware design. As sequences are filmed and written to video tape, for instance, the time-codes identifying their location on the tape are recorded in the database, likewise those of the audio voice-over sequences. When the two tapes are married together and edited to make a master tape, these time-codes are automatically recalculated, and when the material is finally transferred to video disc they are converted to the corresponding frame numbers. So there is no need for any manual indexing procedure.

The video material is first recorded on a *glass master* – -the equivalent of a worm disc on which data can be recorded as a one-off process. This is used for testing during the rest of the development process; if necessary the original master video tape is edited before production of the final version of the video disc.

Page Editing

Using the test disc, the courseware designer now concentrates on the details of overlaying text and graphics on the video image using a *page editor* program. Once again this is a completely interactive task, which involves indicating relevant screen areas and what is to go there. Short messages may be entered immediately; longer pieces of text are often typed separately using a word processor, and then brought into the page editor for final adjustment as to position and appearance.

The end-user will interact with the information via a touch-screen, so very common overlay objects are arrows and labels identifying different parts of the equipment, and associated selection *buttons*. These allow the user to point naturally at the next item he wishes to explore. Alternatively a set of buttons can behave like a conventional menu. (See Figs 8.2 and 8.3.) In either case, each button has a sequence number linking it to a dependent page in the hierarchy, and the system can check for a logical correspondence.

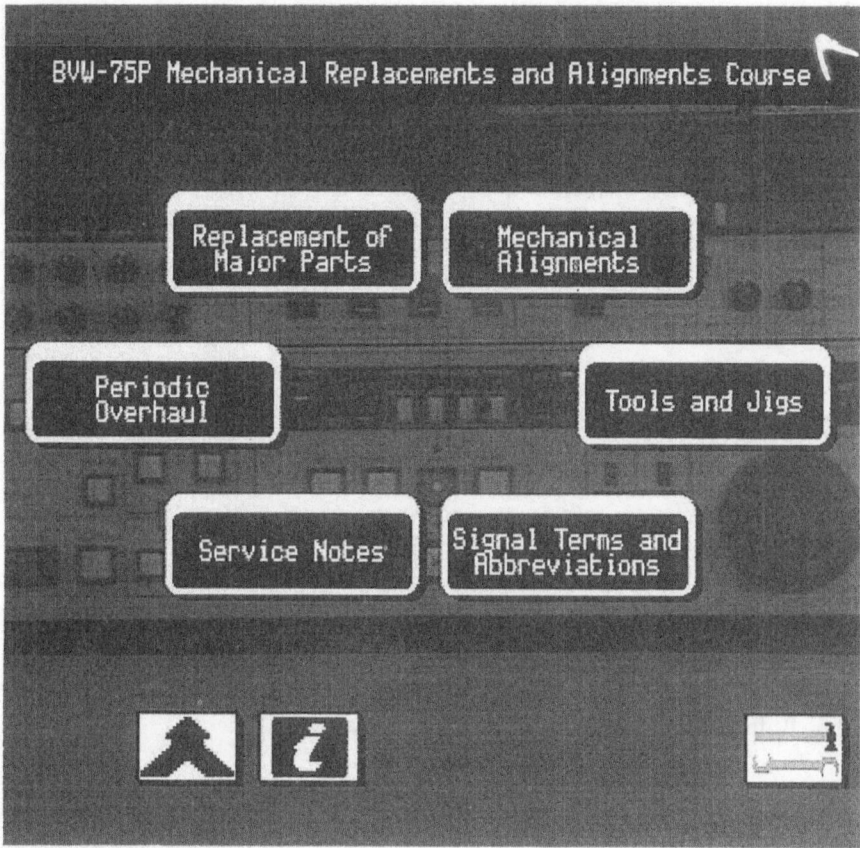

Fig. 8.2. Touch-screen buttons for menu selection.

Note that here the task of describing a page's layout with the page editor is quite separate from that of defining its logical function through the structure editor. This contrasts with the MacAid method where complete frame specifications are assembled within a single script. The IAS system also controls the overall production process; as each stage of the work is completed it is signed off, and the database can be queried to find out what remains to do.

Courseware Presentation

The IKS delivery system calls upon data files built up with the IAS, although some of the descriptive material on the original storyboard now only serves as documentation. The user chooses his path through the information by touching either the buttons already mentioned or one of the standard icons which are used in every application. The following moves are represented through the icons, some of which can be seen in Fig. 8.3:

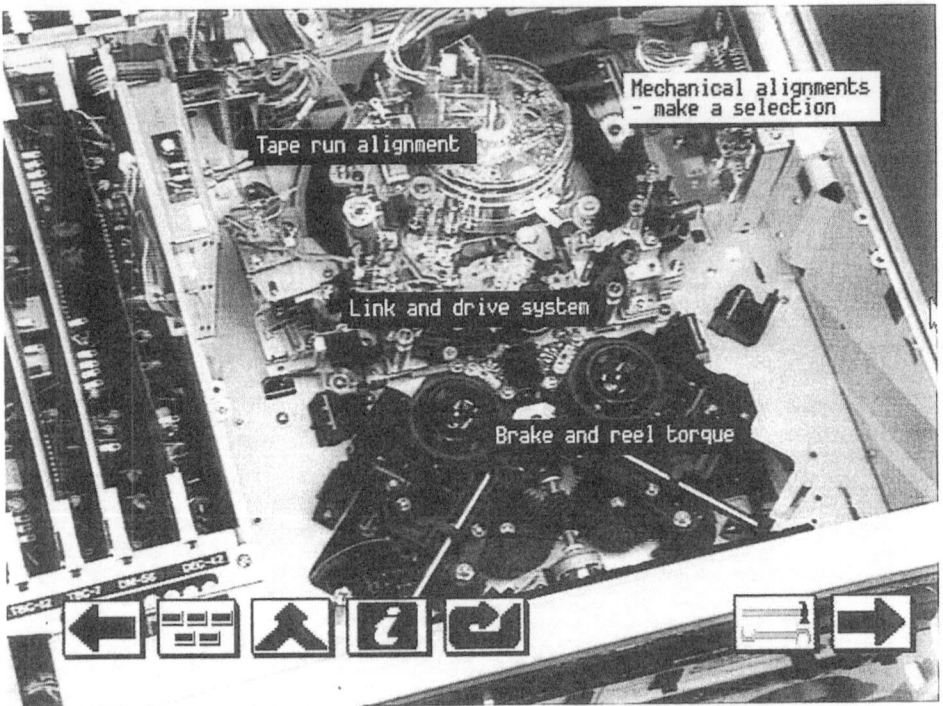

Fig. 8.3. Buttons and icons overlaid on a video image.

- *next/back*: move to next or previous page in a sequence.
- *menu*: return to the previous menu.
- *more/less detail: move down the hierarchy to expand on a topic, or back up again.*
- *help: produce subsidiary information.*
- *map (obtained via help key): show the "path" through the pages followed so far. It is possible to back up through this path with the "less detail" icon.*
- *return/repeat: return from a "help" page or repeat a video sequence.*
- *up/down: move the selection marker up or down through the items on a "list" page.*

Because it does not set out to test the user in any way, or lay down a strict route through the information, there is no need for the software to handle text input, scoring, or complex logic based upon combinations of previous responses. Authoring is much less like programming than with MacAid; there is no equivalent to variables or assignment, and flow of control is most often through the information hierarchy, although the IAS does incorporate general ideas of sequence, selection and iteration, the use of procedural abstraction via macros, and even unrestricted *goto* with the *jump node*.

It is interesting to compare this kind of interactive manual with the British Airways CD-ROM maintenance manuals described in Chapter 6. In that case the starting point was an existing text, and structured in a way which was already familiar to its potential users. There were, as we saw, very precise legal regulations regarding its layout, and the procedures for revising it, to which the CD-ROM version had to conform if it was to be acceptable. The focus in Sony's case was on use for training and familiarisation; the material was designed specifically for presentation by video disc, and was seen as a long-term repository of knowledge about the equipment. The production costs for a video disc are much greater than for a CD-ROM, so there is less scope for the periodic re-issue of updated versions, although minor changes to the courseware can be made by altering files on magnetic disc.

This chapter has diverged somewhat from the main theme of the book to consider databases consisting mainly of video images, with text having a subsidiary role. In fact the ability to mix text and video output will become increasingly important as the demand for *multi-media* systems grows, and the fundamental principles will still be applicable even when cheaper CD-ROM technology proves capable of delivering video sequences of a satisfactory quality. Producers of CBT courseware on video disc were the first to be confronted with technical requirements and design issues which now have a much wider range of application. These topics will be explored further in the following chapter, which deals with hypertext.

Chapter Summary

Video disc was the first optical storage medium to be developed; it stores analogue data which is used directly to generate video images. Discs intended for random access are recorded at constant angular velocity so that each rotation corresponds to a single video frame. The cost of mastering and reproduction, and of playing equipment, is higher than that for CD-ROM, but at the time of writing video disc is still a cost-effective vehicle for CBT. Moreover many of the techniques developed to handle this kind of multi-media output remain applicable when video images are delivered from digital media.

When a video disc player is used as a computer peripheral, an adaptor card is required to enable video images to be mixed with text and graphics output from the PC. Control functions are supplied by a set of routines (e.g. the VideoLogic MIC command library) called through the operating system, and enabling individual frames or sequences to be selected and played. These routines refer to absolute frame addresses, and provide low-level control over factors like playing speed and direction.

The principle application areas for video disc are CBT and interactive manuals, in the design of which it is customary to use special courseware authoring languages or systems. These define the logic of a training session, indicating how input from the user should direct his path through the material, providing feedback and reinforcement of ideas. They also hide some details of low-level device control. A training session is built out of a series of frames or pages which define images, text, and instructions for user interaction.

Two example authoring and delivery systems were described, used to produce medical training material and interactive engineering manuals, respectively. One represented a procedural approach, whereby training sessions were defined as scripts of detailed frame descriptions. Programming constructs were included to allow tight control over the user's choices. The second system was based on diagrammatic interaction, enabling the logical structure of a manual to be separated from the details of individual frame content and layout. More freedom of choice was given to users, so the software needed to support mainly hierarchical and sequential moves through the information.

Investigations

Find examples of the use of video disc outside the area of CBT, e.g. in sales and marketing. Visit the National Interactive Video Centre or one of the periodic exhibitions of interactive video, to see systems in use.

Examine the functions of other courseware authoring systems/languages (e.g. Tencore Plus) which include interactive video facilities. Are they script-based or menu-based? How much understanding of programming do they require? What features do they provide for defining complex logical paths through the material, and extra features such as monitoring and scoring?

References

1 Ahmed K, Ingram D, Dickinson CJ (1980) Software for educational computing. MTP Press
2 Strashun L (1987) Knowledge transfer – what next? Paper presented at the 10th international film and technology conference, June 1987

Nine
Hypertext Principles

*"... to no-one did it occur that the book and the maze were
one and the same thing."*
Jorge Luis Borges

What is it?

The idea of hypertext seems to have a strong appeal to the computing
community; it is for instance a far more visible topic in the popular literature
than other obviously useful but less glamorous applications. A number of very
different systems go under the hypertext umbrella; this chapter attempts to
show what they have in common and where they may legitimately differ,
making comparisons and connections with other approaches to information
management and retrieval.

First, some definitions. Hypertext is a word made up of two parts. We know
by now what a text is – what about "hyper"? This Greek prefix means something
like "beyond", "over", "above", sometimes with the connotation of going to
extremes, or beyond the bounds of acceptability. Thus "hyperbole" is "exag-
geration", "hypercritical" is "over-critical", and every science fiction reader
knows the perils which lurk in "hyperspace".

So hypertext "goes beyond" text. The originator of the term, Ted Nelson [1],
suggested that computer technology should eventually allow the world's
knowledge and literature, now stored as books in libraries, to be assembled into
a single integrated structure. It should be held in a form which would
encourage active exploration, with links between related documents to help
readers follow up topics in the way they find most convenient and natural. Most
current applications of the hypertext idea are rather less ambitious, but the
ability to follow multiple paths within and among different documents is
fundamental. Hence one definition might be:

- A group of interrelated texts which can be read and explored in a non-linear
  way. Even a single document can be so structured that the reader may view
  the material at different levels of detail, or choose amongst different orders
  of presentation.

Another way in which a hypertext may go over and above a conventional text is by including more than just words. So another possible definition is:

- An information structure containing graphics as well as text, and possibly also able to present recorded sound and video, and to trigger off other machine processes. Systems which support these facilities are described as "multi-media" or even "hypermedia" systems.

We have of course met both these ideas in previous chapters without putting this particular name to them. The British Airways manuals gave the user various different paths to a piece of information; so did the Sony IKS system. Computer-based training packages must support non-linear presentation, and often the use of graphics, sound and video as well.

Indeed some of the basic ideas come from books themselves, which it is a mistake to think of as purely linear devices. We can read a book from cover to cover; equally well we can scan and skip, look up topics in a contents list or index, select what to read on the basis of chapter and section headings, execute a return jump to a footnote, and follow up explicit cross-references within a document, or from one document to another. The use of computer technology should make some of these processes more convenient, as well as allowing the inclusion of a wider range of non-textual material.

Printed books have been in use for hundreds of years, and during that time a range of strategies and conventions has developed to enable writers and readers to communicate. The skill with which printed material is produced, and the ease with which it is used, cannot currently be matched by material shown on a computer screen. However the author of a book must choose a single order of presentation; and it is hard to ensure that all relevant facts or arguments come together except through repetition.

Consider for example the chapters in this book dealing with optical storage. At least two possible logical groupings of the material were possible: one based on the device type (CD-ROM, worm, video disc), the other on physical, logical and application levels of data representation. In either case explanations would need to be repeated, or the reader referred forward and back to points treated elsewhere. The solution actually chosen was a compromise between the two, whereas in theory a hypertext version could be viewed from either perspective according to each reader's interests.

A further, very obvious, point to make about a book is that its text is fixed at a particular point in time, then reproduced into thousands of identical copies through the printing and publishing process. A reader can scribble in the margin of one copy (perhaps to the annoyance of later readers), but there is no way to incorporate even the most valuable annotations into the original text. Corrections and additions can be handled only by the infrequent issue of revised editions. And while several different authors may contribute towards a book, it is impossible to allow for multiple layers of commentary over a period of time, which is at least potentially feasible with a text held on magnetic storage and accessed through a computer network.

So another way in which hypertext may go beyond conventional text can be expressed with a third definition:

- A text which is subject to dynamic growth and change, and where in principle there is no distinction between the powers of authors and readers.

Hypertext Systems

A hypertext which fits one or more of the preceding definitions requires software to support its creation and use. Hypertext systems have characteristics in common with other general-purpose software: editors, outline processors and other documentation aids, courseware authoring tools, text retrieval and database management systems. Some current packages are very eclectic, and can be used as graphics or user interface development tools, applications programming languages, electronic mail systems, expert systems, etc. On the whole the following discussion will concentrate on the central issue of text-handling, with other facilities referred to only in passing.

Research and development in hypertext systems was for twenty years concentrated in large US educational establishments or research institutes. Ambitious experimental products were built for mainframe or mini-computers, to serve the needs of researchers and students. A hypertext on the Intermedia [2] system, for instance, gave access to over 800 documents (comprising both text and graphics) to students of English Literature, and there was another for students of Biology comprising 200 documents. The most useful historical survey of this topic is by Conklin [3] – a very full account of important landmarks in the development of hypertext, and an analysis of significant implementation issues.

Direct experience of hypertext has been obtainable for the average computer user only within the last four or five years, when the software started to become available for personal computers and workstations. In this context there are inevitable limitations on the quantity of information to be stored, the number of potential readers, and the extent to which group authorship is feasible, but this software does give the essential flavour of interacting with a document in a non-linear way, and building up heterogenous collections of text and graphics for personal use.

The two packages which will be referred to most frequently in the following discussion are:

- *HyperCard*: available for (in fact supplied free with) the Apple Macintosh, and therefore probably the most widely used hypertext system of all. This is really a hybrid product, combining classic hypertext features with others more typical of a conventional database system [4].
- *Guide*: originally produced at the University of Kent in Canterbury, available commercially as a PC or Macintosh package through Office Workstations

Ltd. The University of Kent has continued independent development, and now supplies a version of the software for Unix workstations – -this is the one which will be described below [5].

Hypertext is a popular and interesting idea and many design approaches are possible; the intention here is not to do comparative product evaluations but to refer to concrete examples as a basis for discussion about general principles.

Before looking in any detail at individual systems we can make a general point about them all: that their communication with the user is likely to be through a *wimp* interface. Historically the development of hypertext and of systems permitting direct manipulation of screen objects went hand in hand – for example the first acknowledged working hypertext system (NLS at Stanford Research Institute [6]) was also the first to use a mouse as a pointing device. A later powerful experimental hypertext system (Notecards [7]) originated at Xerox PARC where research teams also pioneered important advances in human–computer interaction techniques like the desktop metaphor and the object-oriented programming language.

The dependence of hypertext on a wimp environment is hardly surprising. Windows obviously provide a useful mechanism for viewing different parts of a document together, and a "point and click" device will make it easy to navigate around a text. An important control mechanism in many systems is the screen "button" – a small icon or piece of highlighted text which the reader can select in order to change the display or activate a new process.

Data Models

When designing a new hypertext system, or choosing one for a new application, the most important question to consider is the *data model* to be supported. Given that we wish to go beyond a straight linear presentation, what textual units will be recognised, and how will the reader decide what piece of the document to see next?

To the question of textual units, there are two possible answers:

- Require that documents be split into discrete sections which can be displayed in their entirety on the screen.
- Accept documents of variable size, and allow the reader to scroll through them.

The choice between these two approaches turns out to have an important influence on the way systems work in practice, and their suitability for different purposes.

Frame-based Systems

Frame-based systems handle fixed-size structures like the MacAid frame or IKS page described in the previous chapter, where each screen display was separately defined in terms of text, graphics, user interaction, etc. Another analogy often used in explanations is that the basic unit is a "card" – a two-dimensional piece of white space onto which objects may be "pasted". In HyperCard, for instance, an individual card may contain any number and combination of the following objects:

- A bit-mapped image.
- A "field", containing ASCII text or other data.
- A button.

The physical location of these objects on the card is an integral part of their definition. A button, for instance, may be set to coincide with a word of text, but the system recognises it only in terms of its X,Y co-ordinates and if the text is edited later the button will need to be moved independently.

In some respects a card in this system can be treated as a record in a conventional database. Data fields may hold values such as numbers and dates, as well as text, which are referred to by routines written in *HyperTalk*, a procedural programming language supplied with HyperCard. And cards are grouped together in linear "stacks" which can be read through sequentially, like a file. Within a stack, cards are further classified by being given different "backgrounds". HyperTalk routines may be specific to one card, a set of cards with the same background, or all cards in a stack.

So one possible use of HyperCard is for a straightforward database where all cards have a fixed record structure. At the other end of the scale, all cards might have a different structure, or, as in the case where each held a page from a long text, structure as distinct from content might not be very significant. The other major departure from standard database principles is the use of *buttons*.

Following the principle mentioned earlier, these are the main medium for user interaction, having two possible functions. One is to execute a small HyperTalk program. Amongst other things this enables HyperCard to be used as a multi-media system – a process could for instance control a video disc player using the sort of commands described in the previous chapter. The other function is to allow paths from one card to another to be established by the author and followed by the reader – this is of course the crucial point for our current discussion.

A system which handles discrete textual units, and the connections between them, effectively supports a "network" model of data where the basic entities are "nodes" and "links", and the reader's task is to "navigate" through them. This is a very common and in some ways powerful model, although not the only one possible. A detailed discussion of linkages within hypertext will be postponed until an alternative has been presented.

Meanwhile it is worth noting that not all frame-based systems are like HyperCard in insisting on a one-to-one relationship between a card and the screen. Other systems permit two or more (possibly overlapping) windows to be open with a different frame in each. However the basic principle remains that there are definite boundaries between sections of a document, and explicit moves are necessary to go from one to another.

This demands a certain discipline on the part of the hypertext author, who is recommended to divide his material into independent short sections covering one topic at a time. Frame-based systems are very suitable for presenting and testing individual "facts" (like the CBT systems described in the previous chapter), and for other naturally fragmented texts like encyclopedias, cookery books, and adventure games. They allow easy inclusion of pictures and diagrams, either as frames in their own right or as objects pasted onto cards. They may be less successful for sustained argument or narrative; at least they must provide a very unobtrusive page-turning mechanism so that the reader's flow is not interrupted unduly.

To illustrate some of these ideas a small HyperCard example (a stack of six cards) is shown in Fig. 9.1. Links from buttons to cards are shown by connecting lines in the diagram although in normal use only one card would be seen at a time. The buttons implement a series of user choices, and the ease with which this kind of structure can be set up suggests why HyperCard is frequently used to design front-ends for other applications. Note the different fonts and button styles available. HyperCard attaches no particular significance to these but designers of large applications would obviously want to establish consistent conventions. This particular example was put together in a very *ad hoc* way, typical of many people's first attempt at a HyperCard stack. A later example in the section on hypertext authoring will show a more methodical approach, with HyperTalk scripts providing some processing logic in the background.

Scrolling Systems

Scrolling systems do not demand artificial divisions within a document; the reader may look at any section or sections which happen to fit on the screen. They are therefore likely to be better for long continuous texts, especially those originally written for printing in the traditional way. Windowing is essential in this environment to allow different parts of a document to be seen together, and text should be dynamically formatted, so that the display fits the width of the current window.

Buttons must now be thought of as "embedded" within a text, associated with a particular element like a word or picture rather than a fixed screen or card location. And their effect also may be rather different. Some scrolling systems do use them to trigger off a jump to another part of the text, as with the British Airways manual described in Chapter 6 where clicking on a hot link (cross-reference) caused a jump to the appropriate pageblock. However there is an alternative possibility, which is the one we will concentrate on here.

The Guide system supports scrolling documents of any length with embedded (highlighted) buttons, but "selecting" a button normally causes its direct in-line *replacement* by a new piece of text, which also may be of any length.

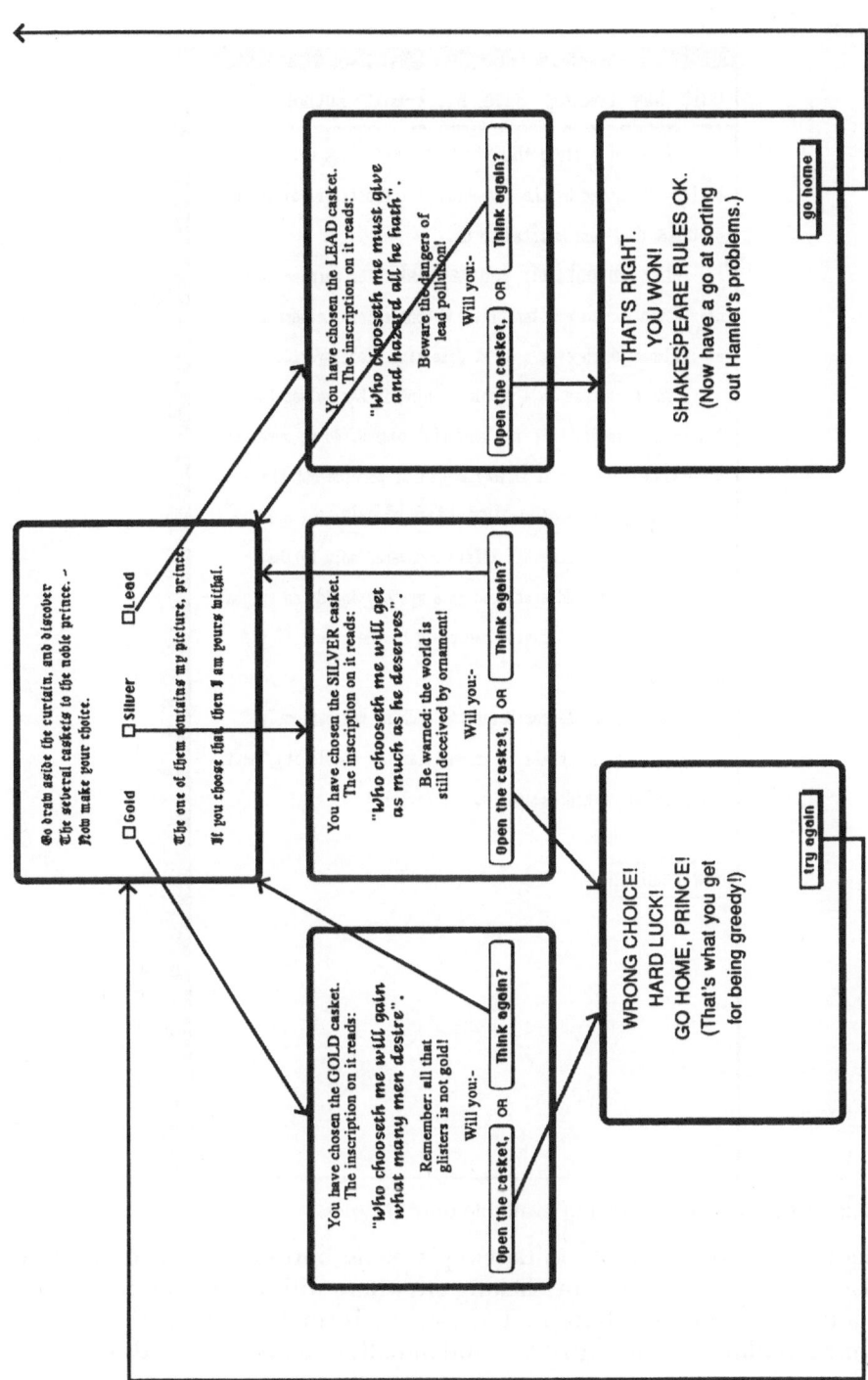

Fig. 9.1. Hypercard cards with linking buttons.

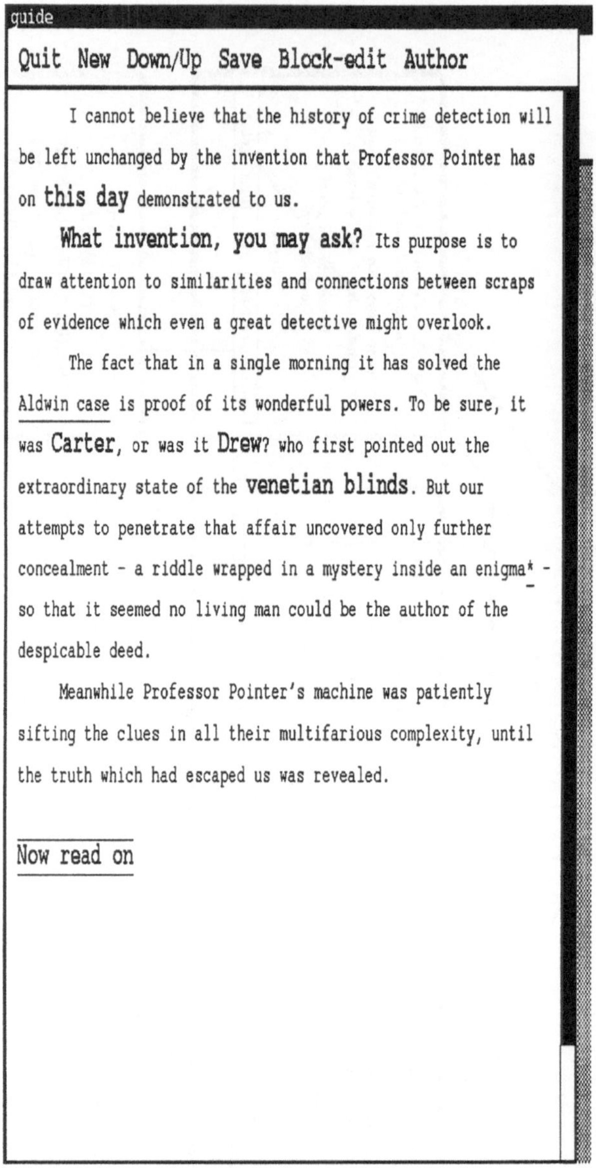

guide

Quit New Down/Up Save Block-edit Author

   I cannot believe that the history of crime detection will
be left unchanged by the invention that Professor Pointer has
on **this day** demonstrated to us.
   What invention, you may ask? Its purpose is to
draw attention to similarities and connections between scraps
of evidence which even a great detective might overlook.
   The fact that in a single morning it has solved the
Aldwin case is proof of its wonderful powers. To be sure, it
was **Carter**, or was it **Drew?** who first pointed out the
extraordinary state of the **venetian blinds**. But our
attempts to penetrate that affair uncovered only further
concealment - a riddle wrapped in a mystery inside an enigma* -
so that it seemed no living man could be the author of the
despicable deed.
   Meanwhile Professor Pointer's machine was patiently
sifting the clues in all their multifarious complexity, until
the truth which had escaped us was revealed.

Now read on

Fig. 9.2. A Guide screen showing available button types.

Replacement text can itself contain replaceable buttons, down to any level. Replacements are "undone" by clicking anywhere within the replacement text with a designated mouse button. The process is similar to that used in some document outliners or *folding editors*, and initially demands some adjustment to

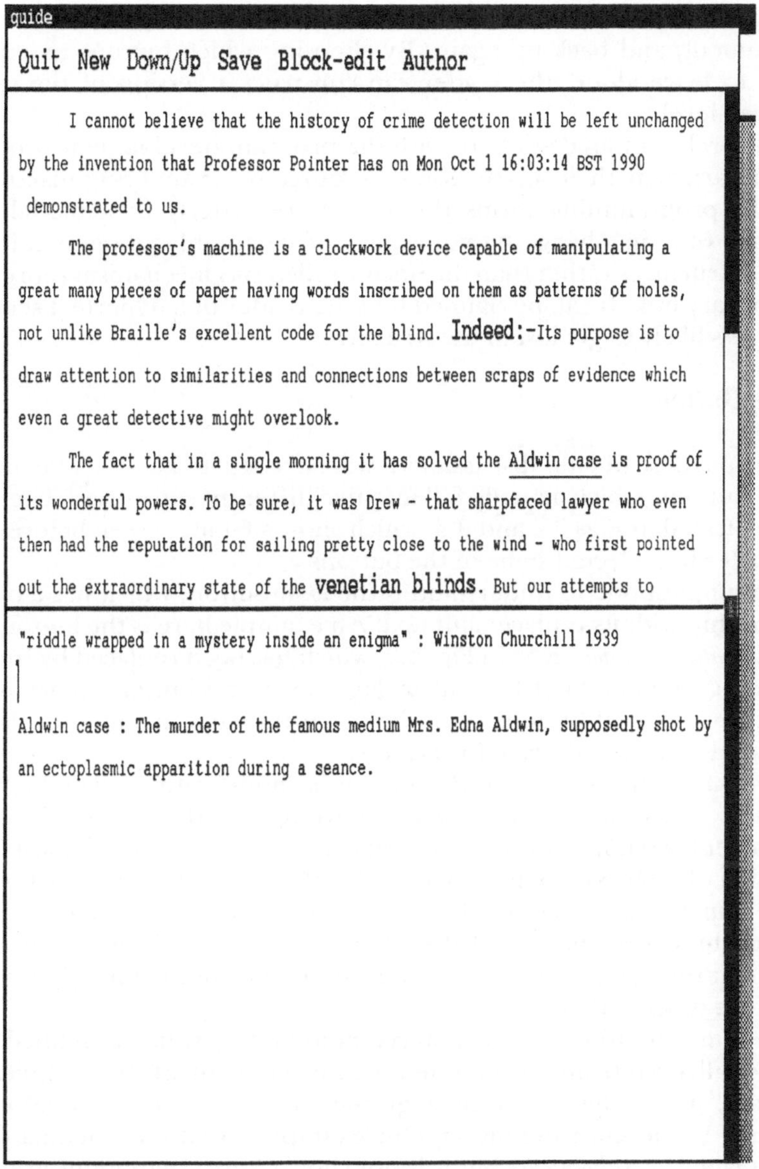

guide

```
Quit  New  Down/Up  Save  Block-edit  Author
```

I cannot believe that the history of crime detection will be left unchanged
by the invention that Professor Pointer has on Mon Oct 1 16:03:14 BST 1990
demonstrated to us.

The professor's machine is a clockwork device capable of manipulating a
great many pieces of paper having words inscribed on them as patterns of holes,
not unlike Braille's excellent code for the blind. **Indeed:**-Its purpose is to
draw attention to similarities and connections between scraps of evidence which
even a great detective might overlook.

The fact that in a single morning it has solved the Aldwin case is proof of
its wonderful powers. To be sure, it was Drew - that sharpfaced lawyer who even
then had the reputation for sailing pretty close to the wind - who first pointed
out the extraordinary state of the **venetian blinds**. But our attempts to

"riddle wrapped in a mystery inside an enigma" : Winston Churchill 1939

Aldwin case : The murder of the famous medium Mrs. Edna Aldwin, supposedly shot by
an ectoplasmic apparition during a seance.

Fig. 9.3. A Guide screen after buttons selection.

the reader's viewing habits, as the screen display changes in a more unpredictable way when selecting and undoing buttons than when scrolling or
windowing.

Quite apart from the superficial visual aspects, we see here a different
underlying model for a hypertext. It can now be thought of as a set of nested
Chinese boxes to be opened and closed at will. The metaphor of navigation

across links is replaced by that of "zooming" down through successive layers of a document, and back up again. By choosing which buttons to expand and which to leave alone, the reader can construct a version of the text at the required level.

Other relevant analogies are with the program development process itself, and in particular the construction of a source program using macro substitution. In programming terms this is a more orderly data model than the previous one, involving the equivalent of commonly-recommended nested control structures rather than the uncontrolled *goto* mechanism represented by an arbitrary link. It can be claimed that the reader of a hypertext set up in this way is less likely to get lost in the structure.

Guide Buttons

For the purpose of later discussions it will be useful to know a little more about Guide buttons, which actually fall into five different categories. Their effect is demonstrated in Figs 9.2 and 9.3, which show a Guide screen before and after the reader has selected some of the buttons.

The simplest one to understand is the *local* button, which has a one-to-one relationship with its replacement text. An example here is the button labelled: *what invention, you may ask?* in Fig. 9.2, which has been replaced by further text (including another local button) in Fig. 9.3. Local button names have local scope; several local buttons could be given the same name even though the associated text was different in each case.

A *glossary* button (displayed with underlining rather than highlighting) produces text in a special *glossary view* window at the foot of the screen. A glossary entry is normally used to explain the meaning of a technical term, and a number of such explanations may be displayed simultaneously in the window. These can be "undone" in the same way as other replacement text. The example here is the button labelled *Aldwin case*, the explanation for which can be seen at the bottom of Fig. 9.3. Glossary text comes from *definition* buttons, which are described next.

A *definition* button is a global object, holding text which is defined once but may be called up from several points within a document. If a technical term is repeated, it may be set up as a glossary button on each occasion, always referring to the same definition. Our example text does contain a definition button labelled *Aldwin case* but it is not shown here. Definitions are normally kept at the end of a document or on a separate glossary file, out of the reader's way rather than mixed up with the main text.

A *usage* button is like a local button in that it is replaced by new text when selected, but the replacement comes from another source. One possibility is to link it by name with a definition button, another is to perform an action which actually generates text. The button labelled *this day* in Fig. 9.2 is a usage button – when selected it calls the Unix "date" command in order to bring up the current date and time which appear in Fig. 9.3.

An *action* button, as its name implies, executes some procedural code when selected. Like the usage button described above it could call upon a Unix command but not merely one to generate text – it might run a complete shell program. Action buttons can also simulate the effect of choosing options from the Guide menus, for instance to load a file containing the next part of a large document. This is in fact the function of the button marked *now read on* in our current example – note how its type is distinguished by lines above and below the label. The effect of selecting this button is not shown here but we shall see later a little more detail about how action buttons work, and other possible uses for them will be mentioned where relevant.

The last Guide feature to mention here is an *enquiry*, used to group together two or more buttons which are really alternatives (e.g. a set of menu options). When any button within the scope of an enquiry is selected, the whole enquiry is replaced, so it is impossible to open more than one at any given time. The phrase *Carter, or was it Drew?* in Fig. 9.2 is defined as an enquiry, giving a choice between the two names marked as buttons. Note that a replacement of the whole enquiry has occurred in Fig. 9.3.

Normally once a button has been selected during a Guide session, its replacement text is stored as a local copy at the relevant point in the document, even if the button is undone again. Any changes made by the user to a replacement text remain in force throughout the session, although they must be saved on file to make them permanent. However sometimes it is necessary to generate the text afresh each time a button is reselected – a usage button calling the system clock is an example – and in this case the author can define the button to be *dynamic*.

Textual Relationships and Their Representation

Having seen two data models supported by typical hypertext software, we now consider what textual relationships we may wish to represent, and how best to do so with the tools at our disposal.

Hierarchical

Hierarchical relationships are the most obvious ones in printed books or papers – there is a long tradition for textual divisions like chapter and verse, act and scene, section and subsection, where parts of a document are identified and numbered according to their hierarchical position. Splitting the text in this way gives it shape for the reader, and allow for ease of reference from elsewhere. Hierarchical divisions are also useful for complex diagrams, and for other graphic representations which help the reader to go from the general to the particular: maps at various levels of detail, for example, or historical "time-lines" which break the past up into named periods to put events into context.

Hierarchical access to a document can be conveniently supported by software, as we saw in previous accounts of the British Airways manuals and the Sony IKS system. Some general-purpose frame-based hypertext systems (e.g. KMS [8]) give a special status to hierarchical (sometimes also called "organisa-tional") links, although HyperCard does not. An advantage of doing so is that moves up or down the tree can be selected through standard icons rather than individually defined buttons on each frame, and that structural outlines of document can be displayed to maintain the reader's sense of direction. Hypertext systems like Guide, based on the idea of textual replacement, obviously also support hierarchical relationships in a very natural way.

However the hypertext author needs to be clear about the significance of his hierarchical subdivisions. The author of a conventional document, when writing, say, Section 3.5.3, is probably justified in assuming that the reader has already seen Section 3.5.2, whereas the hypertext author is not. Recall that the IKS authoring system made a distinction between "choice" nodes, where the lower-level frames were genuinely independent, and "list" nodes, where they were items in a logical sequence. Ideally this point should be made clear to the hypertext reader, whatever the software in use.

Other design choices relate to the question of just where to put flesh onto the skeleton. A conventional document is most likely to have some text associated with Section 3, and some with Subsection 3.5, and yet more with 3.5.1 and 3.5.2 – a hypertext derived from this source will probably look the same. By contrast one designed specifically for interactive use could be based on a strict menu structure, having only section headings in the higher levels of the tree, with all continuous text relegated to the "leaves". Alternatively the higher level frames might contain summary material, covering the same ground as the ones below but in less detail. While helpful to the hypertext reader, the result may not translate very gracefully back into a sequential document.

Sequential

Sequential reading is the norm in printed text, as in a scrolling hypertext document, but systems based on the node and link model must be designed to allow easy movement through a set of nodes representing a logical sequence. The HyperCard stack provides explicit support for sequential access, including standard buttons (and HyperTalk commands) to choose the "next" and "previous" card. In fact HyperCard models a continuously *revolving* structure, the last card in the stack being followed immediately by the first again. Logical order need not reflect the order of entry, and it is possible to insert cards at any position within a stack. Systems with a stronger emphasis on hierarchies, like KMS, have conventions for linearising a tree structure (e.g. for printing) by taking the nodes in top to bottom, left to right order.

The notion of sequence can be extended to enable different paths to be taken, depending on some initial selection. Developers of educational hyper-texts sometimes implement "guided tours" to allow users to become familiar with the material – moving automatically through a few sample frames which explain and illustrate key concepts. Indeed alternative sequences may be defined across a whole database. For example the MacAid courseware presenting basic anatomy on video disc (described in the previous chapter), is used by students of several different medical disciplines: doctor, radiographer, nurse, physiotherapist, dentist. Each chapter is basically linear, but any particular group of students needs to see a different subset of frames, so a special sequence is defined for each. Selecting the "next" frame has a different effect in each case.

This requires some procedural code behind the scenes to test conditions and make choices – to develop the same application on HyperCard for example would require a HyperTalk script. Note that having specified his starting option the user of such an application need make no other choices; all the rest should be under system control. We can distinguish between this sort of non-linear access and the more general kind to be discussed in the following section, where there is a genuine reader choice at each stage.

In Guide, multiple sequences can be set up without writing procedures. Given that all the common material is stored in definition buttons, the selection to be seen by a particular type of user can be set out as a series of usage buttons, which in turn are hidden behind a single button marked with the user type name. A set of mutually exclusive buttons can be grouped together within an "enquiry", so that selecting any button causes the whole enquiry to be replaced. Thus one could prevent a user, for instance, seeing replacements for both a "nurse" and a "doctor" button simultaneously. Another useful function in this context is "automatic replacement".

All replacement buttons in a Guide document have an associated "asking level", while readers entering a Guide session are given a "user level". If a button in a document has an asking level *less than* the user level of the current reader, it is replaced automatically and the reader need not even be aware that the button exists. In general, the higher the user level the more text is made immediately visible, and this can be exploited to allow selective reading. Guide also supports the possibility of "presetting" related buttons so that they can all be opened together by the reader. Using a combination of these functions, multiple sequences can be constructed conveniently for different groups of users.

Referential

The term "referential" is used here, following Conklin [3], to describe textual relationships which are neither strictly sequential nor hierarchical, but which it may be helpful to make the reader aware of. Many of them arise out of actual cross-references within conventional printed text.

For example, we are used to finding notes at the foot of the page or the back of the book, which explain or expand on something in the main text. A hypertext system handles these very well since it enables the reader to see the subsidiary material with very little effort, then return to an uncluttered main text display. Using Guide, the author would define glossary buttons calling up appropriate definitions; in HyperCard he would set a link to another card. There is of course an advantage in having explanations visible along with the main text, so any system which provides more than one screen window scores over HyperCard in that respect.

Looking at footnotes is a fairly orderly process since the reader normally returns immediately to the original point in the document; in programming terms it is the equivalent of a return-jump or procedure call. More serious diversions are possible, taking the reader to another part of the main text from which perhaps he never returns. Once again we can find analogies in printed documents:

- In a long fragmented text like an encyclopedia, there is often a wealth of cross-references between associated entries, (e.g. "see also aardvark"). These are necessary precisely because related information will not generally be located together, the material having been partitioned and arranged in alphabetical order for the convenience of primary look-up.
- In a prescriptive text (whether a piece of legislation or a maintenance manual) explicit references warn the reader of other information which he needs to know in order to carry out a task properly. Otherwise he is directed to the place where it can be found. For example, any Act of Parliament is full of cross-references, both internal: ("in the case of the family of such a man as is mentioned in section 3(1)(b) of this Act"), and external, to related legislation: ("Subject to the provisions of this Act and to section 48(2)(c) of the Insurance Act").
- In a long continuous text, perhaps of a more discursive nature, forward and backward references remind the reader of what has been said and alert him about what is to come, to help him build a mental structure and make sense of what he is reading. They often involve drawing analogies or making contrasts, and may not locate the referred text precisely, e.g. "as described in the previous chapter".
- In a paper written for a scientific or learned journal, references to previous articles on the same topic set the current work in its context, acknowledge intellectual indebtedness, reassure the reader that the author has done his homework, etc. Given an adequate summary of their relevant points, it should not be necessary for the reader to look up references immediately, but they may enable him to continue exploring a topic later.

The above list is by no means exhaustive, but it shows that translating references into hypertext links requires thought. In prose the actual wording of a reference suggests what sort of relationship exists between two pieces of text, and how vital it is to follow it up immediately. By contrast the appearance of a button, with a simple choice as to whether or not to select it, is a relatively unsubtle cue.

Precise references to discrete sections of text with unique identifiers are quite easy to translate into hypertext links, as we saw in the case of the British Airways maintenance manual. They can obviously be implemented with any system like HyperCard by defining buttons and setting appropriate links. And although Guide is not really designed to support random jumps within a document, the effect can also be achieved there in a slightly indirect way. One of the menu options in Guide is to *find* a particular character string within a document and, as we saw earlier, it is possible to associate with an action button commands to simulate the effect of making a menu choice. So a jump to a particular section could be implemented as an action button with associated code to *find <section name>*, provided that the string defined as *<section name>* was guaranteed to occur only once in the document.

By contrast *unlocalised* references present more difficulty – there seems little point in translating every occurrence of the phrase "the previous chapter" into a specific invitation to the reader to jump to the head of that chapter. A more flexible way of supporting such relationships is to have two or more windows onto different document or different parts of the same document, so that the reader can look at related sections side by side. For this purpose, a scrolling system is more convenient than one based on discrete text items. It is achieved very easily in Guide – the Unix version allows several Guide processes to run simultaneously and the PC/Macintosh version implements a special "reference" button which automatically opens a new window and shows the referenced text.

Full support for external references can be achieved only within large-scale databases where a standard method of identifying whole documents is imposed. Suitable cases for this treatment are primary legislation material and reasonably homogenous collections of scientific papers, of the kind currently stored for on-line information retrieval. Here links between documents may complement the searching facilities described in earlier chapters. The references can help to find relevant documents missed by keyword search; while keyword searches within a referenced document help to pin down precisely those parts which are of current interest.

Implicit Associations

So far we have talked about relationships signalled by *explicit* cross-references in the text. Advocates of hypertext wish to go beyond this and support linkages which have no counterpart in conventional writing, but take into account *implicit* associations between ideas or topics. In theory, the ability to define arbitrary connections within a document is potentially the greatest strength of hypertext systems. It lets the reader browse through information in his own way, seeking for specific goals but picking up useful related points *en route*. It is also the most difficult feature for authors to exploit properly, and the one which if badly used can cause confusion and frustration to readers.

The notion originated with Vannevar Bush, a scientist who in 1945 wrote an article: "As we may think" [9], generally acknowledged to be the first proposal for a hypertext system, although not based on computer hardware as we now know it. This article has been extensively quoted in the literature and will not be discussed in any detail here, but there are one or two points of immediate relevance. Bush coined the phrase: "the human mind works by association", which has become the motto of hypertext developers. He proposed, among other things, a device called a "MEMEX" which would enable researchers to build their own libraries of easily accessible documents, annotate them, then link them together in "trails" representing their own personal thought processes.

Nearly fifty years later, Bush's ideas have been implemented in working systems on real computer hardware. Personal information structures involving arbitrary linkages can be created by users on stand-alone machines like the Macintosh – the publicity for HyperCard stresses its suitability and flexibility for that purpose. But here there are inevitable limitations on the size of database which is feasible and, perhaps even more important, on the effort any individual might wish to spend on entering and linking his information.

In publicly accessible hypertext databases on larger machines, it is feasible for individual users to set up their own linkages within an existing framework, and thus organise their material in a way that makes sense to them. It is perhaps less appropriate to do this for prescriptive texts (where the intention is precisely to impose a standard view of the contents) than in more general educational contexts (e.g. as described in [2]), where the student is required both to explore and arrange his material so as to get an intellectual grip on it.

Information structures based on association of ideas are appealing in principle, but not easy to build in practice. Arbitrary linkages made by one person, unless accompanied by copious explanation, may cause confusion when another user tries to follow his trail. Even for the same individual they may be subject to change over time, as his view of the material develops. An interesting comment is made in [7], arising out of experience with Xerox Notecards, that "structures are often obsolete with respect to the user's current thinking ... it will always be easier ... to change one's internal conceptual structures than ... to update the external representations". Just as humans find it necessary to forget as well as remember, in order to avoid confusion and information overload, so maintaining a useful hypertext may involve deleting as well as creating links, as time goes by.

Hypertext System Design Issues

The previous section surveyed some of the relationships which we may wish to represent within a hypertext document – whether hierarchical, sequential, or referential. In the light of that understanding we can return to the issue of hypertext system design, mentioning possible variations in the data models already presented, and seeing how decisions made at that level influence the user interface, and perhaps predispose developers towards certain implementation techniques.

Textual Units or Nodes

A hypertext system designer, as we have seen, has first to decide on the textual units to be handled, and whether they will be of fixed or variable length. If fixed, it will be necessary to decide on their size and shape, which in turn determine some aspects of the user interface, like how many can be seen on the screen at once. For instance HyperCard displays one card, KMS two, Notecards and Intermedia allow for an indeterminate number, occupying overlapping windows.

Other questions about textual units concern the assignment of *identifiers*, and perhaps also *types*. In HyperCard for example a card can be referred to in three ways: (i) by a unique system-allocated identifier, (ii) by a relative sequence number within a stack, and (iii) by a user-defined name. KMS frames likewise have a system-supplied name and a user-assigned title. Some systems impose a fixed classification scheme on cards or frames (e.g. to distinguish a textual element from a picture or a summary card from a detail card), and these are distinguished by their different appearance on screen. Others allow user-defined types, as for instance in HyperCard where allocation of cards to stacks and backgrounds reflects the user's own categories.

These issues are obviously less crucial for a system like Guide – if an author does not partition his document into discrete units the question of node names and types need not arise. Some writers on Hypertext do discuss Guide in terms of the more common data model by defining it as a system where nodes can be of any length, and may include other nodes, but this appears to blur a very basic distinction, so that it is difficult to make positive statements about anything without finding an exception.

Textual Relationships or Links

Next mechanisms must be defined for setting up and examining relationships within a document, and here the first important question is: what exactly gets associated with what?

Once again it is probably more helpful to consider Guide independently from systems based on nodes and links. We have seen that the author can establish a relationship between a button and its replacement text, which will appear either in-line or within a separate window. Any stretch of text (or embedded picture) may be defined as a button, and the same applies to its replacement, so there is considerable flexibility of definition. A button may also trigger off the execution of a piece of code, including a *find* command which relocates the reader at some other point within the document. In that case there is an association between the button and the target of the search. In the commercial version of Guide, this relationship is formally defined using the reference button.

In systems based on the node and link model, the questions focus on the nature of the links themselves. What sort of objects can be the "anchors" of a link, i.e. what textual units act as its source and target? In HyperCard, as we have already seen, the source is a button, defined by its position on the card rather than any particular piece of text. Notecards uses icons related to textual units, and in KMS any distinct block of text can act as a source, and continues to do so even if its location is changed.

It is common (and easy to implement) for the target of a link to be a whole card or frame – this is the case in KMS, HyperCard, and Notecards. However links which involve moving from a small textual unit to a larger one are obviously unsymmetrical, and tend to rule out the possibility of automatic "backward" linking. By contrast Intermedia allows the target of a link to be any point or block "within" a node, thus giving the possibility of more precise crossreference, and the automatic creation of *bi-directional* links.

Another question about links is whether it is appropriate to classify them by type and/or to attach labels or other descriptors to them. Once again, current systems differ in their approach. HyperCard has only one kind of basic link, KMS makes a distinction between *hierarchical* and *referential* links, representing them by different symbols on the screen. Notecards supports user-defined link types. In Intermedia each link is a data object in its own right, having a one-line *explainer* and possibly other properties attached to it at the time of creation, which can be viewed and edited by users.

With the notion of link types comes the possibility of *filtering*, i.e. choosing to see and work with a subset of links. Intermedia supports the notion of *webs*, separate networks of links which may be different for each user. A practical consequence for the underlying system is that link data must be held quite separately from the actual documents in the database.

Surface choices about the user interface involve deciding how link anchors (sources and targets) are distinguished for the reader. Buttons and icons can be highlighted, underlined, and presented in distinctive fonts or shapes. As the reader moves about the text, the appearance of the screen cursor may change according to what object is underneath it. If a link target is not a complete card or frame, the region of text which is being pointed at must be highlighted or otherwise marked at the time when the link is followed. A similar mechanism is necessary for Guide replacement text, which is momentarily displayed in reverse video when the replacement is made.

Obviously all the above details will influence the hypertext author's decisions about how to present his material, and the reader's response to it. Note also that terminal features like size of screen and number of mouse buttons will also dictate some aspects of the user's interaction. As often with software design, there is likely to be a trade-off between power and ease of use. Hypertext systems differ amongst themselves quite as much as other general-purpose packages like spreadsheets and database systems – not surprisingly since they address a wide range of applications areas.

Searching and Browsing

For the hypertext reader the basic ability to replace buttons or follow links is essential, but it often needs to be extended by support for other search activities, and by navigation aids which help in finding one's way through large and complex information structures. We now survey some of the ideas current in this area.

Keyword Search

Word or string searching within the text is an obviously useful function for a hypertext system to supply, often providing a very direct route to the required information. Reference [10] makes an interesting comparison between searching and browsing strategies, suggesting that Boolean queries (particularly if carried out by a professional intermediary) are most "efficient" at finding information of immediate relevance, whereas more informal browsing methods (used by those who actually need the information) may yield long-term benefits in allowing incidental knowledge to be picked up along the way.

Clearly the two approaches are complementary. Reference [7] comments that navigational methods work well within databases which are relatively small (up to 250 cards) or which have a very visible structure, or where the authors have included explicit navigational instructions at each node. In large, unfamiliar and loosely structured networks, readers may be able to describe exactly the information they are seeking, but still not be able to find it. These situations place more emphasis on query-based access mechanisms – the suggestion is made that users should be able to query not only on the basis of *content* (keywords) but also on *structure* – actual patterns of connection between nodes. Intermedia, as described in [2], bases queries not on keywords derived from the main text but on one-line "explainers" and other property lists attached to blocks of text or links between them. What it is feasible to implement depends on the nature of the data – an important question being how much it is subject to change. The user interface for British Airways maintenance manuals allows – as well as link-following and hierarchical access – keyword search with full Boolean query facilities. This is possible because the text is essentially *static*; a complete inverted list index is written to CD-ROM with the rest of the data, giving very efficient search facilities. However we have seen already in the context of other IR applications that it is difficult to maintain up-to-date keyword indexes for a large textual database undergoing continual change.

A different approach to keyword search provides simple *text scanning* facilities like those of a typical word processor or editor. This is the way things work in Guide. When *find* is selected from a menu, the user is asked what string is to be found, and whether the search is to go from the start of text or from the current cursor position. The second option allows each successive copy of a string to be identified, assuming it occurs several times. The search goes through all the text currently in the memory, including replacements for buttons which have not yet been selected. All that happens is that a piece of text containing the relevant string is placed in the current window with the cursor beside it. Another option is to find and select automatically the next button whose name matches the string. Clearly these are much more limited search functions than those in typical IR systems.

In card-based systems a search needs to identify all cards containing the required string, so that the reader can scan them quickly. HyperCard has a *find* option on its menu, allowing the user to enter a string in the message box, then searching forward in the stack to the next card where a match is identified. It is a versatile command which will match characters, words, or lines within nominated fields. It may also be used in a HyperTalk script, along with a function which tests whether a search was successful. A later example of HyperCard authoring will show these facilities in action.

A particularly simple form of keyword search is of course to refer to an individual card by a unique name or identifier, giving a short cut to information whose address the user happens to know. Most card-based systems, like HyperCard, provide a direct *goto* function, useful mainly for small single-user databases with few enough names to be memorable or self-explanatory. If a lengthy prior look-up method has to be used to find them they lose their point.

Navigation Aids

"Getting lost" is a recognised hazard for the reader of a large hypertext, especially one consisting of a network of nodes with no strong hierarchical or sequential structure, and where the author has not provided clear signposts about the linkages. Hypertext systems can provide general-purpose navigation aids falling into several distinct categories:

Histories. Histories help the reader remember how he got to his current position, and retrace his steps if necessary. The system may hold a list of all nodes visited, in order, allowing the reader to repeatedly "backtrack" one step at a time, and perhaps also to "replay" a previous sequence. The designers of Intermedia went further and adopted the principle of "infinite undo" commands whereby the effects of all previous actions (i.e. edits as well as navigations) since the document was last saved could be undone and redone incrementally [2].

On systems using more modest computing resources this approach would not be practical; designers must set a limit on how long a history will be kept, and whether two or more visits to the same node need be remembered individually. For example, HyperCard will show miniature images of the last 20 cards accessed, roughly in their original order of appearance but without repetitions, and with the current card highlighted. The user may click on any card in this display to return to it, but actual changes to the database cannot be undone.

Guide maintains a history based on the hierarchical document structure, to tell the user which button replacements he is currently "inside". If the "undo" button is held down, a pop-up menu appears showing all the relevant button names, and it is possible to select from this menu to undo several replacements at once. As the cursor moves to any button name in the menu, the corresponding replacement text is displayed in inverse video.

Structure Displays.   Another possible requirement is to see a structural overview of the database, in order to decide what else is available and where to go next. This is often discussed in the literature on the original large-scale experimental systems – Notecards, for example, allows the user to see and edit a *browser* card containing a diagram of the network automatically generated by the system. Intermedia also has a facility, to display a particular *web*, but as the example in [3] shows it is hard to make sense of this once there are more than a few interconnections. A strict hierarchy presents fewer problems; KMS confines its graphical displays to those based on hierarchical links, and its designers, in [8], explicitly question whether alternative views are worth the trouble of producing them.

Later applications (e.g. TextVision) have tried to improve the usability of graphic views by exploiting colour and/or three-dimensional images. But systems running on personal computers are limited by the processing power needed to generate graphics dynamically, and – even more significant – by the size of a standard screen. And perhaps in general it is unrealistic to aim for one single-level diagram which tries to show all possible connections within a database at once. The point is often made, e.g. in [11], that arbitrary links between nodes can produce spaghetti structures exactly like the now-discredited *goto* statement in programming. Just as software designers have discarded basic flow-charts in favour of more sophisticated representations of data flow, program logic, and module interdependence, so hypertext authors need to find higher-level constructs to make large documents comprehensible.

Place Markers.   The third kind of aid for the hypertext reader helps him to remember how far he has gone, and to decide whether he has actually seen all the available material, or how much remains unexplored. With a book one is always aware of this – Jane Austen in *Northanger Abbey* can refer to her "readers, who will see in the tell-tale compression of the pages before them that we are all hastening together to perfect felicity". By contrast experiments have shown that hypertext users are bad at estimating the proportion of the material they have read, and at picking up again from a previous stopping-point.

This second problem is of course not unknown to readers of books, but they are helped by the physical memory of having the book open in their hands, and perhaps also of the place (e.g. on the bus or in the bath) where they last read it.

More prosaically, they can use *bookmarks*. These at least can be simulated on a hypertext system, as we saw in the account of the British Airways maintenance manual system. Many general-purpose systems allow the reader to mark and name points of interest in a document so as to return to them directly – this is a first level of annotation which may be extended to the introduction of extra text in the form of notes or memos, for the benefit of the reader himself or (within a multi-user system) later readers.

A function to tell the hypertext reader how much material remains unseen can be provided by automatically marking and counting each node as it is visited, and subtracting the count from the total number of nodes. It is also feasible to keep track of which nodes or sections of text have not yet seen the light of day – Guide certainly does this already. It has been suggested [12] that hypertext systems should be able to respond to the request "show me something new", perhaps by making a random selection from any text unseen so far. (HyperCard does in fact have a *go to any* command, where "any" is a function to generate a random number, but it is not guaranteed to find new material.) Assuming that there was some method in the reader's original navigations, it is unlikely to be helpful anyway to see the remaining nodes or sections presented out of context.

Authoring Hypertext

Part of the original definition of hypertext was that there need be no absolute distinction between authors and readers. In practice, however, hypertext systems show a wide variety of approaches, depending on the nature of the material and the relationship between the different users. At one extreme come those where the two roles are sharply distinguished, because the text is static. Databases on optical storage, as discussed in previous chapters, obviously offer little scope for readers to change them, except in superficial ways like the inclusion of bookmarks. The same applies to electronic encyclopedia systems as described in [9], where any authoring software is quite separate from software to access existing databases.

Indeed, wherever Hypertext is used in a mainly educational context there will be some imbalance between the activities of teachers who create the material and students who use it. However since an "active" reader is likely to remember more of what he has seen, such systems should ideally provide students with a subset of the authoring tools to "re-work" the material in some way (perhaps inserting annotations and new linkages), to demonstrate their understanding in the hypertext equivalent of an essay. In general the author must positively encourage the reader to explore the material in full. Some research work on the usefulness of Hypertext as a learning tool showed, for instance [12], that links to diagrams were often ignored unless the text explicitly invited the reader to follow them. Likewise words whose meanings were imperfectly understood were more likely to be looked up if they were highlighted in the text.

At the other end of the scale are systems designed for group authorship and data sharing, like KMS. As reported in [8], this is intended for collaborative work, and a typical database contains articles, project plans, reports and memos. The system supplies the functions of other special-purpose software like electronic mail and word processing, and covers a range of activities from document production to project administration and software engineering. In these conditions there is no justification for separating authors and readers; all users generate nodes within the database, and access and comment on one another's contributions. Obviously managing such a system demands some of the locking and protection techniques devised for conventional multi-user databases. It also demands the establishment of shared conventions within the group for creating and adding to nodes, sometimes referred to as the hypertext "rhetoric".

In between come systems which cater for both authoring and reading, but may require a switch of *mode*. HyperCard and Guide both fall into this category, and some details are given below of the facilities which they offer.

Authoring with HyperCard

HyperCard has five gradations, allowing users to move in easy stages from very simple to very sophisticated system use. The user-levels are:

- *Browse*: just read and navigate through an existing database.
- *Type*: enter and edit text in fields, create and delete cards.
- *Paint*: create pictures on cards with the paintbox tools.
- *Author*: define new backgrounds, fields, buttons and links.
- *Script*: write HyperTalk scripts to go behind buttons and fields.

The available menus and options depend upon the current user level, and the effect of some actions is context-dependent. Normally, for instance, clicking on a button is a browsing action which causes an associated script to be executed, probably following a link to another card. However once the *button info* function is selected from the *objects* menu, clicking on the same button allows its characteristics to be seen and edited.

The HyperCard menus provide logical groupings of commands and options, which can be summarised as follows:

- *Go*: This gives direct access to other cards. The user may go to the first, last, next or previous card in the stack, or back to the last card visited, or see a display of the most "recent" cards visited, and click on any one to return to it. When authoring, this navigation is required to build up stacks and set links.
- *Tools*: Under this menu comes the paintbox, offering a selection of shape and line-drawing functions to create bit-map graphics and text. It also allows a switch to and from field/button editing modes.

- *Edit*: This gives card-editing functions, e.g. creating and deleting cards, cutting, copying and pasting text from one card to another.
- *Objects*: The most important menu for the author. It has functions to create new backgrounds, buttons and fields, and to see and change information about them through the *Button Info* screen.

The screen for a new button allows choice of its name and various style settings, and for the definition of associated linkages and scripts. A link is made by selecting *linkTo*, navigating to the right destination card, and confirming the link. Alternatively one can select *script* and enter a HyperTalk program to be activated by the current button. In fact a link is itself only a simple script containing an instruction to "go to" another card, to which the author can add extra commands if he wishes, e.g. to specify visual effects.

HyperTalk is a complete programming language in its own right, able to refer to values in fields or parts of fields (lines, words, characters), and having local and global variables, operators and functions, assignment, and standard control structures. In addition it has commands for sorting cards, searching for strings, moving from card to card, producing visual effects like zooming, scrolling and dissolving, and generating sounds. It also provides entry points to external procedures written in another programming language. It is event-driven, in that the execution of a script is triggered off by a particular user action like clicking the mouse on a button.

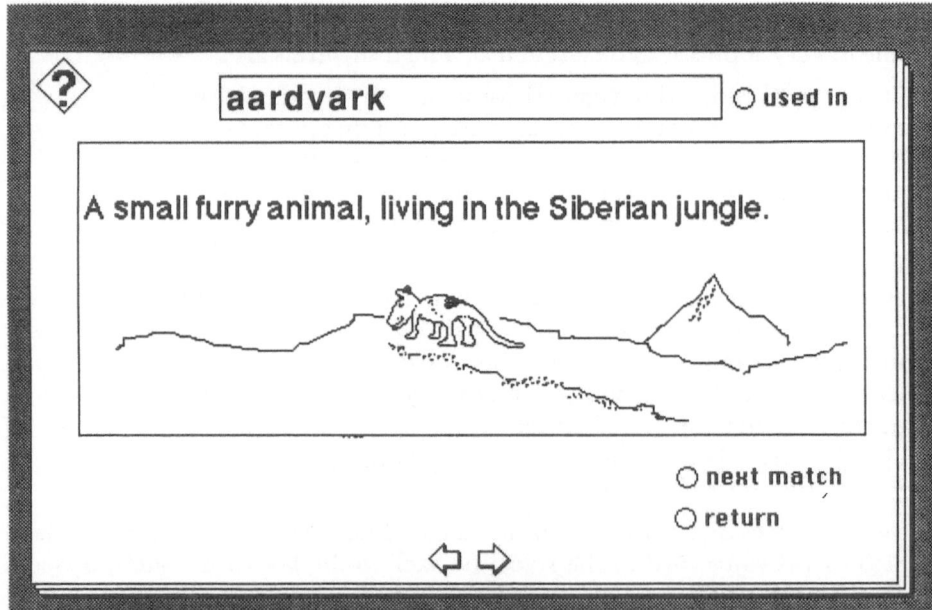

Fig. 9.4. A Hypercard "dictionary" record.

Scripts are associated with a particular object, i.e. a background, card, button, etc. Clearly HyperTalk has been influenced by the principles of object-oriented programming, in the sense that its objects are defined with properties which can be "inherited", and with the capability of responding to "messages" or events. However it is rather more limited in this respect than, for instance, Smalltalk, since the programmer cannot extend the object hierarchy by defining his own object types.

```
21/8/90 10:57 am Script of bkgnd button id 23 = "used in"

on mouseUp
  global SearchKey, StartCard
  put the id of this card into StartCard
  put word 1 of field Headword into SearchKey
  visual dissolve slowly
  find word SearchKey in field Definition
  if the foundText = empty then
    put "Not found" into message
    WaitandClear
  end if
end mouseUp


21/8/90 10:59 am Script of bkgnd button id 24 = "next match"

on mouseUp
  global SearchKey, StartCard
  if SearchKey <> empty then
    get the id of this card
    lock screen
    go to next card
    find word SearchKey in field definition
    if the id of this card <> it then
      unlock screen
    else
      go to StartCard
      put "No more" into message
      WaitandClear
    end if
  end if
end mouseUp


21/8/90 10:59 am Script of bkgnd button id 26 = "return"

on mouseUp
  global SearchKey, StartCard
  if StartCard <> empty then
    go to StartCard
    put "Return to Start" into message
    WaitandClear
  end if
end mouseUp
```

Fig. 9.5. Button scripts for a wordsearch application

HyperTalk Example

To give the flavour of HyperTalk, we show a complete example with half a dozen short scripts written to support a simple dictionary look-up application. Each card in the stack contains two text fields – a "Headword" and a "Definition" – and three buttons (see Fig. 9.4). All these are defined as background objects, giving the cards an identical structure.

Within this stack, the user may check whether a particular headword occurs in the definition field of any other words. Setting explicit links for this purpose would be too laborious, so there are background scripts for the three buttons, which call on the HyperTalk *find* command and the *foundText* function. Each of the three scripts (Fig. 9.5) is executed when the relevant button is clicked, hence all begin with the trigger phrase *on mouseUp*. All have access to two specially declared global variables, *SearchKey* and *StartCard*.

The "used-in" script begins by storing the current card-id in *StartCard* and the current headword in *SearchKey*. It selects a visual effect, then uses *find* to go through the stack looking for an exact match with *SearchKey* in a definition field. If one is found, the relevant card is displayed automatically, with the search key in the definition outlined. Otherwise (*if the foundText = empty*) the script puts a report in the message box and calls a utility routine (shown later) to wait 2 seconds and clear the variables.

```
21/8/90 10:57 am   Script of background id 2802

on openStack
   sort by field 1
   hide message box
   show menuBar
   pass openStack
end openStack


on idle
   hide message box
   get the message
   if it <> empty then
     put empty into message
     visual effect venetian blinds
     find word it in field Headword
     if the foundText = empty then
       put "Not found" into message
       WaitandClear
     end if
   end if
end idle


on WaitandClear
   global SearchKey, StartCard
   wait 2 seconds
   put empty into message
   put empty into SearchKey
   put empty into StartCard
end WaitandClear
```

Fig. 9.6. Background scripts for a wordsearch application.

A headword may be used in more than one definition, and the *next match* button allows the user to see each one in turn. The main function of this script is to move to the "next" card before resuming the search (otherwise the same one would be found again and again). So it locks the screen to avoid showing this (possibly irrelevant) next card, and unlocks it again on completion of the search.

A HyperCard stack is a circular structure so when the *find* command gets to the last card it starts again at the beginning. If there are several relevant definitions, *next match* continues to cycle through them until the *return* button is clicked. However the script can detect if there is only one relevant definition and automatically return to *startCard*. The command *get the id of this card* saves the current card-id in a system-defined temporary variable called *it*, which is later compared with a new card-id to see if they are the same. The *get* command can be used to extract all sorts of object property values, and always puts the result into *it*.

The remaining three scripts (Fig. 9.6) are associated with the whole background rather than individual buttons. *on WaitandClear* is triggered off whenever any of the other scripts calls it – its effect should be self-explanatory. *on openStack* is executed once when the stack is opened for browsing; it will sort the cards into alphabetical definition order (in case any new ones were added in the previous session) then hide the message box until needed. It then passes control to the default HyperCard *openStack* routines.

The *on idle* script is executed when nothing else is happening; it tests continually whether anything new has been put into the message box. This routine provides the opposite of the *used in* search – it will take any selected *definition* word and look for a corresponding *headword* entry. It exploits a useful feature of HyperCard: when the user presses the shift/command keys while pointing at a text field word and clicking with the mouse, that word is pulled out and placed in the message box. The script *gets* it into variable *it* and searches for it, again reporting through the message box if it is not found. Since we expect headword fields to be unique, there is no need for an equivalent of *next match*.

Between them the scripts allow automatic two-way linking between cards, based on the occurrence of headwords in definition fields. Figs 9.7 and 9.8 show example paths through the stack with the two methods. They can of course be used in combination, and all the normal HyperCard navigation facilities remain available – note the standard arrow icons for moving to "next" and "previous" cards.

Authoring with Guide

Texts can be typed directly into Guide or imported from an ASCII file. Normal editing functions for insertion, deletion, block move, etc. are provided,

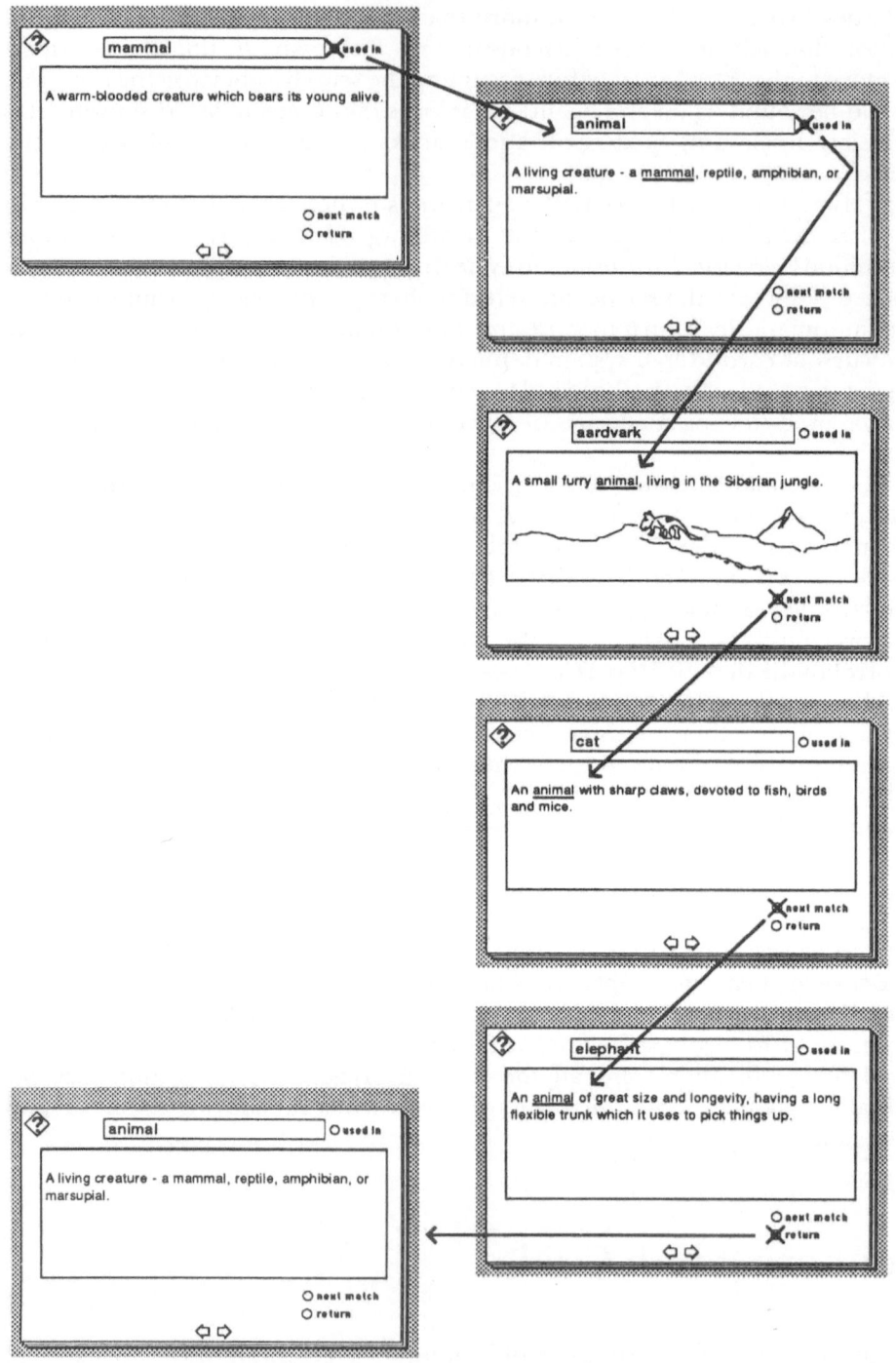

Fig. 9.7. An example path through the dictionary (with the "used in" and "next match" buttons).

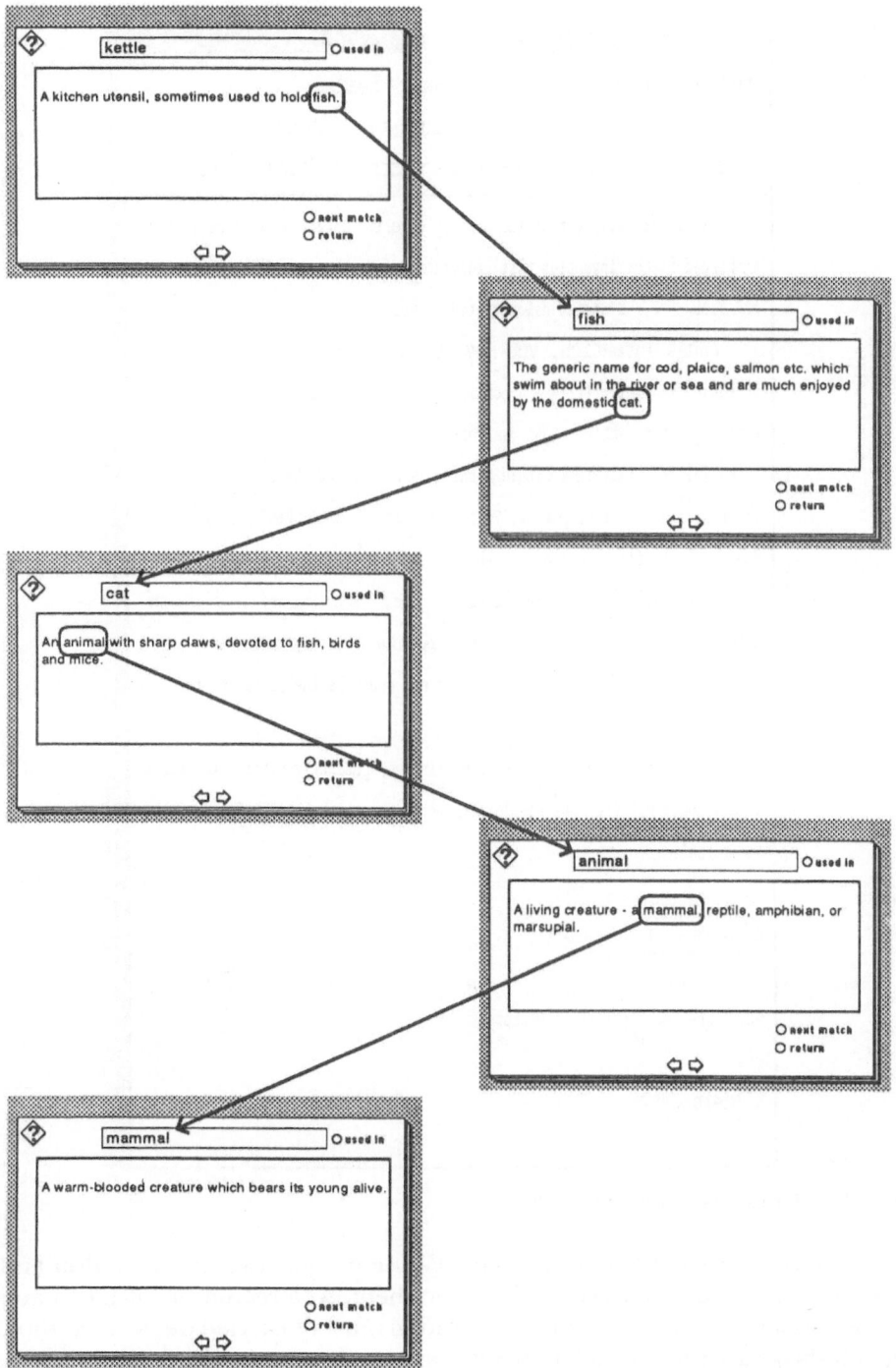

Fig. 9.8. An example path through the dictionary (with the "on idle" script).

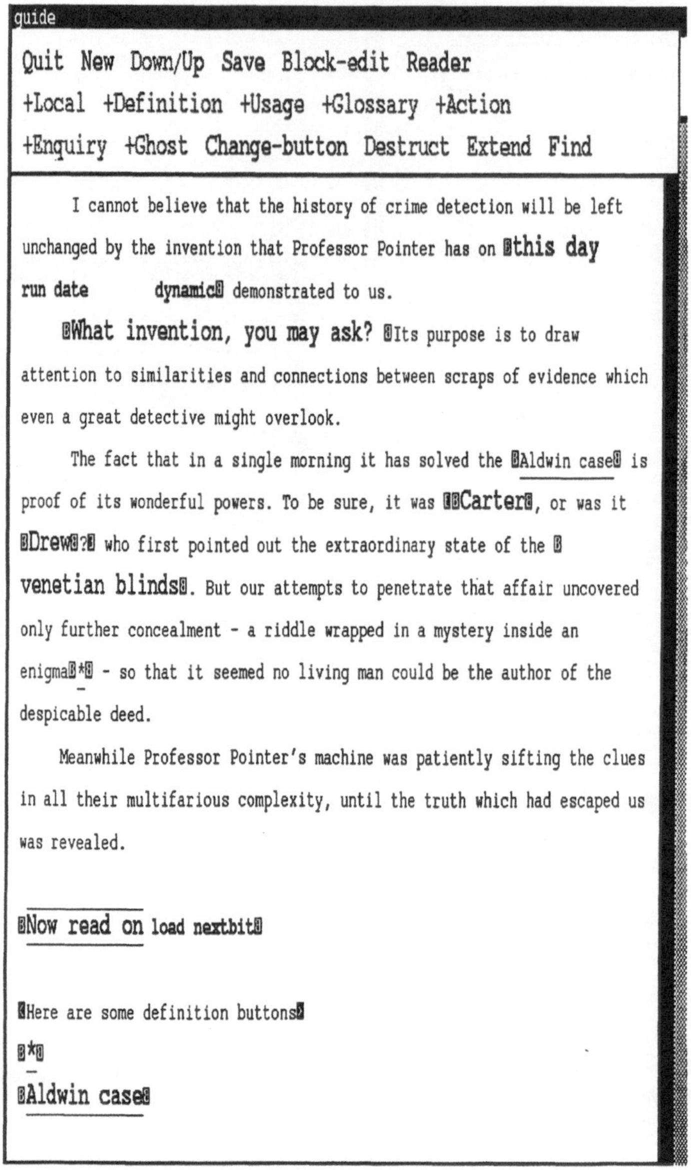

guide

Quit New Down/Up Save Block-edit Reader
+Local +Definition +Usage +Glossary +Action
+Enquiry +Ghost Change-button Destruct Extend Find

I cannot believe that the history of crime detection will be left
unchanged by the invention that Professor Pointer has on ▯**this day**
run date   **dynamic**▯ demonstrated to us.

▯**What invention, you may ask?** ▯Its purpose is to draw
attention to similarities and connections between scraps of evidence which
even a great detective might overlook.

The fact that in a single morning it has solved the ▯Aldwin case▯ is
proof of its wonderful powers. To be sure, it was ▯▯**Carter**▯, or was it
▯**Drew**▯?▯ who first pointed out the extraordinary state of the ▯
venetian blinds▯. But our attempts to penetrate that affair uncovered
only further concealment - a riddle wrapped in a mystery inside an
enigma▯*▯ - so that it seemed no living man could be the author of the
despicable deed.

Meanwhile Professor Pointer's machine was patiently sifting the clues
in all their multifarious complexity, until the truth which had escaped us
was revealed.

▯**Now read on** **load nextbit**▯

▯Here are some definition buttons▯
▯*▯
▯**Aldwin case**▯

Fig. 9.9. A Guide screen in author mode.

although some are a little cumbersome. Guide has just two modes: *author* and
reader, with a menu item to switch between them. As a reader one can edit and
save text, but any kind of structural definition must be carried out as an author.
Fig. 9.9 shows a screen for a Guide text previously seen in Fig. 9.2, but now in
author mode.

Here, obviously, the display is more informative about the underlying structure; it shows the boundaries of each button and enquiry explicitly, and the procedural code associated with usage or action buttons. So the usage button *this day* is linked with the command *run date dynamic* (dynamic to ensure that it is re-executed every time the button is selected), and the action button *now read on* is linked with the command *load nextbit*.

We can also see the definition button for the glossary item *Aldwin case* and this is preceded by a comment or *ghost* which was not visible before. (Ghosts are usually notes of authorial decisions which are not of interest to the normal reader.) There are more options on the menu – surprisingly even the *find* command (keyword search) is available only in author mode. Most of the extra options are there to allow button definition and editing.

To create a button, the author chooses its type (*local, definition, usage, glossary* or *action*) from the menu, and enters its name. The button can then be selected in the normal way to allow entry of the replacement text. As with HyperCard, the effect of selecting a button is context-dependent: in order to change the properties of a button it is necessary to select *change-button* from the menu first and then click on the button to be changed. Recall that two or more buttons may be made mutually exclusive by grouping them within an Enquiry structure, such that if any one of the group is selected the whole enquiry is replaced.

Existing text may be incorporated into an enquiry, a button name, or a replacement using the *extend* function, so it is possible to read in an ordinary document and add structure to it interactively. Conversely there is a *destruct* function which destroys button structure but not text – both the button name and its replacement remain, but now on the same level. Pictures produced with external drawing packages can also be imported into a Guide document – once there they are treated as an indivisible unit which can be moved, deleted, even redefined as a button name or replacement, but not edited in any way.

Unlike HyperCard, Guide does not provide a full programming language, although it allows procedures to be associated with action buttons. These may simulate the effect of a series of menu selections and other user inputs with a command-sequence preceded by *do*. In this context, as well as the normal menu options like *find* (seeking either a text string or the name of a replace button), there are commands which automatically *select* and *undo* buttons, test if a button *is-selected*, *insert* and *delete* text, put out a *message* on the menu-bar (with one or more associated items for selection), and simulate the effect of the user typing in data. Any command can be executed "Shyly", so that the reader does not see the feedback which would normally appear (e.g. scrolling through the text on a keyword search).

For cases which require conditional or repetitive control structures, and even variables, Guide depends upon the Unix shell language. Any shell script may be *run* by an action button, and that script can if necessary interact with Guide using the special program *callguide*, whose function is to feed commands to Guide as if they were entered at the keyboard. So in principle buttons are programmable, albeit less conveniently than with HyperCard. In our current example, the facilities could be used to generate different stories depending on earlier choices made by the reader.

More usefully in the contexts for which Guide is intended, it is possible to set up data entry screens in which action buttons are programmed to control the overall structure of a document by interacting with the user and directing him where and what to type. In particular, they can help to automate the actual process of creating buttons and replacements, if these fall into a regular pattern. We thus see two possible levels of authorship, the first concerned with setting up *templates* by way of command sequences defining dialogues and making menu selections, the second concerned only with the actual text to be entered.

Preprocessing and Verification

In some cases, the authoring process can be streamlined even further. Given an existing set of documents written to a standard, it is possible to map their structure directly into a simple Guide hierarchy without human intervention to define each button explicitly. For example, the Unix *man* documents for system utilities are laid out under general headings:

- NAME: the Unix command name.
- SYNTAX: command syntax showing all possible options/parameters to the command.
- OPTIONS (PARAMETERS): details of the effect of each option, and how each parameter (e.g. filename) is used.
- DESCRIPTION: an overall explanation of what the command does (possibly including references to sources of algorithms).
- EXAMPLES: examples of actual uses of the command with a description of their effect.
- SPECIAL CONSIDERATIONS: limitations and error messages.
- FILES: actual system files or directories accessed by the command.
- SEE ALSO: references to other related Unix utilities.

Most Unix users consult *man* documents in-line, but their order of presentation is not always convenient. Those reading about a command for the first time might prefer to see the overall description before the details of individual options; those who are refreshing their memories on a particular point may simply want to look at a few examples. The Unix version of Guide comes with a pre-processor to format *man* documents so that they can be seen first as a series of headings representing buttons to be selected and expanded in the usual way. This provides a more convenient method of consultation.

Automatic preprocessing is possible here because the *man* texts are held in a standard Unix *nroff* format which indicates the document structure. Text lines are interspersed with *dot commands* specifying document format, including macros for laying out paragraphs, sections, and other structural units, and it is these macro names which are recognised by the Guide pre-processor when performing its conversion. In fact Guide documents are held in a very similar form, with dot commands indicating the start and end of buttons, replacements, enquiries and so on. An example can be seen in Fig. 9.10. Guide reads files like this and formats the text dynamically, displaying lines which fit the width of the current window.

One useful option for authors is *verification* – checking at the time when a source file is loaded into Guide that definitions exist for each usage- or glossary-button which depends on a definition. Note however that the contents of a document will not necessarily all come from the same source; glossary definitions are often held separately, and the replacement for a button may involve loading in the contents of another file. So conventions must be established about which directories are to be searched to find glossary and replacement text. For a small-scale application this can be handled by setting operating system pathnames, but in some cases rather more may be required.

Large Scale Document Management

Our survey of author functions in two current packages has focused on the process of creating a single hypertext document, although in either case more than one data file may be involved. A HyperCard application may use several different stacks, and links can be set from cards in one stack to cards in another. Likewise one Guide source document can call in text from another. In fact many useful applications of hypertext involve the orderly management of very large collections of documents, (possibly subject to change over a period of time), and so demand additional software support. Some possibilities are mentioned briefly below, mainly in the context of Guide.

Preparation/Conversion

An important principle is that documents within a set should have a standard format, and this implies the use of software tools to help create them. An account is given in [13] of the ICL *Locator* project, based on Guide, to support a telephone enquiry system dealing with hardware fault reporting. This involved the consultation of manuals on-line, and using button selection and replacement to find the required information quickly. The text of the existing manuals was converted into Guide format using a pre-processor to, for example, recognise section headings, but human authoring skills were also vital to lay out the material in an understandable way. However discipline in maintaining consistency was very important; the author of [13] remarks that "the haphazard author, even if blessed with flair and imagination, is a menace".

Documents of the kind used for the Locator project are likely to be subject to organisational standards, so it will be feasible to write pre-processing software to convert them. It was noted earlier that a more general standard (Unix *nroff*) also provided a basis for a Guide pre-processor. Now there is a move towards originating technical documents in machine-readable form according to

```
        I cannot believe that the history of crime detection will be left unchanged
.Gu
by the invention that Professor Pointer has on
```
```
  ┌ .Bu u 1 n
  │ this day        run date        dynamic
  └ .bU
   demonstrated to us.
   .Nl
```
```
  ┌ .Bu 1 1 n
  │ What invention, you may ask?
  └ .bU
 ┌── .Re
 │   The professor's machine is a clockwork device capable of manipulating a great many
 │ .Gu
 │ pieces of paper having words inscribed on them as patterns of holes, not unlike
 │ .Gu
 │  Braille's excellent code for the blind.
 │ ┌ .Bu 1 1 n
 │ │ Indeed:-
 │ └ .bU
 │┌── .Re
 ││  (Indeed I have heard of similar automata that can play with special packs of cards
 ││ .Gu
 ││ in the saloons of the United States of America, but none as complex or as useful as
 ││ .Gu
 ││ this.)
 │└── .rE
 └── .rE
   Its purpose is to draw attention to similarities and connections between scraps of
 .Gu
 evidence which even a great detective might overlook.
 .Nl
        The fact that in a single morning it has solved the
  ┌ .Bu g 1 n
  │ Aldwin case
  └ .bU.
   is proof of its wonderful powers. To be sure, it was
 ┌── En
 │ ┌ .Bu 1 1 n
 │ │ Carter
 │ └ .bU
 │┌── .Re
 ││  Carter, if memory serves me aright - a thickset, coarse looking fellow of some
 ││ .Gu
 ││ five-and-fifty years -
 │└── .rE
 │   , or was it
 │ ┌ .Bu 1 1 n
 │ │ Drew
 │ └ .bU
 │┌── .Re
 ││  Drew - that sharpfaced lawyer who even then had the reputation for sailing pretty
 ││ .Gu
 ││ close to the wind -
 │└── .rE
 │   ?
 └── .eN
   who first pointed out the extraordinary state of the
  ┌ .Bu 1 1 n
  │ venetian blinds
  └ .bU
 ┌ .Re
 └ .rE
   .Gu
```

```
    But our attempts to penetrate that affair uncovered only further concealment - a
    .Gu
    riddle wrapped in a mystery inside an enigma
  ┌ .Bu g 1 n
  │ *
  └ .bU
    - so that it seemed no living man could be the author of the despicable deed.
    .Nl
        Meanwhile Professor Pointer's machine was patiently sifting the clues in all
    .Gu
    their multifarious complexity, until the truth which had escaped us was revealed.
    .Nl
  ┌ .Bu a 1 n
  │ Now read on    load nextbit
  └ .bU
    .Nl
    .Nl
  ┌ .Gh
  │ Here are some definition buttons
  └ .gH
    .Nl
  ┌ .Bu d 1 n
  │ *
  └ .bU
  ┌ .Re
  │ "riddle wrapped in a mystery inside an enigma" : Winston Churchill 1939
  └ .rE
    .Nl
  ┌ .Bu d 1 n
  │ Aldwin case
  └ .bU
  ┌ .Re
  │ Aldwin case : The murder of the famous medium Mrs. Edna Aldwin, supposedly shot by
  │ .Gu
  │ an ectoplasmic apparition during a seance.
  └ .rE
    .Nl
```

Fig. 9.10 A Guide text file with embedded commands.

international standards, e.g. the Standard Generalized Markup Language (SGML), which provides a full set of conventions for specifying textual structures and identifying components like footnotes and cross-references. When adopted, this should make the automatic generation of new hypertext documents more efficient and consistent. The principles of SGML are discussed in the following chapter.

Indexing

Given a set of reference documents in hypertext form, some higher level software may be required to help potential readers decide which ones to read. Basically this involves the use of IR techniques discussed in earlier chapters, where document descriptors (including keywords) are indexed and searched on the basis of selection criteria. Reference [14] describes a hypertext document management environment (IDEX), designed as an adjunct to the commercial version of Guide, which enables users to access a large collection of documents in this way. It is implemented as a distributed database on a PC network, and covers the functions of: document conversion (e.g. from SGML to hypertext format), indexing and retrieval, and generation of printed documents according to pre-defined styles. Documents can be classified by type, format and status (e.g. draft or final version), and indexed according to author, date, and keyword descriptors. Higher level document files handle glossaries, bibliographies, contents lists and cross-references between documents.

Revisions

Technical documentation is subject to periodic change, and, as we saw in the case of the British Airways maintenance manuals, formal procedures for updating must be established when systems for on-line consultation are installed. Moreover it may sometimes be necessary to revert to previous document states, or perhaps to maintain a number of variants. The task is similar to that of controlling program source code under development, and can benefit from similar software support. It may be unnecessary, for example, to hold each version in full; instead one complete "root" copy may be kept along with a series of "deltas" or editing specifications which can be applied to create each revision. It must be possible to freeze a version of a document at a particular point in time, and the creation and public release of new versions must be subject to suitable authorisation procedures.

Just as with source program control, a text control system needs to be able to identify dependencies, so that if one document is changed others which refer to it or load it can be checked to ensure that they remain consistent. This was one of the additional features which it was found necessary to add to the PC version of Guide to make it suitable for large-scale applications – along with control of presentation through style sheets, links to graphics stored on external files, and mechanisms for controlling video-disc and for the direct execution of other software packages.

Hypertext in a Broader Context

Further extensions to hypertext systems may be appropriate according to context. Reference [13] stresses the importance of being able to tailor Guide for particular applications and gives several concrete examples from the Locator project. As already stated, this involves the use of on-line manuals by ICL staff answering telephone enquiries from customers; so a by-product of using the system to resolve a query is to log information about it for statistical purposes, and perhaps to send out an engineer carrying the necessary spare parts. It also happens that queries are interrupted while the caller obtains extra information; the Guide user therefore has the option of putting the call on hold, in such a way that it can be resumed at a later time.

Other applications demand quite different extra facilities. CD-Word is a CD-ROM hypertext product, based on PC Guide, which holds two Greek and four

English versions of the Bible, together with important commentaries and illustrations. Users of the system can do full-text keyword retrieval, scroll through two versions of the same passage in parallel, follow references from commentaries, and look up a dictionary entry for each word in the text, which presents a full grammatical analysis. Once again this requires a specially tailored version of the software.

In general, useful hypertext systems must be *open-ended*, providing a core set of facilities but having the potential for interaction with other programs. They may be called upon to present help files or training manuals for financial or administrative software, conversely the may themselves call upon utilities such as spelling checkers. It is obviously not sensible to try to incorporate every conceivable facility into one monolithic package – if a hypertext user wants to do a calculation or display a bar chart he should be able to pull in a spreadsheet or graphics package, perform the task and resume, carrying over any relevant information. In a multi-tasking environment such integration of functions is entirely feasible.

Chapter Summary

Three main characteristics of hypertext systems are that they: (i) allow texts to be perused in a non-linear way, (ii) integrate textual information with graphics (and possibly also sound and video), and (iii) support multiple authorship of, or at least reader commentary on, texts. The first of these points is probably the most significant, in that it must apply to any piece of software offered as a hypertext system. Suitable material for non-linear access includes general works of reference, prescriptive texts like pieces of legislation or technical manuals, and databases with a complex but irregular structure.

A commonly-used data model for a hypertext is of a *network* made up of *nodes* (fixed-length textual units analogous to cards or frames) with arbitrary links between them. Links represent *relationships* (sequential, hierarchical and referential) between pieces of text. The reader chooses which links to follow, in theory seeing the information in the order which suits him best. An alternative format was described, based on a variable-length *scrolling* document with *embedded* buttons. Selection of a button causes either in-line *expansion* of text or the display of glossary definitions in a separate window. Document structure is basically hierarchical but again the reader has a choice as to how he explores it.

As well as browsing through the information, the reader may use facilities for keyword search, direct access to nodes, and backtracking. More ambitious systems provide graphical views of the network structure, and link filtering. Systems differ in the degree to which they separate the functions of author and reader, depending on the intended application area – the two packages described in most detail here provide easy switching between modes and a full set of authoring options for defining textual relationships. Both allow buttons to be linked with executable code for running procedures and external applications, making them potentially open-ended.

Practical large-scale hypertext applications may require extra utilities for automatic document conversion and standardisation, indexing, and the management of multiple versions. These tasks are easier when documents are originated with detailed and unambiguous structural descriptions. Some possible conventions for this are discussed in the following chapter.

Investigations

Try to obtain access to a hypertext system such as Guide or HyperCard. Check what facilities it provides for setting up and following textual relationships, and for incorporating non-textual material. Then try to create a useful hypertext.

- With a card-based system, it is sensible to use material which is already divided into discrete units. One possibility is to take a specialised dictionary, e.g. of computing terms. Select a key entry, and put it onto a card. Look for technical terms in its definition and enter their definitions, setting links to them either explicitly or through a script. Do the same thing with each of the new definitions, and so on *ad infinitum*. Consider what software tools would be useful to help automate this task.

- If you are trying out Guide, take some existing manual or other structured machine-readable text and attempt to fit it into a framework of buttons and replacements. Consider whether explicit jumps within the text are necessary to handle cross-referencing or whether glossary or usage buttons referring to definitions are sufficient. Does the format of the original text indicate its structure unambiguously? If it contains embedded codes, would they provide a basis for automatic conversion into a Guide document?

Implement a simple card-based hypertext system to gain an insight into the main design issues. Your program will probably be split into three parts: (i) an editor to put text onto cards, (ii) a link creator, and (iii) a browser for following links (and possibly backtracking). Use a high-level interpreted language with helpful features for creating the user interface. Interesting questions to decide are: (i) whether link sources are associated with a text item or a card position, (ii) how and where to store link information, (iii) how to maintain the integrity of the network after the deletion of links or nodes.

References

1 Nelson TH (1987) Computer Lib/Literary Machines. Microsoft

2 Yankelovich N, Haan BJ, Meyrowitz NK. et al. (1988) Intermedia: The concept and the construction of a seamless information environment. IEEE Computer 19(1):81–96

3 Conklin J (1987) Hypertext: An introduction and survey. IEEE Computer 20(9):17–41

4 Goodman D (1988) The complete HyperCard handbook. Bantam Computer Books, London

5 Brown PJ (1990) Guide user manual, 8th impression. Computing Laboratory, The University of Canterbury

6 Engelbart D (1963) A conceptual framework for the augmentation of man's intellect. In: Howerton PW, Weeks DC (eds) Vistas in information handling. Spartan Books

7 Halasz F (1988) Reflections on Notecards: Seven issues for the next generation of hypermedia systems. CACM 31(7):836–852

8 Akscyn R, McCracken D, Yoder E (1988) KMS: A distributed hypermedia system for managing knowledge organizations. CACM 31(7):820–835

9 Bush V (1945) As we may think. Atlantic Monthly. Reprinted in Computer Bulletin, March 1988, 35–40

10 Marchionini G, Shneiderman B (1988) Finding facts vs browsing knowledge in hypertext systems. IEEE Computer 19(1):70–79

11 Van Damm A (1988) Hypertext 1987 keynote address. CACM 31(7):887–895

12 Wright P (1989) But are hypertexts useful for "serious" reading? MRC Applied Psychology Unit, Cambridge

13 Brown PJ (1990) Hypertext: Dreams and reality. Computing Laboratory, The University of Canterbury

14 Ritchie I (1989) Hypertext – moving towards large volumes. Computer Journal 32(6):516–523

Ten

Describing the Structure of Documents

" ... therefore let use be preferred before uniformity,
except where both may be had."
Francis Bacon

The Need for Standards

This chapter discusses the process of defining document structure and identifying individual textual units down to any level of detail. It looks at two methods for doing this, developed over the last ten years through the International Organisation for Standardisation (ISO). The aim of any standard for machine-readable documents must be to achieve:

- Portability: documents created in one organisation can be sent to another (over a network or on disc), and be interpreted by a range of different software.
- Reusability: the same source document can be printed in different layouts, or reliably converted for storage in a database.

Let us make the above points more concrete by recalling some of the requirements and problems discussed earlier on in the book.

We began by considering how natural language text can be represented inside a machine. A language's alphabet must be mapped onto internal codes, and for non-ASCII characters it is necessary to define special codings, perhaps using escape sequences. Some researchers also want to mark certain linguistic features so that they can be identified and counted by software. The investment of time involved here is better justified if the machine-readable text can be used later by other researchers.

In the case-study on creating a dictionary, we saw that at different times it must be seen as a continuous text and a randomly accessible database. Applying relational normalisation to the dictionary data forced artificial decisions to split, into separate tables, textual units which were later to be joined together again. A more natural way of representing structure was needed.

When setting up databases for bibliographic and full-text retrieval services, different parts of a document are held in separate fields within variable-length records. Additional indexing structures are then created to aid searching. By the end, any database tends to be firmly bound to a particular piece of retrieval software and its user interface, so that the user of several on-line databases may need familiarity with a corresponding number of different query languages.

This kind of dependency is also evident with text products sold on CD-ROM. Here there are strict standards at the physical level, and at the level of operating system files and directories, but not for the database structures themselves. The same applies to the document images often archived onto worm disc. In this area the only standards in general use concern image scanning and compression; ways of identifying individual parts of documents (e.g. separating textual and graphic information) are application-dependent.

The account of hypertext principles showed the need to represent many different textual relationships – sequential, hierarchical and referential – and to allow texts to be accessed through a variety of paths. It was noted that unambiguous structural definitions are essential if large-scale hypertexts are to be generated from existing machine-readable technical documentation.

Finally – an important topic not yet explored in detail but the subject of this and the following chapters – there is the growing convergence between the worlds of computing and printing. Whereas the original word processing machines were a substitute for the office typewriter, more advanced hardware and software allows complex document layouts to be defined for professional or semi-professional printing. This is achieved, basically, by embedding printer-control instructions within text, but the precise mechanism for doing so varies from one package to another. To make documents prepared in different ways interchangeable and reusable, we must be able to deal separately with their logical structure and physical appearance.

Needless to say, the standard document definition languages to be described here do not solve all the above issues at a stroke, but they represent approaches which will become increasingly important as more and more documents are generated, transmitted, and stored electronically. Whatever its other drawbacks, printed paper is a very portable medium which can be used and read by people widely separated in space and time using conventions which are universally accepted – this is obviously the ultimate goal for electronic text or document processors.

General Principles of Document Structuring

The two standards to be described below are the *Standard Generalized Markup Language* (SGML) and *Office Document Architecture* (ODA). Although rather different in their purpose and scope, they address one fundamental question in the same way. That question is: what sort of descriptive power is needed in a language for defining complex document structures?

The answer can be given by drawing analogies with more familiar forms of description. Most computer science students will have met either or both of the following:

- Jackson structure diagrams – used to define data records and files, and, by derivation, programs to operate upon them. In these diagrams higher level units are broken down into components specified in more and more detail; and organised using sequence, selection, and iteration.
- BNF grammars used to define the syntax of a programming language. A grammar consists of a series of "replacement rules", showing how a whole source program is broken down into smaller syntactic units. Sequences, selections and iterations occur on the right-hand side of a replacement rule; nested structures can also be defined via rules where a component is defined in terms of itself. The BNF definition of a programming language provides a basis for checking the syntactic correctness of any program, and translating it into another form.

Similar ideas turn up in document description languages. A complex document like a book can be defined in terms of lower level elements (contents page, foreword, main body, appendices) which can in turn be broken down further. There is obviously repetition, (of chapters and sections), and choice (indexes or glossaries may be optional, the paperback and hardback editions of a series may contain alternative components). We may also wish to group together elements having a variable sequence; for instance a title page may contain the title, author's name, publisher, date, etc. but not necessarily in that order. This structure is known as a "set" or "aggregate".

The examples above all refer to the *logical* components of a document, but the same principle is applicable to *physical* structures. A book is an iteration of pages, a page in the simple case may be an iteration of lines; however some publications use other substructures like columns and blocks. Separating the logical and physical structure of a document is an important aspect of both the languages under discussion, although they go about it in quite different ways.

As we shall see, SGML document definitions are very much based on replacement rules, while ODA definitions also use graphic representations not too different from the familiar Jackson diagrams. The purpose of both is to provide a framework for whole classes of documents having the same structure. Software can then be written to help authors to create them, check them for completeness, store or transmit them, and translate them into different formats.

The Standard Generalized Markup Language

SGML (ISO–8879) is primarily intended for use within the commercial publishing and printing industry, and many of its ideas and terminology come from that source. The fundamental concept to grasp is that of textual "mark-up".

What is Mark-up?

Mark-up is extra coded information embedded into a text to direct how it should be interpreted. The form it takes depends on who or what is doing the interpreting, and why.

Some forms of mark-up are so common that we are not aware of them as separate from the text. Following Coombs et al. [1], we can distinguish four levels, starting with the punctuation and spaces which normally separate words and sentences in written language. (These are not absolutely essential – medieval manuscripts for example did not always employ them.) At the next level comes so-called *presentational* mark-up, involving, say, indentation and blank lines to distinguish larger units like paragraphs, long quotations, or tables of data. With handwritten or typewritten text this is as far as it goes; but because real printing opens the possibility of introducing other presentational devices (different sizes and styles of type, columns, boxes, etc.) it has been traditional for publishers' copy editors to quite literally "mark-up" authors' manuscripts with instructions to the typesetter as to how the printed text should be laid out.

This is an example of *procedural* mark-up – the copy editor telling the typesetter what to do. In the same way users of word processors and text formatting software often put procedural mark-up in their text to affect its printed layout. Unix *nroff*, for example, accepts instructions about line and page length, justification, vertical spacing, centring and indentation, in the form of embedded commands distinguished by a dot as the first character in the line. To make life easy for users, macros can be defined which group together logically related lower level commands under a mnemonic. Thus the series of events which must occur at the start of a new section (output new numbers and headings, handle indentation and vertical spacing) can be triggered by a single embedded command – which could be considered an example of *logical* mark-up.

True logical mark-up involves the insertion of "tags" to identify textual units, in a way which is quite independent of physical or layout considerations. It is also sometimes referred to as *descriptive* or *generic* mark-up. A document containing logical mark-up can be automatically checked to see whether it is structurally "correct", and then formatted and output in different styles according to the current requirements.

Defining Documents with Replacement Rules

SGML is in fact a *meta-language*: not a single language for describing textual structures but a method for defining such languages. In this respect it is like

BNF, which can be used to define Algol, Pascal, Modula–2, and so on. The task of document definition is quite different from that of using SGML to mark-up a particular text, just as defining a programming language is different from writing a program in it. Any document marked-up according to SGML conventions is preceded by a *document type definition*: a set of rules which show how it should be composed. For this it is necessary to refer to:

- *Elements*: names for each separate part of the document.
- *Meta-symbols*: characters which have a special meaning within the replacement rules.

Elements

The SGML standard does not itself include any particular element names or rules; these are chosen at the time when a class of documents is being defined. Element names are actually used as tags within the text, so they will probably be mnemonics of some kind, e.g. "chapter", "section" or shortened forms of the same. For example the British Library "starter set" [2], a publicly available definition applicable to a wide range of documents, includes:

```
<tp>   : Title Page
<au>   : Author
<int>  : Introduction
<p>    : Paragraph
<sq>   : Short Quotation (to be embedded in the main text)
<lq>   : Long Quotation (set out in a separate paragraph)
<ol>   : Ordered List (in which items are labelled)
<ul>   : Unordered List (in which items are not labelled)
<li>   : List Item
```

The standard does define a set of meta-symbols within its so-called *concrete reference syntax*, although it allows the possibility for even these to be redefined. Some important meta-symbols are:

```
<! >   : mark-up declaration delimiters
< >    : start-tag delimiters
< />   : end-tag delimiters
& ;    : entity reference delimiters (explained later)
```

and, to form expressions in replacement rules:

```
|      : between alternative elements
,      : between elements in a fixed sequence
&      : between elements which may occur in any order
?      : to indicate optional elements (zero or one)
*      : to indicate repeated elements (zero or more)
+      : to indicate repeated elements (one or more)
```

Using the elements and meta-characters, it is now possible to write *rules*. Here are some which might be useful when defining a "thank-you letter" document type:

```
<!ELEMENT letter    (address?, date?, body, signoff)>
<!ELEMENT body      (dear, thanks, gifts, news, cliches)>
<!ELEMENT gifts     (intro, ul) >
<!ELEMENT ul        (li+) >
<!ELEMENT news      (p*) >
<!ELEMENT cliches   (hw? & ss? & sl?) >
<!ELEMENT signoff   ((lf | bw | kr | ys | ttfn), name) >
<!ELEMENT p         (#PCDATA) >
```

A letter consists of an (optional) *address* and *date*, a *body* and a *signoff*. The body contains elements which address the recipient (*dear*), thank him or her for the present (*thanks*), and list other *gifts* received on the same occasion. For this an unordered list (*ul*) is used, containing one or more list items (*li*). News can consist of zero or more paragraphs, so is effectively optional. *Clichés* at the end of the letter are also optional and can occur in any order. Finally *signoff* allows one of five alternative greetings followed by the writer's name. All elements must eventually break down through replacement rules to either #CDATA – simple character data – or #PCDATA – parsed character data which may contain other kinds of mark-up apart from element tags.

Tagging a Document.   A letter written and fully marked-up according to these rules might look like this:

```
<letter> <address> 1 Acacia Avenue, Arundel </address>
<body> <dear> Dear Aunt Anne, </dear>
<thanks> Thank you for the pair of socks you sent me for my birthday. I'm
sure they will be very useful. </thanks> <gifts>
<intro> For my birthday I also had </intro> <ul>
<li> a bicycle </li>
<li> a box of chocolates </li>
<li> a budgerigar </li> </ul> </gifts>
<news> <p> Unfortunately the budgerigar ate the chocolates (wrappers
and all) and I crashed my bicycle when I was taking him to the vet. </p>
</news>
<cliches> <sl> Mum and Dad send their love. </sl> <hw> We hope you
are keeping well. </hw> </cliches> </body>
<signoff> <bw> Best wishes from </bw> <name> John </name>
</signoff> </letter>
```

This is a trivial example (see [3] for more useful and complex ones, including definitions for memos, technical reports and whole books), but it illustrates some basic points. An SGML parser would check that the letter contained all the necessary elements, and an associated formatter could then lay it out properly.

Minimisation.   One thing noticeable here is the high proportion of mark-up to text. In practical applications this would be less evident, partly because normal document tags tend to be shorter (one or two letters only), and partly because SGML employs the principal of *minimisation*. This means that tags can generally be omitted wherever no ambiguity would result. In particular end-tags are often unnecessary if their presence can be deduced from the occurrence of the next start-tag; on that basis almost every end-tag in the above text (except for </letter>) could be left out. So could start-tags for low level elements; for instance a newline symbol could be defined as a "short tag" for the start of paragraphs and list items. Element definitions actually indicate whether or not start-and end-tags can be omitted. So, for instance, according to the following rules:

```
<!ELEMENT letter      – –    (address?, date?, body, signoff)>
<!ELEMENT gifts       – O    (intro, ul)>
<!ELEMENT p           O O (#CDATA)>
```

element "letter" needs both start-and end-tags, element "gifts" needs no end-tag, and the tags for element "p" are both optional (probably because they have been mapped to a "short tag" character like the newline symbol). Mark-up minimisation is an important practical issue, since having to put in too many tags may deter authors from using SGML altogether.

Entities

Another important aspect of SGML is the use of *embedded entities*. These can be thought of as either named constants or macros – often they are short names for longer strings which are used repeatedly in a particular set of documents. If our rules included the following entity declarations:

```
<!ENTITY sendlove "<sl> Mum and Dad send their love. </sl>">
<!ENTITY hopewell "<hw> We hope you are keeping well.</hw>">
<!ENTITY seesoon "<ss> I expect we will see you soon.</ss>">
```

the clichés section of our letter could now simply be coded:

```
<clichés> &hopewell; &sendlove; </clichés>.
```

An SGML parser recognises an entity reference by its ampersand and semicolon character delimiters, and substitutes the long phrase when the document is processed. Note that, as in the above example, expansions of entity names may hold mark-up tags, and indeed references to other *entity* names.

Entities also represent characters which cannot be entered directly at the keyboard. Obvious examples are the meta-symbols themselves: if "<" is interpreted as the start of a tag, how do we include it in a text in its own right? The answer is to declare:

```
<!ENTITY lt "<" >
```

then refer to the entity name:

```
"age &lt; 30".
```

This facility really comes into its own as a way of encoding special characters like mathematical symbols, Greek letters, accents etc. Reference [3] lists details of publicly declared entity sets of this kind, registered in accordance with the ISO standard. The names are mnemonic; e.g. an acute accent is referred to as &*acute*; capital Greek pi as &*Pi*; etc. Obviously at some point when the document is processed these entity references must be converted to real typesetting directives.

At a more abstract level, *parameter entities* can be used as shorthand within element definitions. For instance the British Library starter set has elements *h1*, *h2*, *h3*, *h4*, as tags for headings at four different levels within a document. Likewise there are *hw1*, *hw2*, *hw3*, *hw4* for different kinds of highlighted word – implying perhaps (according to the conventions chosen), underline, italics, small capitals, and bold type. Their occurrence in a document is subject to similar rules so for the sake of conciseness the following entities are declared:

```
<! ENTITY %h "h1 | h2 | h3 | h4" >
<! ENTITY %hw "hw1 | hw2 | hw3 | hw4" >
```

and thereafter only the entity references %h; and %hw; need be used in element definitions.

Attributes

The last important parts of the definition language to mention are *attributes*. Again we can draw on a programming language analogy and think of these as *arguments*: values sent to a procedure to say how a particular document element must be processed. Sometimes they are used to give directives about layout. For example the tag for an element "figure" (which might not itself be coded in SGML), will generally carry with it some attribute values indicating its size and position, as a guide to the formatting software.

Or consider the element "ordered list", consisting of one or more items, each labelled with a number or letter. One advantage of generic mark-up is that the author creating a document need not decide immediately how that list is to be laid out – it can be left to the publisher to say whether there should be a blank line between each item, and whether they should be labelled with arabic or roman numerals, upper or lower case letters. However if the author wants to be more specific he can set some appropriate attribute values. A document definition giving him this opportunity might include the following rules:

```
<!ELEMENT ol (li+) >
<!ATTLIST ol format (compact | spaced) compact >
<!ATTLIST ol label (arabic | roman | alpha) arabic >
<!ELEMENT li #PCDATA >
<!ATTLIST li id ID #IMPLIED >
<!ELEMENT xref EMPTY >
<!ATTLIST xref refid IDREF #REQUIRED >
```

These rules define three elements, each with an associated attribute list. Look first at the ordered list, which has two possible attributes, a *format* and *label*. Format can be *compact* or *spaced*, label can be *arabic*, *roman*, etc. The values outside the brackets, *compact* and *arabic*, are the defaults. The author marking-up a text may choose any option, for example:

<ol format=spaced, label=alpha> <li> Asparagus Soup
<li> Mushroom Omelette <li> Apple Pie <li> Coffee </ol>

would cause the items to be output with a blank line in between and labelled a, b, c, and d. (Note that end-tags for list items can safely be omitted here.) An SGML-based processor could automatically generate labels in ascending order, and if in a later draft some items were inserted, deleted or re-ordered this would again be taken care of.

Cross-referencing.   The other attribute lists in the rules above show a further useful SGML facility: automatic handling of cross-references. Suppose the author wanted to refer to one of the items, but at the time of writing did not know exactly where it would come in the list or how it would be labelled. The solution would be to assign it a unique identifier through attribute "id", and then use the same identifier when referring to it. For example, given:

<ol format=spaced, label=alpha>
<li id=asp> Asparagus Soup <li> Mushroom Omelette
<li> Apple Pie <li> Coffee </ol>
<p> The soup mentioned in item <xref refid=asp) is made from asparagus grown in our own gardens. </p>

an SGML-based processor could translate element "xref" into a reference to the item label associated with identifier "asp".

Note the form of the relevant element and attribute definitions here. Element "xref" has a definition of EMPTY – no actual text goes into it as it is just a linking device. No set of possible values can be given for attributes "id" and "refid" – these must be unique names chosen by the author when making the linkage. Attribute "id" is not always needed since there may be no reference to a list item, so it is declared as IMPLIED, meaning that it can if necessary be system-generated. On the other hand "refid" is REQUIRED, since the only point in having an "xref" element is as a vehicle for this attribute.

This looks like an over-complex mechanism for a trivial example, but it would be useful in lengthy documents with much cross-referencing of different kinds, particularly those subject to extensive redrafting and refor-matting. Then the ability to set up linkages once and for all through unique identifiers could avoid many problems, since cross-references would not need editing if page, section or item numbers were altered. Note also that if the document was converted into hypertext format, the identifiers could act as anchors (sources and destinations) for hot links.

Other SGML Language Features

The above sections have given only a flavour of basic SGML; any reader needing to produce document definitions or use mark-up is referred to [2] and [3]. The full language has many other features, e.g.

- The ability to import complete *file entities* into a document. These may be "subdocuments" which themselves contain SGML coded text. Space can be allocated for non-SGML coded figures or illustrations, using directives which set attribute values to indicate their size and shape.
- The ability to define *marked sections*. Where different versions of a document are being produced, such sections may be included or omitted according to INCLUDE or IGNORE directives in the document definition.
- The ability to define *ranked elements*, for example the four levels of heading *h1, h2, h3* and *h4*. As the document is parsed, any tag consisting only of the stem "h" without a numeric suffix is by default given the same rank as its predecessor. Moreover several elements may be put into a *ranked group*, so that, for instance, paragraphs take on the rank of the section in which they occur. This offers the possibility of consistent automatic labelling and indenting when text is formatted.

Clearly SGML provides a sophisticated method for logical document description, making distinctions which would not be possible at the procedural level. Whereas a a conventionally marked-up document might use italics for certain headings, for references to glossary items, and for general emphasis, one coded in SGML could identify each feature separately, allowing decisions about how to present it to be made independently. That is the point most often made by the advocates of SGML. On the other hand defining and marking-up documents is hard work, and accurate structural description is not an end in itself but a means of producing texts for printing, or perhaps for storage and retrieval. So there is a need to consider not only the language itself but the type of document for which its use is appropriate, and the software required to support that use.

SGML in Use: Creating and Formatting Documents

The design of SGML is based on the assumption that an author applies tags to a text which is then checked by a parser, formatted, and printed. Of these three tasks, only the parsing is actually defined by the ISO standard. In principle tags can be inserted using any word processor or editor, but it is now possible to obtain intelligent software to aid the process by allowing mark-up selection through function keys or menus, limiting the author to tags which are legal in the current context. Alternatively internal control codes generated by popular word processors or desktop publishing packages can be converted to SGML-type mark-up, giving a text in software-independent form which will remain usable with any later technology.

The job of an SGML parser is to check that a document's structure conforms to the relevant definition. This may include inserting omitted tags, making substitutions for locally defined text entities, and ensuring that cross-reference identifiers are unique and match up properly. Other necessary tasks are not strictly speaking part of the parsing process, and require the use of ancillary software before the final formatting stage. These might include, for instance, automatically generating list-item labels, and inserting actual cross-references into the text. (Where such references included things like page numbers, it would not of course be possible to do so until formatting was completed.)

One approach might be to convert first to another mark-up system with the necessary processing power. Barron [4] comments that "it is an almost trivial exercise to map the tags of the BL starter set onto equivalent constructs in LaTeX or troff/mm format". Those systems will be considered more fully in the following chapter; for the moment it suffices to say that they are text-formatters which produce procedural mark-up and, indirectly, actual printer control instructions. They also have full programming language features like variables and control structures, and so can handle such jobs as relocating citation elements, generating successive list item or section numbers, and so on. In practice, however, they are more often used by members of the academic computing community than professional printers; and in that context may well be considered as alternatives rather than adjuncts to SGML.

Within the SGML standard itself, two other mechanisms are relevant to the issue of document formatting. Firstly, the marked-up document may include bracketed *processing instructions* which are ignored by the parser but are in effect typesetting codes. This is not recommended as it reduces the portability of the document, but it may prove a practical necessity in some cases.

Secondly, *concurrent document structures* may be set up by the designer, giving two or more different document type definitions, each with its own tag structure. A text could then be marked-up simultaneously according to each set of rules – a useful option, for instance, if it had to be both printed and stored in a database. Concurrent document structures may also, via *link* declarations, be used to direct the mapping of logical elements like chapters and paragraphs onto physical elements like pages. Reference [3] gives details of these features, which obviously involve some very detailed design decisions. A different approach to the problem of associating logical and layout structures will be discussed later, in the context of ODA.

Apart from SGML, two related standards are in preparation by the ISO: Document Style Semantics and Specification Language (DSSSL) and Standard Page Description Language (SPDL). Like SGML they are interchange formats, but address lower level concepts of formatting and page layout. Eventually it should be possible to convert from the most abstract document description to specific printer directives, using nothing but standard languages all the way. Meanwhile commercial software is already available to assist in the process of creating, parsing and formatting tagged documents. The ultimate success of these products (and of the SGML standard) will be proved when authors routinely generate logical mark-up without being aware of it (because intelligent word processors handle the tagging behind the scenes), and professional printers routinely use the result without further manual intervention.

As things stand now, however, the use of SGML does impose extra overheads, and it is probably worth while only under certain conditions, i.e.

- There are many documents with a similar structure, so it is worth the trouble of creating document definitions (or modifying existing definitions like the BL starter set).
- The document structure itself is complex, so automatic parsing is a useful aspect of quality control.
- The documents are destined for long term use, perhaps involving periodic redrafting, or the construction of variant versions by selection or merging.
- There is a requirement to transmit the material between different organisations, output it in different formats, or consult it on different media (e.g. in print and as a hypertext/database).

We now give brief accounts of two actual text processing applications involving SGML, where at least some of the above considerations were relevant.

The *Oxford English Dictionary*

Chapter 2 of this book described one lexicographic project involving computers; a more recent and well-publicised example is the production of the second edition of the *Oxford English Dictionary* (OED). The OED is intended to be a complete historical record of English language usage from the twelfth century onward. Its first 12-volume edition was finally completed in 1928, and four supplement volumes were published between 1958 and 1986. The objective of the new OED project, carried out between 1984 and 1989, was to produce a new edition incorporating both the original and supplement volumes, together with definitions for 5000 new words and usages which had entered the language more recently.

For the new material, the lexicographers made some use of concordances and searches of machine-readable text, but the role played by this sort of information was much smaller than in the case of the Cobuild project. OED entries carry extensive quotations from printed sources, but these are traditionally supplied by a large body of volunteers who note new words and usages during their reading and send them, with their references, to the lexicographers. The use of computer technology therefore centred on the *merging* of existing dictionary texts, and the *editing* required to produce a new printed edition. At the same time it was intended that the text be stored permanently in electronic form to allow for subsequent revisions and for use as a publicly available database.

A full account of the project objectives and how they were satisfied appears in the introductory section to the first volume of the dictionary itself. From this it is clear that the use of logical mark-up was a central feature of the work:

"It was resolved that the tagging language inserted into the electronic version should do more than simply express the typographical features – layout, typeface, type size, font – of the printed text. It must, as its primary function, identify the structural elements which combine to form a dictionary entry. This was a prerequisite both for the development of the database in the future, and, as it turned out, for the automatic processes applied to the text in the course of integration" [5].

Entries in the supplement volumes were of two kinds; they either defined completely new words or phrases, or specified addition, deletion, transference or substitution in respect of an existing entry. The supplement could therefore be considered as a giant "transaction file" updating records in a "main file" holding the original dictionary. The "key" to an entry comprised a *headword*, and, if the headword was not unique, a *part-of-speech* and *homonym* number. Having found that, the modification could apply to any part of the entry. Using logically marked-up versions of both main and supplement dictionary records, it proved possible to carry out 80 per cent of the merging processes automatically.

The first consideration was the very labour intensive task of data capture. In its printed form the structure of a dictionary entry is expressed using both explicit *labels* (a, b, c, etc.) and *typography* (bold type, capitals, italics, etc.). Optical scanning with text of this complexity was not a practical proposition, so it was all entered manually. The full process involved: copy editing to add minimal logical mark-up to the printed originals, keyboarding, several levels of proofreading, and the application of an SGML parser to produce fully tagged text. Examples of such mark-up, on original OED entries, can be seen in [6] and [7].

The original dictionary structure proved to be so regular that it was possible to produce an SGML document type definition which covered all but very minor variations. The analysis identified between forty and fifty important elements which must be recognised in order to carry out the integration task successfully. We now consider a few specific examples of the tagging, to illustrate the practical use of the SGML elements, attributes and entities described earlier in this chapter.

OED Elements

The principal document element is an <*entry*>, which has four main functions. The first is to identify the basic form under which the word is looked up – the *headword lemma* <*hwlem*>, and its pronunciation <*pron*>; also if applicable its part of speech <*pos*>, homonym number <*hom*> and references to variant forms <*vf*>. Then comes the *etymology*, and *definitions* for each sense and subsense of the headword, with *quotations* illustrating actual instances of those senses in use.

The dictionary aims to show every variation in meaning for each word in the language, not only at the present day but over the last eight hundred years. So it is not surprising that entries for words with a long and complex history are highly nested structures. The mark-up uses ranked sense tags *<sen1>*, *<sen2>*, *<sen3>* etc. to indicate the level of nesting, and the printed dictionary has eight different series of labels to mark the sense-divisions of an entry, each with a slightly different significance. (See "Ordering of Senses" within the "General Explanations" of [5]).

Further nesting occurs within each division; e.g. a set of quotations for a particular sense has the structure:

```
<qpara>                                          (newline)
    <quot>
        <qdat> quotation-date </qdat>            (bold)
        <auth> author           </auth>         (capital)
        <wk>    work            </wk>           (italic)
        <qtxt> quotation-text  </qtext>        (roman)
    </quot>
    <quot>
        etc.
</qpara>
```

The mark-up is mapped onto different printing styles as indicated above, so that readers of the dictionary (which is quite densely packed) can distinguish each item easily. In the equivalent IR database, the tagging allows for retrieval on individual field values, e.g. to identify all quotations from Dickens.

OED use of Attributes for Handling Cross-references

The "etymology" element gives a word's history, showing earlier forms from which it was derived (perhaps in other languages like Latin or French) and words with which it has a close family relationship. This requires the use of cross-references, and hence of the unique identifier attributes already mentioned in the general discussion of SGML. The example entry in [6] shows the following elements in use:

```
<etym>                                          [
    <cf> cited form </cf>                       (italics)
    <xra id= ?? >
        <xlem> cross-referenced lemma </xlem>  (bold)
        <pos>  part of speech </pos>           (italics)
        <hom> homonym number </hom>            (superscript)
    </xra>
</etym>                                          ]
```

Although the combination of lemma (headword), part-of-speech and homonym number may be needed as the unique "key" to a referenced entry, part-of speech and homonym number are optional. Note also that an etymology element may contain any number of cited forms in any order. So the SGML mechanisms to specify sequence, selection, iteration, optionality and aggregation in element definitions would be required here. In fact complete etymology elements may appear at several positions in an entry, with opening and closing tags being mapped to bold square brackets each time.

Not all cross-references are etymological; they may appear also in the parts of the sense definitions, where similar tagging is again required. (It is estimated that there are around 600 000 in the dictionary as a whole.) Each one was assigned a unique numeric identifier by the parser as it created the fully tagged dictionary text, and these identifiers played a vital role in the merging process.

Obviously any reference must match a corresponding entry elsewhere in the dictionary, and as we have seen a combination of *headword, part of speech* and *homonym number* may be needed to identify such an entry uniquely. Some references go further and point at a particular sense *division* within an entry. However one consequence of merging the supplement with the original dictionary, and of adding new words, was to alter the sense division structure of some entries or to insert new homonyms for existing main words (e.g. "bit" in its computing/information-theory sense). This in turn could have the effect of changing or making ambiguous the original target of a cross-reference.

To solve this problem, details of all cross-references generated by the parser were saved onto a file, also details of entry "keys" changed by the merging process. This data was used to match up references with their targets, and either to adjust them automatically or to provide information enabling the lexicographers to do it. Software was also used to check for unsatisfied cross-references between entries, making the new edition of the dictionary more accurate. It is worth noting also that the presence of cross-reference tags in the text could enable automatic link-following in a future hypertext version of the dictionary.

OED use of Embedded Entities for Special Characters

"Between them, the two parent texts (the original dictionary and the supplement) make use of approximately 660 characters apart from the ninety or so available on the typical keyboard. Virtually all these have been retained and some previously wrong have been corrected" [5]. Special characters include those from non-Roman scripts like Greek and Hebrew, and symbols from mathematics, music and astrology. They were first represented by arbitrary numeric codes (see examples in [6]) but converted to SGML-type mnemonic entity references by the parser.

Special characters are particularly important in the part of the entry containing phonetic symbols to define pronunciation. The example entry in [7], for instance, has embedded entities &*breve*. (marking a short vowel), &*mac*. (macron, marking a long vowel), and &*sylab*. (marking a stressed syllable). These formed part of the conventions used in the original OED for representing pronunciation, whereas for the new edition it was decided to convert from this now outdated system to the International Phonetic Alphabet. The SGML tagging within the pronunciation section enabled a large part of that task to be performed automatically, using look-up tables [5].

Overall, then, the use of logical mark-up proved very helpful for the numerous processes which went towards the creation of an integrated OED. The database remains available as a source for smaller selective dictionaries, and for future extended and revised editions of the OED itself. It also of course has great potential for consultation in electronic rather than printed form. At the time of writing a CD-ROM version of the original first edition is on sale for use on a PC; as well as allowing conventional look-up by headword this provides searches through eight extra indexes, so that one can, for example, find all definitions, etymologies or quotations in which a particular word or name occurs.

The new integrated version will also be commercially available on CD, and is expected to have a greatly extended range of search facilities. Reference [7] considers, for example, how to provide a full hypertext interface. The discussion focuses on two issues: (i) how to fragment the text into discrete units given the enormous variation in entry length, and (ii) the desirability of providing automatic link-following for explicit cross-references. We have already noted that the dictionary mark-up would provide a basis for link-following, although the author of [7] expresses some doubt of its value. What may be more useful is *dynamic fragmentation*, allowing users to take *selective* views of long dictionary entries; here again the structural mark-up will support this very well.

The OED is obviously a textual database with a potentially infinite life, and one which is likely to grow in size over the years since new information will be added but very little, if any, thrown away. In these circumstances the investment of intellectual effort in logical mark-up was clearly worthwhile. Our next example concerns text with a similarly long life and wide application: the English law.

Her Majesty's Stationery Office: Statutory Instruments

HMSO is the Government department responsible for official publications, and in particular Parliamentary Bills, Acts, Statutes in Force, and Statutory Instruments. These might be considered the ultimate in technical documentation, since they specify exactly how public affairs are to be conducted and are subject to rigorous acceptance procedures. Obviously they have a complex and strictly controlled structure. An important characteristic of the British legal system is that when a law is amended it is not normally changed and re-issued in full; instead a new Act or Statutory Instrument is produced, referring to the previous text, and specifying the additions, deletions and modifications to be made to it. This results in a very complex network of cross-references across the body of legislation.

HMSO has made its material available in electronic form for twenty years, and was one of the first organisations to adopt a system of logical mark-up rather than pure typesetting codes [8]. As mentioned in Chapter 4 of this book, the earliest examples of full-text retrieval databases were set up to serve the legal profession, and in fact the original database for the Status IR system discussed in Chapter 4 was derived from the logically marked-up text for Statutes in Force. However the mark-up conventions used for that purpose were internal to the organisations concerned. Since HMSO has many actual and potential customers for its material it had a strong interest in the establishment of a standard in this area, and was represented on the ISO working party responsible for developing SGML.

The first application of the SGML standard within HMSO was for the production of Statutory Instruments. These are known as "secondary legislation"; they incorporate regulations which are not considered in detail by Parliament, but passed on the basis of some existing Act or "primary legislation". One of their possible functions, as suggested above, is to introduce additions and amendments to existing legislation.

Reference [8] gives a brief account of the work involved. For an experimental period, experienced typesetters preparing Statutory Instruments for publication were asked to include logical mark-up as well, on the basis of detailed document specifications. In the second stage, the typesetters have reverted to their traditional role, with software being used to generate SGML tags by recognising typesetting codes and fixed textual content. (There are of course very strong constraints on the wording and structure of these particular documents.) The eventual objective is that mark-up will be incorporated at the time when the legislation is drafted, using intelligent software to insert tags automatically.

HMSO is now able to sell copies of marked-up text to organisations who, subject to copyright negotiations, can use the data as they wish. Meanwhile within the Lord Chancellor's Department, preparations are being made to set up a database of UK Law for the government legal service, using as its source the electronic versions of legislation prepared and accumulated over the years by HMSO. This will enable parliamentary draftsmen producing new legislation to access all preceding material which is relevant to it. A complete database of this kind would contain approximately 1.5 gigabytes of raw data. An important requirement will be to retain the dependency relationships between pieces of legislation (e.g. C amends B which amends A), so that anyone consulting the database can see the state of the law either at the present day or at any given time in the past.

In the longer term, there is obviously also potential for publishing the material in database form. Already an official legal database (CELEX) exists for European Community law, available both on-line and on CD-ROM – an equivalent product for British legislation would clearly have a strong public and commercial interest.

SGML Coding

```
<scheds>
<sch>
<nsch>SCHEDULE
<ref>Article_6(1)
<d1>
<h1>Formula_for_determining_payments_to_be_m
ade_by_the_Residuary_Body
<t1>The_formula_for_each_financial_year_comm
encing_with_the_financial_year_beginning_1st
_April_1986_is&enrule;
<formula>
<f3>PY
<f4>
<f5>Z
<f2>&plus;
<f3>RS
<f4>
<f5>T
<where>_where&enrule;
<d2>
<t2>P_is_ascertained_by_applying_the_formula
&enrule;
<formula>
<f2>E&minus;
<f3>GH
<f4>
<f5>J
<where>_where&enrule;
<d2>
<t2>E_is_an_amount_equal_to_the_housing_rece
ipts_for_the_financial_year_in_question,_les
s&enrule;
<d3>
<n3>(a)
<t3>the_amount_which_is_attibutable_to_the_r
epayment_of_housing_advances,_other_than_rei
mbursable_capital_money;
<d3>
<n3>(b)
<t3>an_amount_equal_to_that_part_of_the_reim
bursable_capital_money_received_in_that_year
_which_is_atributable_to_housing_receipts;
<d3>
<n3>(c)
<t3>an_amount_equal_to_the_expenditure_incur
red_by_the_Residual_Body_in_that_year_for_fa
cilitating_the_disposal_of_housing_assets;_a
nd
<d3>
<n3>(d)
<t3>an_amount_equal_to_loans_outstanding_imm
ediately_before_the_first_day_of_that_year_w
hich_that_Body_had_raised_for_the_purpose_of
_financing_expenditure_incurred_by_them_for_
facilitating_the_disposal_of_housing_assets;
<d2>
<t2>G_is_the_amount_paid_in_that_year_by_vir
tue_of_article_5;
<d2>
<t2>H_is_the_amount_equal_to_the_housing_rec
eipts_for_that_year_which_are_attributable_t
o_the_disposal_of_housing_assets;_and
```

```
<d2>
<t2>J_is_the_amount_equal_to_the_direct_capi
tal_receipts_for_that_year_which_are_attribu
table_to_the_disposal_of_relevant_land;
</formula>
<d2>
<t2>R_is_ascertained_by_applying_the_formula
&enrule;
<formula>
<f2>F&minus;
<f3>GK
<f4>
<f5>J
<where>_where&enrule;
<d2>
<t2>F_is_an_amount_equal_to_the_direct_capit
al_receipts_for_that_year_which_are_not_hous
ing_receipts,_less&enrule;
<d3>
<n3>(a)
<t3>the_amount_which_is_attributable_to_the_
repayment_of_the_advances_referred_to_in_art
icle_2(2)(a)(ii)_which_are_not_housing_advan
ces,_other_than_reimbursable_capital_money;
<d3>
<n3>(b)
<t3>an_amount_equal_to_that_part_of_the_reim
bursable_capital_money_received_in_that_year
_which_is_atributable_to_housing_receipts;
<d3>
<n3>(c)
<t3>an_amount_equal_to_the_expenditure_incur
red_by_the_Residual_Body_in_that_year_for_fa
cilitating_the_disposal_of_other_property_an
d_relevant_land_other_than_housing_assets;_a
nd
<d3>
<n3>(d)
<t3>an_amount_equal_to_loans_outstanding_imm
ediately_before_the_first_day_of_that_year_w
hich_that_Body_had_raised_for_the_purpose_of
_financing_expenditure_incurred_by_them_for_
facilitating_the_disposal_of_other_property_
and_relevant_land_other_than_housing_assets;
<d2>
<t2>K_is_the_amount_equal_to_the_direct_capi
tal_receipts_for_that_year_which_are_attribu
table_to_the_disposal_of_relevant_land_but_w
hich_are_not_housing_receipts;_and
</formula>
<d2>
<t2>Y,_Z,_S_and_T_have_the_same_meaning_as_i
n_article_4:
</formula>
```

[Spaces are represented by the underline character]

Fig. 10.1a. SGML coding for a statutory instrument.

1982 No. 39

SOCIAL SECURITY

The Child Benefit (Determination of Claims and Questions) Amendment Regulations 1982

Made - - - -	*15th January 1982*
Laid before Parliament	*25th January 1982*
Coming into force	*15th February 1982*

The Secretary of State for Social Services, in exercise of the powers conferred by section 7 of the Child Benefit Act 1975(a) and of all other powers enabling him in that behalf, after consultation with the Council on Tribunals in accordance with section 10 of the Tribunals and Inquiries Act 1971(b), hereby makes the following Regulations:

Citation, commencement and interpretation

1.—(1) These Regulations may be cited as the Child Benefit (Determination of Claims and Questions) Amendment Regulations 1982 and shall come into force on 15th February 1982.

(2) In these Regulations "the principal regulations" means the Child Benefit (Determination of Claims and Questions) Regulations 1976(c).

Insertion of regulation 6A in the principal regulations

2. After regulation 6 of the principal regulations there is inserted the following regulation –

"**Withdrawal of appeals to local tribunals**

6A.—(1) A person who has appealed to a local tribunal in accordance with regulation 5(1) may withdraw his appeal –

 (a) by giving written notice of intention to withdraw to the tribunal before the date fixed for the hearing of the appeal, if the insurance officer gives his written consent to such withdrawal before the hearing begins, or

 (b) by request made to the chairman of the tribunal for leave to withdraw, if the chairman at a hearing of the tribunal gives leave.

(2) A notice of intention to withdraw an appeal, or a declaration made by or on behalf of the appellant of his desire to withdraw an appeal, may be treated as a request for leave within paragraph (1) (b)."

Amendment of regulation 12 of the principal regulations

3. At the beginning of regulation 12(2) of the principal regulations (persons to be ordered to withdraw while local tribunals consider their decisions or discuss procedure), for the words "For the purposes of arriving at their decision or discussing any question of

(a) 1975 c.61.   (b) 1971 c.62.   (c) S I 1976/962 to which there are amendments not relevant to these Regulations.

[SS81/961]

Fig. 10.1b. Equivalent printed text.

Examples

We now consider a few detailed examples of mark-up in this context, based on reference [9]. The requirements in some cases are rather similar to those of the

OED, but there are some interesting extra features as well.

A "statutory instrument" *<si>*, contains five main elements:

- Text of footnotes.
- Begin section (banner, title, etc.).
- Main regulations.
- Schedules (detailed lists and tables of data).
- End section (explanatory note and ISBN).

Fig. 10.1 shows some marked-up text with the corresponding printed version, and illustrates how the first three of these elements are coded. Firstly, all footnotes are placed at the start of the document. Each is given a unique identifier attribute which will be used in subsequent references to it. Identifiers

SGML Coding

[Spaces are represented by the underline character]

```
<t_cols="c7">
<nt>Table_1:
<ht>Junior_Counsel
<hc>
<r>
<c>Court
<c>Type_of_proceedings
<c>Basic_fee
<c>Full_day_refresher_course
<hc>
<r>
<c_strad="s3">Subsidiary_fees
<r>
<c>Attendance_at_consultations,_conferen
ces_&amp;_views
<c>Written_work
<c>Attendance_at_pre-trial_reviews,_appl
ications_and_other_appearances
</hc>
</hc>
<bt>
<r>
<c>Magistrates'_Court
<c>All_cases
<c>Maximum_amount:_&pound;290
<c>Maximum_amount:_&pound;110
<c>&pound;17_per_hour_Minimum_amount:_&p
ound;9
<c>Maximum_amount:_&pound;35
<c>Maximum_amount:_&pound;65
<r>
<c>Crown_Court
<bt>
<r>
<c>Jury_trials
<c>Maximum_amount:_&pound;350
<r>
<c>Cases_prepared_for_trial_in_which_no_
jury_is_sworn
<c>Maximum_amount:_&pound;200
```

```
<r>
<c>Guilty_pleas
<c>Maximum_amount:_&pound;120
<r>
<c>Appeals_against_conviction
<c>Standard_fee:_&pound;70_Maximum_amoun
t:_&pound;135
<c>Standard_fee:_&pound;85_Maximum_amoun
t:_&pound;120
<c>&pound;19_per_hour_Minimum_amount:_&p
ound;10
<c>Maximum_amount:_&pound;40
<c>Maximum_amount:_&pound;67
<r>
<c>Appeal_against_sentence
<c>Standard_fee:_&pound;50_Maximum_amoun
t:_&pound;70
<r>
<c>Committals_for_sentence
<c>Standard_fee:_&pound;45_Maximum_amoun
t:_&pound;70
</bt>
</bt>
</t>
```

Fig. 10.2a. SGML coding for a table.

Table 1: Junior Counsel

Court	Type of proceedings	Basic fee	Full day refresher course	Subsidiary fees		
				Attendance at consultations, conferences & views	*Written work*	*Attendance at pre-trial reviews, applications and other appearances*
Magistrates' Court	All cases	Maximum amount: £110	Maximum amount: £290	£17 per hour Minimum amount: £9	Maximum amount: £35	Maximum amount: £65
Crown Court	Jury trials	Maximum amount: £350				
	Cases prepared for trial in which no jury is sworn	Maximum amount: £200				
	Guilty pleas	Maximum amount: £120	Standard fee: £85 Maximum amount: £120	£19 per hour Minimum amount: £10	Maximum amount: £40	Maximum amount: £67
	Appeals against conviction	Standard fee: £70 Maximum amount: £135				
	Appeal against sentence	Standard fee: £50 Maximum amount: £70				
	Committals for sentence	Standard fee: £45 Maximum amount: £70				

Fig. 10.2b. Equivalent printed table.

SGML Coding

```
<si>
<tfnotes>
<dept>[SS81/961]
<tfn_num="f001">1975_c._61.
<tfn_num="f002">1971_c._62.
<tfn_num="f003">S.I._1976/962_to_which_th
ere_are_amendments_not_relevant_to_these_
Regulations.
<begin>
<ba>STATUTORY_INSTRUMENTS
<nu>1982_No._39
<sj>SOCIAL_SECURITY
<ti>The_Child_Benefit_(Determination_of_C
laims_and_Questions)_Amendment_Regulation
s_1982
<ma>Made
<da>15th_January_1982
<la>Laid_before_Parliament
<da>25th_January_1982
<co>Coming_into_force
<da>15th_February_1982
<pr>
<dl>
<t1>The_Secretary_of_State_for_Social_Ser
vices,_in_exercise_of_the_powers_conferre
d_by_section_7_of_the_Child_Benefit_Act_1
975
<fn_num="f001">_and_of_all_other_powers_e
nabling_him_in_that_behalf,_after_consult
ation_with_the_Council_on_Tribunals_in_ac
cordance_with_section_10_of_the_Tribunals
_and_Inquiries_Act_1971
<fn_num="f002">,_hereby_makes_the_followi
ng_Regulations:
<main>
<dl>
<h1>Citation,_commencement_and_interpreta
tion
<n1>1.
<t1>&emrule;
<d2>
<n2>(1)
<t2>These_regulations_may_be_cited_as_the
_Child_Benefit_(Determination_of_Claims_a
nd_Questions)_Amendment_Regulations_1982_
and_shall_come_into_force_on_15th_Februar
y_1982.
<d2>
<n2>(2)
<t2>In_these_regulations_
<q>the_principal_regulations
</q>_means_the_Child_Benefit_(Determinati
on_of_Claims_and_Questions)_Regulations_1
976
<fn_num="f003">.
<dl>
<h1>Insertion_of_regulation_6A_in_the_pri
ncipal_regulataions
<n1>2.
<t1>After_regulation_6_in_the_pricıpal_re
gulations_there_is_inserted_the_following
```

```
_regulation&enrule;
<lq>
<dl>
<h1>Withdrawal_of_appeals_to_local_tribuṇ
als
<n1>6A.
<t1>&emrule;
<d2>
<n2>(1)
<t2>A_person_who_has_appealed_to_a_local_
tribunal_in_accordance_with_regulation_5(
1)_may_withdraw_his_appeal&enrule;
<d3>
<n3>(a)
<t3>by_giving_written_notice_of_intention
_to_withdraw_to_the_tribunal_before_the_d
ate_fixed_for_the_hearing_of_the_appeal,_
if_the_insurance_officer_gives_his_writte
n_consent_to_such_withdrawal_before_the_h
earing_begins,_or
<d3>
<n3>(b)
<t3>by_request_made_to_the_chairman_of_th
e_tirbunal_for_leave_to_withdraw,_if_the_
chairman_at_a_hearing_of_the_tribunal_giv
es_leave.
<d2>
<n2>(2)
<t2>A_notice_of_intention_to_withdraw_an_
appeal,_or_a_declaration_made_by_or_on_be
half_of_the_appellant_of_his_desire_to_wi
thdraw_an_appeal,_may_be_treated_as_a_req
uest_for_leave_within_paragraph_(1)(b).
</lq>
<dl>
<h1>Amendment_of_regulation_12_of_the_pri
ncipal_regulations
<n1>3.
<t1>At_the_beginning_of_regulation_12(2)_
of_the_principal_regulations_(persons_to_
be_ordered_to_withdraw_while_local_tribun
als_consider_their_decisions_or_discuss_p
rocedure),_for_the_words_
<q>For_the_purposes_of_arriving_at_their_
decision_or_discussing_any_question_of_
```

[Spaces are represented by the underline character]

Fig. 10.3a. SGML coding for formulae.

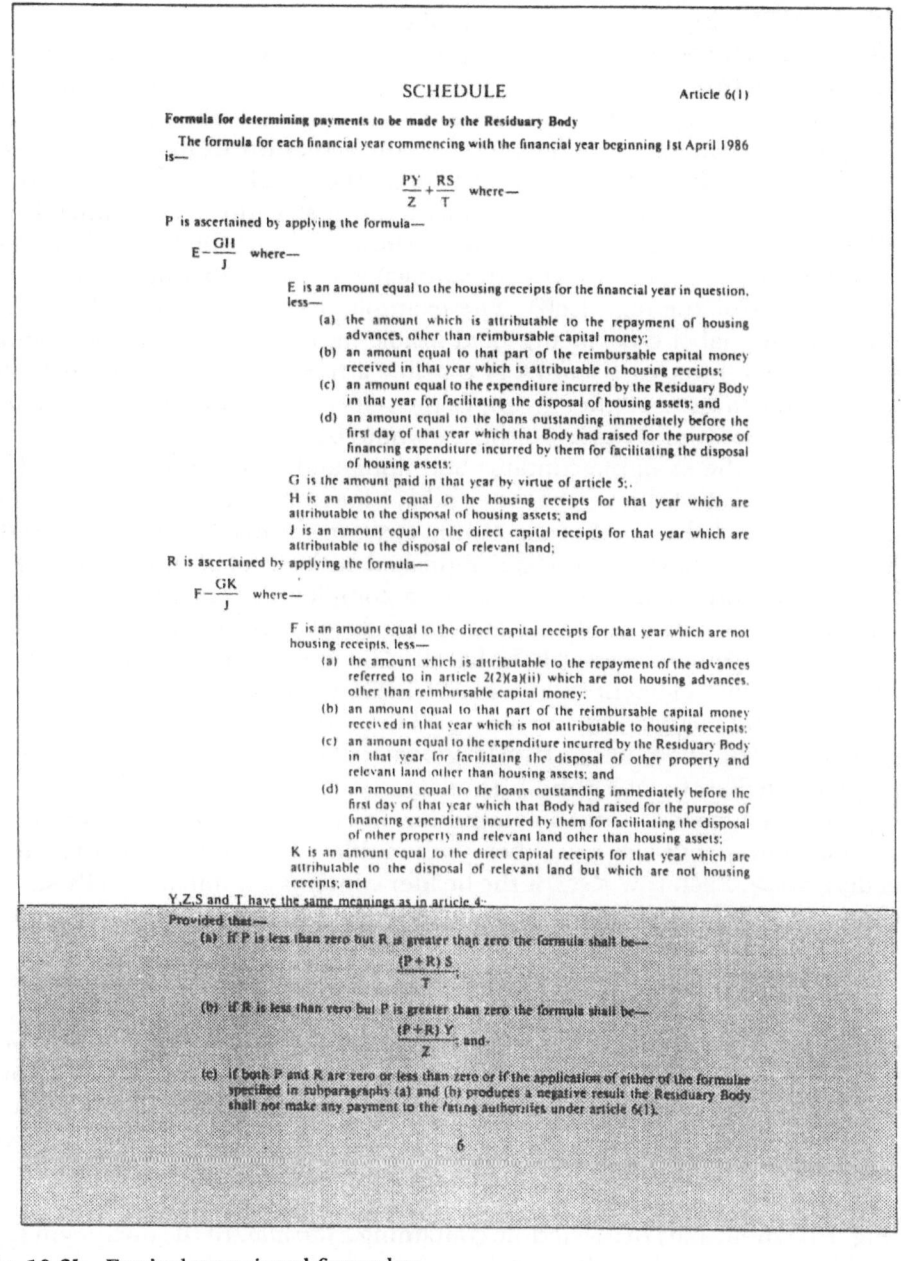

Fig. 10.3b. Equivalent printed formulae.

are numbers in ascending sequence; in the printed text the footnotes are labelled (a), (b), (c), etc. with the alphabetic sequence starting afresh on each new page.

The *<begin>* element in this example contains the banner (STATUTORY INSTRUMENTS), the instrument number, the subject, the title, three dates, and a preamble. Some elements are optional, for example not all dates need be present. Note that in back-conversion from procedural to logical mark-up it would be necessary to look at not only typesetting codes (which do not distinguish each element uniquely) but at the actual words in the text as well.

The main regulations consist, in the simplest case, of a series of "divisions". As with the OED entry, there is a hierarchical structure, with ranked tags *<d1>*, *<d2>*, ... *<d5>* being used to show the current level of nesting. Associated tags are *<h1>–<h3>*, (headings), *<n1>–<n5>* (numbering), and *<t1>–<t5>* (for the text itself). The example here goes to three levels, the corresponding label types being bold arabic numerals, bracketed numerals, and bracketed lower case letters. A possible attribute for a heading is *loc* for location. Headings can either go above the relevant division (the default) or at the side – if the latter is required the tag would be *<h1 loc="side">*.

The text in the example contains both long and short quotations. A short quotation consists of simple character data; a long quotation may itself contain tags, and indeed the one here is a fully structured division in its own right. Typographically, however, it is distinguished by its level of indentation. This illustrates an important point – that in a complex document conversion in either direction between logical and procedural mark-up may be context-sensitive, and cannot necessarily be handled by simple replacement.

The "schedule" element of a statutory instrument contains detailed lists of conditions and actual data values to be used when applying the main regulations. The examples in Figs 10.2 and 10.3 show two new features being handled with SGML: tables and formulae.

A *table* has a tag *<t>*, and a compulsory attribute specifying its number of columns. It may have also a number *<nt>*, a title *<ht>*, and a series of column headers *<hc>*. Each row *<r>* of the header contains a number of cells *<c>* to be tabulated. Some cells may "straddle" several columns – this is indicated by using the cell attribute *strad*.

The body of a table *<bt>* also consists of a series of rows of cells. It may itself contain one or more "sub-tables", as in the current example. Here the cell holding the phrase "Crown Court" is immediately followed by a nested *<bt>* declaration preceding a table of fees for each type of proceeding in the Crown Court. So two closing tags *</bt>* are required, one for the inner body and one for the outer body. Tables of greater complexity are also handled, for example those which contain complete textual divisions, or are split into parts with continuous text between them.

Fig. 10.3 shows part of a schedule containing a *formula*. In the document type definition, a formula is declared as:

$$((((f1?, (f2 \mid (f3,f4,f5) \mid be)+) \mid ((f2 \mid (f3,f4,f5) \mid be)+, f1)), where?)$$

The "where" element is a piece of text defining the parameters used in the formula (which may in turn introduce other formulae), and *<be>* stands for "bracketed element", whose definition is similar to that for the formula itself. Elements f1–f5 are simple formula components such that in the expression:

$$F1 = F2 + \frac{F3}{F5}$$

F1 would be tagged as <f1>, F2 as <f2>, etc. and <f4> tags a line dividing elements of type f3 and f5. This definition covers a large class of possible formulae; anything more complex is handled by inserting a non-SGML coded element with attributes to show its depth and width.

Figs 10.1–10.3 show a few embedded entities for special characters, i.e. *&pound*; *&plus*; *&emrule*; and *&enrule*;. In general HMSO document type definitions use publicly declared sets of entries for this purpose, e.g. Added Latin, Numeric and Special Graphic, and Publishing. Some extras which proved necessary were *&min*; and *&sec*; (for minute and second signs) and *&dotfill*; used when laying out example pro-formas.

That concludes the tagging examples, and the discussion of SGML. The last part of this chapter gives a somewhat briefer account of the other ISO standard mentioned earlier: Office Document Architecture (also referred to more recently as Open Document Architecture).

Office Document Architecture

Contrasts with SGML

As its name implies, ODA is concerned with the kind of documents normally created and filed in offices – letters, invoices, reports, estimates, quotations, agreements – rather than commercially published and professionally printed material. Its purpose is to establish a standard format for such documents when they are passed electronically between different organisations, even though the facilities for processing and printing at each end are incompatible. If every system can translate into and out of this common intermediate format, it will never be necessary to write special software to make one-off direct conversions.

A standard to cover all the possible features supported by real document processing systems must obviously be quite far-reaching, and those responsible for defining it have been chasing a moving target over the last ten years. The early proposals in 1981 were quite modest, dealing with text-only documents printed in one column in a single fixed-pitch font. Their scope has gradually widened to take in the facilities provided by current desk-top publishing packages: multiple fonts, complex page layouts, graphics, and so on.

ODA is very much aimed at systems implementors rather than individual user organisations. The European Computer Manufacturers Association (ECMA) was prominent in the early discussions on the topic, and brought out a preliminary version of the standard in 1985. There have been close links with corresponding bodies within CCITT, and not surprisingly the Group 3/4 data compression standards were adopted in ODA for the transmission of raster graphics within documents. In general, the ODA standard can be thought of as sitting on top of the seventh, or "application" layer of the OSI/ISO reference model for data transmission, and calling upon the file transfer services provided at that level [10].

Most large computer manufacturers and suppliers express support for ODA and have developed, or are developing, products based on it for creating, transmitting and storing documents. However users of such products need not be aware of the internal ODA-type document structuring, any more than they are aware of standard message formats for communications networks. In particular, in the ODA data stream there is no real equivalent of the SGML tag which delimits document structures for both human reader and parsing software.

In its scope, the ODA standard differs from SGML in two important ways:

- It is concerned with more than textual data. The current version defines three so-called "content architectures": for *characters*, for *raster images*, and for geometric or *vector* graphics. There are proposals for other forms of information such as sound, and for data which is subject to numerical processing, like the contents of a spreadsheet.
- It provides a way of describing not just the logical structure of a document but its actual layout, and the mapping between logical and physical divisions which takes place when a text is formatted and displayed. A document formatted on one system can be received by another and isplayed in an equivalent way, even when the software and hardware are quite different at each end.

Reference [11] gives a useful overview of the differences betwen ODA and SGML.

Summary of the ODA Document Processing Model

The standard assumes an abstract model of what happens in document processing – any piece of software based on ODA must in a sense conform to this although detailed algorithms will obviously differ. Some basic assumptions are:

- In a file or data stream representing a document some data will stand for the *content* and some for the *structure*, and the two will be unambiguously distinguished.
- Content data will conform to the rules for one particular *architecture* – currently this may be character, raster graphics or geometric graphics.
- Structural descriptions are of two kinds – *logical* and *layout*. Documents may be represented in one of three ways:

processable form (content plus logical structure),

formatted form (content plus layout structure), or
formatted processable form (content plus both types of structural description).

Depending on the form, the document's recipient will be able to:

- Reprocess it by mapping the logical structure onto a different layout.
- Display it in the nearest equivalent to its original layout.
- Do both of the above.

Creating a document requires three main processes: *editing, formatting,* and *imaging*:

- If a document is in processable form, both its content and structure can be edited, although the standard does not define a set of editing functions.
- Formatting a document involves using its structural descriptions to decide how to lay out its content – a process which will be discussed in detail later.
- Imaging involves displaying the document on a device like a screen or printer. ODA defines some parameters which are used as input to this process but does not set out exactly how it is to be performed.

Fig. 10.4 shows a diagrammatic representation of the overall model.

As the above summary shows, the designers of the model tried to provide a framework for talking about all aspects of the document processing task, using a common terminology. Within this framework, the standard defines an *Office Document Interchange Format* (ODIF), used to encode all structural and content elements for transmission across a network.

To achieve document interchange between two unrelated systems A and B, one piece of software must translate files from A's internal format into the intermediate ODIF, and another one translate from ODIF to B's internal format. If the sending system is more advanced than the receiving system, it may not be possible to carry over all the document's characteristics accurately, but the standard provides for the use of fall-back features so as to capture as much information as possible.

In fact much of the activity undertaken by organisations contributing to the standard has involved defining different *Document Application Profiles* (DAP) which reflect particular levels of capability for sending and receiving systems. A DAP specifies a subset of features from the full ODA model, from those suitable for simple text-only word processors to those which support multiple fonts, graphics, complex layout facilities, structure-based editing, and so on. The intention is that when writing translation software for an existing system, a DAP should be chosen which will reflect its capabilities as closely as possible. New systems can of course be designed to use the full power of the ODA model.

There are, obviously, many possible issues to explore in connection with the ODA standard, and it will not be possible to deal with them all here. We now focus on the question of how the logical and layout structures for a document are defined, bringing out where possible the parallels with SGML. In order to make valid comparisons, the discussion will concentrate mainly on the character content architecture.

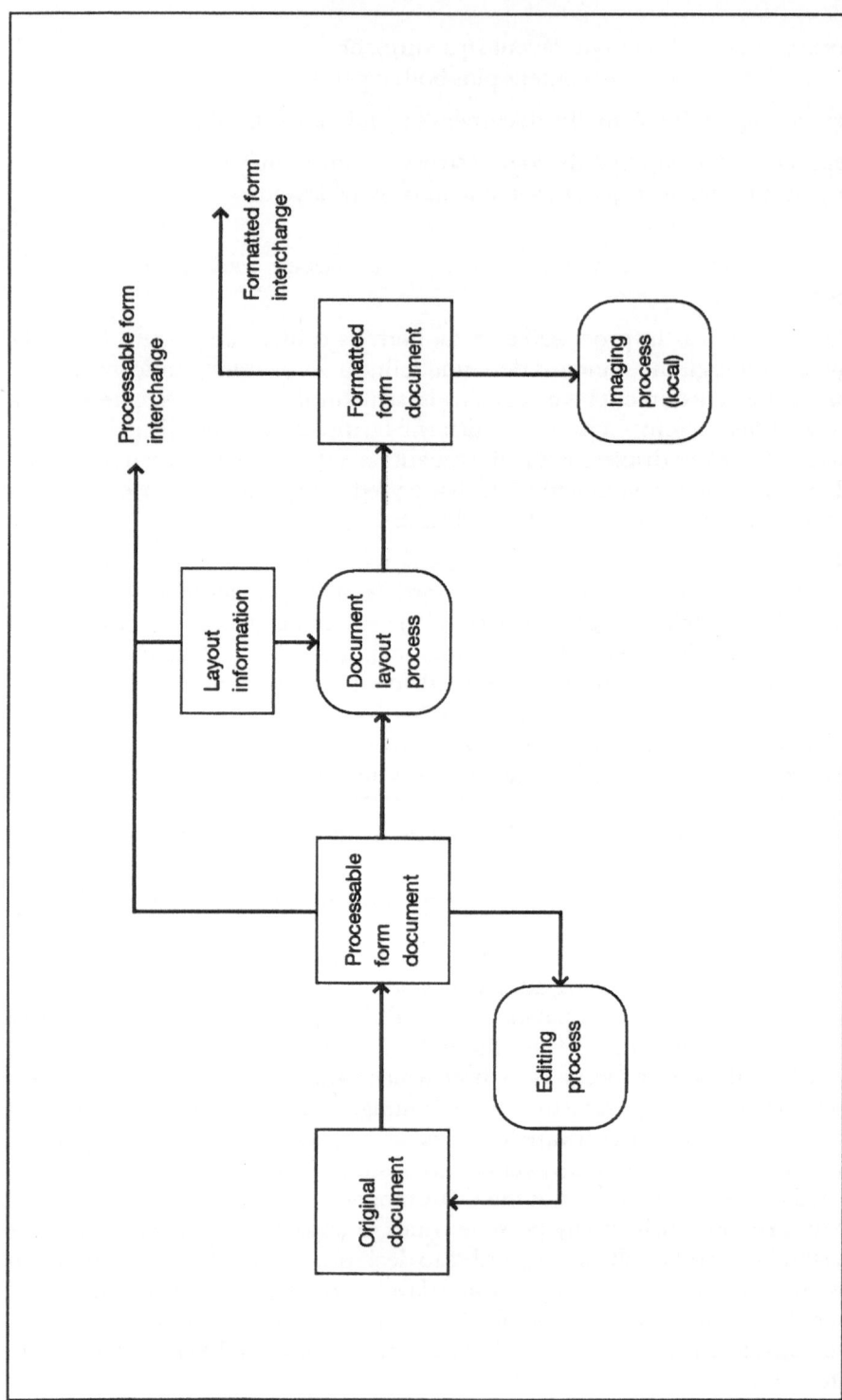

Fig. 10.4. Diagrammatic overview of the ODA processing model.

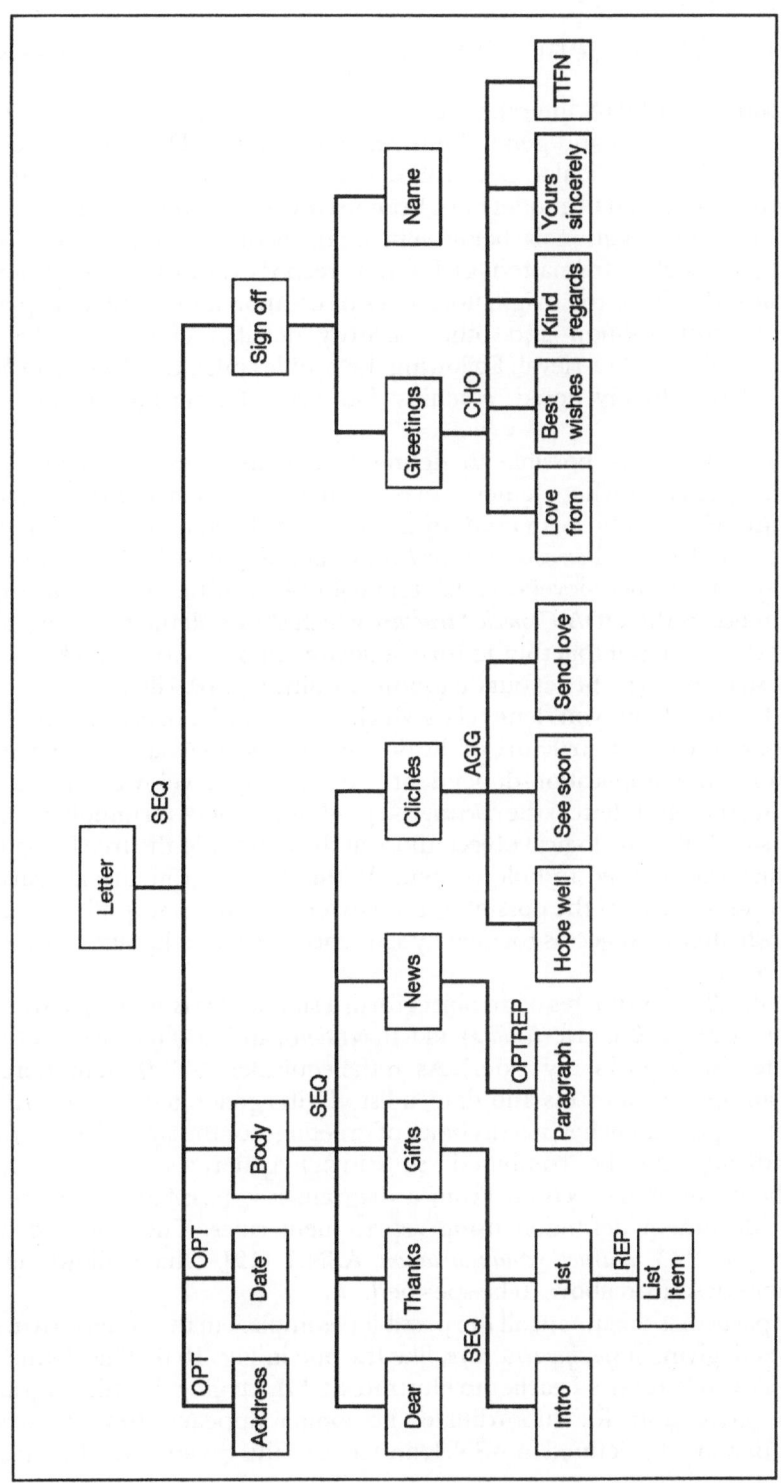

Fig. 10.5. An ODA generic logical structure.

Defining a Document: Generic and Specific Structures

Every document in ODA interchange format is preceded by a *document profile* providing identification and general information about it. The profile specifies, for example, which particular DAP the document conforms to, and therefore which features of the ODA model have been used when encoding it. It also states what structure information is being sent along with the content, i.e. is the document processable, formatted, or both? It records various *document management attributes*: details of the originator, dates of creation and revision, copyright information, authorisation and other security details, reference codes and keywords for filing and retrieval. Following the profile comes the document *body* – this, as we have already noted, contains data representing both content and structure.

As with SGML, it is possible to define a structure for a class of similar documents, specifying what elements may occur in documents of that class and how they are related. The term used for a document element in ODA is an *object*, and objects are described as *composite* or *basic* depending on whether or not they are built up out of lower-level objects. The equivalent to the SGML Document Type Definition is the ODA *Generic Structure* which shows all the possible ways in which objects can be put together to form a document of a particular class.

Generic structures can be set out diagrammatically. Fig. 10.5 illustrates an ODA definition for the "thank-you" letter class which we saw earlier in this chapter. Note that this shows the logical structure of the document, not its layout, and that logical object names are application-dependent. At the top level we have a box representing the whole letter: the *document-logical-root* in ODA terminology. Every other box stands for one logical object, those at the bottom of the tree being basic objects which can be used to hold content. Within the diagram are abbreviated words indicating which of the possible *generators for subordinates* is applicable at that point, i.e. whether an object is formed by sequence, selection, iteration etc. of the objects below it.

By default, all subordinates of an object form a simple SEQ (*sequence*). Otherwise we have OPT (*optionality*), CHO (*choice*), REP (*repetition*), and AGG (*aggregation* or set-subordinates can occur in any order). As in the equivalent SGML definition, our letter has an optional address and date, a list of gifts generated by repetition of items, a set of optional clichés, and a choice of greetings for the signoff. Generators for subordinates can be combined, so OPTREP generates "zero or more" paragraphs in the news section. From a diagram it is possible to generate an equivalent document definition using replacement rules. These are normally written in the ISO *abstract syntax notation* ASN.1 [12], which allows all the constructions described above to be specified.

For any particular document all the possibilities implicit in the generic structure must be fixed, giving a *specific structure*, like the one in Fig. 10.6. This defines the actual thank-you letter used earlier to illustrate SGML tagging. In this diagram of course the generators for subordinates no longer appear. However specific structures may also be defined in ASN.1, and in turn this notation can be encoded into a hexadecimal data stream, which is used for the actual document interchange format. A short example can be seen in [11], and there are more extensive examples in the standard itself, in particular Part 5 which defines the ODIF.

A *processable document* transmitted between systems carries a specific *structure description* along with some *content portions*. A generic structure description is also included, unless the receiving system already holds it and can match the incoming document against it. (This would be economical if many instances of the same document class were to be sent between two organisations.) It is possible also to define "common" or "generic" content portions: text or graphics which will occur with every instance of a particular object type, and therefore need only be defined and transmitted once. Examples might be a name and address appearing at the start of every letter sent by a company, or a copyright notice to go at the foot of each report page. In this respect common content portions are similar to SGML string entities.

So far, then, we have seen how ODA represents logical document structures with a descriptive mechanism basically similar to SGML. However ODA goes farther and provides an equivalent method for describing physical *layout*. We therefore find *generic layout structures*, which specify a framework for laying out all documents of a particular class, and *specific layout structures* associated with particular documents. Once again structures are made out of "objects" which are either "composite" or "basic", depending on whether or not they can be broken down further. The layout objects defined within the standard are:

- The document layout root (the whole document).
- The page-set (a group of related pages).
- The page (either basic or composite).
- The frame (an area of a composite page).
- The block (a basic object).

Obviously these objects have a hierarchical relationship – blocks appear within frames which appear within pages etc. However the number of levels in a structure is not fixed – for a class of documents the designer may choose whether to have page-sets or individual pages, whether a page is a basic object or a composite of frames and blocks, whether there can be frames within frames, etc. (Only pages and blocks are basic objects which can hold content portions directly.) He will often need to specify several types of each object; so for example a title page must be distinguishable from the pages following it, a page header block has different characteristics from a block in the body of the text.

As an illustration of these ideas Fig. 10.7 shows the generic layout structure for a letter which either fits onto one page or stretches over two or more. Once again *generators for subordinates* are used to show the various possibilities. There is obviously a correspondence with the generic logical structure shown in Fig.

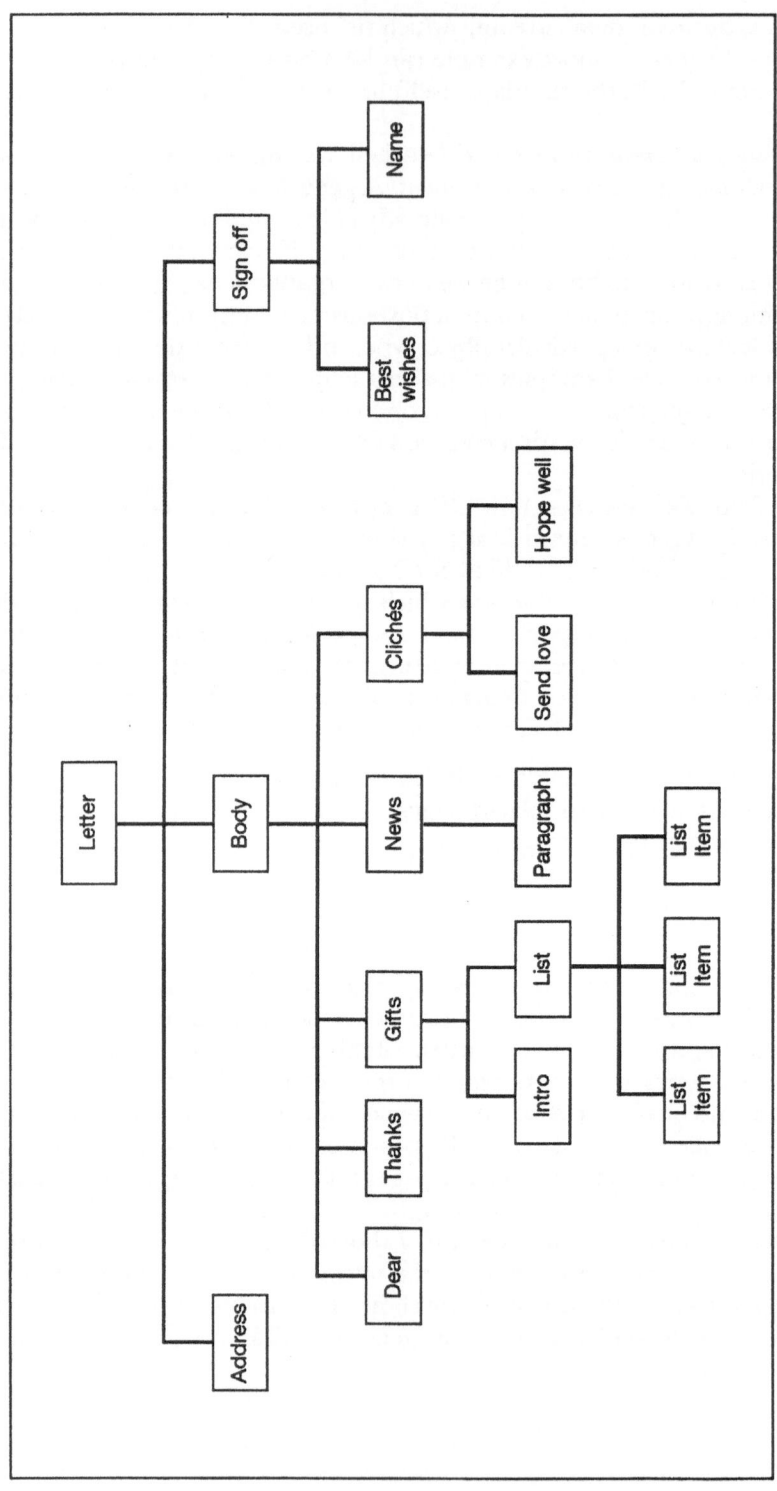

Fig. 10.6. An ODA specific logical structure.

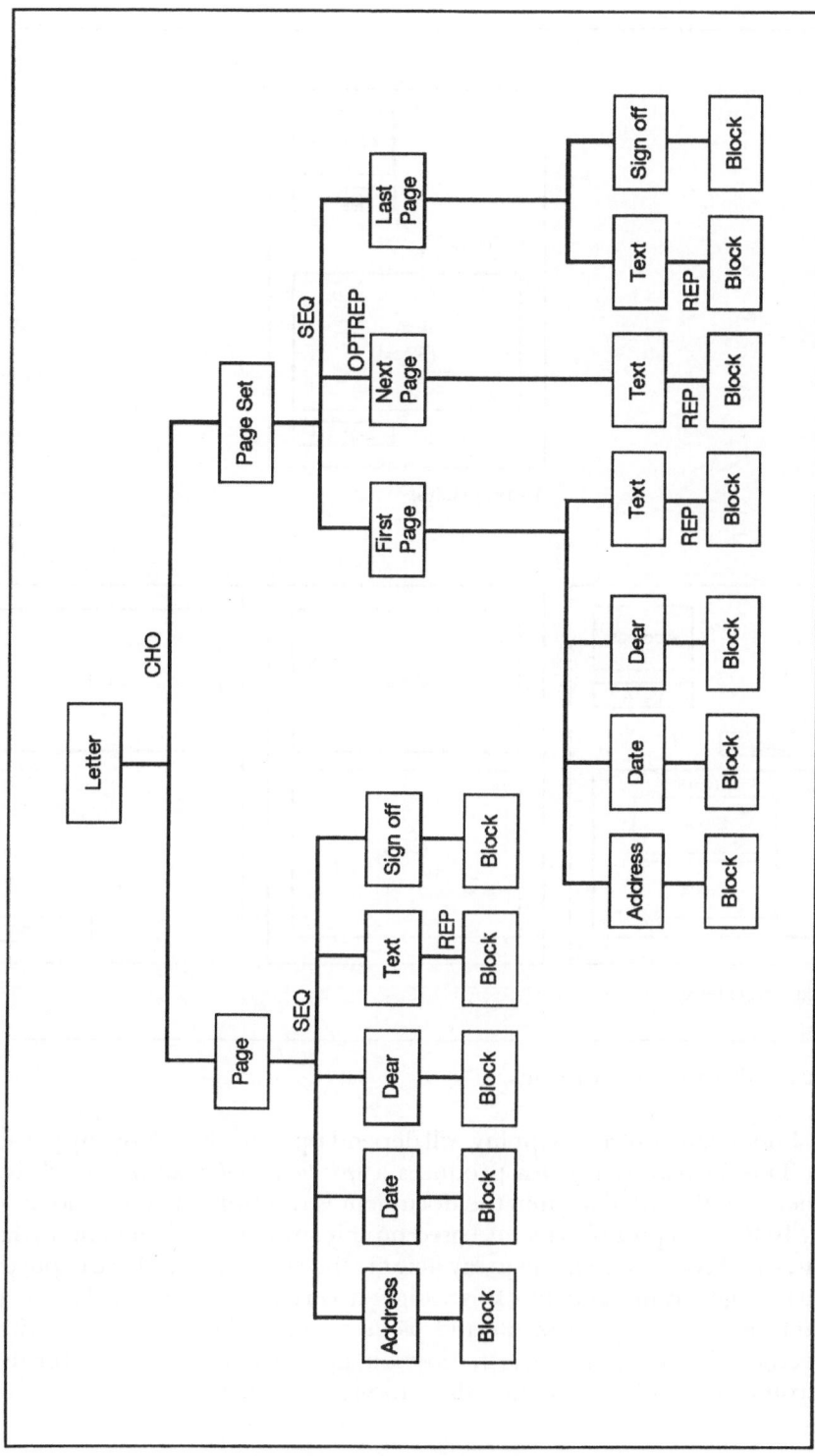

Fig. 10.7. An ODA generic layout structure.

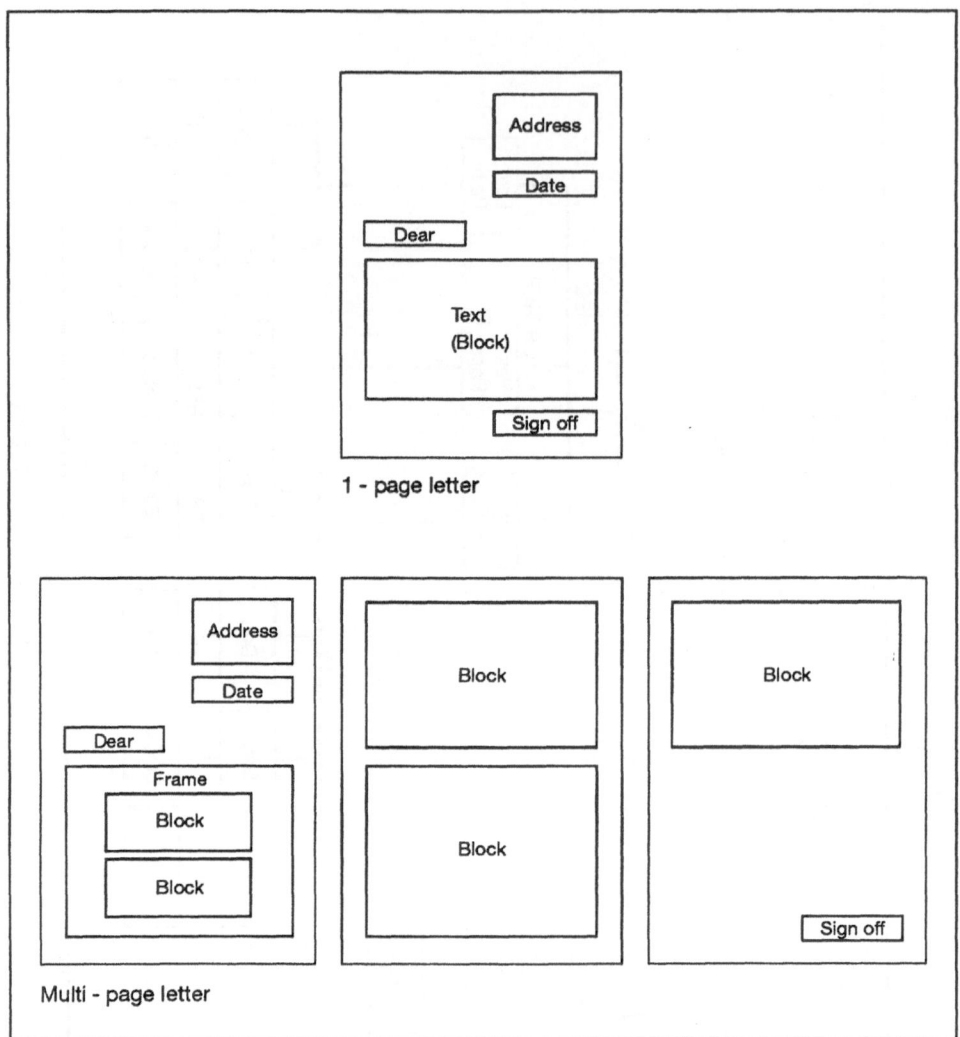

Fig. 10.8. Alternative letter layouts.

10.5, although the precise mapping will depend upon the length of any particular letter. The formatting process produces a *specific layout structure*, which is sent together with the content when the document is transmitted in formatted form.

Fig. 10.8 shows possible layouts based on this structure. When defining layout objects, it is of course important to say how big they will be, and where to put them. So each page, frame and block is assigned certain *properties*, including pairs of numeric values for *dimension* and *position*. Dimension gives the horizontal and vertical length of an object; position gives its start position relative to the containing object, with the top-left corner being used as a

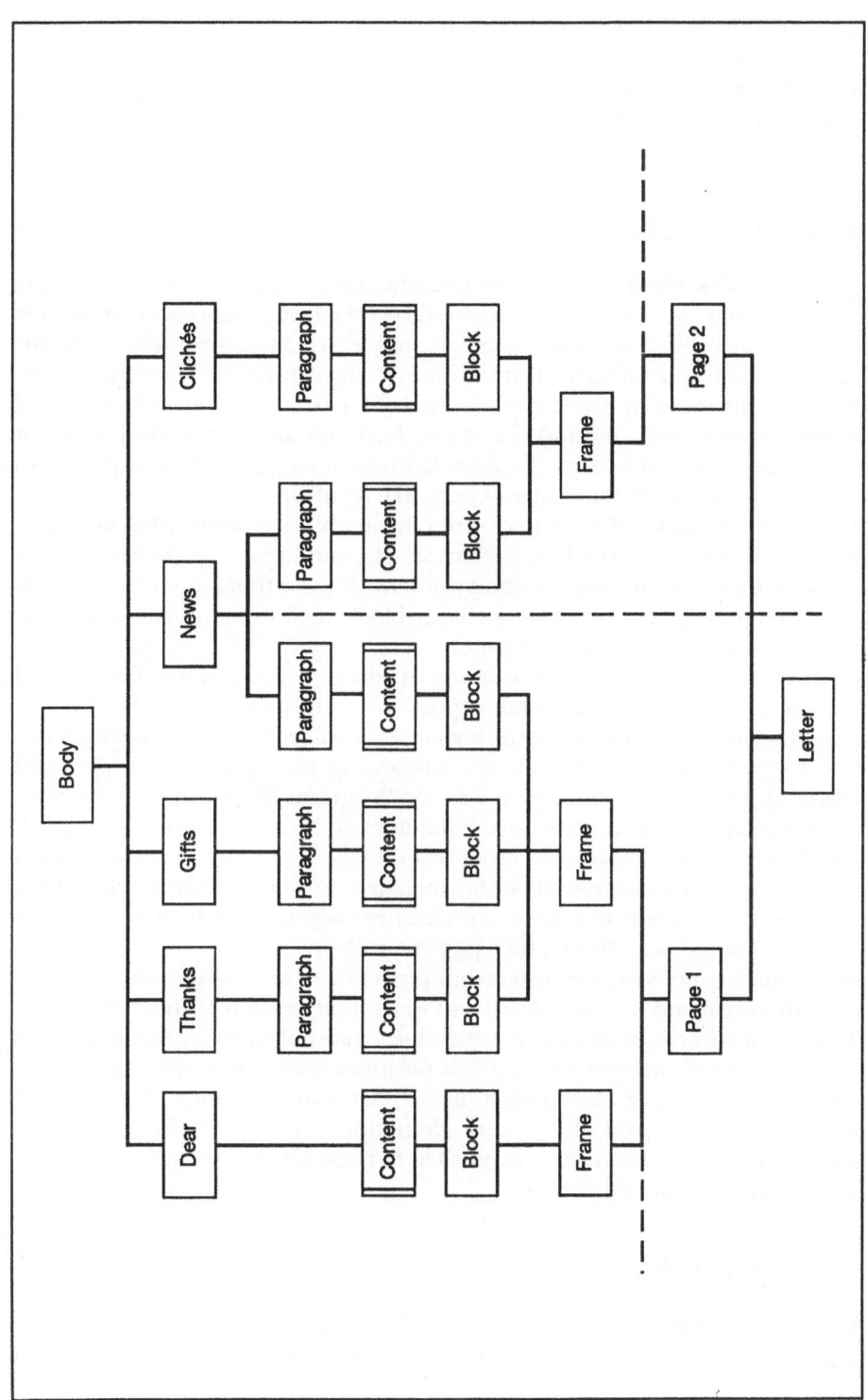

Fig. 10.9. Mapping between logical and layout structures.

reference point. So for a layout page, the position is specified relative to the physical or *nominal* page (effectively defining the surrounding margins), and for frames and blocks it is specified relative to the containing page or frame. Obviously this information is essential to enable a system receiving a formatted document to reproduce its layout accurately.

The Document Layout Process

The properties described above are just one example of an important aspect of the ODA model – the use of object *attributes* to direct the layout process. This process starts with a document matching some generic logical structure, whose specific logical structure has been fixed. It must now produce a specific layout structure, which conforms to an appropriate generic layout structure, but fits the actual document content. Bear in mind that it may have not only text to deal with, but other types of content like raster graphics. Document pages may be complex, with certain areas set aside for particular objects, like headlines.

The task is sometimes likened to that of pouring molten plastic (the document content) into a series of moulds of various shapes and sizes. The choice of which mould to use next is not always straightforward; sometimes for example it is necessary to interrupt the filling of one large block of continuous text in order to insert a footnote at the bottom of a page.

In general the process involves breaking the document down into basic logical objects, using their associated content portions to fill basic layout blocks, and building the blocks up into composite layout objects like frames and pages. Some readers may see an analogy with the processing of input and output data structures as described in Jackson Structured Programming (JSP) Methodology. As in JSP, the ODA formatting process sometimes gives rise to *structure clashes*, with a single logical object being split across several layout objects, or several logical objects being grouped together in one layout object. Fig. 10.9 illustrates part of the mapping from logical to physical for a specific two-page letter structure, where the logical object "news" actually crosses a page boundary.

What actually guides the detailed layout process are the *attributes* which may be attached to logical and layout objects, and to content portions. These direct, for example, what type of content a particular object may hold, how layout and logical objects are matched up, and whether it is permissible or not to split a particular logical object over two or more layout objects. Attributes are most often defined for an object class as part of a generic definition, and then "inherited" by all instances of that class; however it is possible to override the default and give an individual object its own attributes.

Examples of Object Attributes

Some of the object attributes defined by the ODA model are listed below. This is just a representative selection, whose ordering and grouping does not reflect that of the standard itself, but will perhaps give an intuitive idea of the range of possibilities. Actual attribute values may be strings, numbers, or expressions, as appropriate. Some attributes are non-mandatory, in which case the layout process either sets a default or does not use the relevant feature.

Linking Objects to Content

Only basic layout and logical object can be associated with document content. In the generic definitions, object classes may be assigned a *presentation* attribute which determines what type of content (e.g. character, raster image, geometric graphics) they may hold. Within the specific structure, actual objects are linked with their own content via a unique *identifier* attribute which is assigned to each content portion. This makes it possible to send the structure separately from the content in the data stream, but match them up again at the receiving end. The ODA encoding method has no equivalent of the SGML tag, but objects can be assigned a *user-visible-name* in the structure to allow ease of identification, although this has no significance to the processing software.

Some document content (e.g. page numbers, section labels) will be generated by the layout process itself. Definitions of the relevant objects include *content generator* and *binding* attributes – expression involving function calls and references to other objects. So a new page number can be generated by adding 1 to the number of the preceding page. Numerical functions provided are *increment*, *decrement*, and *ordinal*; string-creating functions are *make-string*, *upper-alpha*, *lower-alpha*, *upper-roman*, *lower-roman*.

Linking Layout Objects to Logical Objects

As we have already noted, it is often necessary to ensure that certain logical objects (addresses, headings, figures, footnotes) go into layout objects of the right size and shape, and in an appropriate position on the page. A logical object of this kind can be given a *required category* attribute, which must match one of a set of *permitted category* attributes assigned to the corresponding layout object. If these categories are not set, it is assumed that the two objects are compatible anyway.

Layout Object Attributes

Some layout object attributes, like *dimension* and *position*, have already been mentioned. Their values are often taken from a *default-value-list* assigned as part of a generic structure definition. Other useful attributes are *object path*, *balance* and *transparency*:

- Object path indicates how objects are placed on the page one after another; e.g. blocks within a column normally go from top to bottom while columns on a page go from left to right.
- Balance indicates a layout requirement for subordinate objects, e.g. if there is not enough text to fill a two-column page completely, a balanced layout ensures that both columns are shortened to the same length.

- Transparency indicates whether an overlay block hides the contents of the block underneath. Normal text blocks will be opaque, but one which is to be superimposed on a picture may be declared transparent.

Logical Object Attributes: Layout Directives

These attributes set constraints on how particular logical objects are to be laid out. A few are listed below, with examples of possible uses:

- *New Layout Object*: a new chapter must start on a new page.
- *Indivisibility*: a picture must not be split across columns.
- *Same Layout Object*: logical objects date and time must go into the same block for printing.
- *Separation*: a paragraph must be separated from the preceding paragraph by a blank line
- *Alignment*: a title must be left-aligned, right-aligned, or centred.
- *Synchronisation*: two paragraphs (e.g. English and French versions of the same text) must go side-by-side.

Other attributes relate to the *imaging process*: the final stage when the document is actually put out onto a page or screen. This involves selection of *presentation styles*: with character content these may include vertical spacing, proportional character spacing and right justification, and first line indentation for paragraphs. One can also make a specific choice of *character path* and *line progression*, to handle documents in scripts normally written, say, from right to left or bottom to top. Very low-level presentation information, e.g. font selection, handling of subscripts and superscripts, is incorporated in the document content in the form of control characters.

For non-text content like raster images, many of the same principles apply. An image is sent as a rectangular *pel array* or bit map representing black and white dots, with associated attributes *pel path, line progression, pel spacing* (horizontal) and *line spacing*. It may be in formatted form, with its dimensions fixed by the originating system, or in processable form, so that it can be scaled and re-imaged if necessary by the receiving system. Attributes also indicate whether the bit map is compressed, and if so whether run-length or two-dimensional encoding has been used.

Comments on the ODA Processing Model

The process descriptions in the ODA model are not a specification of how any particular piece of software must behave. They are simply a basis for defining a realistic interchange format between incompatible systems, and it is the job of programmers writing translation software to map the capabilities of existing text processors onto those theoretically available within ODA. (Reference [13] gives an account of practical experiments in this area and notes some of the inherent difficulties of the task.) On the other hand the model definition is obviously detailed enough to act as a basis for new software development if required, and some organisations (see [11]) have adopted it for that purpose.

One general problem about IT standards is mentioned in [4]: that while discussions go on, rapid developments in the outside world alter their terms of reference, so that proposals are often out of date before agreement can be reached. This is certainly a potential hazard in the area of document processing and printing. It is noted in [11], for instance, that the ODA model of the imaging process is less sophisticated than the one currently provided for users of laser printers through the language Postscript. At the time of writing an ISO group is working on a standard page description language; this is likely to be a superset of Postscript and will obviously link up with both the SGML and ODA standards.

Having looked at both SGML and ODA, an obvious question to ask is: "why have two different standards for document processing?" There are historical reasons for divergences of interest between the various bodies concerned with this topic, and as the preceding discussion has shown the two languages do emphasise different aspects of a complex process and address the needs of different members of the computing community. However they are based on similar ideas about how to define document structures, and are basically compatible.

An interesting point not yet mentioned is that SGML actually forms part of ODA. The Office Document Interchange Format (defined in Part 5 of the standard) allows several different orderings and arrangements for objects in a data stream; for instance it is possible to send all the structure definitions first and then the content portions, or to interleave content with structural information. One possible ODIF format consists of a document profile plus SGML entity descriptors and text units, and makes use of SGML's facility for linking two different document definitions to map between logical and layout structures. SGML document elements (identified by tags) are treated as the equivalent of ODA objects. Some ODA attributes can be derived directly from SGML attributes, and the standard specifies other correspondences between the two definition methods.

Chapter Summary

Standards for defining the structure of machine-readable documents enable this kind of data to be freely exchanged between different users and systems. Logical structure is represented independently from printed layout, allowing documents to be output in different formats and used for different purposes. A document definition language must provide a way for the designer to specify components down to any desired level of detail, and show the relationships between them, using the mechanisms of sequence, selection, iteration, optionality, and aggregation.

SGML is a meta-language for defining types or classes of documents, whose internal structure is expressed by the use of logical mark-up or *tags*, delimiting individual components or *elements*. Pieces of text (including tagging) which are used repeatedly, and non-printable symbols, may be declared as *entities* and represented within the document by entity names. Elements may be assigned *attributes* to indicate how they must be processed – one particularly important use for attributes is to provide unique identifiers for cross-references within a text.

A document defined and tagged according to SGML conventions can be *parsed* to verify its structural correctness; auxiliary software can then be used for further processing and formatting. SGML has mainly been adopted for large-scale publishing projects, and is particularly valuable for sets of documents having a complex structure, a long potential life, and a wide application.

The ODA standard was developed to allow the interchange of office-type documents between incompatible software systems. It deals with raster and vector graphics as well as textual content, and potentially covers other types of digital information as well. It is based on an abstract model of the document processing task, involving *editing, formatting* and *imaging*. For the formatting process, it provides methods for defining both the *logical* and *layout structures* of a document, and translating between them.

A class of similar documents is defined using *generic* structure definitions involving *objects* and their possible relationships. From these can be derived *specific* structures for any particular documents of that class. Structure definitions are written in an abstract syntax notation and encoded; they can then be included, along with the content portions of the document, in a data stream for interchange between systems. Translation software is required to convert between this Office Document Interchange Format and the internal format used by any actual word processing or desk-top publishing package.

Investigations

Choose a document type, determine its logical structure by analysing some typical examples, and write a document definition using SGML replacement rules. Then encode one of your examples using appropriate tags. Possible document types to try might be job application forms or CVs, class timetables or appointments diaries, software manuals, or scripts for radio or TV.

Define the same document type using an ODA generic logical structure diagram, and derive a specific logical structure diagram for an example document. Compare the two definition methods. Are there things which it is possible to specify with one and not the other?

Obtain details of commercially-available software to support SGML document tagging.

Take a closer look at ODA standards for non-textual data, e.g. raster graphics.

References

1 Coombs J, Renear A, DeRose S (1987) Markup systems and the future of scholarly text processing. CACM 30(11):933–947
2 Smith J (1987) The Standard Generalized Markup Language (SGML): Guidelines for editors and publishers. Report 26, British National Bibliography Research Fund
3 Bryan M (1988) SGML, an author's guide to the Standard Generalized Markup Language. Addison-Wesley, Reading, MA
4 Barron D (1989) Why use SGML? Electronic Publishing 2(1):3–24
5 Simpson J, Weiner E (eds) (1988) The Oxford English dictionary (2nd edn). Oxford University Press, Oxford
6 Simpson J (1987) The new OED project: a year's work in lexicography. University Computing 9:2–7
7 Raymond D, Tompa F (1988). Hypertext and the Oxford English dictionary. CACM 31(7):871–879
8 Stutely R (1990) The development of HMSO's legal database. Euro-documentation 1(5), Admark Publishing
9 Soutar T (1987) The application of SGML to Statutory Instruments. HMSO Technical Services
10 ISO–8613 (1989) Information processing – text and office systems – Office Document Architecture (ODA) and interchange format
11 Brown H (1989) Standards for structured documents. Computer Journal 32(6): 505–514
12 ISO–8825 (1988) Information processing systems – open systems interconnection – basic encoding rules for abstract notation one (ASN.1)
13 Golkar S (1989) Experience with document interchange. Research Note 89/80, Department of Computer Science, University College London

Eleven
Formatting and Printing Documents

"'Tis pleasant, sure, to see one's name in print;
A book's a book, although there's nothing in't."
Lord Byron

The Development of Desk-top Publishing

The last chapter described some rather abstract approaches to the subject of document processing: this one is about real formatting and printing software. It is not intended to be a users' manual for any of the packages and languages discussed, but to provide an insight into what this kind of software must do to get a document onto paper, and how its users can influence the process.

The convergence between two originally quite separate kinds of printing activity was mentioned in the previous chapter. Printers were first attached to computers as simple peripherals to record the results of calculations; over the years the need to churn out low-cost, low-quality output at high speed has been superseded by the requirement to present a much wider range of information in a more readable way. On small-scale systems this could be partly satisfied by daisy-wheel and dot-matrix printers, but the advent of the page-printer, normally based on laser technology, allowed computers of all sizes to produce output at least comparable to that of professional printing machinery.

At the same time the introduction of computer technology has brought about widespread changes in the printing industry itself. The last thirty years has seen it move from the mechanical setting of hot metal type, through various forms of phototypesetting (using offset lithography, film, then cathode-ray tube) to very high definition laser printing. The degree of electronic control over the whole process has extended correspondingly, at first through hardware only, more recently through special-purpose software, to the point where computer-based techniques now dominate the production of commercial newspapers and periodicals.

Moreover in some cases there may be little or no difference between the equipment used to create masters for printing by professional and "amateur" document designers. Before the launch of a new Sunday newspaper, a decision was taken to handle text input and page layout for its colour magazine using standard Macintosh products [1]. Up until the final printing stage, the equipment used is identical to that found in many commercial organisations for the production of internal reports and publicity. Experienced designers are often critical of the work produced by untrained desk-top publishing (dtp) enthusiasts, but the fact remains that the two groups now inhabit what is recognisably the same world.

The implications of technological change for the printing industry are of course far-reaching, but we are concerned here mainly with facilities which are in theory available to any computer user. An interesting result of the spread of electronic publishing is that terminology and concepts once confined to professional printers have now achieved a wider currency – users talk familiarly of *fonts, kerning, leading, gutters* and so on. And expectations about printing quality and presentation in office-type communications have risen sharply, with typing or dot-matrix printing no longer seen as acceptable, even for quite short-lived documents.

Even more significant is the possibility that wider access to sophisticated document creation software is bringing about a change in our perception of the reading and writing task, putting a much greater reliance than in the past on *visual* clues to meaning. Reference [2] contrasts the qualities of continuous text, such as might be produced on a typewriter or appear in a standard printed book, with "visually informative text". Here different typefaces and sizes emphasise or de-emphasise content, spacing and blocking reflects division of ideas, indentations show dependency relationships, bullets mark parallel items and so on, all perhaps within the short span of a single page. Readers who are accustomed to these conventions in the newspapers now have the technology to put them into practice in their own writing.

Conversely there is less need for complex syntactic structures with conjunctions and subordinate clauses to make connections between ideas – or even for writing in complete grammatical sentences. It is suggested that visually informative text holds readers' attention better, and enables them to skim the page for information rather than read every word to extract its meaning. In the long run, perhaps, the further extension of electronic publishing equipment from the workplace to homes and schools may have a decisive influence on generally accepted standards for the written word, and even the structure of language itself.

At the same time (paradoxically) one of the most important effects of using document processing software is that *content* and *format* can be treated as two quite separate issues. This view was fundamental to the two standards discussed in the previous chapter. Such software allows easy drafting and redrafting of content and an experimental approach to layout, helping the writer to work towards the most effective result. Actual document formatting programs fall into two main classes: those which provide immediate feedback about the appearance of a document as currently specified, and those which enforce a delay between entering a text and seeing how it looks on the page.

Models and Metaphors

We have already seen one abstract model of document layout, defined within ODA. This is based on the notion of *objects* which are related to one another in various ways, and whose job it is to hold document content. However the nature of that content affects the details of the layout process: for instance while continuous text is like a liquid which can be poured into moulds of almost any shape and size, raster graphics has only the limited elasticity given by its potential for scaling along either dimension.

Developers of actual formatting software tend to adopt more concrete metaphors. *Wysiwyg* (what you see is what you get) dtp packages, for example, which allow text and graphics to be directly manipulated on the screen through a wimp interface, obviously try to simulate the physical activities formerly carried out with pieces of paper on a board. Defined page areas are created and positioned using mouse movements, continuous text can be entered at the keyboard or imported from a file, to "flow" down columns and around images. Screen icons represent tools like paintbrushes, pairs of scissors, and clipboards. There are of course many different packages within this category, displaying numerous minor variations in function and user interface, but they all share the same underlying view of what is going on.

By contrast users of other formatting programs must think of themselves as *compositors*, whose task is to embed into the body of their texts codes and instructions to drive a piece of typesetting machinery.

The Unix *troff* program [3] was originally written to output to a particular (now obsolete) typesetting machine, and the basic philosophy remains the same even in its later device-independent version. As a simple illustration of this point, consider the commands ".mk" (*mark*) and ".rt" (*return*), which are used in troff to achieve simple line graphics and multi-column formats. The *mark* request marks a vertical page position as a reference point by saving it in an internal register. The *return* command, referring to the same register, causes a return to that point before doing the next output. These commands fit the underlying model of the typesetter; in a different context they would be meaningless.

The *TeX* program [4] was also designed to generate typesetter control codes from embedded commands, but it presents a somewhat richer mix of metaphors, via terms like "boxes", "glue", "tolerance", "penalty" and "fuzz". It aims to perform high quality setting, using a clever method of hyphenation, and producing printed lines which are neither under-nor over-full. So instead of a simple algorithm which fills one line and goes onto the next there is a more intelligent heuristic approach. The program handles complete paragraphs, back-tracking if a particular result is unacceptable, and adjusting various constraints in order to find the best compromise. These actions are affected by parameter settings which are partly under user control, as will be described in more detail later.

Whatever formatting system is used, the last stage in document creation is "imaging" – actually putting the marks on the page. The basis of our discussion for that process will be *Postscript*: the device-independent "page description language" now used to drive many laser printers and some typesetters. This language is based on the most concrete model of all: a paintbrush travelling across a piece of paper which may itself be rotated through any angle. The brush can move to co-ordinate points, draw straight lines and curves, shade polygonal areas, as well as writing words. At this level there is no real difference between text and graphics; even individual characters can be described in terms of curves and lines, giving Postscript users as much control as they need over font design and the juxtaposition of letters.

In practice of course it is quite unusual to write directly in Postscript; it almost always acts as a *target* language for higher-level software, encoding the document on the final stage of its journey to the printer. Most dtp packages produce Postscript if required, and it can also be generated directly or indirectly from TeX and troff. So a user wishing to do electronic publishing has a first-level choice between a wimp-based wysiwyg package like *Pagemaker*, *Ventura*, *Superpage*, etc. or a program which expects him to behave like a compositor. Apart from questions of availability, how should the choice be made?

One answer is that different approaches suit different types of people. Brailsford [5] suggests that users are divided into "doers", who appreciate the reassurance of direct manipulation and immediate visual feedback, and "describers", probably those with some experience of programming, who feel at home with a more indirect and abstract approach.

The nature of the document being produced is also relevant. A club or departmental newsletter, for instance, is a "layout-intensive" [6] document, in that each page is an individual arrangement of short items, and the choice of where to place each one for maximum impact is a major part of the design task. By contrast a multi-page article or formal report will have a more regular layout, which can be defined once and for all and needs less *ad hoc* interaction.

Finally, there is the question of level of control. In an earlier chapter we noted the contrast between two approaches to specifying interactive courseware, and saw that there was often a trade-off between ease of use and detailed control. It is exactly the same in the present case.

Wysiwyg packages should enable users to start work quickly and exercise individual design flair if they have it. They certainly make it easy to lay out pictures and diagrams on the page, and, although they are not ideal for entering a great deal of text (which is better imported from a word processor), they allow the effects of editing to be checked immediately, and encourage an exploratory approach.

On the other hand they can be frustrating to run on hardware not powerful enough to give immediate response, and certainly at present lack extremely sophisticated filling and layout algorithms like those built into TeX. As usual with a wimp interface, it will be virtually impossible to define and re-use frequently required command sequences. Most important, users will be limited to selecting among a *predetermined* set of possibilities. Too few options here will restrict the scope for design, too many may cause confusion and be hard to combine satisfactorily.

The concepts of typesetter formatting systems are much more difficult to grasp straightaway. Potentially, however, they provide greater power and flexibility by including what are essentially programming language constructs like variables and control structures. Take the example of page numbering. A dtp package will normally hold a page-counter, and provide setting options for such things as its starting value, where it will appear on the page (e.g. at the head or foot), and how it will be printed (e.g. in arabic or roman numerals). The same thing may apply to section and paragraph numbering. On the other hand a typesetter program will support named registers or variables (both system- and user-defined), which can act as counters for any purpose. Their values may be changed or referred to by embedded commands, giving an infinite number of options about how page and section numbers are initialised, incremented, positioned and formatted. Some decisions may be made dynamically, depending on conditions tested during the formatting process.

With this sort of power comes the danger of making mistakes – even simple formatting requires some trial and error and for more ambitious efforts a debugging cycle as in normal programming. For users who want to print documents rather than solve puzzles the effort may seem disproportionate. The usual solution is the use of macro packages embodying higher level constructs, giving explicit support for tricky areas like tables and formulae, and making the underlying programs more manageable by hiding details and restricting the range of options.

Is there a possibility of convergence between the two approaches, giving the future user of formatting software the best of both worlds? Brailsford [5] contends that to advance the art future wysiwyg packages must be based on stronger abstract models of document structure. (The ODA model is one obvious candidate.) In practice some current packages do give partial support for the idea of logical structuring, an example being the Ventura [6] *tag* mechanism.

A tag in this context is a name for a collection of options relating to font, spacing, alignment, and so on. Once defined, tags can be attached to any suitable unit of text, which will immediately take on the defined properties. The careful document designer will define tags for all logically distinguishable elements like list items, section headers and quotations, making it easy to link a typographical description to each, and providing some consistency within the overall document design. So tags in this case give an approximation to logical mark-up, and the tag names are actually embedded within Ventura text files when they are written to disc. However they are always applied at the lowest level (i.e. to a single heading line or continuous paragraph) and there is no equivalent of the hierarchical structuring represented by SGML tagging.

Users of wysiwyg packages needing fine control over their document design may also in future want to specify certain formatting functions through command sequences rather than menu selection. The principle would be to use default facilities as far as possible, but escape into some sort of programming mode when necessary. The development from self-contained packages, where all options are pre-specified, to more open-ended software tools, has for example proved successful in the case of database management systems. In dtp packages it could work in a similar way, giving the designer the ability to associate special formatting routines with particular pages, frames, blocks or tags, to be triggered off when text was entered or imported.

Starting at the other end of the spectrum, the most useful extension to the typical typesetter program would be an interactive front-end for accepting embedded formatting commands and showing their effect at once. Once again there are some existing facilities to build on; for instance TeX already accepts input data values and displays messages while formatting, and there are also previewing programs which can show a close approximation to the formatted page on the screen before printing. A fully interactive version would require at least three windows – one for dialogue, one for text and embedded commands being edited by the user, and a third showing the equivalent formatted text. It should be possible to scroll through the two windows in parallel, adjusting the embedded commands and seeing the effect at once.

Whatever sort of software is used, and whatever future developments occur, it should be stressed that document design is a skill which involves making many separate decisions to contribute towards an effective whole. What counts as effective depends of course on the purpose of the document: for instance whether it is intended to grasp the attention of an uncommitted reader with short, unconnected, easily assimilated items, or to present a sustained logical argument. Some important principles are to maintain an overall consistency of layout and typeface but provide some variety and contrast within the basic framework. New users of dtp software are notorious for trying to use too many unrelated fonts within a short space, giving an untidy effect and distracting the reader from the actual content.

Functions of Formatting Software

Following the above rather broad survey and discussion, it is time to consider in a little more detail what we expect formatting software to do for us. We shall be concerned here with actual operations on the text, rather than the user interface. Naturally a wysiwyg package must contain a great deal of code to handle menus, icons, dialogue boxes, the presentation of enlarged or reduced views of pages on the screen, not to mention direct text entry and editing, cutting and pasting, cropping and scaling images, and so on. On the other hand a typesetter program has to act like a compiler, parsing input commands and translating one or more files from an input to an output format. But in either case the same essential functions are performed and the same essential decisions must be made. These can be grouped and summarised under the following headings.

Overall Document/Page Design

This must include defining the page size, portrait or landscape orientation, sizes of margins, format of headers and footers, also number of columns, their widths, and the width of the "gutters" or spaces between them. There may be titles, numbers and logos to occur on every page, and perhaps slightly different basic layouts for odd-and even-numbered pages which are to appear facing left and right in a book.

It may then be required to override these general options for particular pages, e.g. to say that a title page is not numbered or split into columns, unlike those which follow it. At any level within a document, we can think of formatting instructions having implicit or explicit "scope", and scopes may be nested inside one another as they are in programming.

Representation of Logical Structures

Most long documents are divided into units like parts, chapters, sections and subsections, identified on the page by numbers/letters, headings and indentation. Formatting software should be able to generate number or letter labels automatically, down to several levels. With Ventura, for example, tags may be assigned to section headings at levels 1 to 10, and for each one the user may ask for a label type, saying whether it is to be concatenated with labels at previous levels. Thus a formal report shows its hierarchical structure using section numbers 1.1, 1.2, 1.2.1, etc. while for other purposes the separate sequences 1,2,3, a,b,c, i,ii,iii, etc. may suffice.

In typesetter programs, as mentioned earlier, these functions are based on the ability to operate upon number registers. Neither troff nor TeX provides section numbering directly, but their associated macro packages do, and we shall discuss later how such facilities are built up. Once section headings are identified, it is of course possible to generate contents lists automatically. Again this is an option which can be selected directly from a Ventura menu, whereas the same function is provided for troff and TeX through auxiliary packages.

Selection of Layout Structures

Not all document texts flow continuously down the page line by line and column by column. We have already, in the ODA abstract model, met the idea of objects called "frames" which can be defined and positioned as separate units. Sometimes they are intended for figures or tables, but equally well may hold continuous text which is displayed quite differently from anything else around it. This is an idea which is very easy to grasp in the context of a wysiwyg system. Our example package in this genre, Ventura, has a special icon which

---

1 Example from a WYSIWYG Desk Top Publishing Package

August 1st 1990

1.1 <u>Introduction</u>

Don't you just love the headline? The headline is wearing a chunky, bold, Helvetica like typeface in a big 18 point size set off with a chapter heading tag that gives it that straight number 1 in front. In contrast, the 14 point Introduction subheading sports a short underline for the slimmer figure. Both are daringly sans-serif typefaces and the headline is using just a little bit of kerning. The body text today is respectably done out in a 12 point Times-Romanish typeface with no frills but indenting nicely at the beginning of paragraphs.

1.2 <u>Frames</u>

All text must be placed in a frame. This text is in the default outer frame which includes the whole page. Other frames containing pictures or further

Another frame

This text is in the smaller frame. It is independent of the text in the outer frame and is immune to its typography. It is in italics with a centred title.

text can be overlayed onto it. You can see that the text from this frame automatically flows round them[1].

1.3 <u>Pictures</u>

Pictures can be created by:

- Importing Scanned Images
- Ventura Drawing Functions
- PC drawings & painting packages

A Scanned Image

---

1   *A feature known as "runaround".*

Fig.11.1. Example output from Ventura.

can be chosen to create a new frame or change an existing one. The frame is sized and positioned with the mouse; if it is planted in the middle of some existing text that text will be reformatted to flow around it. (Fig. 11.1 shows a page constructed in this way.) The package also provides a switch for column and line "snap" – which ensures that frame edges are set flush with the nearest appropriate column or line. In its absence they are left exactly where the mouse puts them.

The task of creating a page laid out like Fig. 11.1 with a formatting program is more formidable, since the user must express the spatial relationships required using embedded commands and measurements. In fact TeX has the potential for sophisticated visual effects (setting lines in circular or triangular shapes, for instance), but for most normal purposes the simplest approach is once again through a macro package like *LaTeX* [7]. This allows the user to specify a "minipage" with its own declared width, which can be aligned in various ways with the surrounding text, and having its own internal components like headings and footnotes.

Although on-screen manipulation of spatial units is an easier option in general, it is worth saying that wysiwyg packages should also allow the direct entry of exact measurements through the keyboard. The original version of an otherwise very sophisticated dtp package caused frustration to its professional users by requiring all page and column dimensions to be set with the mouse. Unfortunately the mouse changed its position very slightly as it was clicked, causing inaccuracy in the data entry, and turning what should have been a simple initialisation task into a major test of hand–eye co-ordination.

Text Filling

The main purpose of any formatting software is to fill lines with words and pages with lines. The process is governed by the values of many variables, mostly set as the result of users' choices. To discuss these factors in an orderly way, it will be convenient to consider the horizontal filling (of lines) and the vertical filling (of pages) as separate issues. (We assume text in a language like English which runs from left to right, top to bottom; the details, if not the basic principles, would be somewhat different with another character path.)

Horizontal Filling

This is governed by the characteristics of the current line, and the letters to go into it. Line characteristics include:

- Its position in the paragraph: the algorithm will differ slightly according to whether it the first line, the last line, or comes somewhere in the middle.
- Its width, as given by the current left and right margins, minus any indenting, plus any outdenting, in force.
- The specified alignment: whether text is to be justified right and/or left, or centred.

- Whether hyphenation is allowed or not. (Normally this parameter will be set for the document as a whole, but this is the point at which its effect will be felt.)

In the case of TeX, which has a very complex filling algorithm, a number of other parameters apply as well, some of which are discussed later in this chapter.

The most crucial property of the text to be fitted into the line is the *font* in use, which determines the character widths. A font is a combination of a typeface, e.g. *Times-Roman*, and a type size, e.g. 10-points: a typical size for a book. (Note that there are 72 points to the inch.) With fixed-pitch fonts (like *Courier*) all characters have the same width, just as on a typewriter or lineprinter. For electronic publishing, it is more likely that fonts with proportional spacing will be used, requiring the filling algorithm to allocate a different amount of space to each letter.

Typefaces usually come in *families* – normal, bold and italic – and there is sometimes a change from one to another in mid-line. This may entail small extra adjustments in spacing to maintain the proper distance between a (right-slanting) italic letter and a following upright character. Both troff and TeX allow the user to insert special control symbols to produce this effect.

Another aspect of character-placement is *kerning*. Successive letters can be kerned (moved closer together than their actual widths might suggest) if their shapes are compatible, as in the case of *VA, Po, by.* troff does not support kerning; Ventura and TeX do. Some low-cost dtp packages allow "manual kerning", whereby the careful user may adjust pairs of individual letters himself. This would be worthwhile only for large fonts such as those in headlines. The extreme case of kerning is the use of *ligature* where successive letters (e.g. ff, fi, fl) are actually joined together. This is also handled automatically by TeX, which uses fonts containing composite characters to support it.

Like other characters, inter-word spaces have a width, but one that is potentially variable. If a line is to be both left and right justified, there is usually some spare space to be parcelled out, and the normal procedure once it is seen how many words will fit on the line is to share it between all the inter-word spaces by adjusting the size of each. With fixed-pitch fonts this gives a very crude effect, likewise with very narrow columns, and the best solution in these cases is to use a *ragged right* alignment. Otherwise right justification works satisfactorily, although it always has the potential to produce lines which are too crowded or too sparse. Later we will look briefly at the TeX horizontal filling method, which is intended to minimise this effect.

Vertical Filling

The basic algorithm here involves entering successive lines into a page, column or frame until it is full, then moving onto the next layout object of the same kind. There are exceptions however – consider the fragmented arrangement of popular magazines where narrow ribbons of text make their way between broad blocks of advertisements. Using a dtp package for a publication of this sort, the designer must be able to specify the "routing" for different text-streams, allowing an article starting on page 30 to continue on page 49, and conclude on page 63.

For simplicity, we will consider the filling process in terms of complete pages. In general the two most important factors are:

- The *vertical space* available on the page: its overall height minus anything set aside for margins, headers or footers.
- The *line height*: determined by the type size in use and what is sometimes called the *leading*, the inter-line space, which should be proportional to the type size. Line height will not necessarily remain constant down the page, since headings may take a larger type size.

When no more lines can be fitted onto the current page, the vertical filling process is interrupted. Footer information (e.g the page number) is written, the current page is ejected, and a new page is started, with any headers at the top. Then normal vertical filling is resumed.

An unwelcome result of this process can be *widows* and *orphans*: isolated lines from a paragraph placed at the end of one page or the start of the next. The simple approach here, adopted by Ventura, is to allow the user to say to what extent these are unacceptable, and if necessary move to a new page early so as to avoid them. This in turn has a possible side-effect: pages of uneven length. TeX allows the user to try and avoid both isolated lines and uneven page-lengths, by adjusting inter-line spacing all down the page, or by asking for certain paragraphs to be set more loosely or tightly than usual, so as to generate more or fewer lines.

More serious than isolated lines is the breaking of lists, tables and figures which should be displayed as a unit. The Ventura approach is to expect that these will be placed in a frame which can be moved bodily from one page to another. With typesetter programs the required space must be booked in advance by an embedded command, before the actual content appears. The troff command ".ne", followed by a numeric argument, specifies that the following unit needs that amount of contiguous vertical space. If it is not available on the current page, troff jumps immediately to the next.

A more sophisticated algorithm involves allowing the whole unit to "float" – it is laid out and saved in a buffer while normal filling of the current page continues, then output at the start of the new page. Troff macro packages provide this facility, using its so-called "diversion" mechanism, a description of which will be given later. TeX supports *floating inserts* which behave in a similar way.

Footnotes can also be thought of as insertion units, which "sink" to the bottom of the page. They should be uniquely referenced, so formatting software is often required to generate numbers for them, restarting the sequence at a new page or chapter as necessary. Ventura requires the relevant style and numbering characteristics to be set up initially, after which footnotes can be added by clicking on the appropriate point in the main text, making a menu selection, then entering the actual footnote content, which will be inserted automatically at the bottom of the page.

In typesetter systems it is convenient to be able to enter footnotes along with the text which refers to them, leaving the software to handle cross-referencing and placement. TeX has an embedded command to handle this, which takes an

```
@CHAPTER HEAD = Example from a WYSIWYG Desk Top Publishing
Package

@SUBHEADING = Introduction

@SUBHEADING =

Don't you just love the headline? The headline is wearing a
chunky, bold, Helvetica like typeface in a big 18 point size set
off with a chapter heading tag that gives it that straight number
1 in front. In contrast, the 14 point Introduction subheading
sports a short underline for the slimmer figure. Both are daring-
ly sans-serif typefaces and the headline is using just a little
bit of kerning. The body text today is respectably done out in a
12 point Times-Romanish typeface with no frills but indenting
nicely at the beginning of paragraphs.

@SUBHEADING = Frames

All text must be placed in a frame. This text is in the default
outer frame which includes the whole page. Other frames contain-
ing pictures or further text can be overlayed onto it. You can
see that the text from this frame automatically flows round
them<$FA feature known as "runaround".>.

@SUBHEADING = Pictures

@Z_CAPTION = Pictures can be created by:

@BULLET TEXT = Importing Scanned Images

@BULLET TEXT = Ventura Drawing Functions

@BULLET TEXT = PC drawings & painting packages

@SUBHEADING = Another frame

@INSET = This text is in the smaller frame. It is independent of
the text in the outer frame and is immune to its typography. It
is in italics with a centred title.

@SIDEWAYS =    August 1st 1990
```

Fig. 11.2. Ventura text files with embedded tags.

argument indicating the actual cross-reference symbol to be used. This might be an asterisk, dagger, or other printer's symbol, or a string representation of a number register, which should then be incremented within an appropriate macro.

Like other floating insertions, footnotes must be saved in a text buffer until the bottom of the page is reached. The other notable point for the filling algorithm is that the accumulation of footnotes progressively reduces the amount of vertical space remaining on the page. Complications can arise when a footnote reference occurs low down on the page, leaving no room for the footnote itself, and a formatting program must be able to rearrange the material, breaking long footnotes across two pages if necessary.

Formatting Example

That concludes the overview of the horizontal and vertical filling process. Fig. 11.1 illustrates, via Ventura, many of the formatting options described so far. It shows a page containing frames, different typefaces and sizes, section labelling, bullets for list items, footnotes, and a scanned image. Note that it is not presented as an example of good layout design! Fig. 11.2 shows one of the text files used within this page, complete with the Ventura embedded tags. Similar example outputs from troff and TeX will appear later in the chapter, when there will be more emphasis on the explicit use of embedded commands. Meanwhile we continue with the general survey of formatting software functions.

Document Style/Use of Auxiliary Files

The use of formatting software requires the setting of many parameters, whose scope may cover any text unit from a whole document to a single heading. Together these choices determine the overall document "style". Once a style is defined for one document, it is useful to be able to keep it as a template for future productions of the same type. The Ventura package supports this function by maintaining separate files called *style sheets*, which hold the details of page layouts and tag properties independent of any actual text. Before starting a new document, the user must nominate a style file as a basis for its page make-up, although he may then change it as he goes along and save the modified version under a new name. Organisations may plan a family of styles for related publications, giving some scope for individuality within a basically consistent framework.

Apart from the style sheet, a Ventura document is likely to be composed from a number of separate files, for each content type within each chapter. The preferred method for generating source text is through an ordinary word processor. Precisely because of the wysiwyg interface and on-screen format-ting, actually entering text into a dtp package is a somewhat disconcerting experience, since the line layout is adjusted with each keystroke and inter-word spaces may not show up clearly. Ventura accepts text written by most PC word processors, inserting embedded tags into the original files as the user applies them on the screen. Files of images created by drawing or painting packages can also be imported. The user may scale or crop them to fit into a frame but in that case the originals are not changed; instead details of the transformation are saved and re-applied when the image is next displayed or printed. Unlike some other dtp packages, Ventura does not make its own copies of imported files but creates higher-level reference files tying them all together.

Whatever software is used it is obviously sensible to partition large documents into different files for ease of editing, and perhaps to enable the re-use of text in other documents. Both troff and TeX have embedded commands to switch to different source files while formatting, so large documents can be managed in the same way as large-scale software developments, with a *root* file holding a series of references to lower-level content files. If files are saved in formatted form it may be possible to do selective editing and reformatting before reprinting, perhaps using an operating system utility like Unix *make*. In fact the LaTeX package has a built-in facility for selective reformatting, using *include* and *includeonly* commands.

In the same way, files of macro definitions and associated parameter settings can be kept separately and input as a preamble to any text file, providing global formatting directives. This in fact is how document styles are defined and modified using a typesetter program. LaTeX, for example, consists of a basic file of utility macros, plus additional style files for three main document types: books, reports, and letters. These can be further tailored by resetting parameter values to fit organisational house styles. At the same time other LaTeX users have defined specialised macros for structured documents (timetables, examination papers and CVs) and made them publicly available, so the whole process is very open-ended.

Special Document Elements

Pictures

The ability to include diagrams and pictures in documents is obviously a powerful incentive for many users of electronic publishing software, and a particular selling-point for dtp packages. We have already noted that these objects should be treated by basic filling algorithms as non-divisible, so during the layout process they must carry with them essential information about their size and shape. They may be created either as part of the formatting process or by some entirely independent process.

All three programs under discussion provide some help in constructing simple line diagrams. Ventura has a choice of basic graphics functions, enabling lines, circles, rectangles, etc. to be picked and placed with the mouse. It also allows freehand drawing, which would obviously be impossible for the other two systems. For more sophisticated graphics, pictures created by other software may be imported. Ventura provides commands to crop and scale images to fit into predefined frames, and to attach captions and figure numbers to them.

As might be expected from its origins, troff has only the most primitive facilities for drawing horizontal and vertical lines, allowing the construction of diagrams from lines and boxes but not much else. TeX (via LaTeX) supports the declaration of pictures made up of basic graphics objects, including horizontal, vertical and slanted lines, rectangular boxes, circles and ovals. Once defined, a picture can be saved in a buffer and re-used, and there is a special command to output multiple copies of a picture in a regular pattern, based on the underlying loop structure available within TeX. Once again, anything more ambitious involves importing graphics created by other software. A favourite method is to incorporate a Postscript program into the document before it is finally printed – this is achieved by an embedded macro call referring to a Postscript file.

Tables

Tables of figures or short text entries are another important component of many technical documents. Even the simplest word processor or formatter will imitate the basic typewriter function of tab-setting, but often one wishes to define a table layout in a more abstract form, leaving the software to handle the low-level details of calculating column widths, ruling dividing lines, and lining up entries tidily. Users of troff , for example, can call on the *tbl* preprocessor, which reads a file containing table definitions and their associated data, and translates it into more basic troff commands. A typical simple table definition for tbl includes:

- Begin–end statements delimiting the scope of a table.
- Option selections relating to a whole table, e.g. whether it is to be centred and boxed, whether individuals cells are to be boxed, and if so with what line thickness.
- Format descriptions for table and column header lines, and for body elements. There is an entry here for each column in the table, indicating whether the corresponding data is to be left-aligned, right-aligned, centred, or (for numeric items) lined up on the decimal point. One can also declare that certain entries may span two or more columns, in which case dividing lines are omitted.
- The table data itself, laid out in rows, with elements separated either by the tab character or by another character nominated instead.

There are extra commands for more complex requirements, like switching column formats or fonts in mid-table, multi-line column entries, and vertical centring of entries within cells. Macro packages associated with TeX provide similar functions although the details naturally differ. As with other tasks where the user must first try to visualise what he wants and then specify it, some trial and error may be required to get a satisfactory layout.

Ventura does not provide explicit support for a table as an abstract object; the user must set it out using a suitable mixture of existing facilities. Three different approaches are recommended, depending on the nature of the data. One is to think of it as essentially a graphics task, first drawing boxes, then entering data to fit into the boxes. This gives complete freedom of layout where entries are of different shapes and sizes. The second approach involves setting up tab positions within a frame, then entering successive rows of the table with data items separated by tab codes. This works well for regular tables where each entry is the same size and requires the same alignment. For more complex structures involving multi-line or multi-column entries, a separate tag must be defined for each column in the table, indicating its horizontal start and end positions, and its behaviour with regard to line feeds. Data is then entered into successive rows defined by these tags.

Formulae

Including mathematical formulae in typed or word processed documents has always been considered difficult. Mathematics developed as a hand-written language in which the shape, size and placement of all the symbols is under the writer's control. Systems which support mathematical text processing must not only supply a large repertoire of special characters, but have some understanding of the legitimate ways of putting them together.

Like table definition, this is a task which lends itself more to the descriptive approach than to direct input and on-screen manipulation. Not all possible symbols can be typed in at the keyboard (although the more common ones can be mapped onto function keys, or placed on an overlay). Neither can users be expected to position each subscript, superscript and dividing line in a complex equation accurately on the screen with a mouse (although they may like the chance to make fine adjustments to a provisional display). So the normal solution even for wysiwyg software which handles mathematical text is to accept from the keyboard expressions of the form $c = sqrt(a\char94 2 + b\char94 2)$ and to interpret and lay them out in a mathematically literate way.

Both troff and TeX, because of their origins in research establishments and universities, provide strong support for mathematical typesetting, troff through another preprocessor program called *eqn*. For the developers of TeX, the versatility and quality of its performance in this field has always been a central issue. TeX was designed precisely to give the mathematician total control over the presentation of his work, freeing him from reliance on professional printers and compositors. *The TeX Book* [4] devotes four chapters to this topic – here we can give only a superficial account of the principles involved.

The first thing to say is that TeX incorporates something called *math mode*, normally triggered off by the occurrence of a $ symbol or equivalent keyword in the input stream. Within this environment the normal rules for positioning and sizing characters are suspended and a different set of rules takes over, based on TeX's understanding of the grammar of mathematics.

Spaces in input expressions are ignored, and TeX decides how far apart symbols should be. Letters representing variables go automatically into an italic font, although function names such as "log" and "cos" can be preceded by a backslash to indicate that they are full words to be printed in roman type. In fact backslashes are used to mark all TeX special names, and within math mode this permits reference to around 200 mathematical and miscellaneous symbols. (The principle here is similar to the use of SGML entities, enabling input from a standard keyboard to generate a much wider range of printed characters.) Thus the mathematician can refer to the Greek alphabet (\\alpha, \\pi), accents (\\prime, \\bar, \\hat), logic symbols (\\and, \\or, \\forall, \\exists,), plus the common signs for infinity, integral, root, sum and product, together with brackets of various types and sizes.

The actual placement of symbols in expressions can be described using mathematical conventions: fractions are specified as in $a \setminus over\ b$ and subscripts and superscripts as in x_1, and y^2, with TeX automatically scaling the character sizes as necessary. The scope of any expression is delimited by braces, e.g. $x^\{2y\}$. Sizes of brackets and root symbols are selected according to the length and depth of the expression they enclose, and there are both large and small versions of operators such as sum and integral which can be chosen as needed. TeX provides facilities for including formulae in lines of ordinary text or displaying them on separate lines, for lining up series of equations down the page on their "equals" signs, for automatically numbering equations, and for breaking up long expressions over several lines. A simple example of some mathematical typesetting features can be seen later in Figs 11.5 and 11.6.

Utilities

The last set of functions to consider are those which involve extracting information from the formatted text and creating auxiliary files. One possibility already mentioned is the generation of a *table of contents* from chapter and section headings and their page numbers. The production of *indexes* and *glossaries* is a rather similar task; the writer must mark the items to be indexed in a particular way, so that the software can pull them out into a separate file, then sort them into order if necessary before formatting and printing them.

Even with the aid of software, indexing tends to be a labour-intensive business. In Ventura, for example, the index option is selected from the "edit" menu, then the actual word or phrase to be indexed must be entered through a dialogue box (even though it also appears in the text itself). It is possible to create primary or secondary index entries, to specify a sort key other than the actual index item, and to set up a cross-reference to another index item, e.g. "format: see layout". Alternatively, the wysiwyg approach can be abandoned completely, and the Ventura code for an indexed item can be embedded as a tag into text as it is prepared on a word processor. To produce the file of indexed items, a choice is made from the "options" menu.

With formatting programs such auxiliary tasks are normally handled by macro packages. Troff *mm*, for example, will produce a table of contents and a bibliography, again using embedded commands to identify the relevant items. LaTeX accepts the directives: *tableofcontents*, *listoffigures*, and *listoftables*, each of which writes an appropriate text file which can be edited by the author before printing.

A similar process applies to indexes and glossaries. Any word or phrase to be listed is entered in the text at the appropriate point, preceded by the command *index* or *glossary*. The directives *makeindex* and *makeglossary* cause these items and their page numbers to be written to auxiliary files as a by-product of the formatting process. The files must then of course be sorted and processed further before printing the index: bringing together all entries for the same item, associating main entries with their sub-entries, and turning unbroken series of page numbers into ranges.

Producing a bibliography can be approached in two ways. One method involves entering references in full at the point in the text where they are cited, then using software to extract, sort and print them like the other marked items just discussed. This method is supported by, for example, the troff macro package *mm*. Alternatively only a short citation may be put in the text itself, with full references being placed directly in a separate file. This method (supported by LaTeX and an auxiliary program called *BibTeX*), is especially useful if a database of references already exists (maintained by a research group, perhaps), and writers of new documents have only to set up links to the relevant entries in it.

As with other cross-references, a linkage must be based on a unique attribute attached to the citation. It is introduced by the command *cite*{*label*}, where "label" is a string matching the label of a record in the bibliography database. While formatting, LaTeX converts these tags into unique sequential reference numbers. To make the bibliography, the full references are pulled out of the database and output with their matching reference numbers, either in order of citation, or sorted by author and year of publication.

Behind the Scenes

Following the general survey of formatting functions, we consider selected aspects of their task in a little more depth. This part of the discussion will focus on typesetter programs rather than wysiwyg packages, mainly because they are so much more open to inspection. It is possible for users to look at the structure of existing macro files and to extend and alter them for their own require-ments, so gaining an insight into basic principles and controlling their own document processing in as much detail as they like.

Both programs are large and complex (TeX in particular) so only a few issues can be chosen for examination, and their actual command syntax will not be discussed in any detail. In connection with troff, we shall see how primitives and macro programming structures are used to handle page-breaking. In connec-tion with TeX, we shall look at the ideas behind the filling algorithms which allow it to achieve a high quality of presentation, and then at the exploitation of macro expansion (via LaTeX) to define more specialised document styles.

```
                            1 Acacia Avenue
                            Arundel
                            24 : 8 : 90


         Dear Aunt Anne,
                         Thank you very  much
         for  the  pair  of  socks which you
         sent me for my birthday.  I'm  sure
         they will be very useful.

         For my birthday I also had:
                 a bicycle,
                 a budgerigar,
                 a box of chocolates,
         Unfortunately the budgerigar ate
         the box of chocolates (wrappers and
         all), and I crashed my bicycle tak-
         ing him to the vet.

            I hope you are keeping well. Mum
         and Dad send their love.  I expect
                     we shall see you soon.

                 Best wishes from
                       Alan



                 Page 1
```

Fig. 11.3. Example output from nroff.

Troff/Nroff

Troff and nroff [3] are closely related Unix formatting utilities. Troff is intended for printing documents using real or simulated typesetter systems, nroff simply outputs to devices with fixed-pitch fonts like screens or line printers. The two systems use the same primitives and macro programming facilities, but meanings of command arguments may differ according to

```
.de Da                          \"date macro definition
\n(dy : \n(mo : \n(yr           \"refer to built-in registers
..                              \"end of definition
.ll 35                          \"line-length
.pl 40                          \"page-length
.po 5                           \"page offset (left margin)
.sp 7                           \"space down
.in 15                          \"indent
.nf                             \"no fill mode
1 Acacia Avenue
Arundel
.Da                             \"use date macro
.sp 2
.in 0
Dear Aunt Anne,
.ti 15                          \"temporary indent
.fi                             \"fill mode
Thank you very much for the
pair of socks
which you sent me for my birthday.
I'm sure they will be very useful.
.sp
For my birthday I also had:
.in 5
a bicycle,
.br                             \"break line
a budgerigar,
.br
a box of chocolates,
.na                             \"no adjust (ragged right)
.in 0
Unfortunately the budgerigar ate the box of chocolates (wrappers
and all), and I crashed my bicycle taking him to the vet.
.sp
.ad r                           \"right adjust (ragged left)
I hope you are keeping well. Mum and Dad send their love.
I expect we shall see you soon.
.sp
.ce 3                           \"centre lines
Best wishes from
Alan
.sp 3                           \"refer to page number register
Page \n%
```

Fig. 11.4. An nroff file with embedded formatting commands.

context. For instance the nroff user will specify horizontal and vertical page lengths in terms of number of characters and number of lines, whereas the troff user generally quotes physical measurements. Troff obviously allows a wider range of font selection. But files prepared for one system are normally compatible with the other, with nroff using default rules to translate troff values into those with a lower resolution. Within the Unix community, nroff/troff format provides a standard document interchange medium – it is the one used for all the *man* files of system documentation, and, as noted earlier, also for files created by the Guide hypertext system.

Our example was in fact generated using nroff, and the names of the two systems are interchangeable everywhere in the following discussion. Figs 11.3 and 11.4 show a piece of formatted text and the input file which created it. They illustrate some primitives for handling vertical spacing, indentation, and horizontal filling using different varieties of alignment within paragraphs. Note that automatic hyphenation was put into effect at one point in order to fill a line more tightly. The command lines should be self-explanatory, given the comments to the right of each.

The example also shows references to the contents of some built-in *number registers*: the page number (represented by the % symbol) and the current day, month and year (obtained from the operating system). Day, month and year are called by a simple date macro (DA) defined at the start of the file and used to print the date immediately after the address. It is only by using macro definition and associated programming facilities that raw nroff or troff are actually built up into something usable.

Macros, Conditionals, and Traps

A general requirement might be a "section" macro which defined a space down and a temporary indent: by putting fixed values into the definition the writer could ensure a consistent start to each section. More generally, the macro might take one or more arguments, in the simple case a section heading. Arguments are denoted in the same way as Unix shell script arguments, with a number preceded by a dollar sign. Thus we might have the following definition:

```
.de SE
.sp 2
\$1
.ti 4
..
```

which could be used by the macro call *.SE "Section 1"*.

It is not difficult to imagine how this macro could be made more useful, for instance by handling automatic section numbering, or by testing, before starting a new section, how much space remained on the current page, and jumping to a new page if necessary to avoid an isolated line. This would require reference to another built-in number register and the use of the *.if* command. As in any procedural programming language, alternative commands and text-lines can be selected through conditionals – usually on the contents of number registers which are given values by arithmetic operations and assignment.

However the *.if* command is not enough for all purposes, so the macro writer is also allowed to set *traps*. The *.wh* command introduces a simple event-handling facility so that actions can be triggered "whenever" a certain number of input lines has been read or the typesetter gets to a particular vertical position. This would be needed, for instance, to handle end-of-page processing.

Basic troff has commands to set the page length (*.pl*), and to jump to a new page (*.bp*), but it will not automatically do page throws or put in headers and footers. It may in fact be used to produce galleys – continuously printed sheets which are sometimes used for proofreading or for cut-and-paste layout operations. So for normal document formatting a trap would be set at an appropriate distance from the bottom of the page to trigger off a page throw, and the output of any footer and header information. Trap locations may be changed dynamically while formatting, so the occurrence of a footnote reference should move the nominal end-of-page mark up by the amount of space needed to print the footnote.

Environments

At any time during the formatting process, the current "state" is given by the values of all parameters and registers, e.g. those holding the line length, indentation, font and vertical spacing presently in force. When moving from, say, laying out the body of a page to printing a header or footer, there may be a need to change a whole set of these values temporarily, then change back again when normal page filling resumes. *Environments* provide a way of switching easily between one state and another by allowing all relevant values to be saved and restored as a group.

Troff provides three environments (0, 1 and 2), each with its own workspace, and a command to switch from one to another. The *.ev* command saves the current state in the appropriate workspace, then initialises or restores registers and parameters for the new environment. If used without an environment number it returns to the previous environment. The actual environment numbers are pushed onto a stack on entry and popped off on return, providing an orderly history mechanism and ensuring that macros using different environments can be freely nested inside one another.

The three troff environments are normally used by macro packages to handle page bodies, headers and footers. However the idea of environments or nested scopes is a very general one, both in conventional programming and in text processing. The TeX math mode described earlier is another example – between the $$ delimiters, parameter settings and layout rules are quite different from those outside. The LaTeX macro package extends this idea further, defining environments for quotations, lists, verse, tables, etc. and also allowing users to define their own environments for special purposes. Obviously this requires full stack-management behind the scenes, as for any block-structured language.

Diversions

In the general discussion on vertical filling algorithms, we noted the need for *floating insertions* like footnotes, lists and tables, which must be read from the input file and formatted, but may not actually be output until some time later, at the bottom of the current page or the start of the next one. In troff this task is handled using named buffers or *diversions*. The command *.di BN* (where *BN* stands for a two character buffer name) starts the diversion. Any text following it will be formatted as usual but diverted into the buffer, until the occurrence of the command *.di* without an argument. The command *.da* adds more text to an existing diversion. Its contents are output by using the buffer name itself as a command (e.g. *.BN*), and removed with the command *.rm BN*.

In practice such commands would normally be generated by macros actually processing insertion texts. Troff macro packages supply *floating keep* commands, allowing the user to mark the start and end of blocks of text which must be kept together. A *keep start* macro is expanded into a command to start a diversion, a *keep end* macro will end the diversion, check its length against the remaining space on the page, output and remove it if there is room for it, otherwise resume normal text filling. In this context, any *start page* macro must check for the existence of any outstanding diversions to be printed, and output them before continuing with the current input.

That concludes the brief survey of fundamental troff/nroff concepts. The system documentation for any Unix installation will contain manuals on nroff and any available macro packages, and reference [3] gives a very clear and readable description of how to write one's own macros.

TeX and LaTeX

The TeX system [4] was developed by Donald Knuth to provide computer users with very high quality typographic tools, particularly for mathematical and scientific material. TeX is a portable public-domain product – the complete, fully documented Pascal program is published in book form [8] and the 600 plain TeX macros which build on and supplement the TeX primitives are supplied in a file which can be read and modified if required. In the same spirit of openness, the basic macros for the LaTeX [7] formatting package, and its associated style files, can also be accessed and edited, and useful auxiliary definitions for specialised document types are freely exchanged within the TeX user community.

The system is also used by professional publishers and printers. Cambridge University Press, for example, offers its authors a "TeX to Type" service whereby machine-readable manuscripts can be submitted logically marked up with macros which convert to plain TeX. These macros are designed for book production rather than the A4-type documents principally supported by LaTeX, and they allow printing in conventional font families (Monotype Times, Monotype Helvetica) as well as the "Computer Modern" family originally developed by Knuth for use with TeX.

TeX Formatting

One of the most interesting aspects of TeX is that it encodes aesthetic principles of "good" typesetting into a system based on numeric measurements and calculations. The central algorithm is the one which does horizontal filling of continuous text. This works with the paragraph as a whole, trying to break it up into lines where the words are not too spread out or squashed together, and where end-of-line hyphenation does not occur twice in succession. Similarly there is a vertical filling algorithm which breaks the text into pages in a logical way. We will now explore this process in a little more detail, bearing in mind that one would need to carry out the practical experiments suggested by Knuth to grasp the principles fully, and exploit them for one's own purposes.

As a basis for understanding, the meaning of some TeX terminology must be explained.

Boxes

An analogy is drawn between computer-based typesetting and the original manual activity of slotting pieces of metal type into wooden racks. Within TeX, the smallest "box" is one containing a single character. Characters are put together to make *horizontal* boxes or lines, and lines are put together to make *vertical* boxes, up to the length of a page. The document creator can specify the contents of each horizontal and vertical box so as to control the layout process explicitly. For example, the command \hbox{*A Non-Divisible Heading*} makes the string within braces a single indivisible unit. Going into TeX math mode ensures that a formula embedded within text is treated as a horizontal box, and a displayed formula (like the one shown in Fig. 11.5) is a multi-line vertical box. For continuous text, however, what goes into each successive horizontal box is determined by the filling algorithm.

Glue

Continuing with the physical metaphor, boxes are stuck together to make larger boxes using pieces of "glue". From the programming point of view, glue can be thought of as a data type like "real" or "complex", and a glue parameter as a composite of three values representing distances. A typical example of a glue item is *\spaceskip*, which defines the size of spaces between words. It is made up of three values because it has an ideal distance, and a potential for stretching and shrinking. So, for example, when setting text in a 10-point roman font, the preferred inter-word space is 3.33333 points, but this is permitted to shrink by 1.11111 points or stretch by 1.66666 points. The actual value is calculated for each line in turn, as words are fitted into the available horizontal box. It is considered better to leave more space after punctuation marks, so following a comma, for instance, the potential shrink value is smaller and the stretch value is larger.

Manipulation of glue parameters also generates ragged-right, ragged-left, or centred lines. The control word *\hfil* stands for glue which is infinitely stretchable in the horizontal direction, and this can be inserted at either end or both ends of the line to give the desired effect. Similar principles apply in the vertical direction – the distance between lines on a page (*\lineskip*) can be defined in terms of an ideal length plus or minus stretch and shrink factors, and *\vfil* commands can be inserted in the text to adjust the position of vertical boxes on the page.

Badness, Penalties, and Hyphenation

To identify the best combination of breakpoints within a paragraph, TeX uses a point-scoring system based on the assignment of "penalties" for undesirable conditions. Two main criteria are considered – the appearance of individual lines, and compatibility between adjacent lines. To quote Knuth, "The badness of a line is an integer approximately 100 times the cube of the ratio by which the glue inside the line must stretch or shrink to make an hbox of the required size". A "badness" of zero would imply a perfect fit, higher scores measure the amount of divergence from that ideal.

Where lines are not right-justified, the badness of a line reflects the amount by which *\hfil* has stretched, i.e. the amount of white space on the right. For justified lines, it is based on the stretching or shrinking of inter-word spaces. According to the scoring process, potential lines are classed as "tight", "decent" (acceptable), "loose", or "very loose". To enforce consistency within a paragraph, extra penalties are incurred by breakpoints which would cause adjacent lines to be too dissimilar on this scale, e.g. a tight line next to a loose one or a decent line next to a very loose one. The other penalty on adjacent lines is incurred if two or more of them end with a hyphen.

TeX makes its first pass through a paragraph looking for breakpoints between words – only if this fails to produce a satisfactory result will it try again using hyphenation. The program reads a file of language-specific "patterns" (data giving general rules for determining breakpoints in common character sequences) and an exception file of words with potential hyphenation points marked explicitly. Users may add entries to these files if they wish, and also insert one-off discretionary breakpoints anywhere in the text, where they will cause the normal hyphenation rules to be overridden.

However they are arrived at, hyphens cost a small penalty, and there are more drastic penalties attached to hyphens in the penultimate line of a paragraph or in two or more successive lines. As with other elements of the scoring system, the actual penalty values can be reset by the user, depending upon how he rates the conditions. He may also insert *ad hoc* negative or positive penalties between words wherever he wishes to encourage or discourage linebreaking. At the extreme, the control words *break* or *nobreak* can be used to force or forbid breaking at that point.

For each paragraph, TeX calculates scores for all feasible breakpoints so as to choose the best combination, which it does using a form of *shortest-path* algorithm. The final best score (average badness per line plus extra penalty points) is then tested against a pre-determined *tolerance* parameter. If it is less than or equal to this value, the associated breakpoints are accepted, otherwise a result is produced containing one or more "overfull boxes": lines extending beyond the allotted horizontal space. TeX reports the presence of overfull boxes to the user, who has the option of setting discretionary breakpoints to improve its performance, or adjusting other parameters.

One value which can be adjusted is the tolerance itself. The larger this is, the less fussy TeX will be about tight and loose lines or the other penalty criteria. Another possibility is to change the *horizontal fuzz* parameter – the distance (in terms of points) by which a line can extend beyond its allotted space without being considered overfull. By default TeX sets low values for both *tolerance* and *hfuzz*, but requirements obviously vary according to circumstances – the attention to detail needed for the final version of a published book would be out of place in a draft report or informal letter.

The principle of scoring, penalties, and user-adjustable parameters carries over into the vertical dimension, when pagebreaks are being identified. The main difference is that it is impossible to look at all potential breakpoints before deciding which combination to use – the whole document cannot be held in memory at once, so decisions are made on the basis of local criteria only. These must now take into account the complications of footnotes and floating inserts, which again require the imposition of penalties to avoid inelegant breaks where possible. And there are some direct parallels with the horizontal filling methods just discussed.

For example, TeX by default will attempt to create pages of the same length, but the user may ease the constraints by increasing the value of *vfuzz*, or specify a page with a "ragged bottom" on an analogy with a "ragged right" margin. The *widowpenalty* discourages leaving isolated lines, and the *brokenpenalty* discourages finishing the last line on the page with a hyphen. Users may again enter *ad hoc* penalties, or commands to force or forbid breaking between paragraphs of text.

Isolated lines can sometimes be avoided by shortening or lengthening paragraphs, and TeX provides a special command for this purpose. The *looseness* parameter has a default value of zero. If it is set to 1, the spacing in the following paragraph will be spread out so that it contains one extra line. A higher number gives more lines, and a negative number gives correspondingly fewer lines. The longer the paragraph, the less noticeable is the effect on inter-word spacing.

Exploiting TeX Macro Facilities

The above is a very much simplified account of TeX formatting, but it will be evident that the process depends on interaction between large numbers of parameters, and the user who resets particular values in isolation could trigger off surprising repercussions. TeX is a powerful system, but it is correspondingly difficult to learn as a whole. However the macro substitution mechanism makes it possible to customise and simplify it for users who are happy to give up some of the power in exchange for protection from some of the complexity. This is the purpose of the LaTex package [7], which has been mentioned at intervals throughout this chapter.

One function of LaTeX is to hide low-level details from users. For example it incorporates two commands: *sloppy* and *fussy*, which have the effect of altering the underlying *tolerance*, *hfuzz* and *vfuzz* parameters as a group. These are defined in the following way:

\def\sloppy{\tolerance 1000 \hfuzz .5pt \vfuzz .5pt}
\def\fussy{\tolerance 200 \hfuzz .1pt \vfuzz .1pt}

When TeX meets a macro name in the input stream, it simply replaces it with the substitute text within braces.

A macro definition can also include references to formal *arguments*, marked by a preceding hash sign. The command:

\def\reverse #1,#2{#2 comes before #1}

defines a macro which expects two arguments, separated by a comma, and outputs them in reverse order, separated by some literal text. Thus the command:

\reverse{zebra,aardvark}

generates the string "aardvark comes before zebra". Macro definitions can of course contain nested macro calls, and their arguments can themselves involve macro substitution, so long as the eventual result is a character string.

LaTeX exploits the macro mechanism to introduce a number of higher level document formatting functions: automatic section numbering and list handling, cross-referencing, arrays and tables, graphics objects, bibliographies and indexing. It makes explicit the notion of document "styles", providing structure definition facilities which are somewhat simpler than TeX basic macro definitions, and enabling users to think in terms of logical mark-up rather than explicit formatting commands.

Thanks to the fact that all TeX and LaTeX macros are open to inspection, it is possible to go down through various levels of definition to see how particular functions are carried out. To illustrate these ideas, we will first look at the way automatic section numbering is implemented by LaTeX, and then show a short example of a user-defined document style.

Section Numbering

Automatic section numbering requires that number or letter labels are generated and printed out at the beginning of each separately-identifiable text unit, and that numeric labels can show an explicit hierarchical structure, as in 1.1, 1.2, 1.2.1, etc. For this purpose one or more internal *counters* must be initialised and updated periodically, and the values of those counters must be converted to character strings for printing.

First we consider what is available at the bottom level. TeX holds up to 255 registers for integers, as well as registers for other data types like glue. Symbolic names can be assigned to registers, e.g. the command:

\newcount\sectno=1

declares and initialises a number register *sectno*, which can now be treated like any other TeX parameter. Arithmetic operations can be applied to it, with \advance, \multiply, and \divide. The command:

\advance\sectno by 1

adds 1 to *sectno*, a change which may be either \global or \local in effect. Values of registers can be tested and used with a variety of control structures. TeX supports \if-\else, a multiway \ifcase conditional, a \loop structure, and even recursion in macro definitions.

There is also a set of useful basic conversion functions. The command:

\number\sectno

will generate the value of that register in printable form;

\romannumeral\sectno

will, as its name implies, produce it as a roman numeral. For string values there are functions \lowercase and \uppercase. These conversions may be applied in sequence; if count register \sectno currently has the value 14, then the command:

\uppercase\rommannumerals\sectno

will generate the string "XIV".

One other conversion function needs rather more explanation, since it is bound up with the fact that TeX is a programming language which works by macro substitution. The functions discussed so far – for assignment, conversion, or flow of control – have their counterpart in all procedural programming languages, whether interpreted or compiled. The point about programming with macros is that functions can be evaluated or implemented only by string replacement, and if macros are to be defined with any sort of generality it is impossible to make a hard and fast distinction between "program" and "data".

One requirement must be to allow any character string to be treated as the name of a "control sequence". In TeX terminology any parameter, command, macro name – any word preceded by a backslash and embedded into a text as part of a formatting directive – is a control sequence; in fact one of the main difficulties about reading TeX programs is that no syntactic distinction is made between these different kinds of object!

An arbitrary character string is also treated as a control sequence name when it is surrounded by the words \csname and \endcsname. This string may itself be generated by macro substitution, and the new name will almost certainly form part of a longer control sequence. For example, the command:

\newcount\csname\romannumerals\sectno\endcsname

takes the current value of \sectno, turns it into a roman numeral, and uses the resulting string as the name of a new count register. If \sectno has the value 14, we shall have a count register called \xiv, and can then write commands like:

\advance\xiv by 1.

Taking this idea a little further, a macro can accept an argument which is or evaluates to a character string, and treat it as the name of a control sequence to be defined or executed. This makes possible a very high degree of generality and flexibility, exploited to the full in LaTeX.

Focusing now on the question of section numbering, it is obvious that a counter must be kept for each possible level in the hierarchy, i.e. if the longest section label is of the form x.y.z, we shall need three counters, x, y, and z. LaTeX defines several general macros for declaring numeric counters and their printable versions, and for initialising and incrementing them. Some important examples (which themselves call on other auxiliary macros) are:

- \newcounter: takes two string arguments, "newctr", and an optional "oldctr". It defines \newctr to be the name of a new counter, one level down from \oldctr, which must be already defined. It sets \newctr to zero, and adds its name to a list of counters dependent on \oldctr. This list is simply another TeX control sequence, operated upon using some basic lisp-type macros called \cons, \car, and \cdr.
- \stepcounter: takes the name of a counter as argument and increments the corresponding counter value, resetting all counters in its dependency list to one.
- \arabic, \roman, \Roman, \alph, \Alph, as their names imply, format a counter value into a string for printing. \Roman gives uppercase roman numerals;

\alph and \Alph map from numbers 1–26 to upper and lower case letters respectively, using the TeX \ifcase control structure.

Names of actual textual subdivisions and their corresponding counters are declared as part of a particular document style. For example the LaTeX "report" style file contains the following definitions, which declare all possible section tags, their dependencies, and how counter values are to be concatenated together to form printable labels. Note that chapter numbering is quite independent of part numbering – chapters will run sequentially even if a document is split into parts – but the remaining divisions form a hierarchy:

\newcounter {part}
\newcounter {chapter}
\newcounter {section}[chapter]
\newcounter {subsection}[section]
\newcounter {subsubsection}[subsection]
\newcounter {paragraph}[subsubsection]
\newcounter {subparagraph}[paragraph]

\def\thepart {\Roman{part}}
\def\thechapter {\arabic{chapter}}
\def\thesection {\thechapter.\arabic{section}}
\def\thesubsection {\thesection.\arabic{subsection}}
\def\thesubsubsection {\thesubsection.\arabic{subsubsection}}
\def\theparagraph {\thesubsubsection.\arabic{paragraph}}
\def\thesubparagraph {\theparagraph.\arabic{subparagraph}}

When using this document style, the writer may insert a sectioning command (e.g. \subsubsection) anywhere within his document, causing all relevant counters to be updated and an appropriate label (e.g. 2.3.4.1) to be printed. This action is controlled by a large and complex macro called \startsection, which handles the necessary updating and formatting, including the insertion of penalties to encourage pagebreaking between sections rather than within them.

A User-Defined Document Style

We now consider a short but complete LaTeX document, which illustrates the facility for users to add to existing style definitions. One of the basic styles supported by LaTeX is a "letter". This provides definitions for special elements like the address, signature, opening and closing phrases, which encapsulate lower-level formatting directives. It also prints the current date automatically, immediately after the address. Any extra definitions may be placed either in the input stream immediately before the text to be formatted, or, if they prove to be of more general use, in an auxiliary style file for public access. Such a file has been created for our current example, to support the production of "thank-you" letters.

Fig. 11.5 shows a listing of this file, followed by the text of a document which uses it. The style file comprises five definitions and the assignment of a new value to the parameter \textwidth. LaTeX definitions are actually of two kinds: *commands* and *environments*, both implemented in terms of basic TeX macros. They are similar in that they involve the substitution of text for a control sequence name, and that they may take one or more arguments; they differ in

```
% Special document style for thank-you letters

\newcommand{\hopewell}{I hope you are keeping well. }
\newcommand{\sendlove}{Mum and Dad send their love. }
\newcommand{\seesoon}{I expect we shall see you soon. }
\renewcommand{\thanks}[1]{Thank you {\em very\/} much for
the #1 which you sent me for my birthday. }
\newenvironment{gifts}{For my birthday I also had:
 \begin{itemize}}{\end{itemize}}
\textwidth 3.5in

% A document in LaTeX "letter" style,
% using the extra "thankyou" commands,
% (with a short "math mode" example).

\documentstyle[thankyou]{letter}
\begin{letter}
\fromaddress{1 Acacia Avenue\\Arundel\\}
\signature{Alan}
\opening{Dear Aunt Anne}

\thanks{pair of socks}
I'm sure they will be very useful.

\begin{gifts}
\item a bicycle
\item a budgerigar
\item a box of chocolates
\end{gifts}

{\em Unfortunately} the budgerigar ate the
box of chocolates (wrappers and all), and I
crashed my bicycle taking him to the vet.

Now I have some difficult homework to do.
I have just learned that:
$$x={{-b{+ \atop -}\sqrt{b^2-4ac}}\over 2a}$$
Isn't that interesting?

\hopewell \sendlove \seesoon
\closing{Best Wishes}

\end{letter}
```

Fig.11.5. LaTeX files with embedded macro calls.

that an environment is delimited by explicit \begin– \end markers, and that within that environment other commands may be given a special interpretation.

Looking in detail at the definitions:

- New commands \hopewell, \sendlove, and \seesoon involve simple string replacement (as with an SGML entity).
- \thanks must be declared with \renewcommand, as the underlying style file already has a command of the same name, which does not do what we want here. This command takes a single argument, the name of the present for which thanks are being given.
- The new environment \gifts is built on an existing list formatting environment: \itemize. It outputs some preliminary literal text before entering the \itemize environment, within which all list items are marked with the \item tag, and output in bulleted form. LaTeX also provides the \enumerate environment for numbered lists – once again analogies with SGML-type mark-up should be apparent.

The actual document file begins with a command calling on the main and auxiliary style files, which cause the relevant definitions to be set up before formatting begins. Arguments are sent to the \address, \signature and \opening commands enclosed in braces – note that the newly-defined \thanks command acts in exactly the same way, and that \begin–\end markers must be entered for the \gifts environment.

The letter also contains a short example of TeX math mode for a displayed formula. Within the $$ delimiters are examples of control sequences for the special character \sqrt and the positional directives \atop and \over. Braces show the scope of operators in the expression, which will ensure the correct layout of the quadratic equation formula.

One other point to note is the \em directive, embedded in the \thanks definition and the actual letter text, causing the enclosed words to be emphasised. LaTeX italicises \em text, but allows emphasis within emphasis, in which case a roman font is used. In theory \em could be mapped onto bold, underlined or small caps fonts, simply by a change of definition, supporting the principle of logical rather than procedural mark-up discussed in the previous chapter. However there is one minor difficulty.

A move from right-slanting italics to a roman font reduces inter-word or inter-letter spacing slightly, and TeX allows the control sequence \/ to be inserted anywhere in the text to generate a small extra space to compensate. This trick was used for the emphasised word in the \thanks definition but not in the letter text itself, and it is just about possible to see the two different effects on inter-word spacing in the printed letter (Fig. 11.6). In this case then, the user really should know at the time of writing that \em maps to italics, as the trick is needed only with this font. We thus have a slight conflict between the idea of logical mark-up and the regard for typesetting quality which TeX engenders – a conflict which could be avoided here by a more intelligent definition of \em.

The overall layout of the letter in Fig. 11.6 is governed by the style files, with TeX taking care of the detailed line-filling. Note that inter-word spacing is uniform within lines, but varies from line to line as the glue stretches and shrinks to fit the horizontal boxes. Automatic kerning has been performed (most noticeably before the letter "y") and there is an example of ligature in the word "difficult".

---

1 Acacia Avenue
Arundel
August 8, 1990

Dear Aunt Anne

Thank you *very* much for the pair of socks which you sent me for my birthday. I'm sure they will be very useful.

For my birthday I also had:

- a bicycle
- a budgerigar
- a box of chocolates

Unfortunately the budgerigar ate the box of chocolates (wrappers and all), and I crashed my bicycle taking him to the vet.

Now I have some difficult homework to do. I have just learned that:

$$x = \frac{-b \pm \sqrt{b^2 - 4ac}}{2a}$$

Isn't that interesting?

I hope you are keeping well. Mum and Dad send their love. I expect we shall see you soon.

Best Wishes

Alan

Fig. 11.6. Example output from LaTeX.

The TeX/LaTeX examples demonstrate that it is possible to establish a path from pure SGML-type logical mark-up, through various levels of command and macro definition, down to primitive formatting directives, although establishing the right mappings at each level is not a trivial task. Having formatted the document, it remains to print it out. Normally TeX reads a document file and produces a *dvi* (device-independent) file which can be used to drive a typesetter, or as input to another piece of software. Many installations provide a text previewer to display a formatted document on the screen and a utility program to convert the *dvi* file to Postscript – that is in fact how the example in Fig. 11.6 was generated. The next chapter completes the picture with an account of the document imaging process, based on a survey of the Postscript language.

Chapter Summary

The development of the laser printer, and of generally available formatting software, makes it possible for computer users to create documents which are comparable in layout and print quality to professionally produced material. Desk-top publishing equipment allows printing in a variety of fonts, page layout in multiple columns and frames, and the inclusion of graphics and scanned images into documents. Formatting software falls into two categories: interactive wysiwyg packages, and "typesetter" systems which require the user to control document layout using embedded commands.

Whatever its type, formatting software should enable the user to: specify overall document characteristics like page size and layout, define logical structures like chapters and sections, control details of line and page filling, and include footnotes, graphics, tables, and mathematical formulae. It should support style definitions for classes of documents, the construction of large documents from multiple sources, and the production of contents lists, bibliographies, and indexes.

Interactive packages allowing on-screen manipulation of document contents are easier for the learner than typesetter systems, but provide less flexibility, since choices can be made only from predefined option menus. Typesetter systems are potentially more open-ended, particularly if they provide a macro substitution facility. Macros enable users to set up their own automatic conversion from logical to procedural mark-up, and define nested environments for interpreting embedded commands in a context-sensitive way.

Investigations

Get to know both an interactive dtp package and a formatting system like nroff or TeX. Try to find an inexperienced computer user and teach him or her about each. From this experience, summarise the strengths and weaknesses of the two approaches to document formatting, taking into account the user's background and the type of document.

If you have access to a macro package, look at and try to understand some of the macro definitions. Choose *one* facility (e.g. footnotes, tables, indexing), and see how it is implemented by following macro definitions down to the basic command level.

Take the SGML document style you defined as an exercise from the previous chapter, and map it onto a set of macros for a formatting system. What information is lost on the way, and what extra information must be introduced, as you move from logical to procedural mark-up?

References

1 Green C (1989) Saturday night and Sunday morning. Apple Business, October:23–28
2 Carney TF (1988) Publishing By microcomputer. Education and Human Communication Series, Peter Francis, Cambridge
3 Emerson S, Paulsell K (1987) Typesetting for Unix systems. Prentice-Hall, Englewood Cliffs, NJ
4 Knuth D (1986) The TeX book. Addison-Wesley, Reading, MA
5 Brailsford D (1988) Electronic publishing and computer science. Electronic Publishing 0(0)[*sic*]:13– 21
6 Holtz M (1988) Mastering Ventura. Sybex
7 Lamport L (1986) LaTeX: A document preparation system. Addison-Wesley, London
8 Knuth D (1986) TeX: The program. Addison-Wesley, Reading, MA

Twelve
Postscript

"... like women's letters; all the pith is in the postscript."
William Hazlitt

Postscript is a device-independent page description language, which in principle allows text and images to be rendered on any raster device. It was originally designed for printer control, but it can also be used to control screen displays, as in the NeWS [1] system. The standard references for the language are the excellent Adobe manuals [2].

Normally, Postscript is interpreted by a micro-processor located in the printer itself. Documents are sent to the printer neither as ASCII files with device-dependent control codes, nor as bit-maps representing raster images, but as programs containing definitions of and calls to procedures, interspersed with the actual data. The programs will contain instructions for creating complete page images in memory, and outputting them onto paper. This method is more flexible than the use of embedded control codes, and requires the transfer of much less data than a corresponding bit-map.

The Postscript Imaging Model

The assumption is that there is a blank page ready to be "painted" in black, white, or intermediate shades of grey. (The principle is readily adaptable to colour printing.) A new line or shape, no matter what colour, hides the image underneath, so for instance it is quite possible to paint white or grey on black. The painting commands refer to X,Y co-ordinates in a *user space* which can be mapped to any particular *device space* – thus a properly written program has the same effect whatever the resolution of the printer or screen in use, and Postscript files provide a portable way of transferring document images between machines.

Basic graphics commands include *moveto*, *lineto*, and *curveto*, referring to either absolute or relative co-ordinates. A series of moves and lines comprise a *path* whose start and end points are explicitly defined in the program. Either a *stroke* or a *fill* command must be executed before the lines or shapes defined by a path are actually painted. The complete page image is built up in memory until the execution of the next *showpage* command, when the current image is output, and the memory is cleared in readiness for the following page.

As far as Postscript is concerned there is no real difference between painting graphics and printing character strings. Any piece of text enclosed in brackets is treated as data to be processed – in particular the *show* command will paint it on the page at the current co-ordinate position and in the current shade. Moreover the program may apply scaling, rotation, and translation at any time to modify the effect of subsequent graphics operations on the current page, and these act in precisely the same way on text output. Thus there are no constraints on the size, orientation and direction of printed character strings. Indeed a character shape can be considered as nothing more than a series of lines and curves – a point to be explored later.

Stacks

Before looking at an example program it is necessary to say a little about syntax. Postscript is a language for device control and was designed for efficiency rather than readability, since most Postscript files are generated by other software rather than being hand-coded. It is therefore modelled on the low-level control language *Forth*, using a Reverse Polish (Postfix) notation which evaluates expressions efficiently via stack manipulation. Operands for a command must be placed on the stack before that command is executed, and results are left on the stack for subsequent use. The programmer must ensure that the right values are waiting at the top of the stack when they are needed, and Postscript provides a number of special stack commands – *duplicate, pop, exchange, roll,* etc. – to achieve this.

Besides the operand stack, there are also *dictionary* and *execution* stacks, and a stack for *graphics* states:

- A dictionary is an association list between a name and an object, either an item of data or a procedure. These may be dynamically defined and redefined during program execution – the dictionary actually holds pointers into heap storage where current values are held. By default there is a system dictionary for built-in commands and a user dictionary for user-defined objects. Others may be explicitly declared within procedures, to support locally scoped definitions. Dictionaries are also used within font definitions, as we shall see shortly.
- Procedure calls can be nested, and the execution stack holds partially completed procedure executions. Postscript provides various conditional and looping control structures: *if, ifelse, loop, repeat, forall* etc. These follow the normal Reverse Polish syntax, in that the code which they govern must be put onto the execution stack before the commands themselves are executed.
- A graphics "state" comprises a set of values defining the current X,Y co-ordinates, linewidth, shade, path, font, etc. and the current transformation

matrix which maps from user to device space based on any scaling, rotation, and transformation in force. The commands *gsave* and *grestore* let one save a graphics state before temporary changes are made, then restore it when they cease to apply.

Note the analogy between graphics states and the LaTeX environments discussed in the previous chapter, which allowed sets of related parameter values to be defined and used *en bloc*. In fact Postscript also has a more general pair of commands to save and restore all current procedure and data definitions – in any direct translation from a higher-level formatting language to Postscript these could be used to support the definition and use of environments.

Fonts

Perhaps the most distinctive feature of the language is the freedom it provides for the programmer to select and define fonts for printing. First let us clarify some terminology. Conventionally, printers refer to "families" of related typefaces (e.g. Times-Roman, Times-Italic, Times-Bold), and the choice of a particular font implies a specific type size, i.e. 10-point Times-Roman is one font. (In the days of hot metal printing, each font would be individually cast out of metal.)

In Postscript, however, a font is simply another word for a typeface. Fonts are defined in a size-independent way, then scaled up or down before being used for printing. A number of built-in font families are supplied with the language: Times, Helvetica, Courier, and a "symbol" font containing Greek letters and mathematical symbols. Many other fonts can be purchased for down-loading into a printer, and in addition programmers may define their own fonts. For instance, when a TeX *dvi* file is converted to Postscript, the Computer Modern typeface is simulated by a new font definition which appears in the document header.

Information about a font is held in a font dictionary, which stores, among other things, details of the relative heights and widths of every character, and descriptions of how each is to be imaged on the page. Characters may be defined as bit-maps, but the preferred method is to use the painting operators discussed above to create paths which are then *stroked, outlined,* or *filled.* This obviously allows maximum flexibility and subtlety in the design of letter-shapes.

Using a built-in font, the programmer need know very little about the underlying mechanism, since simple commands are provided to select the required font by name, scale it to the required size, then establish it as the current font for subsequent printing. Here is a typical program fragment:

/Times-Roman findfont   % locate the font dictionary

18 scalefont   % scale up to 18-point size
setfont   % make it the current font

Character definitions are based on a co-ordinate system known as the *character space*. This can be thought of as a 1000 × 1000 grid which defines a one-point character (at 72 points to the inch). The scaling operation maps from the character space to the user space – if the default user space scaling were in force then following the above instruction subsequent printing would be in 18-point Times-Roman.

Each character is painted by executing a special procedure containing the necessary painting commands, i.e. it is built up out of basic graphics operations like *move*, *line*, and *curve*. In principle, the procedure is executed every time the character is printed; in practice this would be inefficient so in fact it need only be done once. Postscript uses a font *cache* which holds a description of characters in rasterised form. The first time a character is used its description is stored in the cache; whence it can be retrieved and used very rapidly next time round.

Programmers can modify the built-in fonts or create entirely new ones, for instance to enable printing in a non-roman alphabet. This obviously requires more knowledge of what is going on behind the scenes. The basic need is to map from any ASCII code to the appropriate character-drawing procedure, and this is the function of the *encoding vector* which is an essential component of a font dictionary. The encoding vector is a one-dimensional string array having entries 0–255, and each entry holds a suitable procedure name. Entries for ASCII codes which are not defined in the current font point to a "null" procedure.

As part of the font definition procedure, therefore, the programmer must:

● Create an encoding vector and enter the relevant procedure names.
● Create a local dictionary in which all these procedures are defined.
● Define a special *BuildChars* procedure which will look up the name of any required procedure in the encoding vector, and execute it.

A new font dictionary is given a unique name or key – it can then be selected, scaled, and set as the current font in the normal way. As each character is printed in the new font, Postscript calls *BuildChars* to identify the correct procedure to use. Information about the character width must also be sent to the imaging process to ensure correct placement. For proportionally spaced fonts this will vary from one character to another so another look-up table (the *font-metrics*) must be defined within the font dictionary to hold this and other related information. In addition, *BuildChars* may ask for the rasterised character to go into the font cache so that it can be imaged more quickly next time.

Font-definition is not a trivial task, but clearly the Postscript approach provides great flexibility, allowing anything from minor modification of coding schemes (ASCII to ebcdic, for example) to the design of a complete new font for a language not yet supported by standard printing technology. It is possible to create composite symbols, use multiple fonts to handle alphabets of more than 255 letters, and ensure consistency of style within a font by allowing the character drawing procedures to call upon common routines.

An Example Program

The program given in Fig. 12.1 produces Fig. 12.2. The page shows a quotation from a poem [3] in a layout which attempts to reflect the meaning of the actual words. No great aesthetic claims are made for this design, but it does illustrate several of the built-in Postscript typefaces, and demonstrates imaging effects which would be difficult to achieve by other means: use of very large fonts, independent scaling of X and Y co-ordinates, character outlining and filling in various shades of grey, and the arbitrary placement and orientation of character strings via rotation and translation.

Although in many ways a low level language, Postscript has a powerful set of string operators which allow quite complex actions to be performed without writing explicit loops. Three which occur in this example are:

- *stringwidth*: returns the length (and height, if required) of a string as imaged in the current font. Used here in two general procedures which centre and right-align strings to be displayed.
- *search*: searches a string for a substring and, if found, breaks the string into three so that the characters before and after the substring can be processed independently. Used here to break a long string up into shorter lengths delimited by commas, so that the angle of rotation can be adjusted before each is output.
- *kshow*: outputs a string, but calls a specified procedure between each character. Used here to give the "stepped" effect for T.S.Eliot and his dates, and to reduce the imaging intensity between the letters of "Quartets".

The *kshow* operator is really provided to assist the process of kerning. A kerning procedure would use a look-up table of correct distances between successive pairs of characters. For this purpose the two current characters are left on the stack by *kshow* – if not required (as in this example) they must be "popped" off. *Kshow* is one of a family of operators which are variants on the basic *show*. Others in the family allow a common space adjustment between all characters or after certain characters – their obvious use being to support line justification by modifying either inter-character or inter-word spacing.

The example program is well commented but some remarks on its structure may be useful. It begins with a "binding definition" of a procedure to select and scale a font. Normally Postscript definitions are dynamic, and commands are executed interpretively; making a binding definition is the equivalent of "compiling" the defined procedure and allows faster execution for processes to be performed repeatedly.

```
%!PS-Adobe-2.0
% POSTSCRIPT EXAMPLE (percent sign indicates a comment)
% Binding Definitions
/bd {bind def} bind def
/F {findfont exch scalefont setfont} bd
%%BoundingBox: 0 0 612 811
% Rotation and translation for a landscape page
612 0 translate 90 rotate
/xlimit 811 def
/ylimit 612 def

% Procedure definitions.
% Values are passed to and from procedures on the stack.

/rectangle{                        % stack: distance from edge
/dist exch def                     % save distance
newpath dist dist moveto           % move to start
/dist 2 dist mul def               % double distance
0 ylimit dist sub rlineto          % create path using
xlimit dist sub 0 rlineto          %    relative moves
0 dist ylimit sub rlineto
closepath                          % join 1st and last points
stroke                   } def     % draw lines

/centre{                           % stack: space, XY, string
/str exch def                      % save string
moveto                             % move to start
str stringwidth pop                % find length of string
sub 2 div                          % (space - length) / 2
0 rmoveto str show       } def     % output at calculated xpos

/align{                            % stack: Y, right edge, string
/str exch def                      % save string
str stringwidth pop                % find length of string
sub exch moveto                    % move to calculated xpos
str show                 } def

/border{                           % two outlines & a header
/outer 35 def                      % offset for outer border
/inner 60 def                      % offset for inner border
outer rectangle
inner rectangle
18 /Times-Roman F                  % choose font for header
xlimit inner 2 mul sub             % space parameter and
inner ylimit inner sub 5 add       %    X,Y co-ordinates
(Postscript Example) centre        %    for centre procedure
                         } def

/step{                             % procedure for use with kshow
pop pop                            % get rid of chars on stack
0 10 rmoveto             } def     % step up
```

1

Fig. 12.1. Postscript program.

```
/stepprint{                              % stack: XY, string
/str exch def                            % save string
gsave moveto                             % save graphics state
1.5 1 scale                              % scale up in X direction
{step} str kshow                         % move up between each char
grestore                      } def      % restore default scaling

/poet{                                   % output poet and dates
24 /Helvetica F                          %     in stepped layout
500 400 (T.S.ELIOT) stepprint
500 370 (1888-1964) stepprint
                              } def

/bigfour{
288 /Helvetica F                         % a 4-inch character!
newpath  70 70 moveto                    % origin at bottom left
(4) false charpath stroke                % stroke outline
titles                        } def      % output inset titles

/titles{                                 % print small titles
10 /Times-Roman F                        %         in big four
/left 195 def                            % left and right edges
/right 160 def                           %     for inset titles
160 right (Burnt) align
150 right (Norton) align
105 right (The Dry) align
95 right (Salvages) align
left 160 moveto (East) show
left 150 moveto (Coker) show
left 105 moveto (Little) show
left 95 moveto (Gidding) show  } def

/fade{                                   % for use with kshow
pop pop                                  % get rid of chars on stack
/darkness darkness .1 add def            % reduce intensity
darkness setgray              } def

/quartets{
/darkness .2 def                         % variable for intensity
darkness setgray                         % start fairly dark
72 /Helvetica-Oblique F
220 120 moveto gsave
1 1.5 scale                              % scale up in y direction
{fade} (Quartets) kshow                  % with diminishing intensity
grestore                      } def      % restore scaling and intensity

/turn{ 22.5                              % turn 22.5 degrees
clock 4 lt                               % 1st 4 turns go clockwise
{360 exch sub} if                        % conditional
rotate                                   % rotate either way
/clock 1 clock add def        } def      % increment count
```

2

Fig. 12.1. (*continued*).

```
/quotation{                            % stack: whole string
13 /Times-BoldItalic F
/clock 0 def                           % initialise count
62 535 moveto gsave
{                                      % start of loop
    (,) search                         % if another comma found -
       {show show turn}                %              print & turn,
       {show exit}                     %      else print rest of
     ifelse                            %    string and exit loop
} loop                                 % end of loop
grestore                    } def

% String data on stack for quotation procedure.
% (Backslash at end of line means n/l characters ignored).

(Words strain, \
crack and sometimes break, under the burden, \
under the tension, slip, slide, perish, \
decay with imprecision, will not stay in place, \
will not stay still.)

% Main Program
% (Procedures could be called in any order)

 border
 poet
 bigfour
 quartets
 quotation
 showpage




                              3
```

Fig. 12.1. *(continued).*

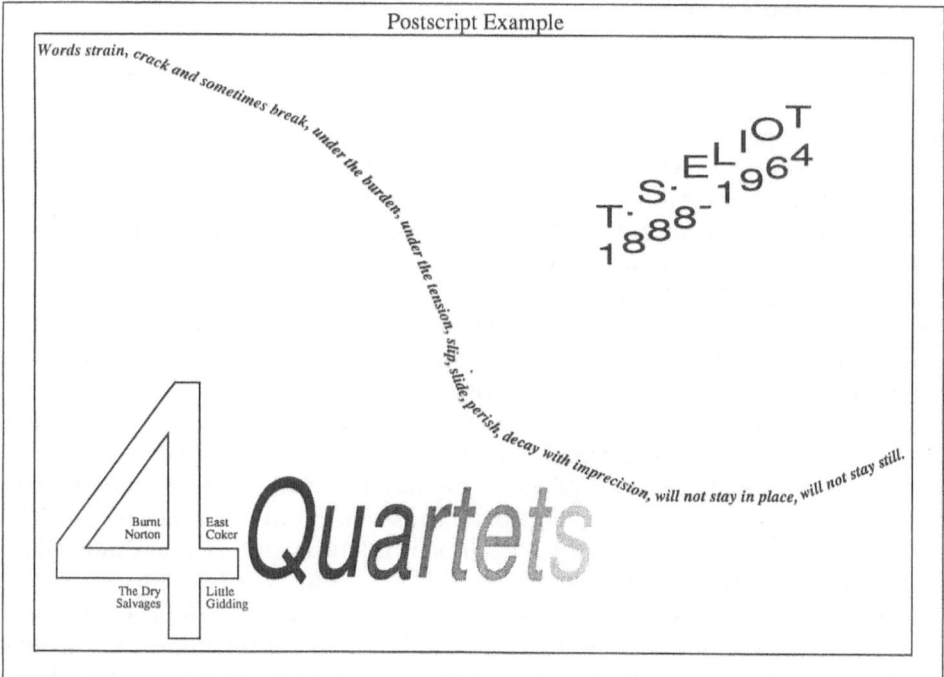

Fig. 12.2. Output from Postscript program.

It has already been noted that imaging involves mapping from a user space to a device space. The default user space consists of an X,Y co-ordinate system with its origin in the bottom left corner, and units expressed in terms of points. At 72 points per inch, an A4 page comprises a bounding box with 612 units on the X-axis, and 811 units on the Y-axis.

The example program starts with a translation and 90-degree rotation so that all subsequent output is in *landscape* rather than portrait orientation. It also defines variables *xlimit* and *ylimit* in this new context, which are used later when fitting text and graphics onto the page. Procedures which do temporary scaling and rotation will always save this initial graphics state and restore it afterwards, so all references to absolute page co-ordinates will be compatible.

The bulk of the program consists of procedure definitions. Those which take arguments fetch them off the stack, and it is conventional to specify through comment statements what sort of values are expected. If the value of an argument is needed more than once, it must be saved in a variable, otherwise it will disappear once it has been used.

The *rectangle* procedure is a typical general-purpose graphics routine, using basic line and move commands to define a path, which is then *stroked* in order to paint it on the page. Likewise *centre* and *align* are simple string-placement procedures which calculate the starting X co-ordinate of a printed string based on its length and the space which it is to occupy, then show it. The *border* procedure prints two rectangles, and centres the 18-point header inside the border.

The *poet* procedure calls *stepprint* twice in succession with starting co-ordinates and strings to be shown. This in turn makes use of *kshow* and *step* to move up the page between each character. The *scale* command scales any subsequent output along the X co-ordinate by 1.5 – a local effect which is undone when the previously saved graphics state is restored.

The *bigfour* procedure selects a very large font for the figure 4, and outputs it in outline, using the *charpath* operator. This operator, when applied to a string, creates a path consisting of the relevant character outlines, which is then stroked exactly as if it had been made up out of basic line commands. This demonstrates clearly the fact that Postscript sees character shapes as collections of graphics primitives like lines and curves.

The *quartets* procedure makes use of *fade* to reduce the intensity level for each successive character in the word. In Postscript the current shade of grey is defined by a value between 0 (black = the default) and 1 (white). The *setgray* operator is provided in the language to set the level; in our example the variable *darkness* is increased by 0.1 between each pair of letters and used as operand to *setgray* to achieve the fade effect.

The *quotations* procedure calls upon *turn* to rotate 22.5 degrees at each occurrence of a comma, so that the text is imaged at different angles. These two procedures illustrate the Postscript control structures *if*, *ifelse* and *loop*, which can, as in this example, be nested. As noted earlier, the body of code contained within a loop must be placed on the execution stack before the loop command itself, and the same applies to a conditional.

Finally, the main program simply consists of a series of procedure calls, followed by the *showpage* command.

Postscript in Practice

Nothing at all is printed from a Postscript file until the execution of the showpage command, so a program with errors in the middle will not usually produce any results. The language contains a few operators which are helpful in tracing and debugging (e.g. one can output the contents of the stack to a message file or convert them to string format and print them), but it does not provide direct high-level support for program development. However software does exist to allow Postscript images to be previewed on the screen while testing, and there are also utility programs which can be pre-loaded into a printer to help track down difficult errors.

The ability to hand-code Postscript is useful for special effects, and essential for new font design, but in practice most real Postscript files for printing are generated by other software. It is possible to examine a file produced by, for

instance, Ventura or LaTeX, although the result is not always very enlightening, particularly if it is actually a translation from some intermediate representation like a *dvi* file. As reference [2] points out, these intermediate files are
often coded at such a low level that the structure of the original document has
been lost, and as a result the real power of the Postscript language is wasted.

As a concrete example of this, consider what happens in the case of LaTeX
graphics. LaTeX allows the definition of simple objects like lines, boxes, and
ovals, and even has a *multiput* operation, which draws repeated copies of an
object on the page in a regular pattern. This facility calls upon lower-level TeX
functions, in particular looping. Because TeX works by macro substitution, a
loop actually generates in the output file multiple copies of the relevant *dvi*
commands, and this replication is carried forward into the final Postscript file.
Obviously a direct translation from LaTeX or TeX into Postscript could map
straight into the relevant control structures and graphics functions, giving a
compact output file which would execute more efficiently.

The designers of Postscript [2] propose the use of certain conventions for
files output from document processing applications. They should consist of a
prologue, containing procedure definitions to implement the layout processes
supported by the package, followed by a *script*, containing the true document
content interspersed with procedure calls.

They should also contain comment lines in a standard format giving general
information about the document. *Header* comments specify its title, author,
recipient and creation date, what fonts it uses, how many pages it contains, and
the maximum vertical and horizontal dimensions of the page (the bounding
box) in terms of Postscript's default user space. *Body* comments mark the start
of each page, and the actual fonts used on it.

Such comments are ignored by the Postscript interpreter, but they enable
other document processing software to perform useful tasks like selecting or
re-ordering pages to be printed, or even nesting one page description inside
another, with suitable modifications of scale. To this end it is also recommended that each page description should be self-sufficient, starting from a
standard "state" and restoring that state when the page is printed.

Postscript is a commercial product, but because of its wide availability on
popular printers like the Apple Laserwriter, and because it permits a high-level
approach to describing document structure and page layout, it has become a *de
facto* standard within certain areas of the computing industry. Moreover the
ISO Standard Page Description Language currently in preparation is likely to
be a superset of Postscript, so the ideas discussed in this section should remain
current for some time.

The language has another important use for describing raster screen
displays, as in the Unix-based *Network Extensible Windows System* [1]. Here the
intention is to handle screen display quite independently of particular
applications, probably running on a server machine within a local network.
Postscript is appropriate in this context once again because it allows text and
graphics to be described in a device-independent manner, and complex

displays to be created by transmitting simple ASCII files. The main difference is that speed is more critical in this environment, since users need faster response from their screens than they will tolerate from a printer. So longer and more complex Postscript routines must be hand-coded and optimised to support such systems, making it desirable to support program development with appropriate language compilers. Reference [4] gives an account of one such system.

Chapter Summary

After formatting, text must be put onto paper, and using a laser printer this involves building up complete page images in memory. An effective means to this end is Postscript, a device-independent (and potentially standard) language for generating page descriptions. The language allows text to be freely combined with graphics images, and printed in any size, colour, and orientation. It provides a number of built-in fonts, and allows users to modify and define new fonts by setting up mappings between ASCII codes and character drawing procedures.

Investigations

Take the set of formatting macros you defined as an exercise from the previous chapter, and map it onto an equivalent set of Postscript procedures. What information is lost on the way, and what extra information must be introduced, as you move down one more level?

Write a Postscript program which will accept a definition of a crossword grid (number of squares, positions of blanks and lights) and a numbered list of words to be entered (across and down) in the lights. Then print it.

References

1 Roberts R, Slater M et al. (1988) First impressions of NeWS. Computer Graphics Forum, vol 7. North-Holland, Amsterdam pp 39–57
2 Adobe Systems Incorporated (1985) Postscript language tutorial and cookbook, Postscript language reference manual. Addison-Wesley, Reading, MA
3 Eliot TS (1944) Four quartets. Faber and Faber, London

4 Gonczarowski J, Paradise O (1989) Inscript – a C-like preprocessor for Postscript. Electronic Publishing 2(3):157– 167

Subject Index